MYTHS AND TRAGEDIES IN THEIR ANCIENT GREEK CONTEXTS

Myths and Tragedies in their Ancient Greek Contexts

RICHARD BUXTON

OXFORD
UNIVERSITY PRESS

OXFORD
UNIVERSITY PRESS

Great Clarendon Street, Oxford, OX2 6DP,
United Kingdom

Oxford University Press is a department of the University of Oxford.
It furthers the University's objective of excellence in research, scholarship,
and education by publishing worldwide. Oxford is a registered trade mark of
Oxford University Press in the UK and in certain other countries

First published 2013
First published in paperback 2018

Published in the United States of America by Oxford University Press
198 Madison Avenue, New York, NY 10016, United States of America

British Library Cataloguing in Publication Data
Data available

Library of Congress Cataloging in Publication Data
Data available

ISBN 978–0–19–955761–5 (Hbk.)
ISBN 978–0–19–881457–3 (Pbk.)

For Mercedes

Preface

The various intellectual and personal debts which I incurred while writing the original versions of these essays are registered chapter by chapter, usually in a concluding footnote. Here it is a pleasure to express gratitude on a more comprehensive scale.

The academic context within which I have worked during the whole of the relevant period has been the Department of Classics and Ancient History (formerly the Department of Classics and Archaeology) at the University of Bristol. My colleagues, and successive cohorts of postgraduate and undergraduate students at Bristol, have taught me more than I can put into words. Beyond that primary location, I am fortunate to have come to know many of the world's leading experts in the literature and mythology of ancient Greece. Their influence pervades the present book, and a list of their names could go on for pages. Instead I single out two only. Jan Bremmer and Pat Easterling have selflessly commented on the whole of this book in draft, saving me from many errors, pointing me towards bibliography which I had overlooked, and encouraging me at every turn. I could wish for no more than that the present book should merit the respect of these two outstanding scholars.

Three more expressions of gratitude are in order. The first is jointly to my OUP editor Hilary O'Shea, for her forbearance and consistently shrewd advice, and to the Press's eagle-eyed copy-editor Richard Mason, who saved me from many an embarrassment. The second is to Lisa Agate who, with superlative efficiency, chased up the images which I wanted to reproduce in this book and secured the permissions to reproduce them. The third is to Mercedes Aguirre, with whom I have talked over countless aspects of myth, tragedy, and much else, to my constant profit and delight.

RGAB

Autumn 2012

Contents

List of Illustrations x
Abbreviations xi

Introduction 1

PART I: THEMES IN MYTH

1. Imaginary Greek Mountains 9
2. Wolves and Werewolves in Greek Thought 33
3. Mythological Names: The Case of *melas* 53
4. The Myth of Talos: Vulnerability, *ichōr*, and Boundary-Crossing 73
5. Movement and Stillness: Versions of Medea 99

PART II: MYTHS IN TRAGEDY

6. Tragedy and Greek Myth 121
7. Time, Space, and Ideology: Tragic Myths and the Athenian *Polis* 145
8. Bafflement in Greek Tragedy 161
9. Blindness and Limits: Sophokles and the Logic of Myth 173
10. Euripides' *Alkestis*: Five Aspects of an Interpretation 201
11. Feminized Males in *Bakchai*: The Importance of Discrimination 219

Envoi 241
Details of Original Publication 243
Bibliography 245
Index 269

List of Illustrations

1. Talos. Silver didrachm from Phaistos. Bibliothèque Nationale de France, Paris, Département de Monnaies, Médailles et Antiques (LUYNES.2365). 79
2. The downfall of Talos. Krater. Museo Nazionale Jatta, Ruvo di Puglia (inv.1501)/photo Luciano Pedicini, Naples. 80
3. Detail of Figure 2. 82
4. Talos. Krater from Spina. Museo Archeologico Nazionale, Ferrara (inv.3092)/su concessione del Ministero per i Beni e le Attività Culturali—Soprintendenza per i Beni Archeologici dell'Emilia Romagna. 83
5. Talos. Krater. Museo Archeologico Nazionale di Montesarchio (inv.28442)/su concessione n.13/2012 del Ministero per i Beni e le Attività Culturali—Soprintendenza per i Beni Archeologici di SA AV BN CE. 84
6. Detail of Figure 5. 85
7. Medea kills her son. Campanian amphora from Cumae. Musée du Louvre, Paris (inv.K300)/photo RMN/Les frères Chuzeville. 108
8. Medea flees from Theseus. Attic pelike. Staatliche Antikensammlungen und Glyptothek, Munich (inv.VAS 2354; J243)/photo Renate Kühling. 109
9. Medea, Theseus, and Aigeus. Apulian krater. © Hessische Hausstiftung, Museum Schloss Fasanerie, Eichenzell/Fulda (inv.FAS AV 179). 110
10. Medea helps Jason overcome the bulls. Apulian krater. Museo Archeologico Nazionale, Naples (inv.81415 [H2413])/photo Luciano Pedicini. 111
11. Medea puts the serpent to sleep. Krater from Paestum. Museo Archeologico Nazionale, Naples (inv.82126 [H3248])/photo Luciano Pedicini. 111
12. Medea sprinkles herbs into a cauldron. Hydria. © The Trustees of the British Museum, London. E163. 112
13. Medea. Detail of Figure 2. 113
14. Medea's aerial escape. Sarcophagus. Antikenmuseum Basel und Sammlung Ludwig (inv.BS 203)/photo Claire Niggli. 114
15. Medea on the serpent-borne chariot. Cleveland Museum of Art (Leonard C. Hanna, Jr. Fund 1991.1). 115

Abbreviations

Authors and titles of ancient works are normally abbreviated according to the practice followed in the third edition of *The Oxford Classical Dictionary*, edited by Simon Hornblower and Antony Spawforth (Oxford, 1996).

AA	*Archäologischer Anzeiger*
ABSA	*Annual of the British School at Athens*
AC	*L'Antiquité Classique*
AJA	*American Journal of Archaeology*
AJP	*American Journal of Philology*
ArchEph	*Archaiologikē Ephēmeris*
BCH	*Bulletin de Correspondance Hellénique*
Beazley *ABV*	J. D. Beazley, *Attic Black-figure Vase-painters*, Oxford, 1956
Beazley *ARV*^{2}	J. D. Beazley, *Attic Red-figure Vase-painters*^{2}, Oxford, 1963
BICS	*Bulletin of the Institute of Classical Studies*
BMCR	*Bryn Mawr Classical Review*
CA	*Classical Antiquity*
CFC	*Cuadernos de Filología Clásica*
CP	*Classical Philology*
CQ	*Classical Quarterly*
CR	*Classical Review*
CW	*Classical World*
Daremberg/Saglio	C. Daremberg and E. Saglio, *Dictionnaire des antiquités grecques et romaines d'après les textes et les monuments*, Paris, 1877–1919
DK	H. Diels and W. Kranz, *Die Fragmente der Vorsokratiker*, 6th edn, Berlin, 1951–2
FGrH	F. Jacoby (ed.), *Die Fragmente der griechischen Historiker*, Berlin and Leiden, 1923–58
FHG	C. Müller (ed.), *Fragmenta Historicorum Graecorum*, Paris, 1841–70
GGM	C. Müller (ed.), *Geographi Graeci Minores*, Paris, 1855–61
G&R	*Greece and Rome*
GRBS	*Greek, Roman and Byzantine Studies*
HSCP	*Harvard Studies in Classical Philology*
ICS	*Illinois Classical Studies*
JDAI	*Jahrbuch des Deutschen Archäologischen Instituts*

JHS	*Journal of Hellenic Studies*
KRS	G. S. Kirk, J. E. Raven, and M. Schofield, *The Presocratic Philosophers*, 2nd edn, Cambridge, 1983
LfgrE	*Lexikon des frühgriechischen Epos*, Göttingen, 1955–2010
LIMC	*Lexicon Iconographicum Mythologiae Classicae*, Zurich and Düsseldorf, 1981–2009
LSAM	F. Sokolowski, *Lois sacrées de l'Asie Mineure*, Paris, 1955
LSCG	F. Sokolowski, *Lois sacrées des cités grecques*, Paris, 1969
LSJ	*Greek-English Lexicon*, compiled by H. G. Liddell and R. Scott, revised by H. S. Jones, 9th edn, Oxford, 1940; revised *Supplement* by P. G. W. Glare, 1996
MD	*Materiali e discussioni per l'analisi dei testi classici*
MDAI(A)	*Mitteilungen des Deutschen Archäologischen Instituts, Athenische Abteilung*
MH	*Museum Helveticum*
OLD	*Oxford Latin Dictionary*, ed. P. G. W. Glare, Oxford, 1982
PCG	R. Kassel and C. Austin (eds.), *Poetae Comici Graeci*, Berlin, 1983–
PCPhS	*Proceedings of the Cambridge Philological Society*
PLF	E. Lobel and D. L. Page (eds.), *Poetarum Lesbiorum Fragmenta*, Oxford, 1955
PMG	D. L. Page (ed.), *Poetae Melici Graeci*, Oxford, 1962
Praktika	*Praktika tēs en Athēnais Archaiologikēs Hetaireias*
QUCC	*Quaderni urbinati di cultura classica*
RA	*Revue Archéologique*
RE	G. Wissowa et al. (eds.), *Paulys Real-Encyclopädie der classischen Altertumswissenschaft*, Stuttgart, 1894–1980
REA	*Revue des Études Anciennes*
REG	*Revue des Études Grecques*
Roscher	W. H. Roscher (ed.), *Ausführliches Lexikon der griechischen und römischen Mythologie*, Leipzig, 1884–1937
TAPA	*Transactions and Proceedings of the American Philological Association*
ThesCRA	*Thesaurus Cultus et Rituum Antiquorum*, Los Angeles, CA
TrGF	B. Snell, R. Kannicht, and S. Radt (eds.), *Tragicorum Graecorum Fragmenta*, Göttingen, 1971–2004
WS	*Wiener Studien*
ZPE	*Zeitschrift für Papyrologie und Epigraphik*

Introduction

The chapters of this book have their origins in eleven papers written over the past thirty years or so. During that time, approaches to Greek myth and Greek tragedy have undergone a number of shifts of emphasis—not, I think, 'paradigm' shifts, but shifts nonetheless. No one writes in a vacuum, and I have inevitably been affected by these successive interpretative trends, whether they have acted as stimuli to explore further where others have gone before, or as provocations to disagreement. Herein lies one reason why the corpus of work here presented is not entirely homogeneous: it reacts to developments in research over the past generation.

Yet the reader will soon discover certain recurrent features of my own approach, features which, while I hope they have not congealed into *idées fixes*, have characterized at least a considerable part of my writing. Whether such features constitute a distinctive contribution to the field is not for me to say, but it may in any case be worthwhile to spell out what, to their author at least, seem to be the central concerns addressed in these chapters.

1. The first concern is with *structure*. Given that several of the chapters deal with tragedy, it will be no surprise that occasionally I refer to aspects of *dramatic* structure; this is especially true in Chapter 11 on *Bakchai*. But that is far from being the predominant sense of 'structure' which I use. Rather, I work with an idea whose origin lies in the structuralist movement, and whose ramifications extend far beyond drama, and indeed beyond texts of any kind.

Although the impact of the structuralist habit of thought on Hellenic studies dates back well over a generation, that habit retains even now the propensity to generate powerful and fruitful interpretations of (among many other things) the stories, texts, and images surviving from classical antiquity. Structuralism makes its presence felt most explicitly in Chapter 9, where I sketch out ways in which the opposition between blindness and sight works as a contrastive pair of terms within what I describe as the 'language system' of Greek myth. Chapter 1 is also concerned with structure; it seems to me incontrovertible that a mountain can be defined only in opposition to what it is not, whether that opposite be (for example) the plain or the *polis*. Indebted to structuralism also is the notion that boundary-crossing is a major aspect of Greek myths and tragedies. I examine this idea in Chapter 4, since the bronze giant Talos literally embodies the crossing of several different boundaries. Tragedy too generates countless instances of boundary-crossing: in Chapters 10 and 11 I discuss this point in relation to the boundaries between, respectively, inside/outside the house (*Alkestis*) and male/female (*Bakchai*).

One more leitmotiv in several of these studies may be traced back to structuralism, in the form of that movement associated with Claude Lévi-Strauss. The idea that an aspect of the empirical world around us may become a tool of thought—making it, in the overused but still valuable cliché, 'good to think (with)'—is an idea I continue to regard as productive. It recurs in several places in Part I, notably in Chapters 2 and 3.

2. A second pervasive feature is a search for *context*, a perspective which I deliberately highlight in my title. Throughout the period when I was working on the original versions of these papers, one of the most influential trends in the study of classical antiquity involved the investigation and theorization of 'reception'—that is, the taking-over/incorporation of the classical world by later cultures. While I recognize the enormous potential of this perspective, it has not been the driver of my own research. Rather, I have sought to replace the material which I am analysing *within its ancient Greek contexts*.

I take it as self-evident that we cannot begin to understand myths which relate in some way to, let us say, a part of the landscape, without considering not only other 'non-mythical' representations of landscape, but also the real ancient landscape itself. Such a deployment of the word 'real' used to be regarded by some as an intellectual solecism: the world of antiquity is (one sometimes heard it suggested) nothing but a text. But the tide has turned, and in any case I have no hesitation in regarding some awareness of ancient real-world contexts as an absolute prerequisite for the kind of research which interests me.

The landscape is one such context; another is the world of fauna, which I investigate in Chapter 2.

Context is relevant in other ways too: not just in real-world terms, but within representational media. To define 'genre' is an apparently simple but in fact fiendishly difficult task; nevertheless, appropriate reference to generic context is crucial if we are to gain access to the horizons of expectation shared by, on the one hand, artists working with words or images, and, on the other hand, their respective publics.[1] In Chapter 6 I isolate some of the features which distinguish tragic versions of myth from versions generated within other contexts. More generally, with tragedy as with myth, I aim to highlight the ancient contexts of the texts. I thus find entirely congenial a comment by Rush Rehm on modern attitudes to, and re-performances of, Greek tragedies: 'To reconnect with the radical nature of Greek tragedy . . . we must . . . engage with tragedy's differences from our own theatrical forms, aesthetic principles, and sociopolitical organisation. We must grapple with unfamiliar cultural assumptions and the peculiarities of foreign dramatic conventions, in order to see our own society and its artifices from a new perspective.'[2]

But the search for context is not an enterprise that goes without saying. That the analysis of context is a gambit, which itself requires contextualization, has been demonstrated by Peter Burke, in an article that discovers ancestors for and exemplars of contextualizing approaches in scholars as diverse and formidable as Marc Bloch, Bruno Malinowski, Edward Evans-Pritchard, and Quentin Skinner.[3] Burke also stresses the role of the interpreter as the ultimate arbiter of what, for any given phenomenon, should be taken to *count* as the context(s). In spite of reservations and qualifications, however, Burke suggests that there is nothing to be gained by rejecting the term 'context'; rather, we should retain it, while being sensitive to its multiple usage. I agree, and would simply reiterate an observation which I recently made in relation to Greek stories about metamorphosis: 'My aim throughout . . . has been always to take notice of the context, but to do so *appropriately*. It is for the reader to judge whether this objective has been reached.'[4]

[1] Genres and their complexity: Genette (1986); Conte (1994) 105–28; Fantuzzi (2004); Mastronarde (2010) 44–62.

[2] Rehm (2003) 37–8.

[3] Burke (2002).

[4] Buxton (2009) 251; italics in original.

3. If 'structure' and 'context' are slippery terms, a third feature common to several chapters is if anything even more elusive: 'theme'. Indeed I am tempted to say that I don't know what a thematic approach is, but I can recognize one when I see it. Within ancient Greece the kinds of themes I have in mind are cross-generic and evidenced from a wide range of historical periods; beyond Greece, they are trans-cultural, offering rich possibilities for comparative analysis—which, however, I hardly need add, needs to be drastically tempered by culture-specific, that is, context-specific considerations.[5] Among earlier practitioners of a thematic approach to the Greek world I would mention R. B. Onians; among contemporaries, three scholars who come to mind are Lloyd Llewellyn-Jones on veiling, Silvia Montiglio on silence and wandering, and Jan Bremmer on numerous themes, though I think especially of his article on walking, standing, and sitting.[6] If we range more widely, I have learnt much from such thematic analyses as those practised by Michel Pastoureau and Theodore Ziolkowski.[7] In so far as I have been able to develop a style of thematic analysis myself, it can be found in any of the chapters in Part I (mountains, wolves, names, (in)vulnerability, movement/stillness), as well as in some chapters in Part II, for instance in the discussions of blindness in Chapter 9, veiling and silence in Chapter 10, and feminization in Chapter 11.

4. Another, related concern is with the *porosity* of myth. One of my main aims in *Imaginary Greece* was to show how the idea of 'myth' was, so far from being neatly circumscribed, in fact integrated in countless ways into the thought and practice of the ancient Greeks.[8] The same objective underpins many of the chapters which follow. Data about the mountains and wolves of mythology must, I argue, be understood in the light of what we know about perceptions of these same themes in 'non-mythical' contexts; the same goes for blackness/whiteness (Chapter 3) and movement/stillness (Chapter 5). Some readers may occasionally feel that the paths I go down in search of the 'non-mythical' are digressive—when, for instance, I look to the

[5] My angle of approach is thus to be sharply distinguished from that of, for instance, Mircea Eliade, whose concerns were above all with themes in their archetypical universality; e.g. Eliade (1954) and numerous other works.

[6] Onians (1954); Bremmer (1991a); Llewellyn-Jones (2003); Montiglio (2000) and (2005).

[7] See for example Pastoureau (2001), (2009a), and (2009b); Ziolkowski (1983).

[8] Buxton (1994).

Hippokratic treatises for help with understanding Talos's vulnerable ankle. Yet I make no apology for such gambits, since, in the words of Louis Gernet: 'One tale leads to another; similarities exist which we should not dismiss because of some a priori fear that connections are arbitrary.'[9]

5. A less pervasive feature of the book, but one which surfaces now and then, might be called, through an appropriately teasing parenthesis, *the (un)certainty principle.* A major trend in research in the humanities over the past generation shelters under the umbrella of 'deconstruction'. To have been impervious to this intellectual movement would have been to adopt the politics of the ostrich. Nevertheless, I remained unpersuaded by the extreme 'infinite play of significance' view of meaning. Instead, it seems to me, we need to differentiate. In some cases, to be sure, we need to allow room for interpretative doubt, indecision, or even bafflement; but in other cases judicious research and reflection can help us reduce our uncertainty to such an extent that we can confidently express a view about probable meanings. These two strategies, apparently contrasting but in reality intertwined, underpin several chapters, but particularly two chapters devoted to tragedy. In Chapter 8 I stress that some elements of that genre—for instance, the causation of events—must remain, on the best evidence before us, simply inexplicable, indeed baffling; in such cases interpretative *aporia* is entirely appropriate. In Chapter 11, on the other hand, I argue that, if we take care to discriminate between the phenomena under review, we can *reduce* our uncertainties and thus understand some aspects of the drama more closely and accurately. In regard to the limits of interpretation, one size emphatically does not fit all.

6. One last common thread is worth mentioning. As its title states, this book is about myths *and* tragedies. What does that 'and' mean? It should not be taken to imply a dichotomy. Virtually without exception, Greek tragedies are retellings of myths: in that sense they *are* myths, or at least versions of myths. So there is something artificial about my division of the book into two sections: 'Themes in Myth' and 'Myths in Tragedy'. Often in Part I the reader will find discussion of mythical themes as explored in tragedy (notably in my account of mountains, but in several other places too). Conversely, several

[9] Gernet (1981) 78; cf. below 97.

chapters in Part II highlight themes found not just in tragedy but also elsewhere in Greek myth. What differentiates Parts I and II is no more than a change of focus, a change which the reader is free to downplay as appropriate.

A further comment about the ordering of the chapters might be useful. This ordering has nothing to do with the original dates of composition of the essays which lie behind each chapter (for the record, those dates are, in chapter order: 1992, 1987, 2010, 2002, 2010, 2007, 2002, 1988, 1980, 1985, 2009). Instead I have wanted to suggest, very broadly and loosely, a spectrum of interpretative emphases, ranging from the cross-contextual analysis of myths at one pole to the analysis of individual literary works at the other. Emblematic of this spectrum is the positioning of the opening and closing chapters. Chapter 1 analyses a mythical theme cross-contextually, yet it also incorporates an account of that theme in specific literary works; Chapter 11 takes as its main focus the dramatic/literary analysis of a single feature of a single tragedy, yet it also explores a mythical theme cross-contextually.

* * * * *

I hesitated for some time about whether or not to update these papers in the light of subsequent scholarship and my own second thoughts. In the event I decided that I *would* make revisions, above all, for obvious reasons, in the case of the less recent publications. Countless small modifications will be found in the footnotes and bibliography, and very many also in the main text. Nevertheless—doubtless under the delusion of vanity—I have seldom felt it necessary, even with the benefit of hindsight, to overhaul the main arguments. To this there are two main exceptions. First, Chapter 3 is, in the form in which it appears here, not so much a reworking of an existing paper as a new one: it is twice the length of the original, since I have added a section on the history of the onomastic interpretation of mythology. Second, I have rewritten some parts of Chapter 8 in order to try to remedy what I now believe to have been defects in the argument.

One final, more cosmetic change is worth mentioning. Since this book aspires to be of interest to non-Hellenists, I have almost entirely eliminated quotations in the Greek alphabet, and proportionately increased the quantity of transliterated (and translated) text. Greek myths and Greek tragedies are too important to be left exclusively in the hands of those able to read them in the original.

Part I

Themes in Myth

1

Imaginary Greek Mountains

My first case study of mythical contexts, structures, and themes concerns a landscape feature which, as any traveller in Greece knows, habitually constitutes the limit to a viewer's line of sight. 'Horizons of expectation' is a metaphor which offers rich possibilities to the cultural historian; in the present instance, literal and metaphorical aspects of those horizons are inextricably interwoven.

One aspect of the mental world of the ancient Greeks relates to their perception of the various elements of the landscape within which they lived: rivers, plains, cities, caves, springs, meadows, mountains. In this first chapter I attempt to show how Greek perceptions of one such feature of the landscape point towards a structure of thought common to many contexts. However, to soften and complicate this sense of structure, I emphasize also several major differences between one context and another, concentrating especially on the distinctive portrayal of mountains in tragedy. Above all, I investigate—with, I hope, due awareness of the pitfalls—the distance between the 'imaginary' world of myth and the 'real' world of life, including that particular form of life which is dramatized in ritual.

1. WHAT IS A MOUNTAIN?

At the outset we have a terminological problem. A mountain is in the eye of the beholder.[1] The Greeks were agreed that, for example,

[1] On the ineradicable role of human perceptions in constructing our idea of even the most 'natural' of landscapes, see the brilliant study by Schama (1995).

Olympos, Cretan Ida, Parnassos, Helikon, Pelion, Kithairon, and Lykaion—which on our reckoning range from about 2,900 metres to about 1,400 metres—were *orē* (plural of *oros*, the Greek word conventionally translated as 'mountain'). But so, according for instance to Strabo, was 'Mount' Kynthos on Delos—a stiff walk if you have a ferry to catch on a hot day, but with the best will in the world only 113 metres above sea level; while at Olympia *to oros to Kronion* ('the *oros* of Kronos'), as Pausanias calls it, can manage a mere 123 metres.[2] An *oros* is not, then, to be defined simply in terms of physical height. Instead we should look to what, in our sources, is contrasted with an *oros*.[3] An *oros* is not the plain (where you grow corn and fight in phalanx), nor is it the city or the village (where you live). The oppositions between *oros* and plain, and *oros* and city, are found in Greek thought of many periods and many contexts. Take the words spoken by Arrian's Alexander to his troops: 'Philip gave you cloaks to wear instead of hides, brought you down from the mountains to the plains . . . made you into *polis*-dwellers, and equipped you with good laws and customs.'[4] But if an *oros* is not a plain and not a city, neither is it an acropolis, that fortified height, often also religious centre and symbol of political power, *within* the city.[5] An *oros* is a height outside inhabited and cultivated space—outside the *polis*, the *astu* (town), and

'Terminology' of Greek mountains: Langdon (2000); Accorinti (2010) 23–5. Although Spencer (2010) focuses on the Roman landscape, the discussions of landscape theory there also have wider relevance, including to Greece.

2 Kynthos: Strabo 10.5.2. Kronion: Paus. 5.21.2; 6.20.1 (altitudes taken from Philippson (1950–9) iv. 111 and iii, 2.340). Fluid meaning of *oros*: Buck (1949) 23; Pritchett (1965) 66. For an apparently anomalous, Argive use of *oros*, see Vollgraff (1914) 333; Caskey and Amandry (1952) 218. For *oros* in Strabo, see Baladié (1980) 124–33.

3 Langdon (2000) 461–2 describes my contrastive definition as 'probably the best approach'. Langdon's article is the most comprehensive analysis of mountains in Greek religion to have appeared since the original publication of my own article; I am pleased to say that it echoes my account in many places, and elsewhere helpfully complements it.

4 Arr. *Anab.* 7.9.2. For the plain/*oros* opposition, see Theophr. *Hist. pl.* 1.8.1 and 3.11.2. For plain/non-plain contrasted in warfare, see Osborne (1987) 144, with reference to Polyb. 18.31. 'Plainsmen' and 'men from beyond the hills' form two political constituencies in the time of Peisistratos: Hdt. 1.59; Arist. [*Ath. Pol.*] 13.4 (with Rhodes (1981) ad loc.); cf. Plut. *Sol.* 13 on the political division between Hillmen, Plainsmen, and Shoremen.

5 Cf. Martin (1974) 32. Like the *oros*, the acropolis may be contrasted with the plain: Arist. *Pol.* 1330^{b} (an acropolis is 'oligarchic' and 'monarchical'; level ground is 'democratic').

the *kōmai* (villages).[6] We might add that, in a specifically Egyptian context, *oros* may signify the desert (near or far) in contrast with the fertile and cultivable Nile valley.[7] Height is once again only part of the story: a contrast with the area of cultivation is equally important.

2. USING MOUNTAINS

What was an *oros* used for?[8] Firstly, for pasturage, particularly (bearing in mind the practice of transhumance) during the summer heat.[9] The inscriptional evidence, meagre enough,[10] tends to concern either the avoidance of damage by flocks to religious property, or disputes between cities over pasturage rights[11]—in other words, cases where the affairs of herdsmen impinged on the wider community. The authentic voice of the herdsman himself is occasionally heard—we have, for instance, a goatherd's votive inscription found on the slopes of Mount Elias on Aigina, and a dedication by another goatherd in the cave at Vari on Hymettos[12]—but such cases are exceptional. Nevertheless, herding was clearly of greater significance than the evidence of our city-oriented sources implies, and will have been the principal activity which drew men to stay in the mountains for long periods.[13]

Mountains were a source of raw materials. Sometimes this is stone or metal (Hymettos and Pentelikon; Pangaion); usually it is wood. Scholars have differed over just how much afforestation of mountains there was in ancient times,[14] but that one of the reasons for going to

[6] One of the referees for the original publication of this chapter made the interesting comment that 'in English the nearest corresponding word [sc. to *oros*] is probably not "mountain" or "hill" but "moor"'. But the connotations of 'moor' are essentially non-Mediterranean; the same goes for 'heath'.

[7] Cf. Cadell and Rémondon (1967).

[8] See Pease (1961); Fehling (1974) ch. 2 ('Fernsicht').

[9] See Georgoudi (1974); Skydsgaard (1988).

[10] The data are reviewed in Robert (1949), (1955), and (1966) 383–4; see also Whittaker (1988).

[11] Cf. Georgoudi (1974) 180–1; Sartre (1979).

[12] Aigina: *IG* IV 127, with Robert (1949) 154–5. Hymettos: *AJA* 7 (1903) 292–3 = *IG* I^2 778. Although in both cases some scholars have read a proper name instead of 'goatherd'—*Αἰπόλου* for αἰπόλου (Aigina) and h*Αίπολος* for hαιπόλος (Vari)—the locations of the finds are at the very least consistent with the sense 'goatherd'.

[13] On herding, see now the excellent article by Berman (2005).

[14] See e.g. Georgoudi (1974); Halstead (1987) 79–81; O. Rackham (1990).

an *oros* was to get timber is not in doubt. A man mentioned in one of Demosthenes' private orations had a farm in an outlying deme and kept six donkeys permanently busy sending wood down to the city.[15] We hear occasionally of woodcutters, whom Theophrastos calls 'mountain-smiters' (*oreotupoi*).[16] Like shepherds, they are usually silent men; though a funerary inscription from classical Athens records the proud boast of a Phrygian: 'By Zeus, I never saw a better woodcutter than myself.'[17] Wood, hence charcoal: like shepherds, charcoal-burners might, from the city-dweller's perspective, be felt to be outsiders. Such an attitude is implicit in a fragment of Andokides: 'May we never again see the charcoal-burners and their wagons arriving in the city [of Athens] from the mountains'—apparently a reference to the consequences of the occupation of Attica during the Archidamian war.[18] Obviously, charcoal-burners came into the city now and again to sell their fuel; it was the *permanent* residence of these outsiders that rankled. As always, of course, the coin of marginality has another side to it, and we glimpse this in the nostalgia of Dikaiopolis in Aristophanes' *Acharnians* (33–6), when the comic hero, 'hating the *astu* (town)', longs to be back in his own 'charcoal' village, which did not cry 'Buy charcoal!' because it had no need to, since it produced everything itself. Indeed so vigorous is the comic portrait of the Acharnians, with their splendid 'Muse of Flame' (665), that charcoal seems to dominate not just their own community but the wider Athenian state too. This is Aristophanic exaggeration; but the play serves as a reminder that the central/marginal distinction has to be used with discretion and elasticity.

Shepherds, woodcutters, and charcoal-burners dwelt on or regularly visited mountains out of economic necessity. Others visited the *oros* more occasionally, in order to hunt. Not all hunting was done on mountains, but most of it was.[19] Xenophon notes that traps for deer

[15] Dem. 42.5–7; Gow (1952) on Theoc. *Id.* 13.25f.

[16] Theophr. *Hist. pl.* 3.3.7; 3.12.4, etc. For woodcutting on Mount Ida, see Theoc. *Id.* 17.9–10, with Gow (1952) ad loc.

[17] *IG* I^2 1084 = P. A. Hansen (1983) no. 87; cf. Himmelmann (1980) 62.

[18] Andoc. fr. 4 Blass. See further Lacey (1968) 53 with 256 n. 13. For a modern example of the charcoal-burner's marginality one may compare the dissident, radical charcoal-burners of the Mount Pelion area in 1921–2. I owe this information to M. Llewellyn Smith. Note also the clandestine movement in 19th-century Italy whose members styled themselves *i carbonari*.

[19] On the question of the 'space' in which hunting was conducted, see Schnapp (1973).

and boar are set in the mountains; up there, as opposed to in the plain, you can catch deer by day as well as by night.[20] According to Pausanias, 'The whole of Taygetos provides excellent hunting for [wild] goats and for boar, and an ample supply of deer and bear.'[21] We do know of a case where circumstances imposed hunting as a full-time necessity, as with Dio Chrysostom's story about shepherds working for a rich Euboian, who were forced to resort to hunting when the Romans killed the man's beasts.[22] But as a rule hunting was part-time. The *oros* was where groups of men went out to pit themselves against beasts, and then return to the city.

Another use of mountains was for travel. In spite of steep gradients and narrow passes, mountain paths were used by both individuals and armies. In a famous article on Greek mountain terrain, A. R. Burn concluded: 'I have shown, I hope, how the chief significance of Helikon in history is as a *route*.'[23] Pausanias tells us often enough of routes that take a direct line across mountains: from Lilaia to Delphi you cut across Parnassos; one road from Mantineia to Orchomenos went via Mount Anchisia; there were two paths over Oita; and so on.[24] It might be risky. A simile in the *Iliad* begins:

> As when upon the peaks of a mountain the South Wind
> scatters thick mist, no friend to the shepherd, but better than night for the robber

A millennium later Lucian reports the story of a wealthy Theban murdered by brigands on Kithairon.[25]

Mountains played various roles in warfare. In time of extreme need the *oros* could function as a kind of temporary acropolis, a refuge for those with no prospect of winning a pitched battle and no safe settlement to which to withdraw. Thus the Phokians fled the Persians by climbing Parnassos; the Messenians sheltered from the Lakonians on Eira and Ithome.[26] We hear occasionally about reconnaissance

[20] Xen. *Cyn.* 9.11; 9.17; 10.22. [21] Paus. 3.20.4.

[22] Dio Chrys. *Or.* 7.11–20.

[23] Burn (1949) 322 (italics in original). This and Burn (1951) are described by Pritchett (1982, 207) as 'the two best articles ever published on Greek mountain terrain'.

[24] Paus. 10.33.3; 8.12.8; 10.22.8.

[25] *Il.* 3.10–11; Lucian *Dial. mort.* 22.2.

[26] Hdt. 8.32, cf. 8.27; Paus. 4.17.10; 4.24.6. On the remote location of places of asylum, see in general Sinn (2000).

ascents, as when Philip V of Macedon went up Haimos.[27] Fire-signalling from beacons on the *oros* was developed with enormous ingenuity.[28] Clearly, though, this is all peripheral to the main issue: fighting. The *oros* was a territory which could be exploited by light-armed troops, but which was wholly unsuited to the hoplite phalanx. It was a place for deception, for ambush, for night combat—witness the tactics of Thracian and other peltasts.[29] Given the strong ideological component in the divide between hoplite and non-hoplite,[30] and given the pervasive rules of appropriateness underpinning Greek warfare,[31] it is surely comprehensible that mountain warfare is as relatively infrequent as it is.[32] It is comprehensible, too—indeed, it is part of the same framework of ideas—that the *oros*, a space which is simultaneously not the city and not the plain, should in some parts of Greece form the backdrop to the military education of the adolescent male, at the stage when he was neither (yet) a full member of the community nor (yet) a hoplite.[33] The *oros* could be an initiatory space (one may compare the wolf-men of Lykaion).[34]

We hear sometimes of what may be described as touristic ascents: at Etna visitors (at any rate in the time of Pausanias) threw valuable objects into the crater, the aim being to be lucky enough to have the gift accepted.[35] Then there were those bent on 'enquiry'. Pliny the Elder writes of people who, in order to do research on plants, 'scoured also pathless mountain peaks, remote deserts, and all the bowels of the earth'.[36] Theophrastos and Philo preserve accounts of persons

[27] Livy 40.21–2. [28] Polyb. 10.43–7.

[29] See Pritchett (1971–91), Part II, 170.

[30] Cf. Ducrey (1985) 110–14.

[31] This has been repeatedly shown by Pritchett in his great study (1971–91).

[32] The absence of a developed mountain strategy in Greek warfare is discussed by Gomme (1945) 10–15.

[33] Cf. Vidal-Naquet (1986a) 108, with particular reference to Crete.

[34] Cf. my remarks at 45–8 below.

[35] Paus. 3.23.9. In his commentary (1898 ad loc.) Frazer's comparatist approach is at its most beguiling: he turns up the propitiatory flinging of tufts of grass (amongst the Masai) and the hurling of 'vast numbers of hogs' (Hawaii) into the relevant volcano. One may compare the anecdotal 'death' of Empedokles, who plunged into the crater of Etna (Diog. Laert. 8.69). For fascinating observations on this story, see Kingsley (1995), index s.v. 'Etna'.

[36] Plin. *HN* 25.1. Much plant-gathering, however, will have had more to do with everyday needs than with 'research': Theophr. *Hist. pl.* 9.10.2–4 (black hellebore best from Helikon, white from Oita).

who observed the heavens from mountains. One such, according to Philostratos' *Life of Apollonios of Tyana*, was the philosopher Anaxagoras, and we have similar reports about Eudoxos and Pythagoras.[37] But to the average Greek village- or city-dweller such eccentricity was irrelevant. What was far more important was the final use of mountains which I want to mention: their role as locations for sanctuaries of the gods.

Zeus was pre-eminent. In A. B. Cook's monumental study of the god there are references to nearly one hundred mountain cults.[38] In a review of the evidence for mountain-*tops* as locations for sanctuaries of Zeus, Merle K. Langdon concluded that, while occasionally these are explicitly dedicated to Zeus as god of rain (e.g. Zeus Ombrios on Hymettos), in most cases no specific divine function of this or any other kind can be identified with certainty.[39] Nevertheless the association between Zeus and the *peak* is worth noting as an example of differentiation in the religious topography of the *oros*.[40] May one go on from this to posit a structuralizing opposition between Zeus, god of the summit of the *oros*, and Athene, goddess of the acropolis, Athene as Polias or Poliouchos, in which role she appears in many cities?[41] I think the answer is 'yes', provided we acknowledge certain facts which soften the rigidity of the schema. For example, Athene herself may be worshipped on an *oros*—on Pentelikon, on Pontinos near Lerna, on a mountain above Kleitor in Arkadia.[42] Nor is Zeus a stranger to the acropolis: he had temples on the citadels of Argos and Akragas, and an altar at the highest point of the Athenian acropolis.[43] Again, Zeus is not the dominant power on every *oros*: Helios, Artemis, Dionysos, Demeter, Pan, Apollo, Hermes, and the variously named 'Mother' goddess of Asia Minor all have mountain sanctuaries.[44]

[37] Theophr. *Sign.* 4; Philo *Prov.* 2.27; Philostr. *VA* 2.5; Petron. *Sat.* 88 (Eudoxos); Iambl. *VP* 3.14–15 (Pythagoras). NB also Hadrian's ascent of Etna 'in order to see the sunrise, which is, so they say, multicoloured like the rainbow' (SHA *Hadr.* 13.3).

[38] A. B. Cook (1914–40) i. 165.

[39] Langdon (1976), esp. 81, to be looked at in conjunction with Lauter (1985), esp. 134–6.

[40] Cf. also Graf (1985) 202–3 on Zeus Ὕπατος.

[41] Cf. Burkert (1985) 140.

[42] Paus. 1.32.2; 2.36.8; 8.21.4.

[43] Paus. 2.24.3; Polyaenus, *Strat.* 5.1.1 (see Cook 1914–40, i. 122–3); Burkert (1983) 136 with n. 2.

[44] Some examples noted by Pausanias: 3.20.4 (Helios); 2.24.5, 2.25.3, 8.13.1 (Artemis); 3.22.2 (Dionysos); 8.10.1 (Demeter); 8.24.4, 8.36.8 (Pan); 9.23.6 (Apollo); 8.17.1

However, notwithstanding these qualifications, Zeus' statistical pre-eminence on the *oros* looks unchallengeable.

It should be mentioned finally that, in addition to divinities who were *associated* with a mountain, there were others who were apparently *identified* with one. But in spite of Korinna's poetical evocation of the song contest between Helikon and Kithairon,[45] and in spite of Wilamowitz's speculations about Atlas and other potential mountain-Giants/Titans,[46] Greek belief (as opposed, for example, to Cappadocian)[47] preferred the model of association to that of identification.

3. IMAGINARY MOUNTAINS

This is not the place to argue in detail the heuristic merits of various definitions of 'myth'. I simply set out baldly two working assumptions. (1) By 'a Greek myth' I shall mean one of the stories related by (some) Greeks about the deeds of the gods and heroes and their interrelations with mortals. (2) The territory of Greek mythology is not hermetically sealed. Many kinds of story ('historical' anecdote, comic plot, etc.) may incorporate patterns of thought analogous to those present in tales about gods and heroes; this material will be raided where appropriate.

To begin with a partial truth: myth 'reflects'. Mythical herdsmen, like real ones, live on mountains. The Euripidean Cyclops had his home on Etna; Paris and Anchises dwelt on Trojan Ida; Apollo was out on the slopes of Pieria when Hermes came to rustle.[48] Herdsmen in myth practise transhumance, like the two in *Oidipous Tyrannos*: 'We herded as neighbours three times', recalls the Corinthian, 'for six months from spring to the rise of Arktouros'.[49] A myth ascribed by

(Hermes). For the 'Mother', cf. Hdt. 1.80, Paus. 5.13.7; *Der Kleine Pauly* (1964–75) iii. 383–9, s.v. 'Kybele' (W. Fauth).

45 The text is very fragmentary, see Page (1953) 19–22 and D. A. Campbell (1992) fr. 654, but Huxley (1978, 71–2) seems to be right in observing that Korinna 'comes close to identifying [the god Helikon] with the mountain'.

46 Wilamowitz-Moellendorff (1931–2) i. 93–5.

47 See Huxley (1978).

48 Eur. *Cyc.* 114; Apollod. *Bibl.* 3.12.5; *Hymn. Hom. Aphr.* 53–5; *Hymn. Hom. Herm.* 69–70.

49 Soph. *OT* 1133–7.

Antoninus Liberalis to Nikandros tells of a herdsman who, when helpfully advised by Pan to take his flocks down from Mount Othrys on account of the impending onset of a harsh winter, declined the advice, and for good measure insulted the Nymphs. The flock disappeared in the snow, and the rash herdsman turned into a beetle.[50]

Mythical mountains are a source of wood: again myth reflects the real world. Timber for the *Argo* came from Pelion; the Trojan horse is of mountain pine; wood for Patroklos' pyre came from the spurs of Ida.[51] Lykos sent servants out from Thebes to gather wood on Helikon and even Parnassos in order to incinerate Herakles' family.[52] Woodcutters put in rare appearances in myths, as in the oracle recorded by Eusebios about nine woodcutters who were stunned 'on the wooded mountains' near Miletos when they heard Pan singing.[53]

As in life, so in myth, men hunt on mountains. Teiresias was hunting on Kithairon when he saw Athene; so was Aktaion when he made an analogous mistake; Endymion hunted by moonlight on Latmos, and was loved by Selene; Peleus and Akastos hunted on Pelion.[54] In Bion's *Lament for Adonis*, the crying of the young man's hounds was echoed by the Oreads (18–19).

Mythical mountains could be used for travel, as when one of Ida's shepherds describes the march of Rhesos.[55] Where there are lonely travellers, there you find robbers: the mythical brigand Autolykos lived on Parnassos.[56] Mythical mountains also provided a refuge. Megaros escaped Deukalion's flood by taking refuge on Mount Gerania; the better-known refuge on the same occasion was Parnassos.[57] In Aratos' *Phainomena*, when Dike abandoned humanity after rebuking it during the Silver Age, she too sought refuge in the mountains.[58]

Even the use of fire-beacons is reflected in myth, in the famous account of the mountain-to-mountain relaying of signifying flame from Troy to Argos in Aischylos' *Agamemnon* (281–316).

[50] Ant. Lib. *Met.* 22; cf. Borgeaud (1988) 61–2.

[51] Eur. *Med.* 3–4; Eur. *Tro.* 534; Hom. *Il.* 23.117.

[52] Eur. *HF* 240–2.

[53] Euseb. *Praep. evang.* 5.6.1; cf. Lane Fox (1986) 131–2.

[54] Callim. *Hymn* 5.74–6 (Teiresias); Apollod. *Bibl.* 3.4.4 (Aktaion); schol. Ap. Rhod. *Argon.* 4.57–8 Wendel (Endymion); Apollod. *Bibl.* 3.13.3 (Peleus, Akastos).

[55] Eur. *Rhes.* 282–316.

[56] Paus. 8.4.6.

[57] Paus. 1.40.1 (Megaros); Apollod. *Bibl.* 1.7.2, Paus. 10.6.2 (Parnassos); cf. Paus. 4.34.10 *re* Asine.

[58] Arat. *Phaen.* 127.

Lastly, the presence of sanctuaries has its mythical counterpart, since many of the gods in the traditional tales can be found on mountains. Zeus' birth and upbringing, his functions as god of rain and lightning, and his supremacy on Olympos all focus his power on the *oros*.[59] The Olympians' foes the Titans fought from Mount Othrys.[60] You find the Muses on Helikon, Pan on mountains everywhere, especially Arkadia; likewise the Nymphs.[61] Artemis loved the heights: a simile in *Odyssey* Book 6 depicts her on Taygetos and Erymanthos; in *Trojan Women* she is *orestera* ('of the *oros*').[62] And in *Bakchai* Dionysos, god of Nysa and Tmolos, sharer of Parnassos with Apollo, comes at last to Kithairon.

Myths, then, 'reflect'. But they also refract, transforming the world by a process of selective emphasis and clarification and exaggeration. In the present case, myths present an image of mountains which is both more extreme and more consistent than that of everyday life, paring down that wide range of uses which men actually made of the *oros*, and coming back again and again to the same few, symbolically productive characteristics.

To what extent can comparative material help us to interpret such characteristics? For the Lele, the forest (opposed both to the village and to the grassland) is the location of spirits, a place of good luck and danger; for the Asante, a visit to the bush (opposed to the village) risks encounters with uncanny powers, and necessitates rituals of transition on one's return; for the Dinka, the homestead (*bai*) is opposed to the wilds (*roor*), which contains harmful anti-social powers, so that Godfrey Lienhardt speaks of a 'distinction between the uncontrolled life of the wilds, without human order and reason, and the orderly and rational domesticated life of men and beasts in society'.[63] Such anthropological 'parallels' could be multiplied almost indefinitely.[64] They do not prove anything, but they may at least encourage us to

[59] Birth and upbringing: see 20 below. Zeus and the *oros:* cf. Burkert (1985) 126.

[60] Hes. *Theog.* 632. Cf. Apollod. *Bibl.* 1.6.3: the combat between Zeus and Typhon moves from Kasios to Nysa to Haimos to Etna.

[61] Hes. *Theog.* 1 (Muses); *Hymn. Hom. Pan.* 6–7, Dion. Hal. *Ant. Rom.* 1.38.1 (Pan); Hom. *Il.* 24.614–17, *Hymn. Hom. Aphr.* 256–68 (Nymphs).

[62] Hom. *Od.* 6.102–9; Eur. *Tro.* 551.

[63] M. Douglas (1954), esp. 4–6; McLeod (1981) 20–40; Lienhardt (1961) 63.

[64] For some biblical material, see Dozeman (1989) 13 n. 48. Bernbaum (1997) offers a much broader perspective, with wonderful illustrations.

look with new attention at existing data, provided we recognize that each individual cultural situation will have its own configuration.

In Greece there are three main aspects to the mythical image of the *oros*. First and most obvious: mountains were outside and wild. Centaurs lived on mountains, as indicated by Nestor's words in *Iliad* Book 1 about an earlier generation of heroes: 'They were strongest, and fought against the strongest, the beast men living in the mountains.'[65] The Sphinx—called an *oureion teras* ('mountain prodigy') in Euripides' *Phoenician Women*—lived, according to Pausanias, on a mountain near Onchestos.[66] An *oros* was a place of wild violence too: on Pangaion, Lykourgos was done to death by wild horses;[67] on Kithairon, Aktaion was torn to pieces by wild dogs, Pentheus by wild aunts. Being outside, mountains are for outsiders. In the discussion of correct naming in Plato's *Kratylos*, Sokrates praises the name 'Orestes' ('Mountain Man') as appropriate since it expresses 'the fierceness, the wildness, and the "mountainous" quality (*to oreinon*) of his nature'.[68] One who commits matricide belongs far away from society. It is revealing that Menander's *Bad-tempered Man*, whose prologue is spoken by Pan, should be set in a mountainous area of Attica on the slopes of Mount Parnes. The misanthrope withdraws up-country.

Being perceived as wild, mythical mountains are the ideal place to expose unwanted offspring: Oidipous on Kithairon, Amphion and Zethos near the same mountain, Asklepios on Titthion, Paris on Ida, Telephos on Parthenion.[69] But exactly what sort of refraction is taking place here? The reality of ancient abandonment is an enormously problematic subject. One starting point for discussion is still John Boswell's study, which has implications for classical Greece even though it focuses on late Roman antiquity and the Middle Ages.[70] Boswell raises the central issue of how far the *topos* of abandonment—rightly distinguished by him from 'infanticide'—was like the modern cinematic motif of 'death by quicksand', in other

65 *Il.* 1.267–8. Cf. Apollod. *Bibl.* 2.5.4 (centaurs on Mounts Pelion and Malea).

66 Eur. *Phoen.* 806; Paus. 9.26.2. Apollodoros locates the Sphinx on Mount Phikion (*Bibl.* 3.5.8); cf. Moret (1984) i. 69 with n. 1.

67 Apollod. *Bibl.* 3.5.1.

68 Pl. *Cra.* 394e; on naming in *Kratylos*, see 55 below.

69 Soph. *OT* (Oidipous); Paus. 1.38.9 (Amphion/Zethos); Paus. 2.26.4 (Asklepios; *Hymn. Hom. Aesc.* 3 gives another version: 'in the Dotian plain'); Apollod. 3.12.5 (Paris); Apollod. 2.7.4; 3.9.1 (Telephos).

70 Boswell (1988).

words basically an 'unrealistic' fictional ploy.[71] Asking the same question about ancient Greece is no less legitimate and important, but the matter is unlikely to be settled while there is so much controversy about what constitutes proper comparative demographic evidence.[72] Notwithstanding this uncertainty, we can, I think, maintain the following: in depicting abandoned infants as male,[73] as always *found*, and as always surviving to experience some notable fate, Greek myths were selecting from the real world in order to construct an *extreme* image of abandonment; in particular, they were representing the *oros* as a place for extraordinary luck (which is not, of course, necessarily to say *good* luck.)[74]

Secondly, mountains are before. They were believed to be humanity's place of first habitation. In the *Laws* (677b–c) Plato's Athenian speculates about a time after a prehistoric flood, when life was preserved on the tops of mountains among herdsmen, since the cities near the sea and in the plains had been destroyed. The same story-pattern applies to Deukalion and Pyrrha on Parnassos, and to the Trojan ancestral hero Dardanos, who left Samothrace to avoid the flood, drifted in a leather bag, and landed on Mount Ida.[75] Before also, in that they are the location of the early lives of gods: Hermes (born on Kyllene); the Muses (born in Pieria, a little below Olympos); not to mention Zeus (born on Cretan Ida or Dikte, reared on Lykaion and Ithome, etc.).[76] If birth is before, so in a different way is

[71] Boswell (1988) 6–7. Along the way Boswell makes some fascinating observations, e.g. at 97, where he questions the fictionality of the *topos* of being saved by a shepherd: 'it is worth noting that there was actually legislation in the later empire prohibiting the upper classes from "handing their children over to shepherds"'.

[72] Cf. the disagreement between Engels (1980) and Golden (1981); see also Patterson (1985). Boswell himself reviews discussions of the Greek evidence, from Glotz onwards, in Boswell (1988) 40–1, n. 96. For bibliography on more recent discussions of infanticide/abandonment of babies in Greece and in other ancient societies, see Dasen (2004) 391–2.

[73] This applies to foundlings in mythology, but not to those in romance (compare Chloe in *Daphnis and Chloe* and the Queen of Ethiopia's daughter in *Aithiopika*) or New Comedy. *If* it is true, as is often taken for granted, that abandonment of female infants was in real life commoner than that of males, it may be that we should see romance and New Comedy as extending mythical patterns in 'realistic' directions (though in each case within a highly artificial framework).

[74] More remarks on exposure in Dillon (1989), ch. 2; he stresses the role played in such stories by a breakdown in the father/daughter relationship.

[75] Apollod. *Bibl.* 1.7.2 (Deukalion); schol. Hom. *Il.* 20.215–16 (Dardanos).

[76] *Hymn. Hom. Herm.* (Hermes); Hes. *Theog.* 53–62 (Muses). For Zeus' Cretan birth see Frazer (1921) i. pp. 6–7, n. 2; A. B. Cook (1914–40) i. 148–54. Paus. 8.38.2 (Lykaion); Paus. 4.33.1 (Ithome).

adolescence. Jason was brought up on Pelion by Cheiron, before descending, aged twenty and clad in a leopard skin, to claim his rights in Iolkos (Pindar, *Pythian* 4). Also socialized by Cheiron on the same mountain were Achilles, Asklepios, Aktaion, and Aristaios.[77] Paris was a young herdsman on Ida before being recognized and accorded his true name and status in Troy.[78] These pairings of Pelion-and-Iolkos and Ida-and-Troy—to which may be added Kithairon-and-Thebes and Oita-and-Trachis—illustrate a common motif, the symbiosis of city and neighbouring mountain. In tragedy in particular, *oros* and *polis* often constitute two of the significant spaces in terms of which the action is oriented: later we shall look at some examples.

Thirdly, a mountain is a place for reversals. Things normally separate are brought together, as the distinctions of the city are collapsed.

The divine and the human come together on mountains. Hesiod meets the Muses on Helikon; Philippides meets Pan on Parthenion.[79] Any hunter or herdsman on an imaginary Greek mountain will probably meet a god. Sometimes such an encounter is momentary and disastrous (Aktaion, Teiresias), sometimes it is briefly prolonged in sexual union (Endymion and Selene, Anchises and Aphrodite). Occasionally, there is the prospect of an extended relationship: Thetis and Peleus *marry* on Pelion.[80] But the distance is unbridgeable: in the *Iliad* they are living apart.

Metamorphosis entails a collapsing of distinctions: and metamorphoses often take place on mountains. Teiresias saw two snakes copulating on Mount Kyllene, struck them, and turned into a woman.[81] On Mount Thornax near Hermione in the Argolid, Zeus turned into a cuckoo and fluttered into Hera's affections;[82] the changing of Aktaion into a stag on Kithairon, and Lykaon into a wolf on Lykaion, are familiar enough.[83]

[77] Apollod. *Bibl.* 3.13.6 (Achilles); Pind. *Pyth.* 3, Apollod. *Bibl.* 3.10.3 (Asklepios); Apollod. *Bibl.* 3.4.4 (Aktaion); Ap. Rhod. *Argon.* 2.509–10 (Aristaios).

[78] Ida/Troy: Eur. *IA* 1283–90, with Stinton (1965) 29–34; Apollod. *Bibl.* 3.12.5. On Ida, see further Elliger (1975) 263–6.

[79] Hes. *Theog.* 22–3; Hdt. 6.105. On Helikon and the Muses, see Hurst and Schachter (1996).

[80] Apollod. *Bibl.* 3.13.5.

[81] Apollod. *Bibl.* 3.6.7. See also 228–9 below.

[82] Paus. 2.36.1.

[83] Aktaion: see Buxton (2009) 98–109. Lykaon: see 41–50 below.

Social relationships and normal social behaviour may be reversed on imaginary mountains. In real life, hunting is for men; although Xenophon in an afterthought praises the virtues of the chase as applying to women as well as men, no mention is made in his treatise of real-life female hunters.[84] Yet myths regularly speak of female hunting, both individual (Atalante, Prokris, Kallisto; Kyrene in Pindar's 9th *Pythian*) and collective (maenads hunt down Orpheus on Pangaion[85] and Pentheus on Kithairon). For *real-life* women to be out on a mountain at all—let alone out hunting—is anyway unusual: observing three striking females, Lucian's Paris remarks to Hermes that 'being so beautiful they are not suitable *oreopolein* ("to go on the mountains")'.[86] The presence of women on the *oros* can even be seen as a symptom of madness. Euripides portrays Phaidra's wish to follow Hippolytos out onto the mountain as the very essence of her mania;[87] the maddened daughters of Proitos run out into the Aroanian mountains of Arkadia.[88] To behave outside the norm, or outside oneself, is to belong on the *oros*, and in a way to belong to it. Here, as elsewhere, myth sharpens the boundary between *oros* and settlement, a boundary which in everyday life will have been blurred; the livelihood of shepherds, and of charcoal-burners like the Acharnians, depended, after all, on the constant crossing of the divide. Such sharpening is an example of the selective emphasis and clarification of which we spoke.

4. RITUAL

So far I have assumed that it is meaningful to separate 'life' from 'myth'. However, it is clear that myths feed back into the perceptions of everyday life, even if the level and extent of this process are hard to pin down and virtually impossible to quantify. (That our ordinary perception of motorway hitchhikers and microwave ovens is at some level and in some contexts affected by their sinister folklore connotations, is as certain as it is difficult to prove.)[89] In the case of Greece,

[84] The afterthought is at *Cyn.* 3.18, and is the concluding sentence of the treatise.
[85] See West (1983); *TrGF* iii, pp. 138–9 Radt.
[86] *Dearum iudic.* 7.
[87] Cf. the Nurse's reaction at Eur. *Hipp.* 232–8.
[88] Paus. 8.18.7.
[89] See Brunvand (1981).

however, there is one aspect of social behaviour into which myths fed back in an unmistakable and literally dramatic way.

In many regions, on certain ritual occasions, the city came to the mountain. The manner of the approach was various: the Plataeans carried wooden images to the top of Kithairon and burnt them for Zeus and Hera; there was a werewolf cult on Lykaion; the Muses received sacrifice on Helikon; and so on.[90] From this variety—for there is no single pattern—I want to pick out two rituals, which will enable us to develop points already made about mythical mountains and to highlight characteristic similarities and contrasts between myth and ritual.

'On the peak of the *oros* there is the so-called "cave of Cheiron", and a shrine of Zeus Aktaios. At the rising of the Dog Star, the time of greatest heat, those among the citizens who are most notable and in the prime of their lives, having been chosen in the presence of the priest, climb up to the cave, clad in thick new fleeces—so cold is it on the mountain.' The mountain is Pelion; the source, the Hellenistic geographer Herakleides.[91] His comment about the cold hardly squares with the time of year: the wearing of fleeces has symbolic rather than practical significance. But what is the nature of the symbolism? Are the participants assimilating themselves to Zeus the Ram God?[92] Or to 'fleecy' clouds in a weather ceremony?[93] Or to the sacrificial *victims* of Zeus?[94] Or is this 'an ancient religious custom whose real meaning we may never know'?[95] The first two guesses embody assumptions which have ceased to be as persuasive as they once were; the third is currently more fashionable, with its emphasis on sacrifice as the semantic heart of the drama;[96] the fourth is clearly the safest. But there is perhaps an alternative. To wear animal skins, whether from cow, goat, or sheep, *can* be a mark of

[90] Paus. 9.3 (Kithairon); for Lykaion, see 41–50 below; Paus. 9.29.6 (Helikon). On mountain shrines, see R. Parker (1996) 29–33, and (2005) 69–70; Accorinti (2010) 20–3.

[91] The fragment from which the passage comes is listed under Dikaiarchos in *FHG* ii. p. 262; for the attribution to Herakleides see *RE* viii (1913) col. 484 (Daebritz), and Pfister (1951), fr. 2.8 (p. 208).

[92] A. B. Cook (1914–40) i. 420–1.

[93] A. B. Cook (1914–40) iii. 31–2, qualifying the scepticism which he expressed at i. 420–1.

[94] Burkert (1983) 113–14.

[95] Langdon (1976) 83.

[96] But there is something over-elaborate about the attempt by Burkert (1983, 113–14), following Pfister (1951, 209–12), to link the Pelion ritual with the story of Aktaion.

'outsiderdom'. To the Arrian passage quoted earlier (*Anab.* 7.9.2: cloaks:hides::city:mountain) may be added Pausanias' reference to Pelasgos, 'who invented sheepskin tunics, which poor people still wear around Euboia and in Phokis'; only at a subsequent stage of civilization do spinning and weaving make an appearance, thanks to Arkas.[97] But, more specifically, the use of animal skins for clothing is associated with herdsmen. Eumaios puts on a hairy goatskin to keep out the North Wind, and at Odysseus' prompting gives him some extra sheep- and goat-fleeces;[98] in Theokritos' 5th *Idyll* a goatherd and a shepherd argue about the respective merits of the fleeces of their own animals.[99] I believe, then, that the Pelion ritual may be read as follows. Once a year the citizen-group turns, through its representatives, into a community of shepherds, which practises what may be described as a one-day ritual transhumance. The highest turn into the lowest, the most prominent citizens into shepherds: for this is the *oros*, where, in ritual as in myth, metamorphoses and reversals take place. And yet this is ritual, not myth: the reversal of the everyday is itself reversible. After the ceremony, the sheepskins are doffed, herding retires from centre-stage to the periphery, and from Outside and Before (shepherds; Cheiron's cave) a return is made to the Here-and-Now.

A still more striking ritual is repeated with variations in many places. The women of certain cities ran 'raving' on the *oros* for Dionysos either at an annual festival, or at the trieteric festival every second year; best known perhaps is the case of the Thyiades, Athenian women who went out onto Parnassos with their Delphic counterparts.[100] A good deal of research has been done in recent years on the ritual aspects of Dionysiac *oros*-cults.[101] Here we need add only that in the mountain-dance for Dionysos the *oros* once more stages a reversal of normal values, as the women wander free, thanks to a temporary legitimation of 'madness'. But this is ritual not myth: the women commit no crime, tear no nephew, behead no poet, and return afterwards to their looms. Through ritual the wildness of the mountain (and of women) is both acknowledged and controlled.

[97] Paus. 8.1.5; 8.4.1. [98] *Od.* 14.530; 518–22.

[99] On Theokritean herdsmen, see Berman (2005).

[100] Paus. 10.4.3.

[101] Henrichs (1978) and (1982); Seaford (1981); Bremmer (1984); Vernant in Vernant and Vidal-Naquet (1988) 381–412.

The ritual for Zeus on Pelion and the mountain-dance for Dionysos exploit as part of their symbolic drama the contrast between mountain and community. Both, as part of that drama, promote to a focal position social groups which are normally marginalized: herdsmen (on my reading) and women.[102] It is not without interest that in the symbolism of Greek religion we occasionally find an overt equivalence between these two groups. A second-century AD inscription from Physkos in Caria records a cult law about a *thiasos* ('ritual group') whose male participants were called 'cowherds' and the females 'maenads',[103] and there are several cases of Dionysiac associations whose members were known as *boukoloi* or *boukolikoi* ('herdsmen').[104] Again, when drunken, mythical shepherds killed Ikarios, the Athenian countryman who introduced them to wine, they did so in 'a maenadic frenzy', as Nonnos puts it in his *Dionysiaka*.[105] Of course the ceremonies for Zeus and Dionysos differ in that, whereas on Pelion a marginal social group (again on my reading) is only *symbolically* central to the ceremony, in the *oreibasia* ('going on the mountain') women *in fact* play the central role. But there is also a fundamental similarity: during the ceremonies, normal social relations are inverted; afterwards, when pseudo-shepherds and women have descended from the *oros*, herding and femaleness resume the marginal positions which they occupied before, and from the perspective of the city the *oros* itself recedes into the distance for a year or two.

5. TRAGIC MOUNTAINS

Hitherto I have drawn on data from a variety of periods and contexts to produce a largely synchronic picture. There are, however, many differences and variations. Not all mountains are always perceived as wild: Pausanias reports that 'the people who live near Helikon say that no herb or root on the mountain can harm human life'.[106]

[102] Let us admit that, although marginality is a useful analytical tool, it can be (and has been) overdone. See the wise remarks of Versnel (1990a), esp. 50–5.

[103] *LSCG* no. 181, pp. 318–19 = Jaccottet (2003) ii, no. 153, discussed by Henrichs (1978) 155–6 and Jaccottet (2003) i. 93, 99, and 139–40.

[104] See Dodds (1960) on Eur. *Bacch.* 654–5; Jaccottet (2003) i. 101–22.

[105] Nonn. *Dion.* 47.117.

[106] Paus. 9.28.1.

Plain and mountain are not always opposed: in Euripides' *Helen* the Mountain Mother is assimilated to the figure of the grieving Demeter to give a picture of all nature—cornfield and mountain—mourning together.[107] Pasturage may take place in the plain as well as in the mountain, in myth as in the real landscape.[108] Then there are differences according to genre. Homer's landscape is not the landscape of Theokritos. Even within one genre, and at one historical moment, the language of Greek mythology can make subtly different statements about the 'same' matters. To illustrate the point I shall discuss three plays and two mountains.

Euripides' *Bakchai* depicts the dangerousness of the *oros*, which invades, seduces, and threatens to overturn the *polis*. Dionysos has arrived at the city of Thebes, but his power extends also over that which is not the city: he has established his dancing among the fields of Lydia and the plateaux of Persia as well as the walled towns of Baktria and the cities of Western Asia Minor (13–20). Above all, his authority is rooted on the *oros*, to which the maddened daughters of Kadmos, and all the Theban women, have been driven. The voluntary maenads too are associated with mountains: they have come from Tmolos (55, 65); they praise the mountain worship of Kybele (78–9) and celebrate the joy of following Bromios on the *orea* (140); later they suggest Nysa, Parnassos, and Olympos as possible locations for their god (556–61). Not the least of the play's paradoxes is the fact that, while part of the city has gone to the mountain, mountain folk are in the heart of the city.[109]

Thebes is a human construction, a place of gates and houses (e.g. 170–2). Yet the power of Dionysos creeps into surprising places: Teiresias and Kadmos—the founder of the city of Thebes himself—are wearing ivy, that parasitic underminer of walls.[110] When Dionysos and Thebes come into conflict, the constructions of the city collapse.

Two narratives characterize Kithairon. From the Cowherd's first words it is clear that the mountain, 'where the bright shafts of snow never cease' (661–2), is perceived as belonging to Dionysos, god of the

[107] Eur. *Hel.* 1301–7.

[108] *Hymn. Hom. Herm.* 491–2; Hodkinson (1988).

[109] See Gould (2001) 243.

[110] Cf. Plin. *HN* 16.62 ('subverting tombs and walls'). On ivy in *Bakchai*, see Gould (2001) 280–1.

winter *oreibasia*. It is a place of *deina* ('terrible/strange things') and 'more than *thaumata* ("astonishing things")' (667): women of all ages in uncanny harmony with nature, miraculously able to turn the *oros* into a source of refreshment and sustenance. On the advice of a man from the city, the dwellers on the *oros* (such as the narrator) are urged to hunt the bacchants. The result is a 'catastrophic' reversal of the norm: a hunt conducted by women, who behave like animals (by tearing apart their prey) and like males (in raiding as an army).

In the eyes of the second narrator the mountain becomes a place of initiation: Pentheus, transformed into a woman, sees the mysteries of Dionysos. As befits an initiatory space, the *oros* is 'other', though its otherness changes as the speech develops.[111] At first Kithairon is a *locus amoenus* ('refreshed by streams, densely shaded with pines', 1051–2), though a note of menace is perhaps already present in its steep crags (1051)—just the landscape in which Pentheus' flesh will be scattered on sharp rocks (1137–8). Perhaps all initiations involve negative as well as positive imagery.

On returning to the built environment of Thebes (1149), Agaue reports that it was Kithairon that killed the lion-cub (1177–8), and calls out the male residents of the *astu* ('town') 'with its beautiful towers' to see her spoils (1202–3). But the spoils are her son: the examples of Aktaion and now Pentheus show Kadmos' Thebans how dangerous their *oros* can be (1291–2). In the *polis* the fragmented body of Pentheus and the fragmented consciousness of Agaue are made whole again; but for the living the city can provide only a temporary resting place: father and daughter must leave forthwith. Agaue's last sentence includes the wish never to see Kithairon again; but apparently she is not to see Thebes again either.[112] The invasion of the city by the mountain has had irreversible consequences: Agaue, unlike the real-life practitioners of Dionysiac ritual, has left her loom for ever.

The space of *Oidipous Tyrannos* is more complex than that of *Bakchai*. The action extends beyond Thebes to Corinth and Delphi.

[111] Here I differ from Bremmer (1984) 276, who observes that 'in the *Bacchae* . . . the mountain appears as a lush place where it is very pleasant to be'. The portrayal of Kithairon in fact varies subtly with different narrators, as I have sought to demonstrate in Buxton (1991). For a subtle study of Kithairon in tragedy and especially as a 'real' place, see Taplin (2010).

[112] Cf. Dodds (1960) 243–4.

In addition, two locations outside the *polis* have shaped Oidipous' destiny: a crossroads and a mountain.

At first the focus is on the sick *polis* of Thebes. Except in Teiresias' allusion to Kithairon echoing with cries (421), the *oros* comes into prominence only after the arrival of the Corinthian messenger. On learning that he was a foundling, Oidipous counts himself a child of good luck (1080–1). It seems that the effect of the *oros*' invasion of the city has been beneficial: is the king, speculates the chorus, a love-child of Pan, or Apollo, or Hermes, or Dionysos?[113] He is, at all events, a lucky find (1106–7). Tomorrow, the chorus is confident, their king will celebrate Kithairon as his 'fellow-native and nurse and mother' (1090–1), as if, extraordinarily, Oidipous' social identity within *oikos* ('house(hold)') and *polis* originated upon a mountainside.

The truth is revealed by the Corinthian's former comrade in transhumance, who saved the baby out of pity. But in tragedy, mountain luck can be double-edged; and so it proves. Oidipous' reaction to disaster is to wish at all costs to leave Thebes. At first this wish is generalized in *ektopion* ('away from this place') (1340), then expressed as a threefold possibility: 'Hide me somewhere abroad, or kill me, or throw me into the sea' (1410–12). (This time it is the sea which represents 'wilderness'.) Kreon's response is to confine Oidipous not just within the *polis* of Thebes, but within Oidipous' own *oikos*, to prevent his pollution from infecting the world outside. Oidipous then makes his request more precise: 'Let me live on the mountains, where this place of mine called Kithairon is situated' (1451–2). The last fifteen lines of the play are the subject of extensive dispute, but an interpretation which is at least defensible is that we are to imagine Oidipous being obliged to leave the stage not in the direction of the *oros*, but back into the palace. If so, having abandoned his second (Corinthian) foster-mother, and seen his real mother hanged, he is denied a last hope of escape—a return to his original foster-mother.[114]

Oidipous Tyrannos overturns assumptions which seemed rock-solid. A citizen, one would have said, is not a stranger; a single brigand does

113 On this chorus, see Easterling (2005a) 37–9.

114 For discussion of the ending of *OT*, with more bibliography cited, see Budelmann (2006), Burian (2009), Finglass (2009), and Kovacs (2009).

not equal several; that which you leave on the mountain does not return to haunt you in the city. This is a tragedy about the disastrous failure of attempts to keep things separate.[115]

The contrast between *oros* and *polis* appears differently again in *Women of Trachis*. This is partly because the city of Trachis is relatively insignificant in the drama.[116] Herakles is not a Trachinian: he is in exile, staying with a *xenos* (40). It is his own *oikos* that his fate predominantly affects; and even then only a few members of it are directly touched by what happens, since most of his children are in Thebes or Tiryns (1153–4). Partly, too, the distinctive quality of the *oros/polis* contrast in *Women of Trachis* stems from Herakles' nature: he belongs in the wild in a way that neither Pentheus nor even Oidipous does.

Although Oita only comes into prominence at the end of the play, it is referred to earlier. When the messenger tells Deianeira that her husband will soon be home, she thanks Zeus 'who have as your preserve the uncut meadow of Oita' (200). This uncut meadow, a precinct sacred to the god, is one aspect of Zeus' connection with Oita. Another is the violence which he can unleash upon it: when urging Lichas to tell the truth, Deianeira swears by Zeus 'who sends lightning down the topmost glen of Oita' (436–7). Both aspects recur after Herakles' arrival. Before he knows the truth about Nessos' deception, he begs Zeus to thunderbolt him (1086); afterwards, more calmly, he asks to be taken to his father's sacred precinct on the mountain—on the *summit* of the mountain (1191), a suitable location for the final exploration of Herakles' proximity to, or distance from, the world of the gods. The wild Herakles will be restored to the wild territory where he belongs, burned on a pyre made partly from wild olive (1197), at a moment predicted by the Selloi, those mountain-dwelling priests of Zeus at Dodona (1164–8). There is a sense of appropriateness about the ending of *Women of Trachis*, even if (as usual in Sophokles) it is an appropriateness free neither from bitterness nor ambiguity.

Bakchai and *Oidipous Tyrannos* present a Kithairon which is threateningly close to the world of human habitation. What of

[115] I borrow the useful notion of 'separation' from Oudemans and Lardinois (1987).

[116] As Pat Easterling (personal communication) points out to me with reference to 188–9, 'at Trachis, even a popular gathering is held in a meadow, not a city space'.

Women of Trachis? It seems to me to follow a different pattern. To be sure, the forces that disrupt Herakles' *oikos*—Love, monsters—are 'wild'; to that extent we are back with the familiar tragic counterpoint of nature and culture. But it is a poor sort of interpretation that reduces every play to the same common denominator. In *Women of Trachis*, the point towards which the action moves is, I suggest, a *separation* of mountain and city, a separation created through the emphasis on the formalized, ritual aspects of Herakles' death. The oath which Hyllos is made to swear; the detail that Hyllos has sacrificed often on Oita (1192); the specifications for the pyre; the procession which ends the play: all this establishes the mountain as a place both distant and characterized by ceremonial order. Why is it this that is stressed, rather than destructive invasiveness? Maybe because Zeus is not Dionysos. The play ends with the affirmation that 'there is none of these things that is not Zeus'. That is (perhaps): there is an order in the relations between gods and men, an order of which Zeus is the guardian. But, as the action of the drama has demonstrated, this order is desperately hard to decipher: Zeus remains for ever distant, 'up in the stars' (1106).

6. CONCLUSIONS

(1) Myths rework, pare down, clarify, and exaggerate experience; to say that they 'reflect' experience is quite inadequate. (2) Clarification is not only not incompatible with ambiguity, but can actually bring it into sharper relief (cf. mountain 'luck'). (3) Perceptions reworked in mythology feed back into ordinary life, even if the way in which this happens can be hard to specify. (4) In ritual, behaviour is articulated through symbols with a comparable 'selectivity' to that found in myths. The two symbolic languages contrast with and complement each other. (5) Overwhelmingly, our evidence, both mythological and non-mythological, bears the stamp of the city or village. Mountains are unsettling for those in settlements; they are to be viewed from afar, visited only to be left again. To this extent, at least, the structuralists are right: we should investigate *contrasts* between the symbolic terms deployed in myths. The *oros* needs to be seen in the light of that

which is not the *oros*. (6) Useful as oppositional analysis may be, however, it must not be allowed to override the nuances of individual texts. Greek mythology speaks with an astonishing range of voices; reductivism is the surest way of muffling them.[117]

[117] Versions of this chapter were put before audiences in Dublin, Lausanne, Oxford, Paris, Strasbourg, and Utrecht; colleagues in Bristol also advised me on various matters. I am grateful to all who have offered comments, in particular to J. N. Bremmer, G. L. Huxley, S. Saïd, F. Shaw, H. S. Versnel, and the *JHS* referees. I am indebted in a different way to the people of S. Vito di Cadore, where I began to learn about mountains.

2

Wolves and Werewolves in Greek Thought

Chapter 1 was about landscape. In Chapter 2 I turn to another aspect of the natural world: its fauna. Once more it becomes clear that the concept of 'the natural' does not exist separately from 'the human', but is defined by it. In this second case study, it will be found to be with wolves as it was with mountains: myth-tellers select from the data of experience and shape them into themes and structures constitutive of the Greek imaginaire.

In this chapter I attempt to show how wolves were 'good to think with'[1] in ancient Greece. In Section 1 I examine a variety of contexts in which wolves appear. My aim is to demonstrate how the complex reality of the wolf was pared down in the tradition to a small number of symbolically powerful characteristics, and how even writers of a 'scientific' type were influenced by features of the wolf as depicted in myth. In Section 2 I investigate how one particular myth-and-ritual complex explored the possibility that a human being might turn into a wolf; and I go on to make some more general points about ways in which myth and ritual can be seen to complement and yet to contrast with each other.

1. GREEK WOLVES, REAL AND IMAGINED

Before mankind's systematic attempts to exterminate it, the grey wolf (*Canis lupus*) was a tremendously widespread predator.[2] In North

[1] On the pedigree of this expression see G. E. R. Lloyd (1983) 8, n. 7.

[2] For general discussions see Mech (1970) and (1991); Zimen (1981); Mech and Boitani (2003).

America it was found coast to coast; in the Old World it extended from Britain south to Spain and Portugal, east across Europe to Russia, China, and Japan. But over the past two centuries—at least until relatively recently—the population of grey wolves underwent a massive global decline. In the New World wolves became virtually extinct except in Alaska: extensive use of strychnine in the nineteenth century, and a decline in the population of the wolf's prey (especially caribou), contributed towards the drop in numbers. A comparable though less drastic sequence of events occurred in Europe. By 1800 wolves were extinct in the British Isles.[3] According to a major investigation published in 1975 by the International Union for the Conservation of Nature and Natural Resources,[4] wolves were by that date extinct in France, Belgium, the Netherlands, Denmark, East and West Germany, Switzerland, Austria, and Hungary; virtually extinct in Finland, Norway, and Sweden; and endangered in Portugal, Spain, Italy, Bulgaria, Czechoslovakia, Poland, and the then USSR. However, at the end of the twentieth century and the beginning of the twenty-first, as a result of conservation measures, including in some countries the reintroduction of the wolf with the status of protected species, the decline in numbers has been halted or even reversed.[5] Yet the situation is fluid, as differences of opinion between advocates of biodiversity, on the one hand, and local ranchers and farmers, on the other, are often impossible to reconcile. While it now seems premature to predict the wolf's extinction, it is also too early to be confident of its long-term survival.

In spite of this halt (or pause) in the decline in global wolf numbers, it is clear that the prominence of the wolf within the broad spectrum of fauna has been very greatly reduced. It is also clear that the animal historically responsible for the reduction has been man. Why this age-old human hostility to the wolf? Normally wolves prey on large, hoofed beasts—the ungulates: caribou, bison, antelope, deer, moose, elk. When these are scarce the wolf turns to smaller mammals such as mice and rabbits, or to man's domesticated herds. It is the fact that since the Neolithic period man has raised stock which has brought him into conflict with the wolf.

[3] Cf. Dent (1974) 99–134.

[4] Pimlott (1975).

[5] See http://en.wikipedia.org/wiki/List_of_gray_wolf_populations_by_country and http://en.wikipedia.org/wiki/Wolf_reintroduction (accessed 2 November 2012).

It is no surprise, then, that in classical antiquity we find numerous references to the wolf as a cruel, predatory enemy. Plutarch (*Sol.* 23.3) reports that 'the Athenians were from of old great enemies of wolves, since their country was better for pasturage than for growing crops'. So Solon introduced a law that 'the man who brings in a wolf is paid five drachmas; for a wolf-cub, one drachma'.[6] (According to Demetrios of Phaleron, cited in the same passage, five drachmas was the price of an ox, one drachma that of a sheep.) Wolves were proverbial for cruelty; hence Orestes' words about his own and his sister's implacability: 'like a raw-minded wolf, our disposition, which we get from our mother, cannot be appeased' (Aesch. *Cho.* 421–2). Already in Homer the wolf is seen as deadly and bloodthirsty, as in the famous simile about the Myrmidons, likened to a pack of wolves who furiously tear apart a stag (*Il.* 16.156–66).

In representing wolves as cruel adversaries of man, Greek thought was simply reflecting the stark fact of the competition between the two species. But other qualities ascribed by Greek tradition to wolves begin to take us away from a direct transcription of 'reality'. It will be convenient to concentrate on the two most prominent qualities: wolves cooperate; and they belong outside.

The perception of wolves as cooperative does far more than simply reflect the existence of wolf-packs. In a range of historical periods and in many different types of source, from the technical to the poetical to the anecdotal, the point is developed and elaborated. Xenophon (*Eq. mag.* 4.19–20) describes how, in attacking a convoy, some wolves drive off the guard while others seize the plunder. An epigram in the *Palatine Anthology* (9.252) tells of a traveller who jumped into the Nile to escape wolves: 'but they continued the chase through the water, each holding on by its teeth to another's tail. A long bridge of wolves was formed over the stream, and the self-taught stratagem of the swimming beasts caught the man'.[7] Aelian too describes how wolves cooperate at a kill (*NA* 8.14), and he also has the tail story: when wolves cross a river 'they fasten their teeth in one another's tails . . . and swim across without harm or danger' (*NA* 3.6). There is, alas, no reliably recorded

[6] Rewards offered in late eighteenth-century France are set out in Molinier and Molinier-Meyer (1981) 228; this is the only serious attempt known to me which offers a historical ecology of the wolf in a particular region. Bounties of £5 per head in Cromwellian Ireland: Fitzgibbon (1971) 37.

[7] Here and several times elsewhere I have followed or adapted the Loeb translation.

evidence of wolf behaviour of this kind—the wolf is in its own right a particularly powerful swimmer.[8] The important thing is that wolves were *perceived* as acting cooperatively.

The tradition of lupine cooperation is a long one. The grammarian Timotheos of Gaza (5th–6th century AD) observes in his *On Animals* that, when two wolves coincide at a kill, 'the shares are equal'.[9] Once more it is instructive to consider the situation at an actual kill. In Greece today—and it is unlikely that things were very different in antiquity—large kills are rare, so the issue of sharing does not arise. (You don't share a mouse.) When a large kill is made, the cubs will usually be allowed in first, and thereafter there is a definite *non*-equality: dominant animals (i.e. those highest in the 'pecking' order) get first go, and so on down the line. But what is true is that there is a structured aspect to a kill, so that the notion of cooperation has a basis in actual behaviour. Myth 'clarifies' an asymmetrical order into equality.

It is a small step from the idea that wolves treat each other as equals to the idea that wolves are all alike; and this step was also taken in Greek belief. Thus we find in Aesop (343 Perry) a story about a battle between the dogs and the wolves. The dog general was unwilling to engage the enemy because they (the wolves) were all alike, while the dogs—some being Cretan, some Molossian, some Thracian, not to mention the variations in colour—were all different. Once more the underlying notion is that the wolves will prove successful by virtue of being able to cooperate more closely than their adversaries.

Like the cooperative wolf, the wolf as outsider has a grounding in observable reality. Not only do wolves in general roam in areas which seem to humans to be outside the confines of human territory, but the *lone* wolf—having dropped out of or been expelled from a pack as a result of being wounded in a fight or infirmity, and thus being a kind of outsider even amongst a community of outsiders—is a recognized part of wolf ecology, known to antiquity as to us (e.g. Arist. *Hist. an.* 594^{a}30). However, as with cooperation, the point is developed so that the wolf becomes a powerful image for the man apart from other men.

[8] For advice on all matters of wolf biology and behaviour mentioned in this article I am indebted to Professor Stephen Harris of the Department of Zoology at the University of Bristol.

[9] Timotheos: Haupt (1869) 8, lines 27–9. On the parallel with 'isonomic' distribution between hoplites, see Detienne and Svenbro (1979).

In his poem about a person in exile Alkaios writes as follows: 'I live a life in the wilds, longing to hear the agora . . . I am in exile, living on the boundary . . . here I settled alone as a *lukaimiais*' (*PLF* 130.16–25). The last word is a puzzle, and the interpretation 'a wolf-thicket man' is far from certain.[10] But for an association with exile, wildness, and solitariness a compound of *lukos* ('wolf') is highly appropriate.[11] There is a similar logic in Pausanias' aetiology for the shrine of Apollo Lykios at Argos, according to which, when Danaos arrived as an outsider in Argos, he found a wolf killing the leader of a herd of cattle. 'It occurred to the Argives that Gelanor'—Danaos' rival for the throne—'was like the bull, and Danaos like the wolf; for as the wolf will not live with men, so Danaos up to that time had not lived with them [i.e. the Argives]'—because he had come from Egypt (Paus. 2.19.3–4).[12] Another mythical exile who had to do with wolves was Athamas (Apollod. *Bibl.* 1.9.2). Having killed his son through Hera's madness and been banished from Boiotia, he was told by an oracle to dwell where he should be entertained by wild beasts. This he duly did when he found wolves 'distributing amongst themselves portions of sheep'. Here a human settlement replaces sharing-between-wolves. Thus on the one hand wolves prefigure human society: to share is to be part of a community. On the other hand they contrast with it as barbarity contrasts with civilization: what they are sharing, after all, is raw meat. The Athamas story neatly embraces both of the principal features of the mythical wolf in Greece: as cooperator, it illuminates the human condition by similarity; as outsider, it illuminates it by contrast.[13]

So far my account has been synchronic, and has drawn together material from a variety of sources without differentiation on grounds of date or context. To what extent do we need to modify that approach in view of the evidence?

We may start with the matter of historical development. In her discussion of the wolf in ancient Greece, C. Mainoldi puts forward the argument that Greek perception of the wolf underwent one major

[10] See Page (1955) 205–6.

[11] Connection between wolf and outlaw: Senn (1982) 16, and Bremmer (1982) 141 n. 35.

[12] On this passage see Mainoldi (1984) 25–6. (Mainoldi's study is careful and extremely interesting.) Apollo Lyk(e)ios: Graf (1985) 220–6.

[13] We may recall that the origins of Rome were perceived as lying with a renegade band of young men, led by the foster-children of the she-wolf—outsiders in cooperation; cf. Alföldi (1974), esp. 119–33; Bremmer in Bremmer and Horsfall (1987) 25–48.

change over time: from being 'le modèle de l'animal fort' in the Homeric poems, the wolf subsequently became marginalized as an emblem of savagery and, above all, of *dolos*, trickery.[14] The post-Homeric association between the wolf and *dolos* is indeed certain: in *Pythian* 2 Pindar expresses the wish: 'May I love my friend; but against my enemy I shall make a secret attack, like a wolf, treading now here now there on my crooked paths' (83–5); a Platonic letter describes a false or tricky friendship as *lukophilia* (318e); Aelian knows how wolves can make up for a lack of strength by feigning a frontal attack, darting aside and leaping on the back of the victim (*NA* 5.19); and perhaps the wolf's best *dolos* is his similarity to a dog, as stated in Plato's *Sophist* (231a).[15] However, not only in the Euripidean *Rhesos* but also in the *Iliad* does the spy Dolon wear a wolfskin during his cunning night exploit (*Il.* 10.334; Eur. *Rhes.* 204–15);[16] and it is hardly coincidence that Odysseus' grandfather, who had been given by Hermes outstanding skill 'in theft and in oath'—the latter on the principle that whoever has power over bonds has power also to break them—is in the *Odyssey* named as Auto*lykos* (19.394–6). In short, the idea that trickery is a later development in the Greek image of the wolf seems to me unjustified. Not only that: in my view *no* development in that image can be isolated and located chronologically until we reach the zoological studies of Aristotle.

Differentiation by context, on the other hand, is possible and revealing. In Homeric epic the emphasis (with the exception of the Dolon episode) is on wolves as a collectivity, fierce in the fight and so suitable for comparison to warriors. In the field of political philosophy Plato characteristically uses the violent aspect of the wolf to think

[14] Mainoldi (1984) 97–103, 127.

[15] Wolves and dogs similar: cf. also Diod. Sic. 1.88.6. But the perceived relation between the two is complex and ambiguous. Although dog can be seen to stand to wolf as tame to wild, the tameness of dogs is problematic. On the one hand, they protect human civilization by warding off wild beasts, and are domesticated to the extent of being regularly eaten; cf. Gejvall (1969) 14–18. On the other hand, dogs are potential killers and may threaten man (NB Aktaion). On dogs see Scholz (1937); Merlen (1971); Zaganiaris (1980); Mainoldi (1984); Franco (2003). NB also Ziolkowski (1983) ch. 3 ('Talking Dogs: The Caninization of Literature'); and, for a brilliant analysis of a medieval cult and legend, Schmitt (1983).

[16] Dolon the wolf: Lissarrague (1980); Gernet (1981) 125–39. The attempt by Mainoldi (1984, 20) to explain away the wolf/trickery link in the 'Doloneia' is unconvincing.

about tyranny.[17] In fable the wolf appears frequently, often with emphasis on its cunning, and often too being presented in contrast with the dog.[18] In such contexts, and in others—for instance the passages from *Libation-Bearers* (on the implacability of Orestes and Elektra) and *Pythian* 2 (on crooked secrecy) cited earlier—the wolf is used as a means for expressing something about human behaviour. But there is another sort of context which illustrates even more strikingly just how pervasive were the patterns of thought embedded in myth. I refer to works which were explicitly about animals, and which we might variously ascribe to the categories 'folklore' and 'zoology'. As we shall see, the distinction is not unproblematic.

We may begin with a report by Plutarch:

> Antipater in his book *On Animals* asserts that wolves give birth at the time when trees that bear nuts or acorns shed their flowers: when they eat these, their wombs are opened. But if there is no supply of these flowers, their offspring die within them and cannot see the light. Moreover those parts of the world that are not fertile in nut-trees or oak-trees are not troubled by wolves. (*Quaest. nat.* 38)

This is a fine example of how Greek thought could combine a traditional pattern of ideas with shrewd empirical observation. Our first reaction is perhaps to find a 'logic of myth' behind Antipater's account, since there was in at least one region an acknowledged religious link between acorns and wolves: Arkadia. Arkadians are perceived as acorn-eaters, hence as pre-civilized;[19] Arkadians are also worshippers of Zeus Lykaios, in whose cult both wolves and oak-trees figure (see below); wolves are outside civilization, and so are associated with acorn eaters, who are before it. But there is sound zoology here too. Wolves do indeed share a habitat with nut- and oak-trees. Good years for nuts and acorns mean plentiful supplies of the small animals eaten by wolves, and this plenty means in turn that wolves produce large litters. But when food is scarce, there is in foxes and rabbits a higher proportion of aborted foetuses than in times of plenty, and it is likely that the same is true for wolves. Antipater's

[17] E.g. *Resp.* 416a, 565e–66a; *Phd.* 82a. Cf. Mainoldi (1984) 187–200, and Lanza (1977) 65–7.

[18] List of references given by Mainoldi (1984) 209–10, n. 12.

[19] See Borgeaud (1988) 14–15. Ancient perceptions of Arkadia: Hartog (2001b) 133–50.

assertion thus provides evidence for a remarkable coincidence between traditional and empirical modes of thought.

We might expect a priori that if any ancient authority is going to privilege the empirical against the traditional, it will be Aristotle. And in some cases we do indeed find him carefully recording data which subsequent zoological research has corroborated: 'polydactylous quadrupeds (such as the dog, lion, wolf, fox, and jackal) all bring forth their young blind, and the eyelid does not separate until some time after birth'; 'the penis is bony in the fox, wolf, marten, and weasel'. More rarely, statements of a straightforwardly zoological kind are simply wrong, e.g. 'the neck is flexible and has a number of vertebrae in all animals except the wolf and the lion, in which the neck consists of one bone only'.[20] In fact all mammals have seven bones in the neck; but, interestingly, some wolves suffer from severe arthritis of the spine, and it is possible that Aristotle's information resulted from observation of an animal so afflicted—it is on general grounds not improbable that infirm wolves offered greater opportunity for close scrutiny than healthy ones.

In addition to findings of the sort just mentioned, though, Aristotle has other things to say about the wolf, and here the mythical representation of the animal becomes visible once more. At one point he describes it as *gennaios* (thorough-bred), *agrios* (wild), and *epiboulos* (scheming) (*Hist. an.* 488^{b}17). At another the direction of the enquiry seems to be affected by the threatening and predatory figure cut by the wolf in popular belief, when Aristotle tackles the matter of wolves eating people. But the specific contribution made by him to this (apparently) endlessly intriguing issue—he asserts that only *lone* wolves eat men, not wolves in packs (*Hist. an.* 594^{a}30)—is zoologically plausible: the lone wolf, which by definition lacks the support of the pack, is likely to have restricted access to prey, and so might in extremity have to resort to human meat.[21] In fact, even where Aristotle's zoological researches are explicitly influenced by the mythical tradition, what is remarkable is the coolness of his judgement:

> An account is given of the she-wolf's parturition which comes very near the fabulous [*pros muthon*], viz. that there are just twelve days in the

[20] Aristotelian references: *Gen. an.* 742^{a}8 (eyelid); *Hist. an.* 500^{b}23 (penis); *Part. an.* 686^{a}21 (neck); translations adapted from Loeb edition.

[21] But see 'A Modern Postscript' below.

> year during which all wolves bring forth their young. The reason for this, they say, is found in a fable, which alleges that it took twelve days to bring Leto from the land of the Hyperboreans to Delos, during which time she had the appearance of a she-wolf because she was afraid of Hera. Whether twelve days really was the time or not has not yet been definitely established by observation; that is merely what is asserted. (*Hist. an.* 580^a14)

It may be added that the situation is identical today: we know nothing about the exact birth-periods of European wolves; but it is zoologically certain that there will be a restricted period for birth, and *it is unlikely that this will be more than 2–3 weeks.* As with Antipater's assertion mentioned above, the coincidence between myth and empirical observation is notable; and so too is the ability of Aristotle to set himself apart from the tradition and to reflect critically upon it.

A few conclusions may be drawn from the material presented in this section. (1) Sometimes Greek perception of the wolf directly reflects the facts of human and lupine existence: humans compete with wolves for food, so wolves appear in myth as cruel foes. (2) In other respects traditional thought works on reality by selective emphasis and 'clarification': wolves share a kill *equally*; they are *all alike.* (3) The tradition is not uniform: in different contexts different aspects of the wolf are stressed, though within the broadly similar image shared by all. (4) Aristotelian zoology represents a marked contrast to the mythical tradition. But the distinction between folklore and zoology is not rigid: we find excellent zoology in anecdote, and mythological patterns and concerns in zoology.

2. THE WEREWOLF OF ARKADIA

Having tried to give a general overview of the place of the wolf in Greek thought, I turn now to one particular aspect of the subject: the cult and myth of the Arkadian werewolf. This complex of religious practice and belief constitutes the single most striking instance of the wolf as 'good to think with' surviving from ancient Greece.

We begin with a point of terminology. It seems sensible to distinguish between werewolfism and lycanthropy. The former may be defined as the belief that people are able to turn into wolves; the latter denotes a psychotic disorder according to which one believes that one has oneself turned into a wolf.[22] Compared with the enormous number of werewolf and lycanthropy cases recorded for medieval Europe,[23] evidence for such phenomena in antiquity is rare. (We are of course at liberty to wonder how representative our sample is, but all we can do is to operate with what information we have.) Instances of lycanthropy are few and late, but Markellos of Side significantly reports that sufferers experienced their symptoms at night (in February) and in cemeteries, i.e. in a context removed both temporally and spatially from that of normal life—we recall that the Petronian werewolf metamorphosed by moonlight and on a road beside some grave-markers.[24] Stories of ancient werewolf belief are again scarce, although there is this time a certain amount of material from Greece. Once more we should note the typical geographical remoteness, as with the Neuri, adjacent to the Scythians in Herodotos' narrative: 'The Scythians, and the Greeks settled in Scythia, say that once a year every one of the Neuri is turned into a wolf, and after remaining so for a few days returns again to his former shape' (Hdt. 4.105). That the Neuri are located by Herodotos next to the Androphagi is wholly logical: in accordance with a pattern of thought common in Greece and in a vast number of other cultures, marginal peoples are perceived as behaving in ways inverse to those favoured by the 'central' people.[25] Whether the story about the Neuri is entirely a product of this sort of inverse projection, or whether an actual ritual lies behind it, is impossible to decide; but the existence of an initiatory *rite de passage* is perfectly plausible, either on the assumption that the participants literally adopted wolf-disguise[26] or on the view that one who temporarily withdraws 'outside' is metaphorically wolfish.

22 Lycanthropy is not unknown to modern psychiatry, although it is very rare: see Rosenstock and Vincent (1977); Garlipp et al. (2004).

23 Ronay (1972) 15 gives a figure of 30,000 cases of lycanthropy investigated by the Roman Church between 1520 and the mid-seventeenth century. On werewolf belief in early modern Europe, see Harf-Lancner (1985). Sconduto (2008) sketches developments from antiquity to the Renaissance; see also Otten (1986); Pluskowski (2006) 172–92. Summers (1933) may still be consulted, though with great circumspection.

24 Text of Markellos in Roscher (1896) 79–81. Petronius: *Sat.* 61–2. Ancient lycanthropy: Piccaluga (1968) 57–64; Ullmann (1976); Burkert (1983) 89 with n. 28. Burkert rightly states that lycanthropy is culturally determined, but his view that it 'no longer plays a role in modern psychiatry' needs rephrasing as 'a *significant* role'; cf. n. 22 above.

25 Cf. Wiedemann (1986). On the 'other' in Herodotos, see Hartog (2001a); on perceived cultural differences between 'same' and 'other', see Todorov (1982).

26 Cf. Meuli (1975) 160.

The Neuri were outside, but the Arkadians were before—in fact, before the moon, *proselēnoi*;[27] and Arkadia was the location of the werewolf cult best known to us from the Greek world. Even today Mount Lykaion has a remote and slightly eerie beauty; how much more eerie in antiquity since, so it was said, a rite of cannibalism was practised there. Pausanias refuses to discuss it (8.38.7); but Plato speaks of a rite in which human innards are mixed with parts of other animals, and the person who tastes the human must turn into a wolf (*Resp.* 565d). One does not need to go all the way with Arens' ultra-sceptical approach to anthropophagy[28] to be doubtful about at least *some* reports of institutionalized cannibalism: as Servius puts it, 'in sacred rites that which is simulated is accepted as reality' (on *Aen.* 2.116). When Konstantinos Kourouniotis dug the site at the beginning of the last century he found no human bones,[29] and, as Walter Burkert has pointed out, only a very few people are going to know exactly what is in the casserole—the rest is suggestion.[30] But more profitable than speculation about the precise contents of the cauldron is some consideration of the symbolism and social context of the ritual. And here we do get a clue from Pausanias, who reports (8.2.6):

> They say that ever since the time of Lykaon a man was always turned into a wolf at the sacrifice to Lykaian Zeus—but not for his whole life; because if he kept off human flesh when he was a wolf, he turned back into a man after nine years; if he tasted human flesh, he stayed a wild beast for ever.

The wolf stands for one who by his behaviour has set himself beyond humanity: so much is clear. But why did the Greeks enact this ceremony of ritual exclusion? Before we can attempt an answer we must consider a ritual which sounds remarkably similar to the Lykaion ceremony. Pliny the Elder reports that, according to the Arkadians, a member of the family of Anthos was chosen by lot, left all his clothes on an oak-tree, swam across a pool, went away 'into a deserted area', and turned into a wolf. After nine years, provided he had eaten no human meat, he swam back across the pool, took up his clothes, and resumed

[27] See Borgeaud (1988) 6–8.

[28] Arens (1979).

[29] Kourouniotis (1904) 169. More on the excavation in Kourouniotis (1905) and (1909).

[30] Burkert (1983) 90. Hughes (1991, 106) inclines to the same view, speaking of 'the cannibalistic meal, real or feigned (but very probably the latter)'.

human shape (*HN* 8.81). A similar version is given by Augustine (citing Varro), though he refers more vaguely to 'the Arkadians' instead of to a specific family (*De civ. D.* 18.17). Two questions present themselves: (1) How do we interpret the ritual described by Pliny? (2) How does it relate to the ceremony mentioned by Pausanias and Plato?

(1) Pliny's ritual centres on two symbolic gestures; stripping and crossing water. Both mark the transition from inside to outside, human to animal. Stripping is associated with animal metamorphosis both in antiquity and later. Pamphile and Lucius in *The Golden Ass* strip before their metamorphoses take place (3.21; 24). The werewolf in Petronius removes his clothes before changing shape; and the crucial importance of the clothes for the transition is indicated by the fact that the werewolf 'fixes' them by urinating around them, after which they turn to stone (62). Numerous medieval werewolf legends confirm the role of clothes as boundary-marker, as in Marie de France's lay *Bisclavret*. A Breton lord changes into a wolf three days a week; before doing so he removes his clothes, without which he is deprived of the means of transition back to humanity. His wife and her lover steal his clothes, but eventually the lord is able to recover them, and with them his human form.[31]

Water is another boundary between the human and wolfish states. Once more there are medieval parallels: in 1580 Jean Bodin recorded a story, set in Livonia, in which crossing water is a prelude to metamorphosis (of twelve days' duration) into wolfish form.[32] One all-too-common reductionist tactic is to link such phenomena to the fact that rabies—a supposed 'origin' of werewolf belief—is characterized by hydrophobia; water thus quite literally marks a barrier between man and werewolf (= rabies victim).[33] But such a realist approach gets us nowhere in our attempt to understand the symbolic role of the supposed 'symptom' in its ritual context.[34] More plausibly one might regard the Arkadian pool in a wholly content-free way as simply a

[31] Bisclavret: Battaglia (1965) 361–89; Bambeck (1973); Suard (1980).

[32] Bodin (1580) 99.

[33] For the werewolf–rabies equation see ch. 12 of Woodward's lurid book (1979).

[34] Equally beside the point is the attempt to explain the religious phenomenon of werewolfism by reference to iron-deficiency porphyria (*New Scientist*, 28 October 1982, 244–5). With this one may contrast the more prudent comments of Ginzburg (1983) 18, on the need to explain the beliefs of the Friulian *benandanti* 'on the basis of the history of popular religiosity not on that of pharmacology or psychiatry'.

boundary between inside and outside; but that would be to ignore the place of water in general, and bathing in particular, in Greek cult.[35] Washing or bathing in water from a spring is an element in several important Greek *rites de passage*. After death the corpse was stripped, washed, and dressed in new robes as a prelude to being 'carried out'; before making the transition back to normal life the mourners would themselves bathe. After a birth, mother and child would bathe as part of the return to normality. Bride and groom bathed before the marriage ceremony. Washing, and sometimes bathing and changing of clothes, was required before the performance of prayer or sacrifice, and preceded other forms of access to the sacred such as prophecy, incubation, and initiation into the mysteries.[36] Thus crossing the boundary between sacred and non-sacred space, and between sacred and non-sacred periods of time, is regularly accompanied by bathing. In one way the relevance of this to Pliny's Arkadian ritual is clear enough, since entering and leaving a sacred space is clearly part of the symbolic drama. But if the ritual as a whole is a *rite de passage*, then bathing becomes that much more appropriate.[37]

In the late twentieth century a good deal of attention was directed towards rituals of transition in ancient Greece. In particular there were investigations into the presence of initiation rituals—or survivals of them—in Archaic and later Greek culture.[38] Fruitful though much of this work undoubtedly was, it was accompanied by an occasional tendency to exaggerate the explanatory value of initiation.[39] It may therefore be worth spelling out that some rituals—consulting an oracle, for instance—were self-evidently not initiatory, while others—such as

[35] See Ninck (1921) 138–80, for the role of water in mythical metamorphoses.

[36] Death: Ginouvès (1962) 239–64; L. R. Parker (1983) 35–6. Birth: Ginouvès (1962) 235–8; L. R. Parker (1983) 50–1. Marriage: Ginouvès (1962) 265–82. Prayer, sacrifice: Ginouvès (1962) 311–18. Prophecy, incubation: Ginouvès (1962) 327–73. Mysteries: Ginouvès (1962) 375–404.

[37] There is a striking parallel with the rite of adult baptism in the early Church. Many fonts had three steps leading down from one side and three steps leading up out of the other side: the initiate thus crossed the font; see Khatchatrian (1962) nos. 83, 136, 194, 270, and 371. The going down into the font was regarded as equivalent to Christ being placed in the tomb, and the going up out of it was interpreted in terms of resurrection: e.g. Ambrose *de Sacr.* 3.1.2; cf. Davies (1962) 22–3.

[38] The major anthropological influence is van Gennep (1909), with important amplification by Turner (1967) 93–111. On Greece, see Jeanmaire (1939); Brelich (1969); Bremmer (1978); Burkert (1985) 260–4; for a comparison with initiatory space in Shakespeare, see Buxton (1992a).

[39] Scepticism about the validity of explanations in terms of initiation has been forcefully voiced in Dodd and Faraone (2003).

the ceremonies surrounding birth, marriage, and death—certainly shared with initiation rituals the pattern of separation/marginalization/reintegration, but were equally certainly not initiatory in the way that, say, the *ephebeia* was. Yet in spite of those reservations it seems to me likely that the ritual described by Pliny was indeed initiatory; at least, the evidence we have is compatible with such a hypothesis. A man—probably, as we shall see, a young man—underwent a rite of separation, left society, and became temporarily a non-person; he subsequently returned and, after a rite of reintegration, rejoined the community, presumably with a different (? adult) status. The negative imagery (wolf; in the wilds) characterizing the liminal period is just what we should expect, given the anthropological parallels.[40] One aspect of the symbolism is particularly interesting: abstention from human meat. The 'wolf' must retain one link with humanity if his eventual return is to be possible.

(2) There are obvious similarities with the Lykaion ritual: the avoidance of human meat, the metamorphosis into a wolf, the period of nine years. At the very least Pausanias and Pliny were reporting rituals which shared some of the same symbols. But were they relating different aspects of the *same* ritual?[41] Perhaps the most persuasive account is that of Burkert, according to whom the Plinian version reflects a watered-down, 'civilized' form of the ritual which became confined to a single conservative family.[42] On this view we should imagine an earlier situation in Archaic Greece in which a whole age-group of young men were initiated into Arkadian adult society. Before they became fully fledged citizens they were obliged to undergo a period of separation from society as 'wolves', i.e. outsiders. When they reached the age of full social adulthood they became true descendants of Arkas, 'The Bear'—Pausanias conveniently tells us that Arkadian warriors wore the skins of two animals, the wolf and the bear (4.11.3). Supporting the initiation hypothesis is the story (recorded by Pausanias, Pliny, and Augustine)[43] of an Arkadian who returned after a nine-year lupine absence to win the Olympic boxing event: it was surely a *young* man who went into the wilds.

The only problem with this interpretation seems to me the nine years. We could of course take it as merely symbolic of 'a period of

[40] See Turner (1967), esp. 96.

[41] For the different views, see Mainoldi (1984) 31, n. 11; Jost (1985) 260–1; Hughes (1991) 100–1.

[42] Burkert (1983) 88.

[43] Paus. 6.8.2; Plin. *HN* 8.82; August. *De civ. D.* 18.17.

time', and leave the matter at that.[44] But if we take it at face value, and if we see the ritual as applying, at least originally, to a whole age-group of young men, then we have to give a reasonable answer to the question, 'What were they *doing* for nine years?'—nine years of 'life as a wolf in the wilderness'.[45] It is not quite the same as withdrawing to the young men's huts for a spell of a couple of months before rejoining the tribe.[46] If we want to regard the Lykaion ritual as being originally an initiation ceremony for an entire age-group, then we have to be sceptical about those nine years, at least until they are explained in a way which makes sense in relation to the real life of a historical Arkadian community.[47] In any case it is unwise to be too dogmatic about what happened on Mount Lykaion. We know, for instance, of a ritual there connected with making rain;[48] we know also that the opposition sunlight/shadow was important;[49] and it is difficult, and probably misleading, to try to incorporate all this material into a single ritual complex. But if we retain the idea of an initiatory rite of passage we have at least a very plausible hypothesis for understanding the logic of the central werewolf ceremony.[50]

[44] Seven years as wolf: Giraldus Cambrensis, *Topographia Hibernica* 2.19. One year: *The Mabinogion*, in J. Gantz (1976) 105. Nine years as a transitional period: Felix's *Life of Saint Guthlac*, in Colgrave (1956) ch. 18. Compare also the Homeric phrase 'for nine days . . . but on the tenth . . .': *LfgrE*, s.v. *ennea, ennēmar*; Richardson (1974) 165–6.

[45] Burkert (1983) 91.

[46] See Sergent (1986) 38, on two months as a common period for initiatory withdrawal.

[47] Cf. J. Z. Smith (1982) 60–1, on the need not to abandon 'our sense of incredulity, our estimate of plausibility' in such matters.

[48] Paus. 8.38.4. Piccaluga (1968) interprets the entire cult activity on Lykaion in terms of drought/water: the first item in her subject index is 'acqua: *passim*'. But her desire to unify the heterogeneous data is over-zealous.

[49] According to Pausanias (8.38.6) no person could enter the precinct of Zeus Lykaios on normal, i.e. non-sacred occasions. If anyone, man or beast, did enter, he cast no shadow—in other words, ceased to be alive. (A variant also recorded by Pausanias makes this explicit: a person entering dies within a year; I am here to report that this is incorrect.) Polybius (16.12.7) and Plutarch (*Quaest. Graec.* 39) confirm the shadow story. Evidently it marks in an emphatic way the boundary between inside and outside the sanctuary. But is there more to it than that? In front of the altar of Zeus there were two pillars 'towards the rising sun', with gilded eagles upon them (Paus. 8.38.7). The detail is enigmatic and, given the state of our knowledge, the sunlight, like the rain, must remain peripheral to our reading of the werewolf rite.

[50] Revisiting the myth-and-ritual complex of Mount Lykaion, Jan Bremmer has highlighted 'a distinctly Arkadian custom', namely 'to leave the region and enlist as a mercenary abroad'; Bremmer (2007) 74. That this practice might help us make sense

We have not yet finished with Mount Lykaion, for associated with it there was a myth. The most dramatically exciting account of Lykaon is in Ovid's *Metamorphoses* Book 1, but the most suggestive from the mythological point of view is in Pausanias (8.1–2). According to his version, Lykaon's father was Pelasgos, the first man who lived in Arkadia. Pelasgos introduced certain aspects of civilization: shelters against the elements and clothing made from sheepskins. Moreover he stopped his subjects eating leaves, grass, and roots, and introduced them instead to acorns. Lykaon continued the civilizing process by founding a city and instituting games in honour of Zeus. At that time, because of their justice and piety, men ate at the same table as the gods. But Lykaon carried out the sacrifice of a child on Zeus' altar on Mount Lykaion; as a consequence he was turned into a wolf.

One way of coming to grips with Greek myths is to identify recurrent themes, and so to observe what Greeks felt to be important. A major theme in the Lykaon myth is the importance of maintaining proper relationships with the gods, and the dangers of not so doing. Countless other myths make a similar point: punishment follows all kinds of transgression against the gods, from failure to honour them (Hippolytos, Pentheus) to ill-advised rivalry (Arachne, Marsyas) to figurative or real violation (Aktaion, Teiresias, Ixion). More specifically, the Lykaon myth narrates the consequences of abusing hospitality, and here it resembles the story of Tantalos, another who was host to the gods at a cannibalistic feast. But Lykaon is a bringer of culture as well as a criminal, and the whole narrative in Pausanias is, from another point of view, the story of the origins of civilization in Arkadia: after relating what Pelasgos and Lykaon did he tells us that one of Lykaon's descendants, Arkas, will invent agriculture, bread-making, and weaving (8.4.1). However, the myth also makes clear that humanity's cultural progress is not unalloyed: part and parcel of the human condition as we know it is that we no longer eat with the gods.

There is a close analogy with Hesiod's account of what happened at Mekone, where Prometheus' attempted deception of Zeus resulted in a definitive end to the commensality of men and gods (*Theog.* 535–57).[51] But the difference is as striking as the similarity: in the Lykaon story the rupture between men and gods is far more drastic. This becomes

of 'the long stay away from home during initiation' is an intriguing possibility, though, as Bremmer admits, given the state of the evidence it must remain no more than that.

[51] See West (1966) 306.

evident if we look at some of the variants—another fruitful way of uncovering the logic of myth. According to Apollodoros, Lykaon's *sons* are the guilty ones, and they (except the youngest) and their father are thunderbolted (3.8); while Hyginus speaks of Lykaon turning into a wolf and his sons being thunderbolted (176). The implications of the equivalence between thunderbolting and metamorphosis into a wolf have been drawn by Philippe Borgeaud.[52] In the case of thunderbolting, Zeus' power is completely manifested (cf. the fate of Semele); in the case of metamorphosis, the guilty party is not simply banished from Zeus' table, he is banished into animality. Coupling the two versions we arrive at a doubly radical break between men and gods: men recede below humanity, the gods' divinity is unanswerably affirmed. Only in future generations will human/divine relations be on a firmer footing—at a more respectful distance.

Another significant theme is the metamorphosis itself.[53] Not only is Lykaon like a wolf, he *is*, permanently, a wolf. Here again is an enormously common pattern in Greek myth: a departure from the norm—often a transgression—is fixed for ever by a change into a non-human state, frequently one (as with Lykaon) appropriate to the nature of the transgression or abnormality. Furthermore the fact that in the Lykaon myth (as usual in Greek metamorphoses) it is a god who effects the alteration is worth bearing in mind if the analogy between classical and medieval werewolves threatens to become too insistent. In both cultures to 'be a wolf' signifies that one has forfeited humanity and is obliged to lead an 'outside' existence. But the medieval werewolf, perceived as being able to change his shape from the God-given human form with which he started, is typically represented as having that power thanks to demonic assistance. The conceptual background to medieval werewolfism is Christianity.[54]

Any Greek myth should be responsive to an enquiry into its themes. But some myths, thanks to the accidents of survival and the character of the stories themselves, may take on added significance when seen in juxtaposition with a ritual. This is undeniably the case

[52] Borgeaud (1988) 27–8.

[53] On this theme in general, see Forbes Irving (1990); Frontisi-Ducroux (2003); Buxton (2009).

[54] Augustine (*De civ. D.* 18.18) ascribes all metamorphoses to demons, who have no power of creation but who change *in appearance* things created by God. On philosophical disputes about the status of metamorphosis in medieval times see ch. 2 of Summers (1933); Ortalli (1973) 286–7; Bynum (2001); Veenstra (2002).

with the myth in question here, which exists in a virtually symbiotic relationship with the werewolf ceremony of Mount Lykaion. On the one hand the myth 'confirms' the ritual, giving it greater resonance. Each time a man leaves the sanctuary to become a wolf, that man in a sense *is* Lykaon: by virtue of the conclusive banishment originally experienced by Lykaon, the exclusion dramatized in the ritual is that much more intense (or so we may surmise—the emotions involved in a ritual are hard enough to assess in a contemporary context, let alone in one sketchily known from antiquity). On the other hand myth and ritual are *contrasting* symbolic languages, the one tending to make explicit and absolute that which the other leaves implicit and temporary. Thus the metamorphosis of Lykaon is permanent, while the exclusion dramatized in the ritual is temporary and reversible. One may note the parallel with the scapegoat: in myth the designated individual is killed; in ritual merely expelled.[55]

A MODERN POSTSCRIPT

At certain points in this chapter I have discussed the far from simple relationship obtaining between traditions about and empirical observation of the wolf in Greek antiquity. My invoking of modern zoology as a control on some of the ancient data may have created an impression that nowadays we have an accurate and tradition-free picture of the wolf. It is true that in recent decades the science of ethology has made quite extraordinary strides; and studies of wolf behaviour are no exception to this generalization.[56] But knowledge of such matters is very thinly diffused. In the industrialized West, at any rate, the wolf is present largely as a residual folklore image, an image which might itself be seen as declining in prominence: in urban folklore, as the motorway has replaced the forest as the location of danger, so the phantom hitchhiker threatens to oust the werewolf.[57] But the continuing popularity of werewolf films and literature[58]

[55] Cf. Bremmer (2008) 179–82.

[56] Cf. works referred to in n. 2 above. I much regret that Hickey (2011) came to my notice too late to incorporate into my argument.

[57] See Brunvand (1981).

[58] See Gerhardt (1977); A. Douglas (1993); Otten (2002).

perhaps suggests that this beast remains good to think with, since it calls into question the boundary between human and 'bestial'. Even ordinary wolves still cause public and media terror if they get out of place. Above all there remains a fascination—the lupine equivalent of the debate over cannibalism—with the question, 'Do wolves make unprovoked attacks on human beings?'[59] The evidence seems in fact to be that, while *rabid* wolves will indeed run amok and bite at random, normally wolves are too terrified of man to attack even when hungry. It is of course hard to substantiate this, since it is often impossible to decide whether any given report, particularly if it is not contemporary, involves a rabid or a non-rabid wolf; and, to add to the confusion, feral dogs can easily be mistaken for wolves.[60] In any case, such cool evaluations of the evidence seem flimsy when confronted with a powerful folklore image. Whether that image would diminish or grow if the current move towards wolf conservation were to end and all the real wolves were to be exterminated, is beyond even guesswork.[61]

[59] Respectable scholars take the matter up eagerly. Eduard Fraenkel (1957, 186 n. 3) added a stop-press footnote: 'I can now add that during the exceptional cold spell of February 1956 a postman was attacked and eaten by wolves . . . in the immediate neighbourhood of Horace's farm'. Peter Levi repeated the *topos* fourteen years later (1971, ii. 324 n. 115).

[60] Molinier and Molinier-Meyer (1981) analyse forty-five attacks by wolves on humans between 1797 and 1817 in six French *départements*. Their guarded conclusion is that non-rabid wolves would attack children, especially those looking after flocks. Less often, adults were attacked; and, according to these authors, the attackers were not always rabid. But all adults fatally wounded or 'partiellement dévorés' were victims of rabid wolves. The authors estimate statistically that the rabid wolf is twenty times more dangerous than the non-rabid wolf.

[61] Versions of this chapter were read at the Universities of Ioannina, Bristol, Oxford, and Swansea, and at an annual meeting of the Classical Association at the University of Nottingham. I am indebted to the many colleagues who offered advice and criticism on each of these occasions. I am also most grateful for help received from Jan Bremmer, Monsignor Renato De Vido, and J. G. Davies.

3

Mythological Names: The Case of *melas*

Chapters 1 and 2 analysed different aspects of the interplay between the natural and the cultural. This third case study, by contrast, deals with a purely cultural phenomenon, one no less distinctive to Greek mythology than its way of imagining the landscape or the animal world. Greek myths do not narrate the exploits of anonymous princesses or foresters: the characters in those myths have individual 'proper' names. Chapter 3 will address the relationship between mythological names and the apparent signification of those names, an issue so far unresolved by scholars. This issue will lead us, not for the first and not for the last time, to context.

I begin by discussing the role played in the history of the interpretation of Greek myths by the search for the *etumos logos* ('true meaning') of the proper names which figure in those myths. The argument then becomes more specific, as it recommends a modification in how we may most fruitfully investigate this 'true meaning', by analysing the particular case of names which contain *melas* ('black', 'dark') as one of their components.

1. NAMES AND THEIR MEANINGS

Already in Homer we find explicit speculation about the true meaning of names. In the *Odyssey* (19.407–9) Autolykos states that he named his grandson 'Odysseus' so as to be *epōnumos* ('named for') the fact that he, Autolykos, had arrived in Ithaca in the condition of being *odussamenos* ('hating'/'hateful') to many. In this passage 'Odysseus' is clearly a 'speaking name'. But signifying what? Is Odysseus a hater, or one who is hated, or both simultaneously? Earlier (5.339–40) Leukothea had wondered why Poseidon *ōdusato* ('hated') Odysseus so much, but before that Kalypso had implicitly gone down another linguistic avenue, by associating Odysseus with lamentation: *odureo* ('you mourned') (5.160).[1] The poem makes no definitive choice between these meanings: in Homer the *etumos logos* of Odysseus' name is multiple, the subject of claim and counter-claim according to the context.

Subsequent mythical texts abound in *etumoi logoi* explicitly provided for the names of mythical characters.[2] Tragedy is a rich hunting ground, not surprisingly: for in tragedy names, like the world in general, turn out, with hindsight and too late, to bear an unexpected significance. But although tragedy is, one might have thought, the context par excellence in which to find multiple meanings, in fact many tragic etymologies are presented as transparently univocal. In Euripides' *Ion* (661–3) the eponymous hero is so named by Xouthos 'because you met me first *exionti* ("as I was coming out")'; according to the same poet's *Phoenician Women* (636–7), Eteokles recalls that Oidipous showed divine foresight when he 'truly' named his other son Polyneikes *neikeōn epōnumon* ('for quarrels'); in the Euripidean *Rhesos* (158–9), Hektor notes that the tricky Trojan spy Dolon is *epōnumos*; in Sophokles' *Aias* (430) the hero follows his exclamation of lament *aiai* with the rueful observation, 'Who would have thought that my name was so *epōnumon* with my misfortunes?'[3]

Sometimes, though, tragedy does make room for less transparent etymological virtuosity, as when the chorus of Aischylos' *Libation-Bearers* (948–51) unpacks the name of Dika (a dialectal form of Dike, 'Justice') as *Di[os] k[or]a* ('daughter of Zeus'). Comparable virtuosity can be found in many types of non-tragic text. Pherekydes of Syros, reputedly the teacher of Pythagoras, explains the name of Zeus' father Kronos by relating it to Chronos ('time').[4] Pindar several times employs etymological expressions to draw out the significance of the names of

[1] See Rank (1951) 51–63; Rutherford (1992) on *Od.* 19.406–9; Calame (1995) 177–8.

[2] As background to his study of Vergilian etymologizing, O'Hara (1996, 7–42) gives a useful review of earlier, Greek examples.

[3] For these and other examples of etymology in tragedy, see Platnauer (1938) on *IT* 32; Dodds (1960) on *Bacch.* 367 (cf. on 508); also on etymologies in *Bakchai*, Segal (1982) and Mirto (2010); on *Aias*, Garvie (1998) 430–3.

[4] F 66 Schibli; see Pfeiffer (1968) 12, and especially Schibli (1990) under 'Chronos' and 'Kronos' in index.

heroes who 'lie behind' the athletic victors he celebrates. Examples of this multi-layering technique are the explicit linkage of the name 'Iamos' to the violets (*ia*) among which this Arkadian hero was found as a baby (*Ol.* 6.53–7), and the allusive punning on the *laoi* ('people') created when Deukalion and Pyrrha threw stones which turned into the original human beings—*laas* being a Greek word for 'stone'—though Pindar sidesteps asserting the equivalence directly (*Ol.* 9.42–6).[5] In his own, much later account of Deukalion in the *Library of Mythology* (1.7.2), Apollodoros would explicitly assert that *laoi* derived their name from the *laas* from which they sprang. Another, earlier Apollodoros, the author of *On the Gods*, had used etymology to explain the characteristics of the gods by reference to their names and epithets. Although always alert to various ways of interpreting a name, this Apollodoros was also ready to express his own preference: in his opinion Apollo earned the epithet 'Delian' not through his shrine on Delos but because he is the god who makes things *dēla* ('clear').[6]

In Plato's *Kratylos* the procedure followed by Sokrates is to begin with a phonetic explication of a name, and then to show how the semantic content so revealed is appropriate to the referent of the name.[7] Sometimes the explication is univocal, as when Sokrates follows Hesiod in deriving 'Aphrodite' from *aphros* ('foam') (406c); but often two or more possibilities are given: 'Artemis' might derive either from the goddess's 'healthiness' (*to artemes*) or from the fact that she 'hates ploughing' (i.e. sexual intercourse) (*aroton misei*) (406b). The etymologies in *Kratylos* have frequently tried the patience of incredulous modern philologists, but David Sedley argues compellingly that there is no need to infer that Plato is systematically presenting the etymologies as ridiculous. The parameters of ancient etymological speculation simply do not—and cannot be expected to—coincide with the practice of philologists able to exploit the findings of comparative and historical linguistics regarding sound-shifts and morphology.[8]

Sometimes the difference in understanding between ancients and moderns about the scope of etymology has led commentators into

[5] See Nisetich (1980, 69–71) for interesting comments on how a translator may try to cope with such Pindaric puns.

[6] *FGrH* 244 F 95.32; Pfeiffer (1968) 262.

[7] Barney (2001) 50.

[8] Sedley (1998) and (2003), above all at 28–30; cf. Mirto (2010) 15 n. 21.

discriminations which sit uneasily with the ancient context. Commenting on that part of Cicero's *On the Nature of the Gods* which sets out the Stoics' elaborate attempts to find the true quality of divinities via an investigation into their names, Peter Walsh describes *some* of these attempts as 'woefully unscientific' and 'fanciful': Saturn because *saturaretur* ('he was "sated" with years'); Jupiter because he was a *iuvans pater* ('helpful father'); Sol because it is *solus* ('unique') (2.64–9). But Walsh finds *other* Stoic etymologies acceptable, for instance Luna, 'certainly cognate' with *lux* ('light') and *lucere* ('to shine'), and Diana, 'connected etymologically' to *dies* ('day').[9] It is, however, very questionable whether it is useful to evaluate such ancient speculations according to a set of criteria dating to no earlier than the nineteenth century. What is certain is that ancient etymologizing was a broad Church, working to make converts through persuasive and plausible argumentation. Not that it convinced everyone. We need go no further than the third book of Cicero's treatise, in which the academic sceptic Cotta ridicules the whole procedure, at least in the bravura version of it practised by the Stoics: 'Your strained interpretations', he observes, 'are quite pathetic' (3.62).[10]

In his book on *Kratylos*, Timothy Baxter follows up an observation by Walter Burkert, who argued for a parallel between ancient etymologizing and allegory. Baxter illuminatingly observes that '[a]llegory by its very nature forces a separation between the surface meaning of a text and its "true" meaning . . . Etymology, by tying the allegorical interpretation more directly to the text, is a way of trying to repair that separation from the surface text. That is why etymology is allegory's handmaiden.'[11] Given space and the necessary expertise, one could profitably prolong the investigation of the role played by etymology, alongside allegory, in the interpretation of myth from the early Christian polemicists through to the medieval period and the Renaissance.[12] Instead I want to look at some more recent attempts to dig beneath the names in Greek myths.

Many of the most august classical scholars of the nineteenth century investigated 'true meanings'. In the main they used one of

[9] Walsh (1997) 181–2, on 2.63–4 and 68–9.

[10] On Stoic etymologizing, see Boys-Stones (2003) 196–9.

[11] Baxter (1992) 119. Cf. Burkert (1970) 450.

[12] There are some pointers in de Vries (1961), e.g. on Clement of Alexandria (46) and Isidore of Seville (57–8). More comprehensive on etymology: Opelt (1966); Klinck (1970); Fontaine (1981). More recent but brief: Katz (2010).

two methods: either they probed the semantics of names within the Greek language, or they identified what they regarded as the non-Greek origins of Greek mythological names.

To illustrate the first of these strategies we may take the example of Gottfried Hermann, who maintained that he could give an interpretation of the myth of the Moliones which would be completely satisfactory, 'since the matter is quite simple and clear'. The conjoined Moliones, the twins Eurytos and Kteatos, are the sons of either Aktor or Poseidon, by Molione. In Hermann's view the name 'Molione' derives from Greek *molein* ('to come') and means 'the one who comes'. Thus the sons of Molione and Poseidon are 'the ones who come from the sea'. Molione's husband Aktor is either 'the man of the shore (*aktē*)', or, in Hermann's view more satisfactorily, 'the one who brings', from *agein* ('to bring'); specifically, he is the one who brings goods (from the sea to the land). As for the names of the twins: Eurytos is 'one for whom goods flow well' (that is, into his possession), from *eu* ('well') and *rhein* ('to flow'); Kteatos is the one who wins or earns something, from *ktaomai* or *kteomai* ('I acquire'). 'So the whole myth means no more than: "people arriving from the sea, bringing goods, acquire wealth through profitable trading".' The underlying meaning of the myth—here etymology really is 'allegory's handmaiden'—is indeed 'simple and clear': it refers to trade by sea.[13]

If we imagine a spectrum which runs from certainty to caution, Gottfried Hermann stood close to the certainty end. So did Hermann Usener. His remarkable study of what he saw as the progression from linguistically transparent *Sondergötter* ('individualized' or 'particularized' gods)[14] to no-longer-linguistically-transparent deities, involved a number of unequivocal affirmations about true meanings. Some names are transparent, as with Iaso ('She Who Heals'), Akeso ('She Who Cures'), Panakeia ('All-cure'), and Hygieia ('Health'). But in other cases, where many scholars would prefer the idea of multiplicity of meaning, Usener was decisive: Apollo *Lukēgenēs* is unequivocally a god of *light*—alleged derivations from either *lukoi* ('wolves'), or from the territory of Lycia, are simply a product of 'the empty game of folk etymology'—a concept which, of course, only becomes meaningful once 'scientific' etymology has come into being.[15]

[13] Hermann (1819) 55–6; my translation.

[14] R. Parker (2011, 105) translates the term as 'special function gods'.

[15] Usener (1896) 166–8, 198–216, 303–4, 333.

Against such certainty, Karl Otfried Müller had already sounded a note of caution. In the course of his *Prolegomena zu einer wissenschaftlichen Mythologie*, while conceding that 'one can hardly doubt the usefulness of etymology as an aid to the elucidation of mythology', he went on to stress that etymology is hardly a mature enough science to be allowed to take the interpretative lead: names, he asserted, like symbols, are often ambiguous and lend themselves to multiple interpretations. Aiolos, for instance, is 'the man of wind' (as Aello is 'a bride of the wind'); but simultaneously Aiolos is the collective noun for the Aiolians. Not, then, quite so 'simple and clear'.[16]

Turning now from intra-Greek to inter-language approaches, we again find a mixture of confidence and caution. About Max Müller it is enough to recall his uncompromising observation that '[i]t is the essential character of a true myth that it should no longer be intelligible by a reference to the spoken language'[17]—in other words, any intra-Greek semantic approach is by definition misguided; the quest for the true meaning of mythological names must be displaced onto Greek's Indo-European predecessor. The point is clearly set out by Müller's British adherent G. W. Cox, in his account of the myth of Prokris, Kephalos, and Eos: 'In this tale, then, we have a series of names, the analysis of which guides us straight to the root of the story and brings before us the phrases relating to the sun, the dawn, and the dew, out of which it sprang.'[18] Simple and clear. But the cautionary note was sounded in the very decade in which Cox was writing, the 1880s, by the Swedish scholar and man of letters Viktor Rydberg, in a book about the interpretation of Germanic myths. Rydberg referred to the 'mistake which has played and still plays a large and regrettable role in the study of mythology', namely 'the immense importance which linguists give to a mythical *name*...If one has established that a name means "He Who Shines" or "He Who Thunders", the assumption has immediately been that one has thereby established *in nuce* all the characteristics of the personality with this name'. To make that assumption is, Rydberg argued, badly to misjudge the true multiplicity of mythical characters.[19]

[16] K. O. Müller (1825) 285, 292; cf. de Vries (1961) 196.

[17] F. M. Müller (1895) 78.

[18] Cox (1883) 22.

[19] Rydberg (1889) 442–3, cited by de Vries (1961) 250–3. For help with the translation from Swedish I am indebted to Ann-Louise Schallin.

In spite of such warnings, the quest for the *etumos logos* continued to flourish in the twentieth century. Robert Graves repeatedly deployed etymology to justify his extraordinary flights of fantasy. Speculating on the names of the Giants Alkyoneus, Mimas, and Hippolytos, all of whom he related to the notion of dreams, Graves commented: 'Alcyoneus ("mighty ass") is probably the spirit of the sirocco, "the breath of the Wild Ass, or Typhon"... which brings bad dreams, and murderous inclinations, and rapes... Mimas ("mimicry") may refer to the delusive verisimilitude of dreams; and Hippolytus ("stampede of horses") recalls the ancient attribution of terror-dreams to the Mare-headed goddess.'[20] This is free association unconfined. The staggering success, in terms of worldwide sales, achieved by Graves' *The Greek Myths* is one of the more puzzling aspects of the recent historiography of myth.

The twentieth century also enjoyed its fair share of etymological interpretations which relate Greek names to non-Greek precursors. Martin Bernal saw the origins of Greek culture in Egyptian, Semitic, and Indo-European—emphatically in that order of priority. As he wrote in *Black Athena II*, 'I believe that many of the Greek divine names, such as Apollo, Athena and so on, were in fact Egyptian'. Thus Rhadamanthys is derived from the Egyptian divinity Mnṯw (Mont) ('*Rdỉ Mnṯw' = 'Mnṯw gives' or 'whom Mnṯw has given'). Semitic origins are also entertained, albeit less often: following Michael Astour, Bernal derives Kadmos from West Semitic *qdm* ('Easterner' and 'ancient one'), Europa from Semitic *<rb* ('west' or 'evening').[21] It is hard to resist the conclusion that Bernal's tendency to derive all things Greek from non-Greek antecedents could be described politely as a panacea, or less so as an *idée fixe*.

For Walter Burkert, too, investigation of names is a major investigative tool, though it is deployed in a much more nuanced way. Almost all the subsections of Burkert's discussion of the Olympian deities in his *Greek Religion* begin with comments on the name of the deity. But Burkert is not dogmatic: where he detects uncertainty or ambiguity or multiplicity, he readily admits it. Sometimes he finds the key to a name in the Greek language, sometimes in pre-Greek, sometimes in a language other than Greek, and sometimes the matter

[20] Graves (1960) 133.

[21] Bernal (1991) 109–10, 178–83, 497; cf. Astour (1965).

is just obscure.[22] For Jan Bremmer, names figure less prominently than they do for Burkert, but Bremmer too invokes them from time to time, in a non-doctrinaire way and on a case-by-case basis. About Pandora, Bremmer is pluralistic, stressing the different meanings exploited by different authors in different contexts; regarding the Titans he follows Burkert, albeit cautiously, in connecting them with the mythical ancestor of the kings in Ugarit, Ditanu (this appeals to Bremmer because he sees a possible North Syrian connection for the festival of the Kronia).[23]

The etymological unpacking of mythological names continues apace; but for the single most seminal, recent gambit in this area we are indebted to Claude Calame. What distinguishes Calame is that he is acutely sensitive to the place of names *within a narrative.* At one point in *The Craft of Poetic Speech* he brilliantly observes that 'the potential meanings that reside in the Greek name turn it into a microstory'; and he concludes his section on names with the assertion that '[t]he name is a metaphor for the identity of its bearer'.[24] I want to pick up the trail where Calame has left it, namely with names not as isolated elements, but as elements within stories. But I want to add a suggestion of my own: that names in narratives should be thought of along a scale ranging from the manifestly and transparently significant, through an intermediate position of multiple significance, to a position in which a name may be regarded as, in a given context, simply *in*significant. I shall illustrate this with names involving the component *melas.*

2. THE MEANINGS OF *MELAS*

In his still useful dissertation on the meaning of the colours white and black in Greek and Roman religion, Gerhard Radke conveys a message which is basically very straightforward: in relation to the gods and their worship, black is negative, white positive.[25] More specifically, the Greek word *melas*—variously translatable as 'black' or

[22] Burkert (1985) 125–70.
[23] Bremmer (2008) 26–7, 86–7.
[24] Calame (1995) 183 and 185.
[25] Radke (1936). Vidal-Naquet (1986a, 112) called this a 'conscientious catalogue'.

'dark'—is associated with the Underworld,[26] with Ate,[27] with death,[28] and mourning.[29] In keeping with this nexus of funereal associations, animals described as *melas* are sacrificed to powers of the Underworld and to the dead: thus at *Odyssey* 11.32–3 Odysseus promises to dedicate an *oin pammelana* ('all-black ram') to Teiresias if he gets back safe to Ithaca, while in Kolophon, according to Pausanias (3.14.9), they sacrifice a black bitch to Enodia, and moreover they do so at night.[30] *Leukos* ('white'), by contrast, is associated not just with divinities of light such as Helios and Day—in Aischylos' *Persians* the glorious day of the victory at Salamis is a *leukopōlos hēmera* ('day of white horses') (386)—but with divinities in general, especially when they are conceived of as 'favourable': the Dioskouroi, those twin saviours, ride on white horses.[31] Again there is a correspondence in the realm of sacrificial ritual: white animals were sacrificed to several of the major Olympian deities, including Aphrodite, Apollo, Hera, Poseidon, and Zeus.[32] Moreover, clothing which is *leukos* may indicate the proper ritual condition in which mortals should approach a god: Diogenes Laertios reports that Pythagoras' prescriptions for ritual purity included *stolē leukē* ('white clothing') and *strōmata leuka* ('white bed-coverings').[33] In all these various data from the world of ritual practice we seem to find ample confirmation of the *melas*-as-negative/*leukos*-as-positive polarity which is also evidenced in myth—in, for example, the black sail of forgetful Theseus, which caused the suicide of his father Aegeus;[34] or in Apollo's changing of the colour of the crow from white to black, to punish it

[26] Erebos is *melamphaes* ('whose light is blackness') at Eur. *Hel.* 518.

[27] Aesch. *Ag.* 770.

[28] Eur. *Alc.* 843–4. On black as generally associated with death in antiquity, see Pastoureau (2009a) 30–5.

[29] The veil of Thetis, as she mourned for Achilles, was *kuaneon, tou d'ou ti melanteron epleto esthos* ('blue-black, the darkest of all garments') (Hom. *Il.* 24.94). Before the destruction of Corinth by the Romans, Corinthian boys used to cut their hair short and wear black in memory of the killing of Medea's children (Paus. 2.3.7).

[30] Similarly, Orestes offers a black sheep to his dead father at Eur. *El.* 513–14.

[31] Pind. *Pyth.* 1.66.

[32] A few examples: Aphrodite: Lucian *Dial. meret.* 7.1. Apollo: Theoc. *Epigr.* 1.5. Hera: *LSAM* 41.6. Poseidon: App. *Mith.* 70; *LSCG* 96.5–9; Pind. *Ol.* 13.69. Zeus: *LSCG* 85.1–2; Dem. 21.53. See Radke (1936) 23–7.

[33] Diog. Laert. 8.19; cf. Aeschin. *In Ctes.* 77, on the wearing of *leukēn esthēta* ('white garments') by a person sacrificing.

[34] Apollod. *Epit.* 1.10. Black is also the colour of the sail of Charon's boat: Aesch. *Sept.* 857.

for bringing the message about Koronis' infidelity;[35] or in the notion of a paradisiacal place known as Leuke (sometimes localized on an island in the Black Sea), implicitly contrasted with the dark realm of Hades.[36] *Melas* negative, *leukos* positive. It seems, at first sight, simple and clear.

Yet as soon as we look more carefully at the evidence from cult, it is not hard to find inversions of our polarity. The colour of death is not *always* black. In a fragment from Aristophanes' *Banqueters*, a white dog is offered to Hekate, notwithstanding the goddess's connections with the Underworld.[37] In the *Iliad* the dead Patroklos is covered with a white shroud (18.353). Not only Patroklos: the Messenians, according to Pausanias, dressed their great men in white cloaks before burial (4.13.2–3), while Artemidoros could interpret a dream of wearing white as a prognostic of death, since 'the dead are carried off in white clothes' (2.3).[38] Nor is it only divinities predominantly linked with death and night who are associated with black: Pausanias' description of Arkadia includes accounts of Demeter Melaina at Phigalia (8.42.4) and Aphrodite Melainis at Mantinea (8.6.5). Again, in relation to sacrificial offerings, Poseidon and other sea deities sometimes received sacrifices of black animals.[39] It seems that the link in cult between *melas*-and-negative/*leukos*-and-positive is far from universal.

And yet, if we really want to, we can come up with explanations to account for all our apparent exceptions. For Hekate's white dog we have no context—so, for all we know, it could have been an Aristophanic joke *para prosdokian* ('against expectation').[40] The fact that the dead are sometimes associated with white might be, not an exception to the normal, symbolically positive connotation of white, but an example of it: white would in that case be apotropaic, to drive away pollution. The blackness of Demeter Melaina could stand for her state of mourning. Pausanias himself explained the blackness of

[35] Schol. Pind. *Pyth.* 3.52b; see T. Gantz (1993) 91. On crows (ambivalent for Greeks and Romans; revered by the ancient Germans; diabolical for Christianity), see Pastoureau (2009a) 36–8.

[36] On Leuke, it was said, Achilles led a blessed existence after death: Pind. *Nem.* 4.49–50; Eur. *Andr.* 1260–2, Eur. *IT* 435–8; Burgess (2009) index s.v. Leuke.

[37] *PCG* Ar. fr. 209.

[38] One may note also that both white and black are associated with ghosts: see Winkler (1980) 160–5.

[39] Poseidon: Hom. *Od.* 3.6. Other sea deities: Porph. apud Euseb. *Praep. evang.* 4.9.

[40] Sternbach (1886, 257) suggested it might refer to a *mangy* dog.

Aphrodite Melainis on the ingenious ground that sex takes place mostly at night. As for marine deities, the sea can be seen as 'dark', so a black sacrifice could be regarded as appropriate for them—a point already made in ancient scholia on Homer.[41] Alternatively, Radke argued that Poseidon's black sacrificial animals correspond to the 'dangerous wildness' of the sea.[42] With a liberal dose of ingenuity, then, the interpreter *can* restore the integrity of the polarity: *melas* negative, *leukos* positive.

But how far is such ingenuity justified? Edmund Leach once wisely observed: 'Even when it is evident that the colour of something has symbolic significance we can never be sure what it is. Each case must be investigated in its particular context.'[43] In my view we should not force all cases of the ritual use of *melas* and *leukos* into one mould: each instance must be taken on its merits. To relate the blackness of Demeter Melaina to mourning is convincing. But to explain—or explain away—the sacrifice of black animals to Poseidon in terms either of the 'darkness' of the sea, or of the sea's 'wildness', seems to me to be special pleading. The data from cult and ritual is *broadly* in line with the *melas*-as-negative/*leukos*-as-positive polarity, but there are genuine exceptions which we must simply accept as part of the complexity of ritual symbolism.

Nor is this surprising, because as soon as we step outside the sphere of cult and ritual to deal with the 'everyday' implications of *leukos* and *melas*, the complexity becomes far more noticeable.[44] It is true that the expression *leukon ēmar* ('white day') was proverbial for a lucky day.[45] But in certain contexts *leukos* and its cognates can have a negative quality. *Leukē* is a disease of the skin, a kind of white eruption like leprosy.[46] For a man, to be *leukos* can be a sign of effeminacy, since it ascribes to a male the skin colour normally regarded as a praiseworthy characteristic of a (properly) stay-at-home woman.[47] To be *leukēpatias*

41 Eust. p. 1454, 4–5, on *Od.* 3.6; other scholia ad loc.

42 Radke (1936) 30.

43 Leach (1976) 59.

44 Some useful material is collected by Irwin (1974).

45 As the Persian queen says in reaction to the news that Xerxes is alive and 'sees the light': 'What you spoke of was a great light for my house and a white day (*leukon ēmar*) after a night that was *melas*' (Aesch. *Pers.* 300–1). The explanation of the expression varied; cf. references in LSJ s.v. λευκός II.3.

46 Cf. 71 below, and n. 77.

47 Ar. *Thesm.* 191, cf. *Eccl.* 428; X. *Hell.* 3.4.19. For an impressive account of black/white skin colour in relation to the male/female polarity, see Sassi (2001) 1–33.

('white-livered'), or, even worse, *leukoprōktos* or *leukopugos* ('white-arsed')—these are signs of cowardice.[48] Although several of the passages linking whiteness with lack of manliness come from comedy, whiteness is presented negatively in other genres too. In Pindar's 4th *Pythian* (109), Jason describes his enemy Pelias as relying on his *leukais phrasin* ('white mind')—obviously a negative quality, though commentators disagree about whether to interpret it as 'foolish', 'superficial', 'cowardly', or 'crazed'.[49]

Melas is no less complex. Already in Homer the epithet is applied to wine, blood, water, ships, and earth. To be *melagchroiēs* ('black-/dark-skinned'), which is the appearance given by Athene to Odysseus when she renders him more handsome, is clearly a good quality in a man (*Od.* 16.175). So is the quality of being *melampugos* or *melampugōn* ('black-arsed')—terms which can be used admiringly, especially in comedy, to describe a tough, Herakles-like individual.[50] More enigmatic is the notion of the person who feels strong emotion around his *phrenes melainai* ('black/dark mind'). In the *Iliad* one's *phrenes* can be black when one feels grief (17.83), but also when one feels courage (17.499) and anger (1.103–4).[51] The quality of being *melas* is not intrinsically negative.

From what I have said so far I draw three conclusions. (1) In relation to cult and ritual, *melas* is usually negative and *leukos* positive; but there are genuine exceptions. (2) In the perceptions of everyday life we find a still more complex picture, with an even less tidy match between *melas* and positive, *leukos* and negative. (3) It follows that we must always *specify the context* in which *melas* and *leukos* appear

[48] *PCG* Callias fr. 14; Alexis fr. 322, on which see Arnott (1996) ad loc. The claim to be 'white-*footed*'—a claim staked by the old men in the chorus of Aristophanes' *Lysistrata* (664), associating themselves with a fight long ago against the Athenian tyrants—involves an epithet whose significance has never been satisfactorily explained. Henderson (1987, ad loc.) sees it as an honorific way of referring to foot-soldiers, citing both *females* who are barefoot (like the bacchants at Eur. *Cyc.* 72) and monosandalism. However (a) one cannot equate the genders over the issue of 'whiteness', and (b) monosandalism is a quite separate and distinctive phenomenon (see 89 below in ch. 4). For Sommerstein (1990, ad loc.) the 'Whitefeet' are aristocrats whose feet have never become dirty or sunburnt.

[49] See Gentili et al. (1995) ad loc.

[50] Archil. 178 West; *PCG* Eubulus fr. 61; Ar. *Lys.* 802–3. On being black-arsed, see Irwin (1974) 139–44.

[51] See Irwin (1974) 135–9.

before reaching conclusions about their signification.[52] No signifier has an intrinsic meaning, only a meaning in context.

Against this background I want now to examine the meaning (or lack of meaning) of some mythological names involving *melas*.

First, three general points need to be made about Greek names. (1) As I said earlier, a name, or part of a name, might not *necessarily* have been felt to be significant. In *Poetics* Aristotle observes: 'In the word "Theodoros", *to dōros ou sēmainei* (the [element] *dōros* doesn't mean anything)' (1457^{a} 13–14). The example Aristotle chooses is a curious one, since in principle there would seem to be nothing objectionable about interpreting the name 'Theodoros' as 'god-*given*'.[53] But what is relevant to us is Aristotle's general point: not every part of a name need be felt to carry meaning. (2) The interpreter, ancient or modern, has a crucial role to play in reading significance into a name. We need look no further than Plato's *Kratylos*, the subject of which is precisely the appropriateness of names in relation to the character of their owner. At one point (395b) Sokrates talks of the name 'Atreus': the form of his name is, Sokrates observes, slightly 'deflected and hidden', but the connection with stubbornness (*to ateires*) and fearlessness (*to atreston*) and ruinousness (*to atēron*) is clear *to those who understand about names*. In other words, the significance of a name does not go without saying. (3) The degree to which a name might have been felt to be meaningful varies not only according to the interpreter, but also according to the context within which the name appears. A name, or an element of a name, might spring into semantic life in one context, but remain dormant in another.

Guided by these considerations, I shall address two questions relating to names involving *melas*. First: is the component *melas* significant in a particular name in a particular context? Second: if it is significant, *what* might it signify?

I begin with a sister-and-brother pair from the *Odyssey*: Melantho and Melanthios, children of Dolios. Melantho is Penelope's maid who sleeps with the suitor Eurymachos and insults Odysseus; Odysseus

[52] For a cross-cultural perspective, see also Pastoureau (2009a) 197 n. 44: whereas the light/dark opposition is 'natural', the white/black opposition is 'totally cultural'. As Pastoureau demonstrates, there are many cultural contexts—medieval heraldry for one—in which the contrast between white and black is far less marked than it is in the ancient classical world, and emphatically *not* aligned with positive/negative.

[53] See Lucas (1972) ad loc.

and Penelope call her a bitch.[54] Melanthios (a metrical alternative is Melantheus) is the arrogant goatherd who kicks Odysseus, helps the suitors in their combat, and eventually suffers humiliating torture and mutilation at Odysseus' hands.[55] Are 'Melantho' and 'Melanthios' significant names? More specifically, does the element *melas* bear meaning within these names? Significance depends on context, and one of the contexts within which these names are situated is the *Odyssey*, a poem replete with names which signify.[56] The insolent suitor with a way with words is Antinoos ('Opposed Mind'), son of Eupeithes ('Effective Persuader') (1.383); the man who willingly supplies Telemachos with his ship is Noemon ('Man of Sense'), son of Phronios ('Prudent') (2.386); the nautical way of life of the Phaiakians is expressed by the names of Nausikaa, Nausithoos, Pontonoos, and all the rest (from *naus*, 'ship'; *thoos*, 'swift'; *pontos*, 'sea'; *noos*, 'mind'); during the Cyclops episode in Book 9 the disguised hero of the poem styles himself as *Outis*, 'Nobody', but at other times this grandson of Autolykos bears the name 'Odysseus', which, as we saw at the beginning of this chapter, is an explicitly significant (albeit ambivalent) name. In the context of such a poem 'Melantho' and 'Melanthios' must surely also be seen as signifying names. But which aspect of *melas* do they evoke? It would seem inevitable to take the implied connotation as, in some general negative sense, 'bad' or 'wicked': *morally* 'dark'. If it were to be proposed that other possible connotations of *melas*—courage, for example—are relevant, I cannot disprove it. I merely suggest that it is highly improbable *in this context*.

Next I turn to the more complicated cases of Melanion and Melanthos. These two mythological figures became jointly famous in 1968, the year when Pierre Vidal-Naquet's rich and deservedly influential article on 'the Black Hunter' was first published.[57] The aim of Vidal-Naquet's paper was to throw light on the Athenian *ephebeia*—an institution involving the ritualized organization of a cohort of male adolescents or 'ephebes'—by investigating a number of myths whose

[54] Hom. *Od.* 18.321–39; 19.65–95.

[55] Hom. *Od.* 17.212–60, 369–73; 20.172–84, 255; 21.175–83, 265–8; 22.135–52, 159–200, 474–7.

[56] On 'speaking names' in Homer, see von Kamptz (1982) 25–35; more generally, Rank (1951).

[57] Translated in Vidal-Naquet (1986a) 106–28. My criticisms of certain aspects of this chapter do not diminish my deep admiration for the work of this fine scholar and great man.

structure may be seen as parallel to the structure implicit in that institution. What makes Vidal-Naquet's analysis relevant to the present inquiry is the fact that the characteristic of 'being *melas*' is common to several of the myths which he discusses.

Melanion *is* the Black Hunter. Vidal-Naquet introduces him by quoting a *muthos* sung in Aristophanes' *Lysistrata* by the chorus of old men, who recall a story they heard in childhood (781–96):

> Once upon a time there was a young man called Melanion, who fled from marriage and went into the wilderness and lived in the mountains; and he hunted hares and wove nets and had a dog, and never came back home again, because of his loathing. So much did he abhor women, as we sensible fellows do, no less than Melanion did.

For Vidal-Naquet, Melanion is an ephebe *manqué*, a lone hunter who goes out into the wilds on an exploit, but who does *not* return to the community afterwards. He is thus *partly* parallel to another '*melas*-hero' discussed by Vidal-Naquet: Melanthos, the mythical opponent of Xanthos.[58] Melanthos uses trickery to outwit his opponent in a border zone between Boiotian and Athenian territory, sometimes named as Melainai (or Melania). In some accounts, Melanthos' victory is ascribed to the intervention of Dionysos Melanaigis ('of the black goatskin').[59] Unlike the Aristophanic Melanion, however, Melanthos does successfully make the transition back from his marginality: he becomes king of Athens. The stories of both Melanion and Melanthos illustrate, for Vidal-Naquet, the negative quality of 'being *melas*' during a period spent in the wilds, segregated from civilization. Taken together, they stand as a kind of composite mythical prototype of the historical Athenian ephebe, whose period of military service on the confines of society preceded his eventual reintegration into the adult community.

Is all this convincing? This is not the place to go into the broader question of the institution of the Athenian *ephebeia*. I restrict myself to a discussion of the two mythical figures Melanthos and Melanion, and, in particular, to the signification of their names.

[58] For the varied and mostly fragmentary sources (which sometimes give the alternative names Melanthios and Xanthios), see Vidal-Naquet (1986a) 123 n. 15.

[59] Cf. *Suda* s.v. *Μελαναιγὶς Διόνυσος*, reporting that Dionysos was worshipped under this epithet at Eleutherai (in the border area between Attica and Boiotia); Nonnos, *Dion.* 27.301–7, with Vian (1990) nn. on 27.301–3 and 304–7.

We must take each character separately. First, Melanthos. In my view Vidal-Naquet's overall analysis of the myth of Melanthos is, from the perspective which concerns us in the present chapter, persuasive. In particular, the threefold occurrence of names containing the element *melas*—Melanthos himself, the place Melainai, and the epithet Melanaigis[60]—reinforces the sense that the myth is indeed exploiting the opposition between the 'fair' Xanthos as opposed to the 'dark' Melanthos. Moreover, the nexus of deception, the wilds, and blackness/darkness does seem to mark out both the behaviour of Melanthos and the location of his exploit as 'marginal' in contrast to that which is associated with the 'central', civilized citizen. Therefore I can see no objection to agreeing with Vidal-Naquet, in relation to the extant narratives about Melanthos, not only that the *melas* component of the name may legitimately be regarded as meaningful, but also that that meaning may plausibly be seen as bearing, in the context of these narratives, an 'initiatory' connotation, in so far as 'being *melas*' may designate symbolically a status which is both chronologically before and structurally antithetical to that which follows it.[61]

With Melanion, however, the case is quite different. After quoting the choral narrative from *Lysistrata*—the story of a lone, woman-hating hunter—Vidal-Naquet recommends that we replace this song within its mythical context. He illustrates this context by citing the association, familiar especially from Apollodoros (3.9.2), between Melanion and Atalante, another character who hunts in the wilds. By the ruse of throwing down some golden apples obtained from Aphrodite, Melanion tricked the usually fast-running Atalante into stooping, losing her race, and thus becoming his bride.[62] That Melanion, like Melanthos, uses trickery is certainly a feature which may encourage us to look for further parallels between the two. What is quite unclear, however, is how the Aristophanic Melanion who hated women can be equated with the Apollodoran Melanion who loved

[60] Cf. Vidal-Naquet (1986a) 111–12.

[61] Several sources for the Melanthos myth explicitly connect it with the founding of the Apatouria (in view of the deception, *apatē*, practised by Melanthos). The Apatouria was an Ionian festival which apparently featured sacrifices on the part of those making various 'passages', e.g. those entering the *ephebeia*. See R. Parker (2005, 458–61) for a judicious account of the extent and limitations of our knowledge of the festival.

[62] For variants of the myths about Atalante and Melanion, see T. Gantz (1993) 335–9.

Atalante—and who even went on, with her, to *over*-value sexual intercourse rather than undervaluing it, when (again according to Apollodoros) the two of them made love in a sanctuary of Zeus, as a consequence of which transgression they were metamorphosed into lions.[63] A more serious difficulty stems from the fact that Vidal-Naquet takes insufficient account of the dramatic context in *Lysistrata.*[64] In response to the men's chorus, who sing about Melanion the *hater* of women, the women's chorus sing about Timon, a wanderer in the wilds who—according to this chorus—hated males, *but loved women* (805–20). However, the usual story of Timon was that he hated everybody—women included.[65] In other words, the chorus of women have invented a largely idiosyncratic version of a traditional story in order to make a polemical point. I suggest that the men's chorus had done precisely the same thing when they re-invented Melanion as a misogynist. To amalgamate the Aristophanic, woman-hating Melanion with the Apollodoran hero who loved Atalante surely devalues the importance of the distinctive Aristophanic context. Comedy is a genre in which significant names are common: Lysistrata, the leader of the sex-strike in her eponymous play, is 'She Who Undoes the Army'; in the same play the forlorn, sex-starved, permanently erect Kinesias is 'He Who Moves' (i.e. sexually); in *Wasps* Bdelykleon and Philokleon are respectively 'Kleon-Hater' and 'Kleon-Lover'; and so on and on.[66] In principle, therefore, we should be well prepared to find significance in the *melas* component of Melanion's name in *Lysistrata*. But in the event I am not confident about ascribing such significance to this name in Aristophanes (or indeed in Apollodoros). In short, whereas I find Vidal-Naquet's account of *melas* in the name 'Melanthos' broadly convincing, I am unable to say the same of his account of the name 'Melanion'.

What we do not have, unfortunately, for either Melanthos or Melanion, is a version of their myths as dramatized in a tragedy, a context no less hospitable than comedy to the explicitly etymologized,

[63] Cf. Sommerstein (1990) n. on Ar. *Lys.* 785.

[64] The same is true of the follow-up article in which Vidal-Naquet reconsidered the argument of 'The Black Hunter', returning briefly at one point to the *Lysistrata* chorus (1986b, 128).

[65] Ar. *Av.* 1548; *PCG* Phrynichus fr. 19.

[66] For 'speaking names' in Aristophanes, see now Kanavou (2011); though note the critical review by Storey (2011).

significant name.[67] The same absence goes for the final and most intriguing figure whom I propose to discuss: Melampous. Is the 'blackness' of his 'foot' significant? If so, *what* does it signify?

Melampous is a seer who can understand the language of animals and birds.[68] Though based in Pylos, he travels to other parts of the Peloponnese and beyond; once he goes on a cattle raid to Thessaly.[69] But his most famous exploit is as a curer of physical and mental illness: according to different versions, he cures either all the women of Argos, driven mad by Dionysos, or just the daughters of Proitos, who are punished in various ways by Dionysos or Hera.[70] Herodotos, who alludes to the curing of the Argive women, maintains elsewhere (2.49) that Melampous introduced divination and the worship of Dionysos into Greece from Egypt. What, though, of the name 'Melampous'? To my knowledge, the only *ancient* interpretation of his blackness/darkness occurs in a fragment by the fourth-century BC historian Dieuchidas of Megara, who relates that Melampous' mother Dorippe placed the newborn baby in the shade, all except his feet, which were said to have 'become *melas*' in the sunshine.[71] We have no context for this, but the story is intriguing, as it locates Melampous within a story pattern reminiscent of that which attaches to baby Achilles, whose heel was accidentally left unprotected by his mother Thetis.[72] Dieuchidas' explanation for Melampous' name is dismissed or ignored by virtually all scholars—too hastily, perhaps, because it is an example (weak, but still just perceptible) of the mythical pattern whereby a seer's special knowledge is balanced by a physical defect.[73] But that is not the only way of reading Melampous' blackness. The Herodotean passage linking him with Egypt would perfectly suit a hero who mediates between Egypt and Greece—being *melampodes* ('black-footed') is a characteristic which we find elsewhere ascribed to Egyptians.[74] Nor is that the end of the possible interpretations. H. W. Parke saw a connection between the blackness of Melampous' feet and the Selloi, priests of Zeus at Dodona who sleep on the ground *and do not wash their feet*; after all, didn't Melampous understand the

[67] See the examples given above at 54 with n. 3.

[68] Apollod. *Bibl.* 1.9.12. On myths of Melampous, see T. Gantz (1993) 185–8, 312–13; Bremmer (2008) 133–51.

[69] Hom. *Od.* 11.288–97; 15.225–42.

[70] Hes. fr. 37 MW; Hdt. 9.34; Apollod. *Bibl.* 2.2.2.

[71] *FGrH* 485 F 9.

[72] See 92–4 in ch. 4.

[73] See 183–7 in ch. 9.

[74] E.g. Apollod. *Bibl.* 2.1.4.

speech of birds (we recall that one channel for Zeus's communications at Dodona was through birds)?[75] Nor is even *that* the end of it: A. B. Cook suggested that 'in primitive times' Melampous was imagined as 'a sacred goat' (a suggestion less likely to carry conviction now that totemism has long since ceased to be a universal explanatory panacea).[76] And couldn't one take yet another explanatory path by recalling that the daughters of Proitos, according to Hesiod, suffered from a leprosy-like skin disease on the head?[77] In that case, Melampous would be acting as a kind of black antidote to a white disease, black feet counterbalancing white heads. What we lack, in order to control this riot of exuberant speculations, is one or more detailed contexts—on the model of the *Odyssey*, in the case of Melantho and Melanthios—which would allow us to be reasonably confident about the significance of the name *in that context or those contexts*. As it stands, the blackness in the name of Melampous cannot be pinned down to just one meaning.

What's in a name? Sometimes more, sometimes less, than we might think. But it is impossible to say *how much* more or less, unless we have a context.[78]

[75] Hom. *Il.* 16.234–5; Parke (1967) 8–9. Parke was followed by Simon (1992) 405 and Jost (1992) 183.

[76] A. B. Cook (1894) 385.

[77] Hes. fr. 133, 4 MW. Borgeaud (1999, 297) is sceptical of ascribing a precise medical name to this affliction.

[78] This chapter is a heavily revised amalgam of contributions which I made to two conferences. One conference was on 'Light and darkness in ancient Greek and Roman mythology and religion', held at Patras in July 2007, and organized by Menelaos Christopoulos and Effy Karakantza. The other took place in Geneva in October 2008, under the guidance of Philippe Borgeaud and Damien Nelis, on the subject of 'Le mythe et ses interprétations: réévaluations de théories anciennes'. I thank my fellow participants on both occasions for their valuable comments, and Jan Bremmer for subsequent help.

4

The Myth of Talos: Vulnerability, *ichōr*, and Boundary-Crossing

The relationship between names and their meaning, the subject of the previous chapter, is by no means the only unresolved issue in the study of mythological onomastics. Another such issue concerns plurality. Many names designate two or more mythological characters; but how are we to understand this? The question has received surprisingly little attention in previous scholarship. Chapter 4 examines the case of the two (or one) Talos(es). Along the way we rejoin a topic raised throughout Chapters 1 and 2. Like mountains and wolves, boundary-crossing giants are 'good to think (with)'.

> In my opinion the very concept of an automaton or robot is a philosophical concept, giving rise to questions about life, thought, and language—and much more. Yes, I sometimes wonder whether robots were not invented in order to answer philosophers' questions.
>
> John Sladek, *Tik-Tok* (1983)[1]

Steven Spielberg, it is said, instructed the technicians who designed the *Jurassic Park* dinosaurs to make them look, sound, and move like animals, not monsters. An animal, he was presumably implying, falls under the definition of a recognizable species, whereas a monster is a cross or confusion between species: an anomaly. But if the population of Spielberg's *Park* is not monstrous, the same cannot be said of the

[1] I am grateful to Neville Morley for this epigraph. Sladek's story, the autobiography of a robot, is dedicated to, among others, Talos of Crete. (The quotation is on p. 53 of the Corgi edition, London, 1984.) Others to whom I owe thanks are my sympathetically critical audiences at Gregynog and Bristol (where versions of this chapter were read), and also Alan Sommerstein, Robert Fowler, and (as usual) Jan Bremmer.

worlds conjured up in many (or many other) traditional tales. Such stories in numerous cultures regularly do exploit anomalies, which allow members of those cultures to play with categories usually kept distinct.

A favourite focus for such thought experiments is the definition of humanity, explored through the medium of creatures which both are and are not human. Our own culture is in this respect no different, not least—indeed, especially—in relation to the tales told by scientists. Is that collection of bones the last ape, or the first human, or (best of all) could it be the Missing Link? While a sophisticated computer may be just a heap of inanimate matter which can in one respect think *like* the world chess champion, what will it take for a computer to cross (or, more intriguingly still, to be situated on) the consciousness threshold (if there is one)? Might it even be that such an issue can be most fruitfully examined, not by philosophers of mind, but in a tale—*2001: A Space Odyssey*, for example?

In this chapter I shall discuss a Greek anomaly, a mythological creature who (or which) embodies many kinds of questions and question marks relating to what it is to be human. The aim of my discussion will be twofold: (a) to highlight what is at stake in one particular mythological narrative about that anomalous creature; (b) to consider certain motifs embedded in that narrative, using them as a springboard towards an investigation of thematic interconnections within the wider network of Greek mythology.

1. TALOS IN APOLLONIOS OF RHODES

We are approaching the end of Apollonios' *Argonautika*. The *Argo* is back in Aegean waters, with Medea and the Golden Fleece safely on board. However, the Argonauts' encounters with the uncanny are not over just yet. One of the eeriest of all their adventures is about to befall them (4.1635–88):

> Rocky Karpathos awaited them next far off, and from there they were to cross over to Crete, furthest out of the other islands in the sea.
>
> But bronze Talos broke rocks off a great cliff and prevented them from attaching their cables to the land when they ran into the sheltered harbour of Dikte. Among the generation of semi-divine men he was the

last survivor of the bronze race of human beings born from ash-trees, and the son of Kronos gave him to Europa to watch over Crete by travelling three times [Hunter: 'three times a day'] around it on his bronze feet. The rest of his body and his limbs were of unbreakable bronze, but below the tendon in his ankle there was a vein of blood, and the thin membrane covering it held the boundary of his life and death. Though they were worn out and exhausted, the heroes quickly rowed the ship back from the land in fright. They would have been carried far from Crete in their wretchedness, bearing the burden of thirst and pain, had not Medea spoken to them as they shrank back from the island:

'Listen to me. I believe that alone I can destroy this man for you—whoever he is—even if his whole body is made of bronze, provided he does not have immortal life. Use gentle oar-strokes to hold the ship here out of range of the rocks, until he yields to destruction at my hands.'

So she spoke. They removed the ship from the danger of the missiles and held it with the oars while waiting to see what unexpected plan she would carry out. She held up a fold of her purple robe on either side of her cheeks and moved towards the stern-deck; the son of Aison took her hand and guided her passage between the benches. Then in her soothing incantation she sought to win over the Keres, devourers of the spirit, swift dogs of Hades who circle through all the sky and are set upon the living. Three times did she beseech and call upon them with incantations, and three times with prayers. She set her mind upon evil, and cast a grudging spell upon bronze Talos' eyes with her malevolent glances; against him she ground out bitter fury, and she sent out dark [or: invisible] images in the vehemence of her wrath.

Father Zeus, astonishment quivers within my mind, if it is true that death comes to us not only from disease and wounds, but someone far off might harm us, as that one, bronze though he was, yielded to destruction through the grim power of Medea, mistress of drugs. As he was heaving up great boulders to prevent the Argonauts from reaching anchorage, he grazed his ankle on the sharp point of a rock, and *ichōr*[2] flowed out from him like molten lead. Not for much longer did he remain standing on the top of the jutting cliff. Like a mighty pine tree high up in the mountains which woodcutters left half-chopped by their sharp axes when they went down from the forest, and at night it first shakes in the wind-blasts, but then topples over, broken off at the base; just so for a while did he sway from side to side on his unwearying feet, but then collapsed strengthless with a thunderous crash.[3]

[2] See 94–6 below.

[3] The translation is based on Hunter (1993a), but with considerable adaptation.

Given her centrality to the poem as a whole, and given the intrinsic fascination (for the reader and for Talos) of her actions here, it is hardly surprising that it has been Medea who has attracted the lion's share of critical attention. Indeed, Apollonios himself leads the reader in that direction: his astonished aside concerns not Talos but Medea ('Father Zeus, could there really have existed an almost invulnerable bronze giant with a fatal weakness in the ankle?', is what the poet *might* have said, but did not). No wonder he is astonished: it is as if, shocked by the power of his own creation, he has to avert his gaze from his text, unwilling to engage with Medea's homicidally baleful eyes.[4] Her malignant magic, as she grinds and glares out her hatred—not exactly telepathic, not quite telekinetic—all this deserves a paper to itself. Fortunately, such a paper already exists, thanks to Matthew Dickie.[5] Noting, as others have done, the correspondence with Demokritean theory,[6] Dickie persuasively argues that the learned invocation by Apollonios of a mechanism by which the Evil Eye could indeed be effectively cast serves not to undermine the horror (thanks to some notional opposition between rationality and magic) but to sustain and enhance it.

Dickie's focus, like that of Apollonios, is on Medea. I wish to look the other way. Apollonios' account of Talos embodies a number of mythically intriguing themes. In order to consider them, we shall need to broaden the picture outside Apollonios, so as to examine the range of stories told in antiquity about this singularly anomalous figure.

2. THE MYTH OF TALOS

Two separate individuals have traditionally been distinguished: Talos the Cretan and Talos the Athenian.[7] Just how distinct they really are

[4] Hutchinson (1988) 140, with n. 97, finds in the aside 'extravagance' and 'laborious simplicity', which 'greatly lightens the effect of the whole passage'; in this he is in disagreement with Paduano (1970) 60–1. But Hutchinson underestimates the power and complexity of the tone: cf. Hunter (1993b) 166 n. 56. On the eerie and disturbing quality of the episode, see Albis (1996) 87–9.

[5] Dickie (1990); see also Buxton (2000a).

[6] Cf. Livrea (1973) on 4.1672.

[7] Cf. e.g. the entries in Buslepp (1916–24a), and *LIMC* (where 'Talos I' and 'Talos II' even have separate authors, respectively J. K. Papadopoulos and I. Leventi).

is a question we shall raise shortly. For now, it will be convenient to retain the dichotomy, and to begin with the Talos about whom there is more evidence.

The genealogy of Talos the Cretan varies remarkably. First, he can be integrated into divine/heroic lineages in a relatively orthodox way, either as son of Kres, father of Hephaistos, and grandfather of Rhadamanthys (Paus. 8.53.5, citing the epic poet Kinaithon) or as son of Oinopion (Paus. 7.4.8). The former version lends Talos great authority of various kinds, linking him as it does with the very identity of Crete (eponymous Kres was either a son of Zeus or autochthonous),[8] with technological prowess (Hephaistos), and with juridical prestige (Rhadamanthys). The second version, which makes Talos a son of Oinopion, thereby adjusts his status. No longer is he father of a god, but grandson either of a god or of a hero: one genealogy cast Oinopion as son of Dionysos (cf. the name *Oino*pion) and Ariadne; according to another, which went back at least to Ion of Chios, the father was Theseus.[9] Either way, the role of Ariadne in Talos' ancestry reinforces the link with Crete.

Other genealogies for Talos are less orthodox than the ones just mentioned. He can, as in Apollonios, be presented as the last survivor of the Bronze Race—not quite Hesiod's Bronze Race, though, since it is not a question of his *using* bronze, but of his actually being *made* of bronze. Alternatively, he can be entirely without ancestry: something fabricated, artificial, a work of art crafted by Hephaistos and given to Minos as a present to guard Crete. Indeed, as reported by Apollodoros (1.9.26), matters are even more complicated than that: the work of art was said by some to have been a bronze man, by others a bronze bull. Those alternatives throw into greater relief something clear already from Apollonios: that Talos was implicated in all kinds of mixtures of categories. His various genealogies point to radically different positionings within the spectra constituted by the oppositions between divine/heroic, natural/artificial, and even human/animal.

When Talos is integrated into Cretan heroic lineage, whether as son of Kres or son of Oinopion, no mention is made of any metallic peculiarity on his part; his only 'borderline' characteristic in these cases is the fact of his belonging to Crete—situated at what is, at least

[8] Steph. Byz. s.v. *Κρήτη* (p. 384 Meineke), Diod. Sic. 5.64; cf. Stoll (1890–4).
[9] Apollod. *Epit.* 1.9; Plut. *Thes.* 20.2; cf. Wörner (1897–1902).

from some perspectives, the 'edge' of the Aegean. But for those myth-tellers who describe Talos as made of bronze, the problem of how to classify him raises all kinds of issues relating to borderlines and boundaries.

For Apollonios, Talos' implied 'gigantic' size—he is like a 'monstrous [*pelōriē*] pine tree' (1682)—does not mean that he is 'racially' a Giant.[10] Rather, he is one of the race of *anthrōpoi* ('human beings') who has outlasted his time, to live now amongst the *hēmitheoi* ('demigods')—in other words, the heroes. Indeed, he is not just an *anthrōpos* but an *anēr* ('man'), or so Medea calls him (1655). This is by no means unprecedented, for the status of several mythologically intermediate groups, such as Silenoi and Cyclopes, is similarly negotiable:[11] while not quite human, they are not quite divine either—or not necessarily, or exactly, or always, divine.[12] It is in this area of the 'not quite' that the unique fate of Apollonios' Talos is worked out.

Apollonios is by no means the only author to explore Talos' anomalous physiology. Apollodoros records several variations on this theme (1.9.26). According to one such, Talos was a 'bronze *anēr*'. He had a single vein running from neck to ankle, secured at the bottom by a bronze nail (a cultural variant of the more natural membrane mentioned by Apollonios). His thrice-*daily* circuits of Crete were halted by Medea, who made him mad with drugs, or promised to make him immortal but then removed his nail: as in Apollonios, what flowed out was *ichōr*. Or he was shot—in the ankle, of course—by Poias. Simonides portrayed Talos as both bronze and *empsuchos* ('animate'), as did Sophokles in his play *Daidalos*.[13] In the pseudo-Platonic *Minos*, humanity and bronze are reconciled quite differently, in a manner worthy of the arch-rationalizer Palaiphatos himself. Talos was simply a legal administrator, appointed by Minos: while Rhadamanthys looked after the *astu* ('town'), Talos travelled through outlying districts carrying laws written down on bronze tablets. In fact he was quite literally a circuit judge, doing the rounds of Crete thrice *a year*.[14]

[10] Though according to the Orphic *Argonautika* 1351 he is *trigigas* ('triply a Giant'). On Giants, see Vian (1952).

[11] See Brelich (1958) 326–7.

[12] Thus the Cyclopes are *andres* ('men'), according to *Od.* 6.5, and Polyphemos in particular is an *anēr* (9.187), yet in so far as he is monstrous (*pelōrios*, 9.187, 190–1) he does not resemble an *anēr* who eats bread; cf. Baldry (1965) 204 n. 5.

[13] Schol. Pl. *Resp.* 337a = *PMG* 568, *TrGF* iv, fr. 160 Radt.

[14] [Pl.] *Min.* 320c. Cf. 75 above, on the Apollonian version of 'three times'.

Fig. 1. The winged figure of Talos (named here as 'Talon') wields a stone in his right hand. Silver coin (*c.*300–270 BC) from Phaistos, Crete.

I add two last features of the myth of Talos the Cretan from the written evidence. In one group of sources, Talos, along with his lover Rhadamanthys, was responsible for introducing homosexuality into Crete, like Laios in the equivalent Theban story.[15] Here Talos appears in the typical hero's role of inventor or 'first finder', with no suggestion of anything metallic about him. We shall return later to the question of what it was that he invented. Secondly, another tradition explained the phrase 'sardonic laughter' in relation to Talos, whose preferred method of despatching his foes was to fold them in his burning embrace, after leaping into fire to heat himself up. The resulting grimaces on the faces of the victims (*sairein*, 'to grimace') allegedly generated the phrase in question. This too will occupy us briefly later, in relation to 'origins'.[16]

What we know from texts is amplified in several respects by the visual evidence. On fifth/fourth-century BC coins from Phaistos (Fig. 1), Talos/Talon is depicted as a menacing figure, sometimes threatening to hurl the stones which he is holding. So far, so familiar, but Talos' *wings* are something new. These wings are the visual expression of his ability to complete a circuit of Crete with unnatural

[15] Athen. 603d = Ibykos *PMG* 28; Suda, s.v. *Θάμυρις*; see Buslepp (1916–24a) 27.
[16] See refs. in n. 13 above; cf. Buslepp (1916–24a) 28.

Fig. 2. Painted white to distinguish his metallic form, the figure of Talos is in a state of collapse. Kastor and Polydeukes restrain him. Medea (left) holds a box, perhaps containing a magical substance. To the right are Poseidon and Amphitrite (both seated); below is a fleeing female figure (Crete personified?). Krater from Ruvo di Puglia (c.400 BC).

rapidity;[17] they suggest a perception of Talos as distinctly superhuman—a powerful Cretan daemon, well worthy of the literary genealogy which made him son of Kres.

Vases tell a story closer to that recounted by Apollonios: a story of metal and mortality.[18] A famous amphora from Ruvo (Figs. 2 and 3) gives a magnificent sense of the bronze quality of Talos, as he faints away under the relentless gaze of Medea.[19] Exactly how she secured his downfall is unclear, though it is difficult not to be suspicious of that casket she is carrying. Equally unclear is the role being played by Kastor and Polydeukes, on either side of the man of bronze. A krater from Spina (Fig. 4) shows a near-identical Talos, but with two significant variations: in the bottom left-hand corner, Medea (almost completely lost, but confirmed by inscription [*MH*]*ΔEIA*) sits at his feet, with a box on her knee and a blade in her hand; adjacent to Talos' feet is a winged figure (probably Thanatos).[20] Most intriguing of all is a krater in Montesarchio, at first thought to portray Philoktetes, but convincingly identified by Lesky and Robertson as depicting Talos (Fig. 5).[21] A hero is operating on something small and circular—a nail?—on the inner ankle of Talos (Fig. 6). A woman with a bowl is also present. The identification of the hero and the woman as Jason and Medea is virtually certain, though the identity of the small winged figure near Talos' foot is tantalizingly problematic; as with the krater from Spina, Thanatos seems the likeliest candidate.[22] All three vases demonstrate just how central to the Talos myth is the manner of his death, together with the incomplete invulnerability which forms the context and rationale of that death.

Before concluding our survey of the variants, we must mention yet another doubleness on Talos' part: he is both Cretan and Athenian. According to some versions, the Athenian in question is called Talos; according to others, Perdix, 'Mr Partridge'—the bird into which he is metamorphosed.[23] But several sources agree both on the name 'Talos'

[17] Wings and rapidity: cf. Hermes and Perseus; see Buslepp (1916–24a) 25.

[18] See esp. Papadopoulos (1994); also Robertson (1977).

[19] Papadopoulos (1994) no. 4, with Robertson (1977) and Sparkes (1996) 123–4.

[20] Papadopoulos (1994) no. 5.

[21] Papadopoulos (1994) no. 6; Lesky (1973) Figs. 1–2; Robertson (1977).

[22] See now Kossatz-Deissmann (2009) add. 5, discussing an Apulian krater on which the small, bearded, winged figure of Thanatos (inscriptionally identified), knife in hand, flies down to cut a symbolic lock of hair from the dead Memnon.

[23] Yet another variant is Kalos, e.g. at Paus. 1.21.4; cf. Höfer (1902–9) col. 1947; Frontisi-Ducroux (1975) 123 n. 20 and 128 n. 49.

Fig. 3. Detail of Fig. 2. A teardrop can be seen falling from Talos' right eye.

and on his connection with another mythological figure who linked Crete and Athens: Daidalos.

Diodoros (4.76) has the story in detail. Daidalos, an inventor, was especially good at carving life-like statues. 'Since he was the first to represent the open eye and to fashion the legs separated in a stride and the arms and hands as extended, it was a natural thing that he should have received the admiration of mankind.'[24] He had a nephew called Talos, who came to the home of his maternal uncle as an apprentice.[25] Talos was even more gifted than Daidalos, contriving to invent, among other things, the potter's wheel and the draftsman's compass. In a fit of envy, Daidalos treacherously killed the boy by

24 Trans. C. H. Oldfather (Loeb edn.).
25 Maternal uncle: see Bremmer (1983).

Fig. 4. On this fascinating but fragmentary Attic krater from Spina (end of fifth century BC), Talos is again restrained, presumably (as in Figs. 2 and 3) by Kastor and Polydeukes. Medea (bottom left, her presence confirmed by an inscription) holds a box and a blade. Near Talos' feet is an enigmatic, small, male, bearded, winged figure—Thanatos?

throwing him down from the Acropolis (Apollod. *Bibl.* 3.15.8). Metamorphosis followed, at least in Ovid (*Met.* 8.236–59).

Between Talos the Cretan and Talos the Athenian, overlaps and inversions abound. The Cretan is just the kind of creature whom/which supreme artisans—Daidalos or his nephew—were expert at fabricating. The *fall* of the Athenian parallels the fall of the Cretan. The skill in *circularity* of the Athenian (potter's wheel, compass) parallels the Cretan's ability to run *around* the island;[26] furthermore, as Françoise Frontisi-Ducroux observes, the partridge was believed to avoid its enemies by feigning lameness and by adopting a circular, rolling motion.[27] Then, Apollonios' Cretan giant is remarkable for his ability to *move*, and he is struck down through the *eyes*—the two features singled out by Diodoros as exemplifying Daidalos' craftsmanly skill in statuary. Finally,

[26] Cf. Frontisi-Ducroux (1975) 124.

[27] See Ar. *Av.* 1292–3 (lameness), 768 ('partridge tricks'), with notes by Dunbar (1995) ad loc.; Ael. *NA* 3.16 ('rolls about'); cf. Frontisi-Ducroux (1975) 163.

Fig. 5. Talos collapses again, held by Kastor and Polydeukes. A youth (Jason) kneels in front of Talos, apparently trying to remove the head of a nail from inside the giant's ankle. Medea steps forward, holding a bowl. A small winged figure assists Jason. Attic krater from Montesarchio (440–430 BC).

there is a parallel between Medea's use, in Apollonios, of *baskania*, evil eye (which scholars have rightly connected to the notion of 'envious grudge'),[28] and the rivalry which leads to the downfall of the Athenian Talos.

[28] Bibliography in Burkert (1996) 198 n. 19.

Fig. 6. Detail of Fig. 5. A mini-figure, perhaps Thanatos, helps Jason to ‘undo’ Talos.

It can of course sometimes be problematic for us as observers to reassemble a composite picture out of a range of variants, each responding to different contextual demands, and to call the result ‘The Myth of ’, as if it went without saying that such a composite picture was available and meaningful to the original actors also. But in the present case not only are there unusually compelling parallels between the Athenian and the Cretan Talos, but we happen to know that, as early as the fifth century BC, at least one individual (and, presumably, his audience) was aware of both stories: namely, Sophokles, whose *Kamikoi* spoke of the Athenian murder on the Acropolis, and whose *Daidalos* mentioned the bronze guardian of Crete.[29] Nevertheless, given that the focus of the present chapter is

[29] *TrGF* iv, frr. 323 and 160–1 Radt. (I am indebted to Alan Sommerstein for this point.)

Apollonios' narrative set in Crete, the Athenian Talos will occupy us less than his Cretan opposite number.

3. 'ORIGINS'?

One time-honoured interpretative strategy has been to look for Talos' hypothetical 'origins'. J. Schoo opted for the volcano on Santorini, which 'lies as a guardian north of Crete'. Volcanoes, he argued, throw out stones, and molten lava can be seen as their blood.[30] R. F. Willetts, by contrast, followed A. B. Cook in detecting a progress in the island's religion from Talos-as-Sun-God to Talos-as-Zeus.[31] Such evidence as there is, is handled with considerable freedom: glosses in Hesychios, and Hellenistic epigraphical references to 'Tallaios' as an epithet of Zeus in Crete,[32] are used to construct a historical development *from* Sun *to* Zeus, with the name Talos standing successively for each.[33] Others have detected behind the Talos story a colossal statue of the Sun God, perhaps even as a shelter against the Sun's heat,[34] or a statue to which human sacrifice was made (compare 'sardonic laughter').[35] The problem with all this—whether the emphasis be volcanic or solar—is to know how such hypothetical origins might conceivably make a difference to our reading of the mythical narratives.[36] For instance, whether or not Talos might have been 'originally' Zeus, Apollonios tells us clearly enough that Zeus *gave Talos to Europa as guardian of Crete*: here, and in all our extant narratives, Zeus and Talos are wholly distinct.

About one other hypothesis relating to origins a little more deserves to be said. This concerns the so-called 'lost wax' method of casting bronze statues.[37] The process varied, and not all the details are

[30] Schoo (1936–7) 264.

[31] A. B. Cook (1914–40), i. 728–30; Willetts (1962) 52, 100–1, 248–9.

[32] Hesych.: *Talōs: ho hēlios. Talaios: ho Zeus en Krētēi* ('Talos: the sun. Talaios: Zeus in Crete.') Epigraphy: quoted in Höfer (1916–24).

[33] Verbruggen (1981) dismisses these hypotheses as unfounded.

[34] Buslepp (1916–24a) 24.

[35] Cf. Buslepp (1916–24a) 29.

[36] Federico (1989) makes as reasonable a case as can be produced for seeing the Sun as representing *some* point of reference in the myth.

[37] A. B. Cook (1914–40) i. 723–4; Frontisi-Ducroux (1975) 127–34.

known, but one technique involved the making of a preliminary model, perhaps in wood or clay; this was then covered with wax, and subsequently in clay to make a mould; when the wax was melted out, bronze was poured in to form the final sculpture.[38] There is no precise analogy with the *ichōr* as Apollonios describes it, 'flowing out like melting lead' (4.1679–80), but *this* explanation in terms of origins has at least the merit of focusing on what is peculiar to this myth, as opposed to the countless myths which might or might not be about the Sun.

4. THEMES

More productive than an inquiry into origins is an investigation into how Talos was used, in particular narrative contexts, as a vehicle for thinking about the world—specifically, about the nature of humankind and the boundaries which define it. It is to such an investigation that I hope to offer a contribution in the rest of this chapter. Along the way I hope to demonstrate something of the complex associative logic which underlies and binds together various strands of the mythical web which we have been considering. I turn, then, to two themes raised by the Apollonios passage: (i) vulnerability and (ii) *ichōr*.

(i) Vulnerability

There are three related issues: (a) vulnerability in general; (b) vulnerability more specifically in the lower limbs; and (c) vulnerability most specifically in the ankle.

(a) Vulnerability in general

The place to start is still Berthold's 1911 treatise on *in*vulnerability.[39] This has a store of helpful information, some of it comparative. Several

[38] R. M. Cook (1972) 79–80. Also, on constructed metal figures (interpreted as apotropaic): Faraone (1987).

[39] Berthold (1911); see now also W. F. Hansen (2010).

of the examples Berthold cites are well enough known (Siegfried, vulnerable between the shoulder-blades; Baldur, susceptible to attack by mistletoe—presumably an equivalent of the 'kryptonite' by which alone Superman can be harmed); some are less familiar (such as an invulnerable herring).[40] As for Greece, Berthold rightly observes that 'invulnerability is only there to be broken or circumvented'; in other words, the mythical logic of invulnerability is that it should be incomplete.[41] (In the same way, the logic of the mythical exposure of infants is that it should fail.) The classic schema is: 'hero manages to defeat adversary who is vulnerable in just one spot, or just one respect'. The applicability of this schema to Talos is plain enough. A parallel case is Herakles and the Nemean lion: according to one version of the combat, the hero had to club and throttle the beast, since it was impervious to arrows.[42] But the adversary does not have to be monstrous. Or, let us put it differently: as we know from Angelo Brelich's masterly work *Gli eroi greci*, heroes themselves, who test boundaries beyond the limit, have something of the monstrous about them. So the otherwise invulnerable Lapith Kaineus was overcome by his foes the centaurs when they hammered him into the ground with rocks and fir trees. Kaineus, too, was a boundary-crosser: he had been female before he was male.[43] The wholly male Aias, by contrast, was vulnerable in just one spot (shoulder blade, armpit, or neck; as usual there are variants), the rest of him having been rendered invulnerable when he was covered as a baby with—perfectly logically—the skin of the Nemean lion.[44] Localized vulnerability has been plausibly seen as implying an assumption that what one might call the life-spirit can be concentrated in a specific place, a view found already in antiquity: the Hellenistic historian and geographer Agatharchides observes in relation to Talos that 'alone of

[40] Berthold (1911) 66, citing Meyer (1884) 278; comparative material is also reviewed in West (2007) 444–6.

[41] Berthold (1911) 62, followed by Brelich (1958) 304: 'Il senso del motivo è sempre, chiaramente, questo: "pur essendo invulnerabile, l'eroe muore".'

[42] [Theoc.] *Id.* 25.

[43] Cf. Pind. fr. 128f Maehler; Ap. Rhod. *Argon.* 1.57–64 with schol.; schol. *Il.* 1.264; Apollod. *Epit.* 1.22, with Frazer (1921) ad loc.; Berthold (1911) 17–21.

[44] See e.g. *TrGF* iii, fr. 83 Radt (= schol. Soph. *Aj.* 833 etc.), schol. Lycoph. *Alex.* 455, schol. Hom. *Il.* 23.821; Berthold (1911) 6–26. Compare also Pl. *Symp.* 219e, where Aias is 'invulnerable to iron'. Dover (1980) ad loc., commenting that 'Aias was not invulnerable to weapons in any magical or supernatural sense', seems to have overlooked the fact that the *Iliad*'s portrayal of Aias was not the only one current in the fourth century BC.

living creatures he had his life in his ankle'.[45] There are certainly analogies with Pterelaos and Nisos (who die when their hair is pulled out) and with Meleager, whose weak point is not his leg, but his log.

(b) Vulnerability in the lower limbs

We can consider the matter from two theoretical perspectives.

The first was developed by Angelo Brelich and later by Jan Bremmer. Brelich's paper 'Les monosandales' started from the observation that many Greek mythological figures exhibit a weakness or imperfection in the leg, which may be anything from a gash or a gangrenous wound to a defect as mild as 'lacking one sandal'—from Oidipous and Philoktetes and Hephaistos, through to the single-shod Jason.[46] Brelich wants to make sense of these tales by replacing them within an initiatory context: on this view, the imperfection highlighted by these myths would place the figures concerned on the side of chaos and disorder, the temporary state into which initiates are plunged, only to re-emerge into wholeness and adulthood. Jan Bremmer takes this further:[47] such wounds as those of Adonis and Odysseus in the thigh, or Philoktetes and Achilles in the foot, are reflections of symbolic wounds inflicted on young hunters and warriors as a prelude to adulthood. Myth reflects hypothesized ritual: in Bremmer's words: 'it seems then that the wounding of the leg was originally a symbolic laming to contrast the novices with the adult hunters for whom running was of such great importance'.[48]

Might such an approach illuminate the Talos story? Here it will be useful to cite an acute article by Eduardo Federico.[49] Federico recalls the myth about Talos as inventor of homosexuality in Crete (in his role as Rhadamanthys' *erastēs* ('lover')), and relates that myth to Strabo's account (10.4.21, based on Ephoros) of the initiatory practice of Cretan homosexuality, according to which an adult *erastēs* took a younger *erōmenos* ('beloved') outside the space of the city; after a liminal period, the two returned, with the change in status of the novice being sealed by, amongst other gifts from the older man, that of hoplite armour. However, as Federico also points out,[50] there is a paradox here: if the myth casts Talos as the adult partner, the *erastēs*,

[45] *De mar. Erythr.* 1.7 (= *GGM* i, 115).
[46] Brelich (1955–7); cf. Ogden (1997) 32.
[47] Bremmer (1978).
[48] Bremmer (1978) 13.
[49] Federico (1989).
[50] Federico (1989) 108.

how do we explain his figuration as a naked ranger over the margins (coasts), wielding as weapon of choice not the sword but the rocky crag?[51] These details suggest that Talos is being cast as a mythical embodiment of the initi*and*. However, as Federico again observes, this time citing Bernard Sergent's study of homosexuality in Greek myth, Talos is not the only character to embody such ambiguity: the same is true of Aristomenes: young, mountain-roaming, yet an *erastēs* and originator of the Messenian phalanx.[52] Probably the best we can do is to appeal once more to that overriding characteristic of Talos: his doubleness. True, he is naked, and throws crags: but he is also 'of bronze'—anti-hoplite and hoplite simultaneously, bestriding, like the colossus he is, the boundary between wild and civilized, between initiator and initiand. *Very* good to think with.

An alternative approach to imperfect lower limbs is prompted by an article by Jean-Pierre Vernant about lameness.[53] Vernant argues that in two households, those of the 'mythical' Labdakos and the 'historical' Corinthian tyrants, two themes interweave: first, lameness or inability to walk straight—Labdakos ('the lame'), Laios ('lefty'), Oidipous ('swell-foot'), and the descendants of Labda ('the one bent like the letter Λ'); second, blocked or deviant succession between generations, often because of abnormal sexual relations. So in Greek imagery the Corinthian tyranny is figured as a 'limping kingship'. Aspects of the etymological argument have been questioned, for example by Claude Calame: no *ancient* author plays on the names Labdakos and Laios in the way suggested, while for some modern etymologists too the interpretation of this pair of names as signifying 'lameness' is insecure.[54] Nevertheless, there is no reason to place in doubt Vernant's general establishment of the link, in Greek

[51] Rock-hurling, as depicted by Apollonios and on coins (see Fig. 1), puts Talos on the side of nature rather than culture; cf. Buslepp (1916–24a) col. 26. On the rock/metal opposition, compare the Makhimoi, a race who can be wounded by rocks and wood, but not iron; see Ael. *VH* 3.18, with Gernet (1981) 114.

[52] Federico (1989) 108, with n. 93, following Sergent (1986) ch. 1. Aristomenes' exploits are set out at length in Pausanias, Book 4.

[53] Vernant in Vernant and Vidal-Naquet (1988) 207–36.

[54] Calame (1986). Calame explicitly rules out (from the point of view of the *modern* etymologist) any derivation of Laios from *laios* ('left'), preferring to connect the name with *laos* ('the people'). On the differences between 'ancient' and 'modern' etymology, however, see 55–6 above.

perception, between physical defects, especially limping, and irregular generation.[55]

Might we borrow from this analysis in order to throw more light on our giant? Could there, in the events of the Talos story, be an implicit link between imperfection in the lower leg and blocked or abnormal generation? Like Laios, Talos is associated with the origin of homosexuality. Moreover, as is clear not least from Apollonios, Talos is the last of his line (1642). Here, it could be argued, are two details which imply the 'blocking' of generation. We may notice also the similarity to Hephaistos.[56] Not only do the themes of craftsmanship, the creation of automata, and the fall from a height, already link Talos to the divine smith,[57] but there is also the fact that lameness and lack of success in procreation are two of Hephaistos' most prominent characteristics.[58]

A reservation, however, needs to be entered, relating to the suggested association between homosexuality and 'blocked' generation. For this association to be valid, it must be the case that in Greek perception homosexuality and procreative heterosexuality were felt to be mutually exclusive alternatives. Yet it is clear that in Greek tradition, at least in the Archaic and Classical periods, homosexuality was commonly perceived as an *aspect* of male development rather than as a permanent lifestyle diametrically opposed to heterosexuality. If the proposed link between blocked generation and homosexuality is to hold, it must be true either that such a link reflects post-Classical social developments,[59] or, in the instance under consideration, that Talos is, so to speak, a case of arrested development—cut down *before* his marital prime.

[55] See Ogden (1997).

[56] For this god in myth and ritual, see now Bremmer in Bremmer and Erskine (2010) 193–208.

[57] Javier Uría Varela has brought to my attention the perceived link between metal-working and unhealthiness, specifically arsenic poisoning: see Charles (1980) 178; Lehmann (1986) 87; also Rosner (1955), discussed by Uría Varela (1997) 487–90. Fall from a height: Delcourt (1982) 159–60.

[58] I make no comment for or against a possible Freudian reading of lameness as symbolic castration, except to observe that Talos has double trouble, in that he is afflicted (in Apollonios) in two places: the ankle, certainly, but also the eyes—where Medea's influence first penetrates. Blinding, of course, is another classic castration-equivalent in the opinion of those who adopt that theoretical stance; cf. 196 below.

[59] Cf. Bremmer (1991b) 22–3.

It should be emphasized—although it should hardly need emphasizing—that not every narrative about Talos exploits every aspect of the potential material. No myths are raw; all are cooked by the context. In Apollonios' narrative, greater and certainly more explicit narrative attention is given to Talos' mode of action as a warrior than to any hypothetical association with blocked generation. To that extent, for this narrative at least, the perspective developed by Brelich, Bremmer, and Federico would seem to be the more effective.

(c) *Vulnerability in the ankle*

It is time to give more than a passing mention to Achilles. Yet his case is problematic. Since the earliest literary source to evoke the (to us) familiar tale of the dipping in the Styx, etc., is Statius (first century AD), a lot hangs on interpretation of the earlier visual evidence. Jonathan Burgess has argued that '[u]ndoubtedly Achilles was wounded in the lower leg in the early [visual] tradition of his death on the battlefield, but this does not necessarily suggest he was imperfectly invulnerable'.[60] Lilian Balensiefen comes to a similar conclusion, pointing out that only by the time of Hyginus (second century AD) and possibly Apollodoros the mythographer (also second century AD) do we have unambiguous evidence for the notion of Achilles' fatal vulnerability in the ankle.[61] Berthold had already noted that Palaiphatos (fourth century BC) mentioned as types of invulnerability Aias, Kaineus, and Kyknos, but not Achilles, and that this might be a significant silence.[62] What one can certainly say of Achilles, as of Talos, is that his pre-eminence *as a runner* marks out the lower leg as a particularly crucial part of his anatomy (this is already part of the tradition in the Archaic period).[63] But might a less obvious logic lie

[60] Stat. *Achil.* 1.133–4, 269–70, 480–1; Burgess (1995) 240 and (2009) 13, cf. T. Gantz (1993) 625–8. As is implied in the title of his article ('Die Ferse des Achilleus—ein skythisches Motiv?'), Thordarson (1972) believes he can detect the influence of Ossetic epic.

[61] Balensiefen (1996) 88, with n. 41; Hyg. *Fab.* 107 ('talum quem mortalem habuisse dicitur'), cf. Apollod. *Epit.* 5.3, with Frazer (1921) ad loc. Date of Apollodoros: Bremmer (2008) 75, following Carrière and Massonie (1991) 9–12.

[62] Berthold (1911) 37. Brelich (1958) 303–4, admits that the invulnerability motif is explicitly related to Achilles no earlier than Statius and Hyginus, but still regards an 'origine antica' as plausible; similarly Janko (1992) on *Il.* 16.777–867.

[63] Richardson (1993) on *Il.* 22.396–7 follows Leaf in arguing that the term 'Achilles' tendon' goes back to the passage where Achilles pierces Hector's feet 'in the space

behind the location of Achilles' and even Talos' vulnerability just there?

A computer search through *Thesaurus Linguae Graecae* for the collocation *phleb-* ('vein') and *sphur-* ('ankle') in significant proximity reveals one recurrent context: blood-letting.[64] Sites of choice, from the Hippokratics to Galen, are the crook of the arm and . . . the ankle. But *where* on the ankle? The Hippokratic *On the Nature of Man* (11) offers the following analysis and recommendation:

> The thickest of the veins have the following nature. There are four pairs in the body. One pair extends from behind the head through the neck, and on either side of the spine externally reaches to the hips and legs, and then stretches through the shanks to the outside of the ankles and to the feet. *So bleeding for pains in the back and hips should be made on the outside, behind the knee or at the ankle.* The second pair of veins extends from the head by the ears through the neck, and are called jugular veins. They stretch right and left by the side of the spine internally along the loins to the testicles and thighs, then on the inside through the hollow of the knee, and finally through the shanks to the ankles on the inside and to the feet. Accordingly, *to counteract pains in the loins and testicles, bleeding should be performed in the hollow of the knee and in the ankles on the inner side . . .*[65]

(We may recall the Montesarchio krater (see Fig. 5), with the nail on the inside of the ankle.) If failure of normal procreation could indeed be seen as an implicit characteristic of the Cretan Talos, then Hippokratic assumptions would supply a convenient physiological rationale: the ankle, being literally connected to the genitals, would become a logical place in which a procreative weakness might manifest itself. Inverted confirmation of a perceived link between ankles and sexuality may be found in two mythological details, though this time it is heightened rather than defective procreativity which is at issue. First, one version of Achilles' death explicitly connected his ambush and shooting by Paris with his love-meeting with Polyxena: erotic ardour leads to a wound in the ankle.[66] Secondly, the partridge—

between the ankle and the heel' in order to drag him. For Achilles' *speed* as related to the wound in the lower leg, see Burgess (2009) 13–15.

64 For this theme see Siegel (1972) and in general Duminil (1983).

65 Trans. slightly adapted from Loeb edn.

66 Servius on Verg. *Aen.* 6.57; cf. Onians (1954) 528–9. Achilles and Polyxena: T. Gantz (1993) 628; Burgess (2009) 15.

the bird into which the *Athenian* Talos was changed—was proverbially salacious.[67] Nor may it be irrelevant that for numerous later writers, from Fulgentius onwards, there was a symbolic connection between the ankle or heel, and the genitals; between wounds in the foot and sexuality.[68] However, let us concede at once that to move from the Athenian to the Cretan Talos is not an automatic associative step; the same goes a fortiori for the step from the Hellenistic period to Fulgentius, and, for that matter, for the step from Hippokrates to Apollonios. Furthermore—to the extent that we are attempting to elucidate Apollonios in particular—it should be stressed that his surface narrative makes no perceptible allusion to sexuality, except perhaps for that 'last-of-the-line' detail. But nor does the surface narrative raise the question: Why a wound *in the ankle*? We could, of course, ourselves refuse to ask that question. But the moment we *do* ask it, we must be prepared to find some surprising things below the surface.

(ii) *ichōr*

In Homer, *ichōr* is explicitly *contrasted* to human blood: it is what the gods have in their veins, standing to human blood as ambrosia does to human food. So *ichōr* is what flows out of Aphrodite when Diomedes grazes her hand in *Iliad* 5 (340, 416).[69] (We learn nothing about what this *ichōr* is, merely what it is not—as with ambrosia.) But the Homeric distinction is by no means constantly maintained in subsequent texts. Towards the end of Aischylos' *Agamemnon*, Klytaimestra, referring to the persistence of harm in the household, speaks of the 'new *ichōr*' which appears 'before the ancient pain has ceased' (1479–80). Marie-Paule Duminil rejects the possibility that *ichōr* here signifies 'blood' (so LSJ), preferring the sense of 'noxious organic fluid' such as that from an abscess (so Fraenkel, Headlam, Wilamowitz).[70] Indeed it certainly looks as though we have here an echo or anticipation of one of the central Hippokratic senses of *ichōr*, namely, noxious fluid. But this is not its only Hipppokratic sense: it can designate a *non*-noxious fluid,

[67] See Pollard (1977) 60. One myth about the mythological Perdix/Perdicca(s) had him desire his own mother, like swollen-footed Oidipous: Fulg. *Mit.* 3.2 = 1st Vat. Mythogr. 3.30 (Zorzetti and Berlioz); cf. Höfer (1902–9) col. 1953.

[68] See Onians (1954) 528–9, on e.g. Fulg. *Mit.* 3.7.

[69] Onians (1954) 506–7.

[70] Duminil (1977) 65–6.

for example the serous part of the blood. However, what is constant is that *ichōr* is distinguished from ordinary human blood.

When Apollonios' Talos loses *ichōr*, then, this might simply mean, on the Homeric model, that he is non-human. But might it alternatively—or additionally—signify that he has been the victim of a harmful attack, which has a pathological effect on him? Consider a passage from, once more, a Hippokratic treatise.[71] In *Epidemics* 5.74 (echoed in 7.36), we hear of a naval commander whose forefinger has been crushed by an anchor. Inflammation, gangrene, and fever ensue; part of the finger drops off. After the seventh day, 'a satisfactory quantity of *ichōr* came out'. *Opisthotonos* (a particularly dramatic form of tetanus) is predicted, and duly follows. Death occurs some days later. A finger is not an ankle, and the doctor records no malevolent minds or baleful glances which might have precipitated the commander's undoing. Yet, in a Hippokratic treatise as in a Hellenistic epic, a flux of *ichōr* can be a sign of mortality.

Ichōr is in fact almost as ambiguous as Talos himself. We may conclude this part of the discussion by quoting an intriguing anecdote about Alexander. As Plutarch reports, of the numerous places in which Alexander was wounded, it was allegedly an arrow wound *in the ankle* which drew this response from the young general, directed smilingly at his flatterers: 'This that you see is blood, not "*ichōr*, such as flows from [the wounds of] the blessed immortals"'—a quotation from the *Iliad* which we just noted.[72] Like Talos and Achilles, Alexander is wounded in the ankle. Unlike Talos, but like Achilles, Alexander has blood, not *ichōr*, in his veins. Like both Talos and Achilles, Alexander is mortal; and yet, also like them, he has characteristics which could be felt to bring him perilously close to the boundary between mortality and immortality—after all, what gives the anecdote its point is Alexander's felt proximity to divine status.[73] We have insufficient information to reconstruct a detailed network of allusion and cross-reference between narratives about Achilles, Talos, and Alexander. But it would surely be perverse to deny that the

[71] Brought to my notice by Geoffrey Lloyd.

[72] Plut. *Mor.* 341b, with n. on pp. 233–4 of the Budé edition by Frazier and Froidefond. The *Iliad* reference is 5.340. Cf. also the similar passage at *Mor.* 180e.

[73] On the anecdote in the context of Plutarch's view of the Alexander ruler-cult, see Scott (1929) 119.

Alexander anecdote might have been perceived as standing in a tradition which echoed the fates of both these mythical antecedents.

5. REFLECTIONS ON METHOD

Man and metal, Athenian and Cretan, initiand and initiator. For real-world experiences of lost wax and blood-letting to be combined through *bricolage* in an image of lost *ichōr* flowing from a not-quite-human not-quite-statue—all this serves to reinforce a sense of the multiple doubleness which is at the core of this constitutionally ambiguous being.[74] 'The Talos myth'—whatever we say or refrain from saying about its origins—is about anomaly and the mixing of categories.

It goes without saying that in the work of any individual teller of 'the Talos myth'—epic poet, mythographer, designer of coins, painter of amphorae—generic and idiosyncratic emphases from within this range of possibilities are going to express themselves. Some aspects irrelevant or tangential to the context will be downplayed or ignored; others will be highlighted. This is as true of Apollonios as of anyone else. Let me repeat that I am not concerned to argue for the felt presence in Apollonios of all the elements which I discussed in relation to the wider myth. *Some* matters which we touched on in discussing the wider myth are indeed relevant to the Apollonios narrative—for instance, the ramifications of the notion of vulnerability, and the role of *ichōr* as a marker of boundary status. By contrast, other avenues which we followed seem to lead more readily *away* from Apollonios into the broader mythical web, rather than generating any direct interpretative spin-off for the *Argonautika*. To observe this is just to reinforce something on which I have insisted already in print: that we need to resist the temptation to impose methodological straitjackets on the prodigal richness of Greek mythology.[75]

Now it might be objected that my general approach—looking for 'mythical logic' in narratives about Talos—is better suited to 'pre-literate' material than to a sophisticated 'literary' author like Apollonios. The reply to this can be brief. It is a mistake to overemphasize

[74] Cf. P. Vidal-Naquet, introduction to Frontisi-Ducroux (1975) 10.
[75] See Buxton (1994) *passim*.

the contrast between Hellenistic and pre-Hellenistic Greece: (1) oral performance *continued* to play a major role in the transmission of Hellenistic myth; (2) given the undoubted *interrelation* between oral and written tale-telling even in the Hellenistic period, it would be quite unjustifiable to use one methodology for 'oral' myth and another for 'written'. *All* contexts cooked myths, oral no less than written.

It might also be objected that my approach assumes the possible existence of allusions or implied cross-references between different types of text, without it always being possible to *demonstrate* such links—without, for instance, our being able to *demonstrate* that Apollonios had read a specific passage of Hippokrates. Of course, this objection has some potential force; however, given the richness of Hellenistic cultural resources, one should never underestimate what an author might have expected an audience to know. But in any case, a student of myths is obliged ceaselessly to negotiate Skylla and Charybdis. Skylla is over-interpretation, going implausibly beyond the evidence; Charybdis is failure to register the incredible intricacy of the language of Greek myth. We can only follow the course set by Odysseus: avoid Charybdis at all costs, and then keep our heads down so as not to get them bitten off.[76]

[76] I append a note about the name 'Talos'. The Latin for ankle is *tālus*. Was there a cognate Greek equivalent, so that the very name of our giant ('Mr Ankle') might be expressing the location of his vulnerability? Unfortunately, the total silence on this possibility in LSJ, *OLD*, and Roscher, as well as in Frisk (1960–72) and Chantraine (1968–80), was corroborated when I asked the advice of the distinguished Cambridge linguist, the late Robert Coleman. In the view of all these experts, *Τάλως* (*Tălōs*, with short alpha) is linguistically a world away from *tālus*, with long 'a'. In the absence of a Greek cognate, Alan Sommerstein has suggested to me that the Talos story might have been generated in Magna Graecia, in an environment where there was contact between Greeks and Italic-speakers. Such a possibility is at once thoroughly intriguing and completely speculative. As usual, the most problematic feature of a myth is its 'origin'.

5

Movement and Stillness: Versions of Medea

In the course of Chapter 4 I discussed an episode from Apollonios' Argonautika. *In the present chapter I return to the same poem, focusing this time not on Talos but on Medea. But I aim to go beyond the literary analysis of a single text. As well as investigating myths about Medea in many of their non-Apollonian manifestations, artistic as well as literary, I examine a cultural polarity which has been largely neglected by scholars.*

1. APOLLONIOS: HOW MEDEA MOVES

Unlike the *Odyssey*, which, as its first word indicates, is the story of a man, the *Argonautika* is the story of a ship, whose journey is evoked in the first sentence of Book 1, and whose return to home port in Greece is celebrated in the last line of the final book, Book 4. Medea is with us for two books: Book 3, when the arrow of Eros compels her to fall in love with Jason, whom she then helps to yoke the fire-breathing bulls and to cut down the Sown Men; and Book 4 when, with the Golden Fleece safely captured, she sails at Jason's side back to Greece.

As dozens of scholars and thousands of other readers have noticed, Apollonios' Medea is a juxtaposition of opposites: on the one hand, the woman tormented by personal anguish, torn between her Kolchian family and her Greek lover; on the other hand, the manipulator with uncanny powers. But a more specific polarity has received comparatively little attention, at any rate from scholars; and it is this second, more specific polarity that I want to explore. What I have in mind is the opposition between the Medea we see for most of the poem—a Medea in constant, restless movement—and the Medea who very occasionally asserts magical control, and in so doing becomes calm and composed in her physical movements, while simultaneously exercising power over the movements of others.

Although Athene and Hera have already mentioned Medea near the start of Book 3 in relation to their plan to make her fall for Jason and so aid him in his exploits, the first time that Apollonios brings Medea before us in action and in person is the moment when the Argonauts too first catch sight of her (3.248–56):[1]

> Jason and his companions came across Medea as she was going from room to room looking for her sister. For Hera had kept Medea at home; before, she did not use to spend much time in the palace, but rather she would be busy all day at the shrine of Hekate, since she was the goddess's priestess. When Medea saw them approaching, she screamed. Chalkiope heard it clearly; the maidservants dropped their wool and spindles in front of their feet and all rushed out together.[2]

These few lines encapsulate the Apollonian Medea. First, she is looking for her sister Chalkiope: Medea, unmarried, still lives at home, and is bound to her siblings, as also to her parents, by strong social and emotional ties. Next, Medea is kept at home on this particular day by Hera: Medea's emotional life is and will be largely at the mercy of the gods. Thirdly, the fact that Medea is priestess of Hekate already hints at her possession of a special kind of power, which we might locate somewhere in the definitional quicksand between religion and magic.[3] Finally, and for us most relevantly, Apollonios has chosen to present Medea to us in the act of moving from one room to another (*ek thalamou thalamonde*): even when at home, she is not—unlike the maidservants with whom Chalkiope is linked here (254–6)—associated with spinning, and therefore seated; rather she is in transit.

Medea's restlessness intensifies exponentially when Eros shoots her with his arrow. It expresses itself in her eyes: she glances repeatedly at

[1] From now on, all line references will be to Book 3, unless otherwise specified.

[2] As in Chapter 4, I draw on the translation by Hunter (1993a); however, I also make many adaptations to it, often in order to render the Greek more literally.

[3] This quicksand has brought about the downfall of many victims; for a guide one may consult for example Fowler (1995). Fortunately, I believe that the argument of the present essay does not necessitate any addition to the enormous quantity of discussions as to the definition of magic.

Jason (as opposed to staring at him unswervingly) (287–8). It expresses itself in her complexion: one moment her cheeks drain of colour, the next she blushes (297–8). It expresses itself in her feet: 'For a long time she remained there in her ante-chamber: shame would not allow her to go further. Then she turned around and went back in again, but then came out again, and then hid away inside again; her feet carried her this way and that, all to no purpose.' (648–51) It expresses itself in her production of speech: 'Words rose to the very tip of her tongue, but then flew back again deep into her chest' (683–4). It expresses itself in her perceptions: Medea sees the world as a place of fluttering, dancing indecision: in what is probably Apollonios' best-known simile, Medea's heart trembles like a sunbeam which darts this way and that within a house when reflected from the rippling surface of water just poured into a cauldron or bucket (756–60). It is true that—perhaps for us counter-intuitively—Medea's *dreams* are clear and unambiguous: in her sleep she imagines that her parents allow her to choose whether or not to go with Jason, at which point she unhesitatingly decides to leave with him (630–1). Yet her waking consciousness is in turmoil (766–9):

> At one moment she thought that she would give him the drugs as charms against the bulls; then she would not, but would herself face death; then she would not die and would not give the drugs, but with calmness would endure her misery just as she was.

Eyes, complexion, feet, speech, perceptions: all oscillate—they move, but they do not progress.

What happens, though, when the narrative brings us closer to Medea the devotee of Hekate—when she does not just speculate about using her uncanny powers, but actually goes to fetch the casket which contains her drugs, both beneficent and destructive? To begin with, her habitual condition persists, as she is at first on the point of opening the casket and swallowing drugs which will end her life—but then, remembering the joy of living, pushes the casket away from her. However, the pattern of her obsessive oscillation is broken by Hera, who causes her to *decide* (818–19):

> Through Hera's urging she changed her mind, nor did she have further doubts which took her mind in another direction

Now that Medea is set upon helping Jason, her movements become, for the first time in the poem, purposeful and controlled. True, she is not static; in fact she moves quickly (on a mule-drawn cart) to a meeting with Jason at which she can confer on him the power which will make him temporarily invulnerable. But, though not static, she is in control: she puts up her hair, which had previously been loose (829); she holds the reins and whip to control the mules (871–2); and, whereas previously her eyes were perpetually darting here and there, now it is the people of the city who turn their eyes aside to avoid meeting Medea's (886).

But it is a constant in the character of the Apollonian Medea that, whenever she is not focussed strictly on practising magical control, the turmoil generated by the conflicting claims of *erōs* and family removes all fixity, and condemns her to oscillate. While waiting for Jason, she plays games with her maidservants, games which Apollonios evokes through a broken, anacoluthic syntax that Malcolm Campbell rightly saw as enacting Medea's fidgety state of mind (949–51).[4] But it is the games played by her eyes to which the narrator gives greater emphasis: 'Nor could she keep her eyes fixed on the crowd of maidservants, but constantly turned her face away and peered into the distance along the paths' (951–3). Just for an instant, when she and Jason meet, the narrative brings Medea to a halt beside him, and, through a simile, it seems as if the equivalence between Medea's domestic conflicts and her restless motion is going to be undermined (967–70):

> The pair then faced each other, silent, unable to speak, like oaks or tall firs, which at first when there is no wind stand quiet and firmly rooted on the mountains

However, even within the vehicle of this simile, the pause is immediately followed by an evocation of continuous oscillation:

> like oaks or tall firs, which at first when there is no wind stand quiet and firmly rooted on the mountains, *but afterwards stir in the wind and rustle together ceaselessly.* [emphases added]

And sure enough, when the main narrative resumes, Medea begins to move to and fro: under Jason's flattery, she first turns her eyes aside, then looks into his face (1008–10). Even as she hands over to him the drug of invulnerability, the sign she lives under is not that of control but that of mobility, a mood which affects Jason too (1022–3):

[4] M. Campbell (1983) 66.

> At one moment they both stared coyly at the ground, at the next they cast glances at each other

After explaining to Jason how he should appease Hekate and then smear himself and his weaponry with a drug which confers invulnerability for a day, Medea is once more a prey to oscillation: she fixes her eyes on the ground, then looks up into Jason's face (1063–8), begging him to tell her about his home.

Jason's successful exploits with the bulls and then with the Sown Men make Medea's departure from home inevitable. Apollonios presents that departure as a mixture of rushing and tearing (4.35–40):

> Like a young girl, recently separated by fate from her homeland, who was torn as a prisoner from a rich house and who has not yet tasted wearying labour, but unused to wretchedness and the work of slaves, she goes in terror into the harsh control of a mistress; this was how the lovely girl rushed from her home.

Accompanying Jason on board the *Argo* as he goes to seize the Golden Fleece, Medea loses none of her restlessness (4.106–7):

> She rushed back and stretched out her hands towards the land in helpless despair.

But now comes the second moment for Medea to assume control, a moment for her eyes no longer to be restless. And this time there is no mule-cart, no journey to make. A stillness falls over the narrative. As the serpent which guards the Golden Fleece slithers towards her, Medea fixes it in the eye, and invokes Sleep in a lovely song. Then (4.156–61):

> But she, dipping into a potion a freshly-cut sprig of juniper, sprinkled untempered drugs down over the snake's eyes as she sang; and, all around, the overwhelming scent of the drug cast sleep. Just where it was, the snake dropped its jaw to rest on the ground. Far into the distance its countless spirals were stretched out through the dense wood.

No wonder the poor beast falls asleep: Medea has prepared an irresistible, three-pronged assault—fixing with the eye, invocation in song, and potion.

But the stillness lasts only as long as it takes Jason to seize the Fleece. Thereafter the narrative suddenly accelerates (4.241–3):

> The goddess Hera caused the wind to blow so strongly that Aiaian Medea should reach the Pelasgian land with all speed, to bring disaster upon the house of Pelias.

Medea resumes her characteristic state of anguish and movement—because the competing presences within her of Kolchis and Greece have surfaced once again: her brother Apsyrtos has appeared with a force of pursuing Kolchians. Will Medea deploy against him the same techniques which lulled the serpent to sleep? In fact she opts for a different method. Apsyrtos is enticed into an ambush by means of gifts, above all a robe, a robe such as that which Deianeira, in Sophokles' *Women of Trachis*, sent to Herakles in order, she thought, to reawaken his love (but which turned out to be impregnated with murderous poison). It is the same erotically charged robe which Hypsipyle gave to Jason as his going-away present; originally the Graces had woven it for Dionysos, and he and Ariadne had lain on it while they made love; to enhance its effect still further, Medea now sprinkles drugs of enticement into the air. But what follows this interlude corroborates my main point: whenever her mind is torn between Kolchis and Greece, Medea cannot remain still. As Jason leaps from ambush and stabs Apsyrtos, Medea averts her eyes, while her brother's blood spurts over her veil and robe (4.465–7).

This grubby little murder drives Medea-the-controlled-and-controlling sorceress yet further out of narrative view. When the *Argo* puts in to the coast where Medea's aunt Circe dwells, in the hope that she will grant Jason and Medea absolution for the killing of Apsyrtos, the movement of Medea's eyes mirrors the failure of their quest: first she looks downwards in shame, then she raises her eyes, then she covers her eyes with her robe in shame once more (4.697–8; 726; 749–50). Nor does the next port of call, the Phaiakian kingdom of Alkinoos and Arete, bring her rest (4.1061–5):

> In her breast her aching spirit whirled like a spindle turned in the night by a toiling woman whose orphaned children cry all around her; her husband is dead, and as she weeps at the awful fate which has seized her, tears drip over her cheeks.

There is an all-too-glaring contrast between the rootless, childless, spindle-less Medea and the labouring, widowed mother to whom the simile compares her; but what the two women have in common is not only suffering but also constant, repetitive motion.

In Phaiakia, Medea's relationship with Jason is consummated (which is why Alkinoos agrees not to surrender her to the pursuing

Kolchians); but this does not elevate her to any new prominence within the action. On the contrary, she recedes into narrative invisibility for almost the whole of the rest of the epic. But there is one more episode, the third and last such in the poem, when Medea steps forward to display an eerie and unnerving poise. Significantly, this episode is as completely removed as can be from her own domestic conflicts and anguish, a free-standing contest between her and another formidable creature, the bronze giant Talos.[5] Talos' role in life is to run around Crete as its guardian; the only vulnerable spot in his otherwise metallic body is a small vein in his ankle, covered by a penetrable membrane.

The *Argo* glides to a halt, held motionless by the crew's gentle oarstrokes. Then (4.1661–72):

> [Medea] held up a fold of her purple robe either side of her cheeks and moved towards the stern-deck; the son of Aison took her hand and guided her passage between the benches. Then in her soothing incantation she sought to win over the Keres, devourers of the spirit, swift dogs of Hades who circle through all the sky and are set upon the living. Three times did she beseech and call upon them with incantations, and three times with prayers. She set her mind upon evil, and cast a grudging spell upon bronze Talos' eyes with her malevolent glances; against him she ground out bitter fury, and she sent out dark [or invisible] phantoms in the vehemence of her wrath.

One can instantly recognize the race of Helios, as the narrator had pointed out earlier in Book 4, because their eyes throw out sparkling rays into the far distance (4.727–9). But Medea turns this inherited quality into something more specific and personal. Staring unflinchingly at Talos, she unsteadies the movements of this normally tireless runner, causing him to graze his ankle on the sharp point of a rock; the membrane covering the vein is pierced, and all the life-sustaining *ichōr* flows out.[6] The Talos encounter shows us Medea at her furthest remove from her condition of domestically generated anguish, and at her most eerily impressive: the unmoved mover. (We shall come back to this phrase). Thereafter, for the hundred or so lines that remain, we hear nothing more of Medea's thoughts, emotions, or actions: the returning *Argo*, in this poem about a ship, becomes the centre of attention once again.

[5] See 73–97 above.

[6] For a detailed analysis of this episode, see 74–6 above.

2. A NEGLECTED POLARITY

Having analysed the specific opposition in Apollonios between restless movement and controlled stillness, I propose now to reflect on some questions which grow out of this discussion. These questions will take us beyond Apollonios, but we shall not stray far from the idea of movement.

When he narrates the episodes of Medea's principal uncanny exploits as moments when she is *in control of the movements of others* (notably, the movements of the serpent guarding the Fleece, and of Talos), Apollonios is echoing a fundamental aspect of the representation of ancient magical practice. Numerous surviving papyri contain spells which employ the imagery of binding, spells designed to restrict and hobble the movement of another.[7] Again, archaeologists have unearthed tiny lead figurines whose bodies have been distorted or pierced so as symbolically to hamper their movement; by a perhaps pardonable shorthand they have come to be known as 'voodoo dolls'.[8] Then, we have numerous literary references to sorceresses drawing down the moon or other heavenly bodies, or using the *iunx* ('magic wheel') to 'drag that man to my house'.[9] In the three cases I have mentioned—binding curses, hobbled figurines, the power to draw or drag—the aim of the practitioner is to control the movement of others. But what is far from clear is the extent to which self-control and stillness *on the part of the practitioner* are perceived to be a necessary part of the procedure, as they are in the case of Apollonios' Medea. In fact it seems that this stillness may be a distinctively Apollonian emphasis, reflecting in particular the poet's decision to single out the theme of bewitching the eyes as a technique for controlling others. That theme in turn is integrated, first, with a series of other connotations of eyes and looking in the poem (shame or shamelessness in the avoidance or engagement of direct eye-contact with another; concealment of one's intentions from view; the erotic gaze; the inner sight of the blind prophet Phineus, and so on);[10] and

[7] See e.g. Ogden in Flint et al. (1999) 26–9. On binding, see Johnston (1999) 79.

[8] Cf. Jordan (1988).

[9] On the notion of magical 'dragging' or 'drawing down', see e.g. Ar. *Nub.* 749–50; Pl. *Grg.* 513a; Hor. *Epod.* 5.45–6; Verg. *Ecl.* 8.69; Sen. *Med.* 674; Luc. 6.499–500. *Iunx*: Gow (1934); Pirenne-Delforge (1993); Johnston (1995).

[10] Eyes in the *Argonautika*: Dickie (1990); Buxton (2000a).

integrated, secondly, with other connotations of *oscillation* in the poem, particularly the often-discussed theme of Jason's habitual condition of being *amēchanos*, in a state of aporetic indecision.

But does this actually amount to Apollonian distinctiveness vis-à-vis other tellings of the myth? Let us glance at some of these other versions. The *general* opposition between Medea-the-victimized-woman and Medea-the-sorceress recurs in most ancient narratives about Medea. Of course it permeates Euripides' tragedy, where we have, on the one hand, Medea the manipulator of men—capable of the calculated use of grim and deadly *pharmaka* ('drugs', 'medicines', 'potions') to destroy Jason's new bride and her father, or of beneficent *pharmaka* to restore Aigeus' fertility—and, on the other hand, Medea the self-tormenting infanticide. In Ovid's *Metamorphoses* the same general opposition is, if anything, even more starkly present; Carole Newlands goes so far as to use the metaphors of 'the fractured woman' and even cubism to describe the Ovidian disjunction between Medea the lovesick girl and Medea the witch.[11] But the specific Apollonian opposition, between the restlessness generated by domestic chaos and the composed stillness of the practising sorceress, is much harder to parallel. It cannot, I believe, be found in Euripides or in Ovid. In Pindar's *Pythian* 4 we do meet a *victimized* Medea (indeed she is the victim, as opposed to the manipulator, of the *iunx*), but we are given little sense of the manner in which she practises her arts, and certainly no sense of any controlled composure on her part.[12] In Seneca, Medea is fuelled by a constant supply of highly enriched, weapons-grade *furor* both in her supra-normal practices: Nurse: *Vidi furentem saepe et aggressam deos,/caelum trahentem* ('I have often seen her in fury and assailing the gods, drawing down the sky') (673–4); and in her frenzied personal emotions: *Quonam cruenta maenas/praeceps amore saevo/rapitur? Quod impotenti/facinus parat furore?* ('Whither is this blood-stained maenad carried away headlong by crazed passion? What crime is she preparing with uncontrolled fury?') (849–52). Seneca, that is, presents us with a *continuity* of Medea's temperament between furious sorceress and furious and vengeful victim, rather than with a juxtaposition of composed sorceress and distraught, oscillating, wronged woman.

[11] Newlands (1997) 207. [12] Pind. *Pyth.* 4.213–19.

Fig. 7. Medea in the act of killing her son. Campanian amphora (*c.*330 BC).

Fig. 8. Medea flees from Theseus. Pelike (*c.*450 BC).

But I believe we do find something similar to Apollonios' specific polarity in iconography. Several images of Medea depict her being driven to violent action because of her domestic turmoil. One example is a Campanian amphora which represents her killing her son (Fig. 7); another is an Attic pelike which shows Medea fleeing from Theseus after she has attempted to poison him (Fig. 8),[13] a scene captured also in another image, this time on an Apulian krater (Fig. 9), where Medea's gestures indicate her agitation as Aigeus recognizes Theseus. However, on another set of images we find the composed Medea, the Medea who is capable of maintaining a state of poised self-control while exercising her uncanny powers. For example, on another Apulian krater she helps Jason overcome the bulls (Fig. 10); on yet another fine south Italian krater she is in the act of putting the serpent to sleep (Fig. 11); or else, as on a hydria in the British Museum, she sprinkles herbs into a cauldron to rejuvenate an old ram (Fig. 12)—the

[13] The scene has been plausibly identified as Theseus-and-Medea by Sourvinou-Inwood (1979) 35–47.

Fig. 9. Medea's failed poisoning of Theseus. Aigeus (right) recognizes Theseus by the token of the sword. Apulian krater (*c.*380 BC).

same cauldron into which Pelias will be induced to step, only to end up as goulash; again, as on the famous Talos vase in Ruvo di Puglia, she is shown launching deathly glances at Talos while holding a container which symbolizes her uncanny power (Fig. 13). It looks, then, as if we have found in iconography something comparable to Apollonios' 'specific' polarity.

However, one other strand of visual imagery complicates the picture, since it effectively combines, within one and the same representation, both Medea in the act of exercising magical superiority and Medea in implied vigorous movement: namely the image of *aerial flight*. (Agreed, flight represents a different order of supra-human capability from that displayed by Medea in her magically agonistic

Fig. 10. Medea helps Jason overcome the bulls. Apulian krater (*c.*370 BC).

Fig. 11. The serpent licks a potion which puts it to sleep. Medea stands to the left, in control; Jason, seizing the Golden Fleece, is to the right. Paestan krater (*c.*320–310 BC).

Fig. 12. Medea rejuvenates a ram in a cauldron. At the right, a gesticulating Jason (inscription). Attic hydria (480–470 BC).

mode; but still, even granted that it is the serpents which have wings and not she herself, flight does set Medea uncannily apart from the humans with whom she has been interacting.) A Roman sarcophagus in Basel depicts the serpent-borne chariot in which Medea bears the corpse of one of her children slung dramatically over her shoulder (Fig. 14): it is an image which, so far from separating the Medea of domestic turmoil from the Medea of controlling, superhuman power,

Fig. 13. Medea holds an ornate and mysterious container, symbolic of her power to undermine Talos. Detail of the Ruvo krater (see Fig. 2).

emphasizes what amounts to an identity between the two. In very different style is a Lucanian krater, probably the best known of all representations of Medea in flight (Fig. 15), an image which gives us (i) the controlling sorceress, (ii) the visible results of the domestic chaos which she has precipitated, and (iii) the representation of movement through aerial flight. This image too, like the sarcophagus, seems *prima facie* to be going against an Apollonios-type disjunction between movement and magic. Yet perhaps, at least in this vase-painting, we can also detect a qualified *similarity* with Apollonios: note how Medea the controlling sorceress is hermetically sealed off, by the ring of Helios' rays, from the Corinthian family disaster below. (We might recall Apollonios' description of Medea's departure from the Kolchian palace on her mule-cart: not static, but in control.)

Fig. 14. Medea in flight, with her infant son flung dramatically over her shoulder. Roman sarcophagus in Basel (*c*.190–200 AD).

Overall, then, iconography can yield a partial parallel for Apollonios' specific polarity, but not a complete one.

The idea of Medea's aerial flight will steer us towards the final part of this chapter. Medea's flight is a recurring theme in many versions of her story. In Ovid she first flies for nine days and nine nights from Iolkos in search of magic herbs; then, after the daughters of Pelias have put their father into the casserole, she flies to Corinth (looking down, as she does so, on the locations of numerous previous metamorphoses, and thus reminding us that flight constitutes for Medea an alternative to the different form of escape represented by metamorphosis); then she takes off yet again on the short flight to Athens.[14] Euripides and Seneca give us finales in which Medea

[14] *Met.* 7.234–6, 350–92, 398–9.

Fig. 15. Medea again in flight, with a scene of domestic carnage below. Lucanian krater (*c.*400 BC).

appears above the stage *preparing* to fly off.[15] In Euripides, the fact that she retains her children's corpses in the chariot symbolizes her continuing emotional attachment to them;[16] in Seneca, her gesture of dropping the children's bodies down onto the hapless Jason—*recipe iam natos, parens* ('Receive your children now, you who are their father')—suggests that, whatever else the Senecan Medea may be, she is no longer a mother.[17]

[15] Eur. *Med.* 1321–2; Sen. *Med.* 1022–7.
[16] Eur. *Med.* 1402–4.
[17] Sen. *Med.* 1024.

Now a Medea in aerial flight is not the Medea of Apollonios: in Apollonios she translocates by conventional means. Yet translocate she does, in Apollonios and in every other ancient telling of her myth. This brings me to my final point, which concerns what seems to me to be a notable difference between Medea and other ancient sorceresses. It is a difference concerning, once more, movement.

Typically, ancient sorceresses use their special powers to manipulate substances in the world in order to produce astonishing effects. They employ the same household items as do ordinary, domesticated women: cups, bowls, cauldrons, clothes, containers such as chests or baskets normally used for storing food or for other everyday commodities. But sorceresses distort the purpose of these objects. Circe uses a cup not to sustain her guests but to transform them into animals.[18] The bowl used by Theokritos' Simaitha stands as the focus for an act of symbolic dragging of the beloved to the lover.[19] We might add that in Sophokles' *Women of Trachis* the unwitting and deeply reluctant sorceress Deianeira keeps a deadly robe smeared with Nessos' poisoned blood, concealed in a casket.[20]

Where does the Medea of the ancient tradition stand in relation to these other female possessors of uncanny powers? In many ways she is typical. In her attempt to poison Theseus she uses a jug and a cup; with the daughters of Pelias she sprinkles *pharmaka* into a cauldron; to dispose of Apsyrtos, and later of Jason's Corinthian wife, she uses enticing robes; she habitually keeps her *pharmaka* in a casket, and a box with mysterious contents is her regular attribute in visual imagery. Add to this her use of the bewitching gaze and her invocations of Hekate, and we seem to have a sorceress who is the complete article. And yet Medea also has one quality which makes her *un*typical.

Of all ancient sorceresses, Medea moves her base of operations the most often. Circe's home may be located by different myth-tellers in different parts of the world, but home is where she stays. Theokritos' Simaitha also works from home: she repeatedly invokes the *iunx* to

[18] See for example the illustration of Circe holding a cup and stirring the contents, amid a group of already metamorphosed humans (Attic black-figure cup, Boston Museum of Fine Arts 99.518 = *LIMC* vi 'Kirke' 14).

[19] Theoc. *Id.* 2.2.

[20] Soph. *Trach.* 692. I owe the expression 'deeply reluctant' to Pat Easterling, who also points out to me (personal communication) that Deianeira lacks both the training and the lifestyle of the sorceress, whence our sense of her combined boldness and vulnerability.

bring that man *emon poti dōma*, 'to my house'.[21] Deianeira has moved from her father's home to Herakles', but that is the extent of her wanderings.[22] Lucan's ghastly witch Erichtho is Thessalian to the core of her hideous being.[23]

Medea, by contrast, is a compulsive mover: from Kolchis to Iolkos to Corinth to Athens, and back to Kolchis. As the Senecan Medea puts it to Jason: *Fugimus, Iason, fugimus; hoc non est novum/mutare sedes* ('We are fleeing Jason, fleeing; changing our home—this is nothing new').[24] She may use robes as enticements, but she has not woven them on her own loom; she may stir ingredients into a cauldron, but she does so in another woman's kitchen. From the day she leaves Kolchis, the principal moments in her career when she is able to impose some measure of control over her continually displaced existence are moments of magical self-composure. At these moments she takes charge of her own destiny and that of others, by bending the world to her will. The irony—and in some narratives it is a tragic irony—is that it is precisely the uncanny deeds which she accomplishes, with total success, during those brief interludes, that drive her headlong to flee, and sometimes to fly, from one stage of her extraordinary career to the next.

Earlier in this chapter I described Medea as 'the unmoved mover', a phrase with evidently Aristotelian, and theological, overtones.[25] This expression was designed to act as a hint that movement and stillness might be mapped onto a much more general issue, relating to the representation of power in Greece in terms of two contrasting models. On the one hand, there is the capacity to move effortlessly and instantaneously, a capacity which the gods display on countless occasions, shifting at will their physical location and their physical form. On the other hand, in a less widespread but still influential tradition, we find an association between the highest divine authority and *im*movability.[26] This occurs not just in Aristotle, but also in the Presocratic philosopher Xenophanes, for whom '[god] always... remains in the same place, moving not at all; nor is it fitting for

[21] Theoc. *Id.* 2.17 etc.

[22] See though n. 20 above, for the limited sense in which Deianeira can be seen as a 'sorceress'.

[23] E.g. Luc. 6.485–6, 589.

[24] Sen. *Med.* 447–8; cf. 1022: *sic fugere soleo* ('This is how I am accustomed to flee').

[25] Cf. Arist. *Ph.* $258^{b}10$–16; G. E. R. Lloyd (1968) 140–2; Manuwald (1989) 9.

[26] For some excellent preliminary remarks see Jaeger (1947) 44–5.

him to go to different places at different times, but without toil he shakes all things by the thought of his mind'.[27] Even more intriguingly, in the Pythagorean table of opposites *rest* appears on the same side of the table as male, right, light, and good, whereas *motion* is located in the company of female, left, dark, and bad.[28] To all this we may add the numerous images which show a person in a dominant social position *seated*, as opposed to standing or moving.

These issues might be addressed as part of the following framework. There exists in every culture a rich and complex repertory of symbolic/expressive modes upon which members of that culture may draw in order to represent their experience. One of these modes can be visualized as a spectrum ranging from composed stillness to frantic movement. Different artists or writers can exploit this opposition differently. In the specific case which we are discussing, the poles of the spectrum may, for example, be used as Apollonios uses them, to highlight a contrast between two aspects of the same character; here the spectrum intersects with the notion of 'magic', since magical control is associated with stillness. But the poles may also be used in quite different ways: for instance, in the case of characters such as the mourning, motionless Achilles or Niobe, their stillness represents a kind of 'degree zero' of engagement with the world, symbolizing not so much control as rejection. Again, as we have just noted, the stillness/movement opposition offers contrasting ways of imagining the power of divinities. It would thus be quite wrong to claim for this opposition a univocal meaning even within the limited context of one culture, let alone more broadly, let alone universally. A more reasonable claim, however, is the one made in this chapter, that of attempting to shed some light on the way this opposition is used in certain specific literary and visual contexts.[29]

[27] KRS fr. 171. [28] KRS fr. 438.

[29] For insightful comments on the original version of this chapter I am indebted to Heike Bartel and Anne Simon, and also to the audience of a lecture which I gave on this subject at a meeting of the Hellenic Society in London.

Part II

Myths in Tragedy

6

Tragedy and Greek Myth

In two genres at least, Greek myth-telling achieved a profundity and power unsurpassed in the history of the human imagination: epic and tragedy. To the second of these the rest of this book will be devoted. We have already considered tragic retellings of myth at several points, especially in relation to mountains, significant names, and the myth of Medea. As the argument of the book turns now more directly towards tragedy, I offer next a general chapter about the genre, in order to establish what distinguishes tragic ways of retelling a myth from other forms of myth narration.

The theatre of Dionysos in fifth-century BC Athens provided a unique context for myth-telling.[1] At the annual festival of the City Dionysia, myths were re-embodied in performances by members of the citizen group. In these re-embodiments, as heroes and divinities walked the stage, myths were not just narrated as past events: they were actualized as present happenings. Then and there, but also now and here; remote enough to allow room for pity, but close enough to inspire awe.[2]

In the present attempt to characterize tragic myths, I begin with a discussion (Section 1) of an apparently simple question: what happens in Greek tragedies? In order to suggest an answer, I contrast tragedy with the non-tragic mythological tradition, examining in particular the kinds of actions and sufferings ascribed to heroes and heroines. In Section 2 I ask another seemingly straightforward question: where

[1] See Pickard-Cambridge (1988); Csapo and Slater (1994).

[2] However exaggerated one may consider the reverence paid to Aristotle's *Poetics* over the centuries, the composite Aristotelian concept of pity-and-fear remains a pointer towards reconstructing the experience of Greek tragedy (cf. 145–6 below). On the whole question of the role of the *Poetics* in the history of the interpretation of tragedy, see Lurje (2004).

are Greek tragedies imagined as taking place? My answer involves politics and psychology as well as topography and geography. Finally, in Section 3, I discuss ways in which tragedy represents the gods. Throughout the chapter, my aim is to ask how far it is possible to isolate features which are distinctively tragic.[3]

1. WHAT HAPPENS IN GREEK TRAGEDIES?

Across a wide range of Greek mythological narratives, in both texts and visual representations, the mighty heroes Herakles, Theseus, Agamemnon, and Oidipous are credited with formidable and triumphantly successful exploits. Herakles is the monster-slayer par excellence; Theseus, champion of idealized Athenian values, rids the world of unpleasant villains and puts an end to the Minotaur; Agamemnon leads the expedition which captures Troy, so justly avenging Paris' abduction of Helen; Oidipous destroys the oppressive power of the Sphinx. These same heroes appear, more specifically, in tragedies, including four which survive to the present day: Euripides' *The Madness of Herakles* and *Hippolytos*; Aischylos' *Agamemnon*; Sophokles' *Oidipous Tyrannos*. What is noticeable about the way in which these heroes are represented in tragedy is the kind of *selection* of mythical material which tragedy practises. When in Euripides' play the peerless Herakles returns home after his culminating twelfth Labour (the seizing of the hell-hound Kerberos), he is struck by a frenzy sent upon him by Hera; while out of his senses he slaughters his wife and children, and is only prevented from killing his father Amphitryon when Athena hurls a rock at him. In *Hippolytos* Theseus witnesses the utter destruction of his family: when his son Hippolytos slights Aphrodite, the goddess' punishment leads to the suicide of Theseus' wife Phaidra and to the death of Hippolytos, intemperately cursed by his father in the false belief that the young man had raped Phaidra. In *Agamemnon* Troy's conqueror is humiliatingly stabbed to death in his bath by his vengeful and unfaithful wife Klytaimestra. In *Oidipous Tyrannos* the saviour of Thebes becomes an abhorred

[3] There are many ways of asking and answering this question: two examples, complementary both to my own approach and to each other, are the general account by Burian (1997) and the more specific one by Calame (2000).

outcast, revealed as the killer of his father Laios and as the husband to whom his own mother Jocasta bore four children.

This pattern is typical. Greek tragedies do not narrate heroic exploits: instead, they explore the disruptions and dilemmas generated by such heroism, disruptions and dilemmas which almost invariably involve the catastrophic destruction of a household. Of course tragedy is not the only genre to highlight the problematic aspects of heroism. We need only think of the *Iliad*, where heroic values are put under enormous strain by the conflict between Agamemnon and Achilles; where Achilles' clear-eyed awareness of the brevity of his glory contrasts with the all-too-human, indeed 'tragically' limited vision which characterizes Hektor;[4] and where one of the poem's greatest affective climaxes, in which Priam ransoms from Achilles the body of his dead son Hektor, precisely exemplifies the kind of emotional intensity later exploited in Attic tragedy.[5] Or we may think of the *Odyssey*, in which Odysseus' slaying of the suitors is by no means morally unambiguous (this is especially clear in Book 24, where the suitors' grieving families step forward to exact vengeance for their murdered brothers and sons). Nevertheless, it is above all in tragedy that the underside of heroism, albeit counterbalanced by largely 'dignified' language and costume, becomes pervasive, not simply as a 'theme', but as the predominant perspective from which mythical events are selected and depicted. It will be useful to illustrate this in more detail, by examining one myth, that of Jason and Medea, in three different versions.[6]

In *Pythian* 4 the praise-poet Pindar honours Arkesilaos of Cyrene, victor in the chariot-race at Delphi in 462 BC. The poem includes what is, for Pindar, an unusually extended account of a myth, namely Jason's quest for the Golden Fleece. In spite of its length, this account is not a detailed narration, but rather a spotlighting of significant moments. Given that Pindar is celebrating the return of a victorious

[4] See Redfield (1975).

[5] Plato (*Resp.* 602b9–10) significantly takes 'tragic poetry' to be a quality of *both* epic *and* drama. Plato identifies a 'tragic' viewpoint which stresses humanity's subjection to indifferent or hostile divine forces—the opposite of his own metaphysical and ethical position, which locates happiness exclusively in the individual soul's capacity to choose between good and evil. On this, see the excellent discussion in Halliwell (2002).

[6] See also Chapters 4 and especially 5 above, for complementary accounts of the story of Medea.

athlete after a competitive triumph, the choice of the myth of the Argonauts makes perfect sense as a paradigm of success in the world of heroic adventure: Jason left home in search of glory, and returned having won it.[7] The Pindaric Jason is formidable, handsome, and gentle of speech, even when he confronts Pelias, who has forcibly usurped sovereignty from Jason's 'rightfully ruling parents' (110). Thanks to his trust in the god (232) and to Medea's passionate assistance, Jason wins the Fleece, and is wreathed by his comrades like a victor in the Games (240). What of Medea? It is true that Aphrodite teaches Jason how to induce Medea to lose her shame for her parents and to desire a country—Hellas—which is not her own, so that she shall be 'burned and whirled by the lash of Persuasion' (216–19). It is true, too, that her chaotic and disruptive emotions have been taken to exemplify her 'disturbing ambiguity'.[8] Nor can it be denied that at one point Medea is described as 'the murder(ess) of Pelias' (250), presumably an allusion to the later brutal episode in which she deceived Pelias' daughters into butchering and boiling him, in an attempt to effect his rejuvenation. Nevertheless, although this allusion has been cited as evidence of Medea's 'infamous duplicity',[9] there is surely no implication that to be a murder(ess)-of-Pelias is necessarily a negative quality, since earlier in the poem Pelias has been portrayed as unlawfully and violently insolent (*athemin, biaiōs, hubrin*) (109–12). Moreover, about any possible future dissension between the Kolchian princess and her Greek lover, Pindar is silent: Jason took her away secretly but *sun autai* ('with her acquiescence') (250). To put the matter in broad and direct terms: in *Pythian* 4 the central function of the myth of the *Argo* is to shed lustre on the human victor Arkesilaos by praising the mythical hero who stands as his exemplar.[10]

Apollonios' *Argonautika*, already the subject of scrutiny in Chapters 4 and 5 above, narrates the tale of Jason and Medea in far richer detail than anything we find in Pindar; and in Apollonios it

[7] For an insightful account of the motif of the return home in Pindaric poetry, see Crotty (1982), esp. 104–38.

[8] O'Higgins (1997) 121.

[9] O'Higgins (1997) 103.

[10] On the whole I am sceptical of attempts, e.g. by Segal (1986, 15–29), to emphasize at every turn the craftiness and duplicity of the Pindaric Jason-with-Medea; I prefer Burton's more straightforward reading (1962, 150–73). To find ambiguity *everywhere* is to risk bleaching out its impact when it does occur.

does indeed become imperative to recognize ambiguity. The portrayal of the two principals is subtle and complex: for the bright light of Pindaric heroism Apollonios substitutes something far more troubling. Jason can only achieve his goal by relying on others: even though, before yoking the fire-breathing Kolchian bulls, he exults in the strength of his limbs like a proud war-horse (3.1259–62), he has by that stage already been sprinkled by Medea with potions which confer invulnerability. Not only is Jason far from self-reliant, but he also enters deeply worrying moral territory: his treacherous and religiously polluting murder of Medea's brother Apsyrtos overshadows the latter part of the epic, and partly determines the return course taken by the *Argo*, as Jason and Medea visit first Circe, and then Alkinoos on Phaiakia, in a quest for purification.[11]

The differences between the Pindaric and the Apollonian Medeas are even greater than those between their Jasons. Compared to the near-evanescence of Medea in *Pythian* 4, the Medea of Apollonios is a strong and disturbing presence from the moment that she appears. When she abandons her home, she is torn apart by grief (4.34–40); she threatens Jason with the terrible consequences of breaking his oath to her, when it seems that he will negotiate with the pursuing Kolchians (4.383–93). There is even a subtext which hints at the future rupture between Jason and Medea, since the myth of Ariadne, mentioned several times (3.997–1004, 1096–1108; 4.430–4), cannot but recall Theseus' abandoning of *his* foreign princess. Nevertheless, in spite of these darker characteristics of Jason and Medea, as the *Argo* sails into its home port of Pagasai at the end of the poem there is no mention of impending trouble. Indeed about Medea's future career we have learned explicitly only two things. First, according to Hera's plan, Medea will arrive in Iolkos as a *kakon* ('bane') to Pelias (3.1134–6). Secondly—so Hera assures Thetis—Medea will ultimately marry Achilles in the Elysian Fields (4.810–16).[12] Whatever has gone before, the ending of the epic is serene, concluding as it does at the moment when the *Argo* itself bows out of the story (4.1778–81):

[11] For a fascinating treatment of the Apsyrtos story, see Bremmer (1997).

[12] According to the scholiast on this passage in Apollonios (Schol. Ap. Rhod. 4.814–15, p. 293 W), this intriguing detail was apparently also found in Ibykos and Simonides (*PMG* 291 Ibycus = *PMG* 558 Simonides); cf. T. Gantz (1993) 133.

> You sailed untroubled past the coast of Kekrops' land, past Aulis inside Euboia, past the towns of the Opuntian Lokrians, and joyfully you stepped ashore at Pagasai.

Chronologically intermediate between the Pindaric and the Apollonian narratives is Euripides' tragedy. As might be expected from a story incorporating so many episodes of violent conflict, the myth of Medea was a favourite with the Greek tragedians;[13] but the only play on this theme to survive to the present day is the Euripidean masterpiece. Within the world of this play, the expedition of the *Argo* is just a memory; equally remote is the recollected love between Jason and Medea. From the perspective of the tragedy's Corinthian setting, Kolchis and Iolkos lie in the past; Athens, Medea's eventual refuge, lies in the future. Concentrated into the transitional Corinthian present is an episode of horrifying cruelty, which encompasses the destruction of two families.

Jason has decided to put Medea aside in favour of a new bride, the daughter of the Corinthian king Kreon. When Medea cunningly obtains from a nervous and reluctant Kreon the permission to remain for just one more day before leaving Corinth, she seizes the opportunity to inflict a ghastly vengeance on her former lover and his prospective second family. As wedding presents to Jason's new bride, Medea sends a lovely gown and coronet, conveyed by her own little sons to make the gifts more persuasively welcome. But the gifts turn out to contain a fiery, flesh-eating poison, which causes the excruciating deaths of the girl and her father. A Newsbringer[14] recounts the final stages of the torment (1195–1203):

> Overcome by disaster, she fell to the ground;
> Except to her father, she was indeed hard to recognize;
> The form of her eyes was not clear, and her face was disfigured;
> Blood mingled with flame dripped down from her head; her flesh,
> Eaten away by the invisible jaws of poison, flowed away
> From the bones, like drops of pine resin—
> A terrible sight. Everyone was afraid to touch
> Her corpse. We had learned the lesson from what had happened.

Going beyond even these horrors, Medea then kills her own two young sons—acting not as a monstrous psychopath, but as a mother

[13] See Moreau (1994) 174.

[14] Modern critics usually refer to such characters as 'Messengers', but as often as not there is no message: just news from elsewhere.

torn apart by conflicting drives.[15] At first she had found the thought of infanticide hideous beyond imagining (1042–7):

> What am I to do? My courage has gone,
> Women, when I saw the bright eyes of my children.
> I could not do it. Farewell to the plans
> I had before. I'll take my children from this land.
> Why should I cause harm to my children in order to make
> Their father suffer, when I shall suffer twice as much myself?

But finally, overcome by the urge to punish the partner who has betrayed her, Medea convinces herself that she has no choice (1236–43):

> Friends, the deed is decided: with all speed
> To kill the children and then leave Corinth;
> Not to delay, giving the children up to another
> More malevolent hand to murder them.
> At all events, they must die; and since they must,
> It is I who shall kill them, I who gave them birth.
> Arm yourself, my heart: why do I hesitate
> To perform wicked deeds that are terrible, yet inevitable?

With the boys lying dead, it might seem that any possibility for still greater cruelty has been exhausted. Yet as a final refinement Medea conveys her sons' corpses away from Corinth, in order to prevent Jason from embracing them in a last farewell. 'You are not yet mourning,' she chillingly informs Jason (1396): 'Wait until you are old.'

In exploring the catastrophic underside of heroism, Euripides' *Medea* exemplifies the inflection typically given by tragic playwrights to the mythical tradition. Tragedy is a world in which the tensions which ordinarily beset family life are unbearably intensified. In marriages, ancient and modern, husbands and wives quarrel and even fight: in tragedy, Klytaimestra goes further: she slaughters Agamemnon. In families, ancient and modern, children often face conflicts of loyalty towards their father and mother: in tragedy, Orestes goes further: he kills his mother Klytaimestra because she killed his father. Tragedy is a crucible, a burning glass, an arena which displays events so terrible that one can hardly bear to contemplate them, yet so compelling that one cannot but watch to the end.

[15] On Medea the filicide, see now Hall (2010).

2. WHERE DO GREEK TRAGEDIES HAPPEN?

We turn now to the *location* of tragic myths. The action of Greek tragedies is, I shall suggest, imagined as unfolding 'in between'. The Euripidean Medea may once more serve as our initial guide.

Medea is in many senses an outsider. Not only is she a stranger to Corinth: this Kolchian princess is a stranger to the Greek world altogether. At first she relies on Jason; later—for her escape plan—she relies on Aigeus. But throughout, her status is that of one who is *apolis* ('citiless') (255, cf. 644).[16] This condition of exclusion applies, literally or metaphorically, to a large proportion of the protagonists in Greek tragedy. In Sophokles' *Philoktetes* the eponymous hero, abandoned on the island of Lemnos after being bitten in the foot by a poisonous snake, lacks all the comforts which would have brought his life closer to that of a civilized human being; only his magically unerring bow raises him above the level of a brute. (The desolation and isolation attributed to Lemnos in this play constitute another example of tragic 'selection': inhabited since prehistoric times, the real Lemnos was by no means devoid of human population.) Another Sophoklean work, *Aias*, depicts a hero whose position at the very edge of the beached Greek ships (*Aj.* 4) reflects his martial indomitability—the extremity of an army's lines is one of its points of maximum vulnerability—but also symbolizes other aspects of his marginality, including his madness and his attainment, albeit briefly, of a sublime linguistic register unparalleled elsewhere in the play;[17] eventually he commits the ultimate act of self-exclusion by falling on his sword. In these and many other tragedies, explorations of the moral and emotional implications of exclusion and marginality illustrate the genre's predilection for 'testing to destruction' the concepts and categories of ordinary Greek life.[18] By dramatizing the experiences of individuals driven out of their usual frameworks for living, tragedies depict actions which are simultaneously extreme and representative—just as the chorus of *Oidipous Tyrannos* can characterize the utterly extraordinary events surrounding Oidipous as a 'paradigm' of human existence (*OT* 1193).

[16] Compare also the Nurse's remarkable expression at 34–5, where she observes that Medea has realized what it means *not* to have been uprooted from one's native land.

[17] I have explored the unique language of Aias, comparable to that of Macbeth, in Buxton (2006).

[18] See 155 below.

There are various ways in which tragic actions may unfold in the gaps between states. Sometimes these states are *city* states, as in Sophokles' *Oidipous at Kolonos,* in which the plot concerns an outcast wandering in the no-man's-land between Thebes and Athens. Will hospitable Athens agree to admit a wanderer with a horrific past? Will Kreon and Polyneikes, with their threats and persuasion, draw Oidipous back to Thebes? At the end Oidipous mysteriously crosses an even more dangerous, because sacred, boundary, that between life and death, eventually to occupy a *post mortem* position between the two poles—as a dead hero with the power to affect the living.

A similar sense of the precarious balance between states typically underlies works which turn on the acceptance or rejection of a ritual supplication. Central to Aischylos' *Suppliant Maidens* is the dilemma faced by the Argive ruler Pelasgos, obliged to decide whether to accept a group of refugees in a crisis where such acceptance will entail the dangerous enmity of those angrily pursuing them. The asylum-seekers in question are the daughters of Danaos, desperate to avoid being forced into marriage with their cousins, the sons of Aigyptos. To intensify Pelasgos' dilemma still further, the Danaids threaten to commit suicide by hanging themselves within the city's holy shrines. As Pelasgos expresses it to the chorus of Danaid maidens (468–79):

> Yes, I see difficulties everywhere, hard to wrestle with;
> A surge of troubles overwhelms me like a river.
> I have entered upon a sea of ruin, bottomless and dangerous,
> With nowhere a harbour to escape from misfortune.
> If I do not fulfil this duty to help you,
> You threatened us with pollution unsurpassed;
> But if I stand against your cousins, Aigyptos' sons,
> Before our walls and fight the matter out,
> Is the cost not a bitter one, that men
> Should soak the earth in blood for women's sake?
> Yet I must fear the wrath of Zeus, the suppliants' god:
> For mortals that is the supreme fear.

The boundary between one community and another is a place of tension, and potentially a powerful generator of dramatic meaning.[19]

[19] This kind of 'boundary decision', while typical of tragedy, is certainly not exclusive to it. A classic case from epic is that from Book 4 of Apollonios' *Argonautika.* The Phaiakian king Alkinoos has to find a criterion by which to determine

The gaps-between-states explored in Euripides' *Trojan Women* are at once political and more than political. The action is suspended between Troy and Greece, but also between past and present and, for the Trojan women themselves, between one male and another. The surviving women of Troy find themselves in a city whose past already lies in smouldering ruins, and whose future will consist of a slave existence across the sea in Greece. Kassandra will be transferred from the service of Apollo to the bed of Agamemnon; it is proposed that Hekabe and Andromache shall serve Odysseus and Neoptolemos. The Trojan men, it is true, died good deaths, achieving 'the most beautiful glory' by dying for their country (*Tro.* 386–7). But dead they are: the only living Trojan male to appear in the play is Astyanax, Hektor's baby son, a silent victim soon to be hurled to his death from the city walls. In so far as a *polis* is defined by the presence of its male citizens, Troy is a *polis* no longer; rather, it is an empty space, abandoned even by Poseidon and Athene, who had ended their prologue by walking away. The minimal scope for the expression of personal preference which had momentarily opened up earlier on ('I would rather go to the famed and blessed land of Theseus'—i.e. Athens—the chorus had observed at line 207) has given way by the end to an ineluctable trek toward the Greek ships.

Yet another boundary explored in tragedy is the problematic interface between 'Greek' and 'Barbarian'. *Medea* again provides a reference point. In the face of Medea's accusations about broken vows, Jason retorts that moving to Greece has introduced her to a society which respects justice and the rule of law (*Med.* 536–8). Yet, notwithstanding the 'barbaric' cruelty of Medea's revenge, Jason's breaking of his vows to her hardly allows such a dichotomy to stand unchallenged: there is heartlessness on either side of the division between Greek and non-Greek. An equivalent overlap between these two categories pervades Aischylos' *Agamemnon,* whose subtitle might be 'A Tale of Two Cities'. The play evokes a series of characters who travel, or who once travelled, from Argos to Troy or vice versa, and one of the questions implicitly raised in the play is: will the generalizations which applied in Troy (for example, that the gods

whether to return Medea to the pursuing Kolchians, or to allow her to remain with Jason. His Solomon-like judgement is that, if Medea is still a virgin, she must go back to Kolchis; but if she has already been united with Jason, she should not be forced to leave him (1106–9).

punish mortals who are impious) apply also in Argos? When Agamemnon is persuaded by Klytaimestra to perform the symbolically tremendous gesture of trampling on rich fabric as he re-enters his palace, he admits that this is exactly what Priam would have done (*Ag.* 935–6)—another example of the characteristically tragic collapsing of boundaries.

In several other plays an analogous to-ing and fro-ing takes place; but in these cases the opposed locations are features of the landscape rather than different communities. More often than not, the *skēnē* ('stage building'), in front of which tragedies were played out, was designed to represent part of the built environment such as a house or palace, which in turn usually belonged within a *polis*.[20] Yet it often happens that significant action takes place in the offstage space imagined to lie beyond the *skēnē*—typically in a mountain region adjacent to and contrasting with the world of human habitation. The reciprocal relationship between mountain and city constitutes yet one more permutation of the interstitial status of tragic action, since the action of many tragedies oscillates between an ostensibly civilized household/city and the sacred wildness of a mountain. The most obvious example is the role of Mount Kithairon in myths based in the city of Thebes. In both *Oidipous Tyrannos* and *Bakchai*, this mountain is where human beings come unusually and dangerously close to the sacred. For Oidipous, this proximity is strange and eerie: Kithairon is where he was left to die and then miraculously saved. For the mortals swept up in the arrival of Dionysos in Greece, Kithairon has a more sharply defined role: it is where the women go in search of Dionysos, abandoning their proper domestic role in a civilized community. By the end of the play, the mountain has become a place of nightmarish carnage, and yet the religious experiences which take place there are, at least when properly channelled through ritual, an integral part of the world of civilization.[21]

'Spaces between' are found not only in the physical world, but also in the mind. Several tragedies are shaped by the interplay of sanity

[20] The imagined location of the building need not be Greece: cf. Euripides' *Helen* (set in Egypt) or Aischylos' *Persians* (set in Persia); and there may be *equivalents* of a house, such as a more-or-less permanent warrior-tent (*Aias*, set in the Greek camp at Troy). But there are exceptions: the scene of *Prometheus Bound* is the extreme wilderness of the Caucasus; that of Sophokles' *Philoktetes* is before a cave on the seashore of Lemnos.

[21] For more on tragic mountains, see 25–30 above.

and madness, though there are marked variations, from play to play, about what constitutes being out of one's 'right' mind, and what the causes and effects of such a condition might be. For Io in *Prometheus Bound* (attributed to Aischylos), the distortion of her mind is provoked by the jealousy of Hera, whose agent is a fly which stings unremittingly. Being driven out of her senses is for Io analogous to other disastrous upheavals which she endures, namely metamorphosis from human to cow, and exile from her homeland as she wanders from continent to continent. Throughout all this, Io is a victim: she suffers but does not act. To some extent comparable is the madness of Kassandra in *Agamemnon*: she too has become a victim, having lost credibility as a prophetess after refusing to satisfy Apollo's lust. Io and Kassandra have in common the linguistic turmoil which the playwright lends to each: as they lurch in and out of frenzy, their utterances alternate between reasoned lucidity and tormented, wordless exclamation, whether it be the *otototototoi popoi da* of Kassandra (*Ag.* 1072) or Io's *iō moi moi; he he* (*Prom.* 742).

For Herakles in *The Madness of Herakles* and Agaue in *Bakchai*, the sufferings produced by madness are even more 'tragic' (if we take that word to signify, this time, a quality of experience, rather than 'that which is represented in a tragedy'). The agent of Herakles' delusion is once more the jealous Hera (acting now through Lyssa, goddess of madness); the result is Herakles' commission of acts no less terrible for being unwitting. As for Agaue, the god she offends is Dionysos, whose divinity she, like her sisters, denies. Her punishment is to be maddened, and in that state to dismember her still-living son Pentheus. Both of these explorations of madness involve the agonizing return of the protagonists to their normal condition of mind, a process guided in each case by their father. Herakles' guide is Amphitryon (*Her.* 1131–5):

> *Amph*: There: look at the bodies of these children, lying where they fell.
> *Her*: Ah! What is this that I see? Ah no!
> *Amph*: They were no enemies, these children you fought against, my son.
> *Her*: Fought? Who killed these children?
> *Amph*: You did, my son: your bow—and whichever god is responsible.

For Agaue, it is Kadmos who gently steers her mind onto the path of horrified recognition (*Ba.* 1273–82):

> *Kadm*: Whose house did you go to when you were married?
> *Agaue*: You gave me to Echion, one of the Sown Men, so they said.
> *Kadm*: What son was born to your husband in your home?
> *Agaue*: Pentheus, the product of my union with his father.

Kadm: Whose head are you holding in your arms?
Agaue: A lion's head—at least, so said the women who hunted it.
Kadm: Look directly at it: it is but a small labour to look upon it.
Agaue: Ah! What am I looking at? What am I carrying in my hands?
Kadm: Gaze at it; learn the truth more clearly.
Agaue: I see the greatest pain. I am wretched.

That Herakles was out of his 'right' mind when he slew his children is clear enough. But was Agaue really deluded, while she was ecstatically worshipping Dionysos? How is 'true wisdom' to be defined? These are some of the many disturbing issues which *Bakchai* confronts.

In summary: tragedy does not occupy a comfortable space within accepted concepts and assumptions. The distinctive location of tragic myths is in the gaps between certainties. Tragedy is a place of edges and margins, an in-between territory where boundaries—literal and metaphorical—are ripe for exploration and contestation.

3. DIVINITIES AND MORTALS

I turn finally to a question fundamental to any attempt to clarify tragedy's distinctiveness within the mythical tradition: how are the gods portrayed?

The actions of divinities are highlighted in every narrative genre which retells Greek myths.[22] In Homeric epic, and in all subsequent Greek epics down to Nonnos, the gods play a decisive part.[23] Hesiod's *Theogony* self-evidently centres on divinities, but the same poet's *Works and Days* also accords a crucial role to the gods, for example through the interrelated fates of Prometheus and Pandora—the gods' gift to humanity. Pindaric praise-poetry—composed for victors in the Games celebrated for Zeus, Apollo, and Poseidon—depends on constant reference to the gods' transcendent power, as a foil and a paradigm for the deeds of mortal heroes and the victors who strive to emulate them. Herodotos' *Histories* may focus on the glorious exploits of mortals in the Greco-Persian War, but the backdrop to these events is a structure of religious assumptions anchored in the

[22] See Bremmer and Erskine (2010).
[23] On Homer, see e.g. Griffin (1980) 144–204; Kraus (1984); Kullmann (1992); Kearns (2004). On post-Homeric epic, Feeney (1991) is fundamental.

mythical past.[24] As for comedy, Aristophanes' plays take the existence of the gods as read, even if the nature of the reading allows for outrageous mockery of the rulers of the universe; half a millennium later, in a quite different comic vein, the dialogues of Lucian still mine the deeds of the gods in order to extract humour.[25] To all this textual evidence must be added countless visual images from every period of classical antiquity, including objects as disparate as temple friezes, statues, coins, vases, and gems, all of which embody or are adorned by representations of divinities involved in mythological episodes.[26] Each of these genres, indeed each individual poet or artist, works from a particular perspective; the same is true of tragedy and tragedians. What, then, can we identify as distinctive about the tragic portrayal of gods and goddesses?

First, a crucial preliminary. It must be stressed that the gods only very rarely form the centrepiece of a tragedy.[27] They are, rather, its framework, its backdrop, that which is beyond and behind the action—action which is carried forward by the mortal heroes and heroines, who choose, are deluded, come to grief, struggle courageously, in fear or madness or generosity or hatred. Nevertheless, those human actions always resonate against a more-than-human background, and it is this which we shall now investigate.

No single 'voice' dominates this portrayal. Tragedy was competitive: in the contest at the City Dionysia, each playwright staged his own version of the mythological past, striving to be adjudged superior to his rivals. Just as the music, choreography, and costuming of tragedies varied between play and play, so too did the representation of the gods. This variety is evident even in the tiny proportion of the total tragic output constituted by the surviving plays. To take one example: the dramatic device found in so many Euripidean works, whereby, during the prologue or epilogue, a divinity speaks authoritatively from the stage apparatus known as 'the machine', is by contrast unusual in extant Sophokles, where we encounter a

24 For an incisive contribution to this much-discussed topic, see Gould (2001) 359–77. See now, with extensive further bibliography, Fowler (2010).

25 Aristophanes: see Bowie (1993). Lucian: see Dickie (2010).

26 The first and usually the best place to turn for information about visual evidence for Greek mythology is *LIMC*.

27 Even in the case of *Prometheus Bound*, it could be argued that the central character is not simply a Titan, but also a kind of honorary, quasi-human hero, by virtue of his steadfast support for humankind.

predominant sense of the *difficulty* of determining the gods' views and intentions.[28] Even within a single work we find changing emphases. In Aischylos' *Oresteia*, the first play of the trilogy offers a picture of divine action which is at best enigmatic and at worst baffling;[29] only in the third play do the gods stride forth upon the stage, as Apollo, the Furies, and Athene argue their cases and defend their individual, explicitly stated perspectives on the action.

Making every allowance for such variations, however, we may still plausibly suggest a number of generalizations about the gods in tragedy. I shall mention four.

(1) Tragedy explores conflicts among the gods

Emphasis on conflict between divinities is far from being unique to tragedy. We need only think of the cosmic wars narrated in Hesiod's *Theogony*; of the battles between the gods in the *Iliad*; of the struggle between Athene and Poseidon in the *Odyssey* over the homecoming of Odysseus; of the squabble between Hermes and Apollo in the *Homeric Hymn to Hermes*, concerning the theft of his brother's cattle by the newborn trickster god. Nevertheless, tragedy does show a marked interest in such conflicts—another aspect of tragedy's location in 'the space between'. Sometimes these conflicts are about power and sovereignty; sometimes they are generated by boundary disputes over the various provinces of interest with which the gods are associated. In both kinds of conflict, human beings play the role of victims.

A classic struggle over sovereignty is dramatized in *Prometheus Bound*, in which Zeus, the new and (as depicted by his adversaries) tyrannical ruler of the universe, is pitted against the no less divine Prometheus. For having dared to champion humanity in the face of Zeus' intention to annihilate them, Prometheus is subjected to an interminable and horrible punishment: fixed to a rock in the Caucasus, he will have his endlessly self-regenerating liver torn to shreds daily by an eagle. However, the Titan, whose suffering is compounded by his knowledge of the full duration of his future

[28] The two appearances of divinities in the extant plays are those of Athene at the beginning of *Aias* and the deified Herakles at the end of *Philoktetes*. For four other instances in the fragmentary plays, see the discussion in R. Parker (1999) 11–12.

[29] On tragic 'bafflement', see 161–72 below.

torment (his name means 'Forethought'), refuses to defer to his tormentor, or to his tormentor's lackey (999–1006):

> *Hermes*: Bring yourself, rash fool, at last
> To think correctly in face of your present anguish.
> *Prom*: You exhort me in vain, as if you were talking to the waves.
> Never convince yourself that I, in fear
> Of Zeus' intent, will become feminized in my mind,
> Begging my greatly hated enemy, with hands
> Upturned in womanish supplication, to free me from these bonds.
> No, never.

One aspect of the cosmic power-struggle dramatized in *Prometheus Bound* is the clash between two successive generations of gods. The same is true of the *Oresteia,* though here the climactic struggle is fought not over the fate of humanity as a whole, but over the fate of a single individual. Orestes' act of matricide is defended by the 'younger' god Apollo and attacked by the 'older' Furies, the goddesses whose primordial authority to punish kin-murderers long pre-dates the coming to power of the Olympians. When Apollo's side of the argument is confirmed by the casting vote of his fellow Olympian Athene, the Furies' resentment is couched in terms of generational conflict (*Eum.* 778–9):

> You younger gods, you have ridden down
> The ancient laws, and torn them from my hands.

Seniority was not the only reason for a divinity to assert a claim to honour, or to resent the behaviour of a fellow god. Differences in spheres of operation between deities also held ample potential for clashes of interest. In *Hippolytos*, the conflict between Artemis and Aphrodite works itself out through the lives and deaths of the family of Theseus; the goddesses themselves merely frame the action by appearing in the prologue (Aphrodite) and in the finale (Artemis). When the young hunter Hippolytos prefers the chaste pursuits associated with the virginal Artemis to the world of sexuality presided over by Aphrodite, his agonizing death at the hands of the goddess of love leads Artemis, at the end of the play, to locate the action firmly within the context of the eternal rivalry between the two goddesses. As she says to the dying Hippolytos (1417–22):

> Let be. For, even when you are under the dark of earth,
> Aphrodite's zealous anger shall not fall upon you

Unavenged; your piety and noble spirit deserve requital.
I, by my own hand, with these unerring arrows
Shall wreak vengeance on the mortal she holds dearest.

The time of gods is not the time of mortals. Human lives may come and go, but Artemis and Aphrodite will forever embody antithetical perceptions of sexuality.

(2) In tragedy the gods' use of power can be openly criticized, yet at the same time that power must be acknowledged, because it is omnipresent and unavoidable

One feature of ancient Greek religion which can be particularly difficult to comprehend for a modern observer—especially one from a morally polarized monotheistic background—is its readiness to tolerate overt criticism of the gods' behaviour. In few works of Greek literature is the conduct of a god placed under more intense scrutiny than in Euripides' *Ion*. The plot narrates the consequences of the god's rape of Kreousa, an event which she recollects in an aria of extraordinary bitterness (887–901):

You came with hair flashing
Gold, as I gathered
Into my cloak flowers ablaze
With their golden light.
Clinging to my pale wrists
As I cried for my mother's help
You led me to a bed in a cave,
A god and my lover,
With no shame,
Doing a favour to the Cyprian.
In misery I bore you
A son, whom in maternal terror
I placed in that bed
Where you cruelly forced me.[30]

[30] Adapted from translation by R. F. Willetts, in Grene and Lattimore (1958). The other translations from tragedy in the present chapter—which make no claim to literary merit—are my own.

This is not, to be sure, the only view of Apollo which the play presents. In the opening scene a servant of the god's Delphic temple, a young man by the name of Ion—who (it will turn out) was born from Kreousa's union with Apollo—associates this shrine and its patron deity with the qualities of brightness, healing, and, above all, purity—in a very literal sense (Ion reports that his duties include frightening away birds from the temple, and sweeping the floor of the shrine when it has been fouled). Moreover, after many twists and turns in the plot, mother and son will recognize each other, and Apollo's paternity will be cast in a positive light when Athene pronounces *ex machina* that 'Apollo then has managed all things well' (1595). However, such a view is expressed only after the goddess has excused Apollo's own attendance at the denouement in highly equivocal terms (1556–8):

> I have come here in haste, sent by Apollo,
> Who did not think it right to come himself
> Into your sight, in case there should be blame
> For what has happened in the past

When Kreousa does at last utter praises of Apollo, it is because he has restored her son to her, not because she feels any differently about the sexual mistreatment which she herself received at the god's hands (1609–10). The weight of the play leaves Apolline morality in at best an ambiguous light.[31]

Though the criticisms of Apollo in *Ion* are especially sustained and strident, in other tragedies too the conduct of various divinities is presented, at least by some of the characters, as worthy of censure. Sophokles' *Women of Trachis* highlights the ritual importance of Zeus, in relation to his oracle at Dodona and his altar at Kenaion; Zeus is the addressee of numerous invocations, prayers, and oaths; Zeus holds sway over Mount Oita, the location of the funeral pyre to which Herakles will be conveyed. But as an agent within the drama the father of the gods is noticeable by his complete absence, even when his son Herakles cries out to him in anguish ('O Zeus, where in the world have I come?'—the hero's very first words, 983–4). Furthermore, although Herakles' expression 'Zeus in the stars' (1106) does not necessarily imply a tone of irony or resentment, the

[31] See ch. 3 of Zacharia (2003) for an exploration of the ambiguity of Apollo in this play.

concluding reference by Herakles' son Hyllos to 'the great cruelty of the gods displayed in what is being done, gods who beget children and are called fathers but who can look upon such sufferings as these' (1266–9) can only be taken as a bitter accusation by Hyllos of a state of divinely ordered affairs which can tolerate such a waste of human life. And yet the seeds of a perception which counterbalances Hyllos' outburst are already present in the choral coda to the play (1278):

> There is none of these things which is not Zeus.[32]

The gods are *there*, and they are powerful: mortals ignore them at their peril.

Two other Sophoklean plays bring home this realization with particular force. In *Aias*, long before the eponymous hero made his attempt on the lives of the Greek commanders, he had (so a News-bringer reports) made a reckless boast about his lack of need of divine help: 'Father, together with the gods even one who is nothing could win mastery; but I trust that I shall grasp this glory even without them!' (767–9). When seen in the light of Athene's concluding words in the opening scene ('Look, then, at such things, and never yourself speak an arrogant word against the gods . . . For one day brings down all mortal things, and one day raises them up; the gods love those who think sensibly and hate the wicked' (127–33)), Aias' arrogance shows a fatal misunderstanding of the proper relationship between mortals and gods. Equally heedless of the divine framework of human ethical behaviour is Kreon in *Antigone*. Though Antigone herself might merely be using self-justifying rhetoric when she invokes 'the unwritten and unfailing laws of the gods' (454) to back her defiant burial of her traitorous brother Polyneikes, her position receives unequivocal support from the seer Teiresias, who describes how a horrific distortion of sacrificial practice has been precipitated by the exposing of Polyneikes' corpse (1016–22). Kreon rescinds his decree forbidding burial, but too late; his refusal to comprehend how the world works culminates not only in the death of Antigone but also in the suicides of his own son and wife.

[32] In spite of the views of some scholars who assign this and the preceding three lines to Hyllos, I believe that the concluding voice of the play should be that of the chorus. See also 163–4 below.

(3) The omnipresence of divine influence on human action in tragedy does not negate the importance of human choice

Contrary to a common misperception of what Greek tragedy is like, tragic myths do not simply illustrate the inevitability of 'fate'. It is true that spectators and readers are often confronted with the subjecting of human beings to irresistible pressure from the gods: Herakles is sent mad by Hera, and Aias by Athene; Phaidra does not choose to fall in love with her stepson—her passion is caused by Aphrodite; when Pentheus suddenly expresses a desire to see the maenads on Mount Kithairon, it is because his mind has been invaded by Dionysos. But such cases must be set against those where the preponderant dramatic meaning is borne by actions which are squarely the consequence of human choice.

Two plays by Sophokles will exemplify this point. *Oidipous Tyrannos* has often been taken to be the paradigm of a work in which a human being is shown to be powerless against fortune. And yet the *plot* of the play—as opposed to the mythical events, and in particular the oracular predictions, which constitute its *antecedents*—concerns a man who, whatever the cost, is bent upon two interrelated courses of action: at first, doing everything necessary to free his city from the pollution which has engulfed it; then, finding out his own identity, from the moment when this has been called into question. These courses of action are, to put it crudely, what the play is about; and they are the product of Oidipous' own choosing. Even when the now blind king cries out to the chorus that 'It was Apollo, friends, Apollo who brought about these cruel, cruel sufferings of mine!' (1329–30), not only is it unclear in what sense Apollo can possibly be 'responsible' for what has occurred, but also Oidipous immediately goes on to maintain his own responsibility for the most shocking deed to have taken place within the time-frame of the play—his self-blinding ('And no other hand but mine struck my eyes, miserable that I am!', 1331–2). Whatever Apollo's oracle may have predicted, and whatever the putative relationship between such predictions and the eventual outcome, what is undeniable is that nothing in the play for a moment suggests that the truth was 'fated' to come out *in this way*—and it is the *manner* of the revelation of the truth which bears the weight of the work's dramatic significance.

Aias offers another example of the overriding importance of human choice. The play begins with a demonstration of the cool, terrifying power of a divinity, Athene, first to drive a great hero mad, and then to mock and toy with him while he is in that condition: mighty Aias ignominiously drips with the blood of sacrificial sheep, which he believes to be the blood of the Greek commanders whom he has, he thinks, put to death because (in his view) they had slighted him. But this state of helpless delusion, of powerless submission to the gods, soon gives way: initially to a consciousness of profound shame, and then to a decision to commit suicide. This decision is Aias' alone: a decision taken with deliberation, like the deliberation with which he fixes in the earth the sword upon which he will fall (815–22). Nor is this the only crucial moment in the play for which the frame of reference is presented as completely within the hands of mortals. The rancorous debate about whether or not to allow burial to Aias is driven exclusively by human feelings: anger, loyalty, together with the ultimately decisive ingredient of self-interest added by Odysseus ('I too shall come to that need', 1365). Athene's controlling presence has left the stage long ago.

We have mentioned some cases where the gods evidently compel, and others where mortals unambiguously choose. But in still other cases tragic action occupies an intermediate ground between compulsion and choice. When, in *Agamemnon*, the chorus recalls the episode in which the Greek commander sacrificed his daughter Iphigeneia in order to appease the anger of Artemis, the words they use are: 'When he had put on the yoke-strap of necessity' (218). The paradox could not be more stark. Agamemnon *put on* the yoke-strap: it was a freely chosen act. But the yoke-strap which he put on was that of *necessity*: he had no choice. In representing the involvement of the gods in human life, tragic myths dwell on crises in which precisely this kind of paradox comes into focus.

(4) The gods of tragedy are partially comprehensible, but aspects of them remain unfathomable, incommensurable, and unknowable

We have already encountered several instances in which the role and attitude of the gods is explicitly set out in the tragic action. Usually this is when the gods themselves appear on the scene and speak.

Sometimes a divinity will set out the ground rules of the action only to depart for good (e.g. Athene in *Aias*, Hermes in *Ion*, Athene and Poseidon in *The Trojan Women*); in other cases it will be left to a divinity at the end of a play to reintegrate the action into the audience's experience by referring to ritual (Artemis at the end of *Hippolytos*; Athene at the end of *Iphigeneia in Tauris*) or by placing the events of the play in a wider mythical context (Kastor in Euripides' *Elektra*; Apollo in *Orestes*; Thetis in *Andromache*). Less often, divinities express their own point of view either throughout the action or at its mid-point, rather than at its beginning or end: Dionysos is onstage for much of *Bakchai*; Iris and Lyssa appear midway through *Herakles*; in *Eumenides* Apollo, the Furies, and Athene dominate the action in person.

But there are also cases in which what receives emphasis is not the gods' visibility but their ultimate unpredictability and unfathomability. Of the three great Athenian tragedians, Euripides is the one who most insistently confronts spectators with what they seemingly could not have anticipated, so much so that a choral coda to this effect becomes a refrain in several of his works:

> Many are the shapes of the divinities;
> The gods bring many matters to surprising ends;
> The things we thought would happen do not happen;
> For the unexpected the god finds a way.
> Such was the conclusion of this story.[33]

Although it is usually impossible to determine precisely how far the spectators' background knowledge of mythology might have shaped their expectations, the manner in which Euripides introduces abrupt changes of dramatic direction suggests that even an audience acquainted with the general outlines of a myth might have reacted with astonishment: one example is the shocking arrival, in *Herakles*, of Lyssa, goddess of madness; another—this time narrated as opposed to enacted—is the appearance of the monstrous bull from the sea as reported by the Newsbringer in *Hippolytos*. Such epiphanies sharpen an audience's sense of the gulf between mortals and divinity, and dramatize the ultimate incommensurability of human with divine,

[33] This passage occurs at the end of *Alkestis* (1159–63), *Andromache* (1284–8), *Helen* (1688–92), and *Bakchai* (1388–92) and, with a variation in the first line (which now runs: 'Zeus on Olympos is dispenser of many things'), *Medea* (1415–19).

even in a medium such as tragedy, in which god and mortal visibly tread the stage side by side.[34]

Fundamental though the unexpected may be to Euripidean dramaturgy, some of the most striking illustrations of the gods' unfathomability are to be found in works by the other two great tragedians. Near the beginning of *Agamemnon*, in the course of the chorus' monumental opening ode, the old men of Argos recall an episode from the outset of the Greek expedition against Troy. When the fleet was gathered at Aulis, two eagles were seen devouring a pregnant hare. The beginning of any military campaign was a sensitive and dangerous time, when—given a belief-system in which human and cosmic events were perceived to be mutually interconnected[35]—anything remotely unusual would be interpreted as ominous. The Greek seer Kalchas duly read the strange occurrence as a sign: in this case, a sign of the displeasure of Artemis, who 'hates the eagles' feast' (138). But why Artemis should not only 'hate' this natural event, but also, if the Aischylean text is taken to mean what it says,[36] take it as a justification for her subsequent injunction upon Agamemnon to sacrifice his own daughter—these matters are left opaque. At the origin of the action of the *Oresteia* is an enigma wrapped in a riddle; and at the centre of the enigma is the attitude of the gods towards humanity.

But it is neither Aischylos nor Euripides who presents the purposes of the gods at their most inscrutable. The tragedian who does *this* is Sophokles; above all, in *Oidipous Tyrannos*. 'To the gods', Oidipous maintains, just as the play is about to end (1519), 'I am most hateful.' If Oidipous *is* hated by the gods—as opposed to simply *feeling* that he is hated—then there must be a reason for it, since it would be out of keeping with everything we know of Greek religion if one or more divinities were to conceive an *unmotivated* hatred for a mortal. And the reason is not far to seek: the sending of the plague upon Thebes, an unambiguous indication of divine displeasure, follows inexorably upon the miasma generated by Oidipous' hideous transgressions. But that is far from being the end of the matter. For why should it have been precisely Oidipous, and not someone else, who has been put into

[34] See Gould (2001) 203–34, on the partial incommensurability of the divine with the human.

[35] A thought-provoking study of 'interconnectedness' is to be found in Oudemans and Lardinois (1987).

[36] Cf. Denniston and Page (1957) xxv. On this episode as an example of tragic 'bafflement', see 165–6 below.

the position, unwittingly, of incurring this displeasure? Did the gods will *that*? Nothing in the play entitles us to give an answer; indeed, nothing in the play raises the question at all. What the gods want for Oidipous remains as enigmatic at the end of the play as it was at the beginning.

Tragic myths offer a spectacle of a world in which mortals try to cope with events at the limits of or beyond their comprehension; even when these events *are* comprehended, they are comprehended too late. But Greek tragedy is not just a record of human inadequacy. The sense of limitation is offset by a whole range of positives: Oidipous' moral strength in his relentless quest for the truth; Neoptolemos' change of heart when he decides to abandon his deception of Philoktetes and to take him home (even though the decision is eventually countermanded by Herakles); Theseus' generosity of spirit towards Herakles and Oidipous; the linguistic sublimity of Aias and Kassandra when they gain insight into how the world is.[37] Most of the characteristics which I have described as 'distinctively tragic' can be paralleled in one or more other genres of myth-telling. But the combination of all of them in tragedy is what makes the genre unique. It is nothing less than an exploration, through the medium of traditional tales, of the place of humanity in the world, an exploration both popular and profound. To rephrase the point I made at the head of this chapter: of all the ancient forms of myth-telling, only the Homeric poems can rival the tragedies in their continuing power to hold, enchant, shock, and unsettle.[38]

[37] *Aj.* 669–77 and *Agam.* 1327–30.

[38] Several friends and colleagues have helped me to think through the issues developed in this chapter. In particular I must single out Michael Lurje, whose detailed and thoughtful comments enabled me to remove at least some of the shortcomings in my argument.

7

Time, Space, and Ideology: Tragic Myths and the Athenian *Polis*

This chapter offers a second general account of myth-in-tragedy. Having already (Chapter 6) addressed the question of tragic space, I return now to this topic in more detail, in order to investigate a problem which has been high on the agenda of recent scholarly debate, namely the extent to which tragic retellings of myth may be seen as 'distinctively Athenian'.

1. INTRODUCTION

Aristotle's *Poetics* is a remarkably consistent work. If you accept its two unargued premises—that tragedy's characteristic effect upon an audience is achieved through the arousing of pity-and-fear; and that the best way of achieving that arousal is through the *muthos* (myth; plot-construction)—then everything else follows with remorseless logic. Not only a consistent work, though: also a paradoxical one. It manages to talk about tragedy without paying any explicit attention to politics (this from the author of the *Politics*!). In this chapter I shall not discuss Aristotle directly, but I do want to use Aristotle as a way into tragedy. I propose to start from the combination of emotions which he isolates, and to relate it to the object of that silence of his: the life of the *polis*.[1]

There is a widely held view, which I share, that one can get some idea of how Aristotle intends the pity-and-fear combination to be understood by looking at the way he deploys it in Book II of the

[1] On Aristotle's silence, see Hall (1996).

Rhetoric.[2] Fear is said to arise when people contemplate a situation that is near at hand and threatening; an orator will arouse it by making the audience feel that '*that* sort of destruction might happen to *me*' (2.5.15). Pity, on the other hand, is felt when the perceiver senses a distance between himself and the object of the pity (2.8.12), though there is still a pressure of inference from the victim's fate to his own. In brief: that which people fear in relation to themselves, they pity when others are the victims (2.8.13). In other words—if we take as applying to the *Poetics* the position maintained in the *Rhetoric*—Aristotle sees tragedy as centring on a combination of the individual's sense of emotional distance from the scene observed, and his sense of emotional closeness to it.[3]

I want to borrow this notion of combined proximity-and-distance in order to explore three features of represented tragic action not discussed by Aristotle, or at least not in the relevant way. These three features are *time*, *space*, and *ideology*. I shall argue that one of the many ambiguities inherent in Greek tragedy concerns the simultaneous proximity and distance, in terms of these three variables, of the scene set before the spectators. Tragedy is both now and not now, here and not here, and—most intriguingly of all—both supportive of the dominant values of the Athenian *polis*, and (apparently) critical, perhaps even subversive, of them.

2. TIME

From a very basic standpoint, tragedies are re-playings in the audience's present of happenings from the mythical past.[4] Yet this is only the beginning of the story.

With a few well-known kinds of exception (such as re-stagings of Aischylos' works after his death, second versions of initially unsuccessful tragedies, like *Hippolytos*, and re-performances at deme

[2] See for example Stanford (1983) 23, and in general 21–48, a wise and thoughtful account of the emotional dimension of Greek tragedy.

[3] Among the enormous bibliography on Aristotelian pity-and-fear one may profitably consult Nehamas (1992), esp. 296–7 and 300–1; Halliwell (1998) 170–84; Konstan (2001) 49–74 and 128–36; Rehm (2003) 43–4 and more generally 40–64.

[4] Reflections on tragedy and time: Rehm (2003) 119–39.

festivals),[5] fifth-century tragedies are new works, new versions of the past—the past constantly updated, re-'present'ed. However, that the *muthoi* are thought of as in some sense *having happened* as well as happening now before the audience's eyes is clear from passages in which future events are referred to: both events which are future in relation to the dramatic action, but past in relation to the audience's present (as with the impending destruction of the Greek fleet predicted by Athene and confirmed by Poseidon already in the prologue of *Trojan Women*, 73–97), and also events whose validity through repeated re-enactment is predicted as continuing into the dramatic future and—there is no reason to rule out—into the audience's future too (as with Artemis' prediction at the end of *Hippolytos* that the fate of the young hero will be remembered *for ever* in ritual song by Trozenian maidens, 1428–30).

In so far as they are, in the well-known although hardly transparent phrase attributed by Athenaios to Aischylos, 'cuts from the mighty banquets of Homer',[6] tragic reworkings of themes adumbrated in epic are, this time in a poetic sense, echoes of a past genre: one thinks of the Sophoklean scene featuring Aias and his son Eurysakes, and of its precursor in Book 6 of the *Iliad*, the episode involving Hektor and baby Astyanax. And yet, as every Attic schoolboy knew, and as everyone who had attended a rhapsodic contest knew too, Homer was a living part of the poetic present; we may recall the anecdote about Alkibiades who, when he went into a school and failed to find a text of the *Iliad*, punched the teacher.[7] So when Bernard Knox eloquently tells us that 'Aias is presented to us in this play as the last of the heroes. His death is the death of the old Homeric . . . individual ethos which had for centuries of aristocratic rule served as the dominant ideal of man's nobility and action', we do well to remind ourselves that, even at the height of the fifth-century democracy, Homeric poetry was a feature of the audience's present as well as of their past, albeit a feature which (to complicate matters further) looks back from its own narrative present to an earlier, heroic age.[8]

Jean-Pierre Vernant famously defined tragedy's 'historical moment' as occurring when 'a gap develops at the heart of the social experience.

[5] See Pickard-Cambridge (1988) 99–100; Whitehead (1986) 212–22; P. Wilson (2000) 279–302.

[6] Ath. 8.347e; cf. Gould (2001) 158–9.

[7] Plut. *Mor.* 186d; Ael. *VH* 13.38.

[8] Knox (1979) 144. *Aias* is of course undated, so we do not know how 'high' the democracy actually was.

It is wide enough for the oppositions between legal and political thought on the one hand and the mythical and heroic traditions on the other to stand out quite clearly. Yet it is narrow enough for the conflict in values still to be a painful one and for the clash to continue to take place.'[9] This still seems to me to be an extremely useful model, but the same can no longer, I think, be said of another opposition proposed in the same essay: 'on the one hand the chorus, an anonymous and collective being whose role is to express . . . the feelings of the spectators who make up the civic community; on the other the individualized figure whose action forms the centre of the drama and who is seen as a hero from another age, always more or less alien to the ordinary condition of a citizen.'[10] But Phoenician women, Salaminian sailors, old men of Argos, even old men of Kolonos (who live under Theseus' monarchy), cannot be regarded as the mouthpiece *tout court* of *any* fifth-century *polis*, let alone of Athens, at least not as contrasted with 'non-civic' heroes. Being forced to see the Erinyes in *Eumenides* or the chorus in *Bakchai* as embodying the 'civic present' is as awkward as being forced to *deny* the element of 'civic presentness' in the argument between Haimon and Kreon in *Antigone*.

From the perspective of social time, then, tragedy incorporates a complex interweaving of past and present. This emerges also from Pat Easterling's study of what are sometimes rather misleadingly referred to as 'anachronisms' in tragedy: she shows how 'modern' references to, for example, literacy and coinage are kept 'under control', and always tempered by a certain 'heroic vagueness'.[11] Nicole Loraux expresses the general point beautifully: 'The city retold the myth all over again, in a different way, so as to hear its own voice in a tale of long ago.'[12]

3. SPACE

If tragic time is far from simple, its complexities pale beside those of tragic space. This is a territory in which many scholars have taken an

[9] Vernant and Vidal-Naquet (1988) 27.

[10] Vernant and Vidal-Naquet (1988) 24.

[11] Easterling (1985) 7. Cf. also de Romilly (1968) for more on the complexities of tragic time; though some of the ideas she deploys in relation to *developments* in Greek concepts of time need considerable revision.

[12] Loraux (1993) 235.

interest. From the scenic angle, N. C. Hourmouziades' account of the on- and off-stage worlds of Euripides was followed by Oliver Taplin on exits and entrances, and Ruth Padel on the drama of inside and outside.[13] On representations of the *polis* there have been, among many others, Pierre Vidal-Naquet on *Philoktetes*,[14] Froma Zeitlin, Paola Angeli Bernardini, and Daniel Berman on tragic Thebes,[15] Suzanne Saïd and Guido Avezzù on tragic Argos,[16] the present author on *polis*/mountain relationships and on tragic seashores,[17] and Neil Croally on Troy in *Trojan Women* as an 'other place'.[18] Studies of tragic space, whether general or particular, continue unabated.[19]

No shortage of cartographers, then. But is it really feasible to generalize about the 'here and there' aspect of our general 'remoteness/proximity' polarity? After all, without looking beyond the extant plays we can list a remarkable variety of locations: Persia, Argos, Thebes, Athens/Attica, Delphi, the Caucasus, Troy, Trachis, Lemnos, Pherai, Corinth, Aulis, Trozen, Phthia, the Crimea, Egypt. Is it not the variety, rather than the contrasts, which strikes us? Deserted, extra-political Lemnos; the Caucasus, hardly a political centre; Trachis, where Herakles has an *oikos* (household), true enough, but where the *polis* is almost an irrelevance; and, at the other end of the spectrum, the Argos of Aischylos' *Suppliants*, where the king must take a supremely political decision; not to mention the Argos and Athens of the *Oresteia*, both quintessentially political locations. Just what generalizations can we make amid all this diversity?

Richard Seaford's edition of Euripides' *Cyclops* has a thoughtful introduction in which he speculates that satyr-plays may be reintroducing an element—specifically, a non- or pre-political, wild element—which tragedy possessed in its 'original' form (compare Aristotle's brief remarks about tragedy's origins) but which it had lost by the time of the institutionalized production of the plays that have survived to us.[20] In other words, the argument goes, extant tragedy has a politicalness

[13] Hourmouziades (1965); Taplin (1977) and (1978) 31–57; Padel (1990).

[14] In Vernant and Vidal-Naquet (1988) 161–79.

[15] Zeitlin in Winkler and Zeitlin (1990) 130–67; Bernardini (2000); Berman (2002), (2004), and (2007).

[16] Saïd (1993); Avezzù (2004).

[17] See 25–30 above, and Buxton (1992b).

[18] Croally (1994).

[19] General: Rehm (2002) and Easterling (2005b). One among many particular studies: Rodighiero (2011).

[20] Seaford (1984).

about it which satyr-play does not. Seaford's contrast is admittedly speculative, but it is impossible to deny that again and again tragedy does come back to the question of what it is to live in a *polis:* its claims (*Antigone*), its tensions (*Eumenides*), its being necessary to a civilized life yet, like any collectivity, fraught with drawbacks (*Philoktetes*).

If we assume that tragedy is, centrally, about what it is to live in a *polis*, how do we relate this to our 'here-and-there' opposition?

We may begin with the easier pole: 'here'. Tragic Athens is unlike anywhere else. Its democracy is glorified as early as *Persians* (241–2):

> *Queen*: Who shepherds them? Who acts as master over their army?
> *Chorus*: They are called the slaves and subjects of no man.

In *Eumenides*, Athens is the home of Athene, where persuasion enables the reaching of an end unattainable either by the ensnaring intrigues of *dolos* ('trickery') or by the bloody right hand of *bia* ('violence'). In *Medea*, Athens is a refuge, a paradise, the home of sweetness, harmony, and wisdom (824–45). In *The Madness of Herakles*, Theseus promises the slayer of wife and children that Athens will offer him acceptance, dignity, and fame (1322–35):

> Obey the law and leave your native Thebes,
> And follow after me to Pallas' city.
> There I shall purify your hands from pollution,
> Give you a home and a share of my wealth
> And when you die and go to Hades,
> . . . .
> All Athens' citizens shall raise you up a monument
> Of stone, and honour you with sacrifice.
> For thus my people, helping a noble man,
> Shall win from the Greeks a lovely crown of fame.

These are not the only examples, nor are they untypical. (It is no coincidence that the authoritarian Theseus of *Hippolytos* acts out his grim confrontation with his stepson not in Athens but over the sea in Trozen.) I agree with Simon Goldhill when he observes that 'I do not think Athens is seriously challenged as the home of [the] civilization of the *polis*.'[21] That is not, of course, to say that Athens as portrayed in tragedy is 'here', in the sense of being in some way an authentic representation of Athenian life. On the contrary, the picture is

[21] Goldhill (1987) 68.

aspirational and inspirational, no less than, although not in the same way as, the image projected by the Funeral Speeches.

Issues relevant to the Athenian 'here' are explored in dramas located elsewhere. Contrasts between persuasion, deception, and violence are as relevant to life on Lemnos as they are on the Areopagos; the duties and conflicts attaching to the accepting of suppliants perplex Argive Pelasgos no less than Athenian Theseus; the political and moral dilemmas relating to decisions about burying dead warriors bother Aias' former comrades at Troy and Kreon in Thebes, just as they do Theseus near Athens in Euripides' *Suppliants*. But can we characterize these other places, these 'theres', in order to arrive at a clearer understanding of the kind of relationship in which they stand to Athens?

Froma Zeitlin analysed the portrayal of Thebes in tragedy. In her view, 'Thebes' is a *topos* in the metaphorical as well as the literal sense: a distinctive place, the focus of recurrent images and concepts which constitute it as 'the negative model to Athens' manifest image of itself with regard to its notions of the proper management of city, society and self'. Zeitlin sees this Thebes as a quintessentially *tragic* place: 'Thebes consistently supplies the radical tragic terrain where there can be no escape from the tragic in the resolution of conflict or in the institutional provision of a civic future beyond the world of the play'.[22] (The contrast with the end of the *Oresteia* could hardly be more evident.) On this challenging reading, Thebes becomes an elsewhere in polar opposition to Athens, in such a way that 'there' is not only *contrasted* with 'here', but actually *more tragic*.

Zeitlin's account is well worth reading; what I find ultimately unconvincing in it is its schematicness. Zeitlin sets Thebes up as *the* other place par excellence, where, dominated by the transgressive Dionysos and the doomed house of Laios, disaster reigns and escape is impossible. Argos, by contrast with both Athens and Thebes, is a middle term: witness Orestes, riven by conflict yet ultimately redeemable. But how, then, are we to draw onto this polarized map all those other places which are 'not-Athens'? Troy, for instance: in *Aias*, it is a male space, a space for honour-disputes between heroes; in *Trojan Women*, it is a limbo for females, between a past of dead Trojans and a future of live Greeks; in *Agamemnon*, it is yet a third kind of space,

[22] Zeitlin (1990) 131.

contrasted with Argos yet terribly, tragically like it. Where does Troy fit into the Thebes/Athens polarity? Or Trachis? Or Corinth? Best then, I suggest, to keep much of Zeitlin's description of Thebes, without accepting the total polarity which it seems to entail.[23] I would be happier to follow Suzanne Saïd's more nuanced and less schematically ambitious approach in analysing 'tragic Argos',[24] and to see this followed up with work on tragic Troy, tragic Delphi, and so on. Thebes is not *the* 'other place'.

4. IDEOLOGY

So far, I have tried to suggest how intricate is the temporal and, even more, the spatial *va-et-vient* to be found in tragedy. I turn now to the third and most perplexing heading under which to consider tragic proximity-and-distance. To what extent do tragedies corroborate dominant *ideological* positions which might be thought to be common ground for the viewing public; and to what extent do they stand outside them, to question or even subvert them? Are tragedies, ideologically speaking, 'here' or 'there'?[25]

We may begin with the (I assume) uncontentious observation that tragedies often echo ideological assumptions embedded in the life of the *polis*. For example, women behaving mannishly or men womanishly are

[23] Similar criticism in Croally (1994) 38–42, 188–91, 205–7, 213–14; Rehm (2003) 27–9; Easterling (2005b); Taplin (2010).

[24] Though even Saïd goes a bit too far towards Zeitlinesque schematism when she asserts (1993, 174) that 'Argos is not per se a tragic space: at least in all the "return-plays", tragic action always comes to Argos from the outside'. Where, if not from outside, does Dionysos 'come from' in *Bakchai*?

[25] In talking of ideology I shall broadly follow the example of Cartledge (1993), in his series of studies of 'ideological oppositions' in Greek thought [Greek/barbarian, free/slave, man/woman, etc]. Cartledge says at one point (121) that he intends to leave open the question of whether the Aristotelian doctrine of natural slavery should be 'classed properly as philosophy... or rather as ideology, *that is a doctrine consciously or unconsciously overdetermined by social rather than philosophical imperatives*'. It is with such a general sense of 'ideology' that I shall operate, viz. one which implies a structure of ideas, consciously or unconsciously held, and underpinned by social factors. Cf. also Rehm (2003) 87: ideology is 'the nexus of basic assumptions that members of a society hold (or are expected to hold), into which they are educated or indoctrinated, and for which they are rewarded'. Some notes on the history of the concept can be found under the relevant entry in Kuper and Kuper (1985) 375–6; more detail in Dierse (1982). Helpful too is Freeden (2003).

represented with animal imagery which portrays their conduct as monstrous and therefore unnatural (as in Kassandra's description of Klytaimestra and Aigisthos in *Agamemnon* (1223–34)). Again, slaves may be instrumental in the tragic deaths of others (*Hippolytos*), and are often sensitive to the sufferings of their social superiors (the Theban shepherd in *Oidipous Tyrannos*, the nurse in *Libation-Bearers*, and many others), but they do not themselves experience a tragic reversal of fortune, or commit suicide—that is reserved for the free and noble. But let us immediately go on to make another and (I imagine) equally uncontentious assertion: that tragedies often call ideological assumptions into question. We need look no further than *Medea*, where any preconceived ideas about the automatic rightness of Greek husband against barbarian wife are rendered highly problematic by the play. How do we come to terms with this paradox?

A helpful place to start is Simon Goldhill's article on the Dionysia and civic ideology.[26] Goldhill looks first at certain elements of the ceremonies preceding the tragic festival, such as the self-glorification of the city of Athens through the bringing of tribute into the theatre by representatives of Athens' imperial subjects, and the praising of orphan sons of men who had died in battle, orphans who now, having reached the threshold of manhood, parade in full hoplite uniform; and he then considers some examples of the content of the tragedies. Goldhill conclusively shows how the tragedies may undercut the ceremonies. A clear instance is the contrasting role of the ephebe, the young male on the verge of manhood, in the preplay ceremony and in Sophokles' *Philoktetes*. In the ceremony, '[t]he herald at the parade of orphans proclaims the city's education and support of the boys, and the boys' future support of the city as hoplites and citizens... Yet Neoptolemos' involvement in the *Philoktetes* dramatizes a conflict between moral and social values and a commitment to the collective need of the Trojan expedition. Neoptolemos is put in the position of refusing his military role in order to maintain his notions of what is right.'[27] Goldhill's view is that tragedy's role is to 'problematize the norm', which role is in turn linked to the patronage of smiling/dangerous, boundary-collapsing Dionysos. To quote Goldhill again: 'It is the *interplay between norm and transgression* enacted in the tragic festival that makes it a Dionysiac occasion.'[28]

[26] Goldhill (1987). [27] Goldhill (1987) 73.
[28] Goldhill (1987) 76; the italics are his.

On this I would say three things. First: the contrast between preplay ceremonies and tragedies is indeed an important one. Second: the analysis of this contrast as an 'interplay between norm and transgression' looks ultimately more like a redescription than an explanation. Third: it is characteristic of the 1980s and 1990s that the preferred level of analysis is 'superstructural' (in terms of religion) rather than 'infrastructural' (with reference to socioeconomic conditions).

To point the contrast, it may be instructive to look back to a book published in 1978, V. Citti's *Tragedia e lotta di classe in Grecia*.[29] After discussing a series of polarities explored in tragedy (male/female, citizen/foreigner, old/young, Greek/barbarian, immortal/mortal, etc.), Citti concluded that Athenian tragedy is an 'apparato ideologico dello stato' (269) which reinforces in the ruling class a sense of its own superiority, and confirms in the ruled a sense of their own natural inferiority. Citti did allow for exceptions and 'contradictions', but did not, to my mind, evolve a satisfactory model to accommodate *both* the 'apparato ideologico' perspective *and* the 'exceptions'. He could, in fact, have retained his general, Marx-oriented, approach *and* accounted for exceptions/contradictions if he had borrowed the approach exemplified in *Ways of Seeing*, a study written by the novelist and art historian John Berger. For Berger, himself inspired by Marx, great artists can call into question the ideological preconceptions of their age even while apparently sharing them. An example is Rembrandt who, while seeming to follow a painterly tradition of celebrating ownership of private property, actually, through the impression of transience conveyed among other things by his brushwork, questions the permanence of such values.[30] Citti would have been more convincing if he had followed Berger's implied explanatory model, which incorporates the notions of 'confirming', 'questioning', *and* 'individual genius'.[31]

But we still have problems. For can we, as the Berger model would suggest, equate the questioning aspect of the tragic genre with artistic greatness? Is it only when they are calling ideology into question that Greek tragedians reach their most impressive, Rembrandtesque heights? I wonder. Do we not, in that case, have trouble with the end of *Eumenides*, where celebration of an Athenian ideal looks

[29] Citti (1978). [30] Berger (1972) 110–12.
[31] I made this point in Buxton (1981).

compatible with what (on most criteria) one would want to recognize as the culmination of a towering artistic achievement? Like any pair of hermeneutic spectacles, the ones whose lenses are labelled 'ambiguity' and 'paradox' can lead us to see some things but miss others.

I do not propose to offer a radically new model for understanding the mixture of celebration-and-questioning to be found in tragedy. Instead, I would start from the position set out by Goldhill, but would modify it in two respects.

First, in spite of my reservation about ambiguity/paradox there is indeed much to be said in favour of stressing the importance of Dionysos, an emphasis which attributes the centrality of questioning *to the whole genre*, and not just (as the Berger model would have it) to the particularly insightful bits of it. Nevertheless, we still have to *explain* the anomalousness of this extraordinary, institutionalized, radical, public, profound, popular self-examination. Dionysos, after all, was to be found all over Greece: why was it specifically in Athens that tragedy developed?[32] To account for *that*, we need, it seems to me, to retain an explanatory element involving social tensions—to add, in fact, a dose of Vernant and Vidal-Naquet, with their emphasis on the socially generated dislocation between a heroic past and a radically politicized, Athenian present.

Secondly, I would accept Goldhill's notion of 'norm-testing', which rightly makes tragedy do in extreme form what other types of myth-telling do in less extreme form; but I would take the notion further. I suggest that, borrowing the engineers' phrase, we might speak of 'testing to destruction'. What we find in tragedy is a kind of drastic experimentation, resulting in a controlled catastrophe. Through the medium of tragic myth, Athenian society was able to test the weaknesses in its own structures in such a way that, however terrifying the consequences *within* the dramatic frame, the society which held that frame could continue to function.[33]

[32] See now Carter (2011), a very substantial volume devoted to precisely this question.

[33] Testing weaknesses: cf. the not dissimilar view of Meier (1993, 4): 'It seems possible that we have here a rather special example of a social body carrying out quite publicly *the maintenance and development of its mental infrastructure*' (my emphasis). Society continues to function: cf. Osborne (1993, 34), who goes so far as to suggest that the city's tolerance of competition in relation to the 'promotion of issues' in drama is to be seen as a sign of *confidence*.

I would like to make one more observation about the debate over ideology; and this brings me to the final part of this chapter. I wish to urge that we register the *complexity* of the concept of 'ideology in tragedy'.[34] My chosen example is designed to show that any talk of a tragedy's straightforwardly 'confirming' or 'subverting' the ideology of the *polis* is likely to be wildly simplistic:

> This I will tell you—see how right I am.
> The woman you call the mother of the child
> Is not the parent, just a nurse to the seed,
> The new-sown seed that grows and swells inside her.
> The man is the source of life—the one who mounts.
> She, like a stranger for a stranger, keeps
> The shoot alive unless god hurts it.
> I'll give you proof that all I say is true.
> The father could produce a child, without a mother.
> Here she stands, our living witness. Look—
> Child sprung from Olympian Zeus,
> Never bred in the darkness of the womb
> But such a stock as no goddess could conceive![35]

How is Apollo's famous argument from *Eumenides* to be taken? After suggesting two points of orientation from the scholarly literature, I shall offer my own comments.

On the one hand, there is the approach exemplified in an article by Froma Zeitlin. 'If Aischylos is concerned with world-building,' she writes, 'the cornerstone of his architecture is the control of woman, the social and cultural prerequisite for the construction of civilization. The *Oresteia* stands squarely within the misogynistic tradition which pervades Greek thought, a bias which both projects a combative dialogue in male-female interactions and which relates the mastery of the female to higher social goals.'[36] Subsequently, W. Blake Tyrrell and Frieda S. Brown, building on Zeitlin, sought to expose what they saw as a patriarchal hijacking of the interpretation of the *Oresteia*, and in particular of the interpretation of Apollo's argument. For Tyrrell and Brown, those who seek to minimize the importance of

[34] Peter Wilson (2011, 19) has recently put the matter well: not only was 'ideological complexity, even tension' fundamental to Athenian democracy, but also tragic *representation* 'exceeds any simple ideological or historical determinism'.

[35] Aesch. *Eum.* 657–66; trans. adapted from Fagles (1966).

[36] Zeitlin (1978) 150.

Apollo's case by casting it as mere sophistry are masking the true, central import of what is said: 'Apollo's theory,' they say, 'coincides with the democracy's restriction of meaning-making to the male'.[37] Now there is some rather curious logic in Tyrrell and Brown's analysis: for example, they interpret Athenian belief in autochthony exclusively as an escape from the mother as parent, without mentioning that it hardly does much for the father's role either.[38] But let us concentrate on the general point, namely that Tyrrell and Brown, as well as Zeitlin, represent what has become a popular, and certainly politically correct, view of Apollo's argument. For these scholars, Apollo is giving an authoritative codification of a scientific theory with profound ideological ramifications: we have to take it seriously as expressing a deep-seated, male-oriented view of the cosmos and the male's dominant place within it.

In the opposite corner there is Alan Sommerstein, who wrote the commentary on *Eumenides* in the Cambridge Greek and Latin Classics series. Sommerstein's conclusion is as follows: 'The audience thus probably saw Apollo's argument as a clever and specious but fallacious piece of forensic pleading; and so apparently do half the all-male jury. Not so easily can motherhood be argued out of existence.'[39] This is exactly the kind of position attacked by Zeitlin, and by Tyrrell and Brown. How does Sommerstein reach his conclusions, and what do we make of this clash of views?

The first point first. After noting that Apollo's theory closely resembles that attributed by Aristotle to Anaxagoras and other *phusiologoi*, and that 'it is arbitrary to deny that [Anaxagoras'] teachings could have been known to educated Athenians of the late 460s and early 450s' (that is, the time of the *Oresteia*), Sommerstein argues on several grounds that the audience is unlikely to have found this dramatized scientific theory convincing. Some of Sommerstein's arguments are linguistic, and relate to the verbal landscape of the trilogy. For example: in denying that the mother is the *tokeus* ('bearer') of the child, Apollo goes against the trilogy's frequent linkage of the related verb *tiktein* ('give birth to') with, precisely, the

[37] Tyrrell and Brown (1991) 127.
[38] Tyrrell and Brown (1991) 127.
[39] Sommerstein (1989) 208, n. on lines 657–66.

mother. Then there are more general arguments, relating to what we can hypothetically reconstruct of assumptions likely to have been shared by audience and playwright. Sommerstein points out that Apollo's theory was a minority one even amongst scientist/philosophers, most of whom affirmed that male as well as female contributed 'seed' in the process of generation.[40] Moreover—an interesting point, this—we apparently know of no instance of an *actual* forensic case in ancient Greece being built on a scientific theory. Perhaps, bearing in mind the mass nature of juries, it was simply too dangerous to expose oneself to ridicule or prejudice (we may think of Aristophanes' *Clouds*) by aligning oneself, and therefore one's client, with a particular, fashionable, potentially controversial view.

Some of Sommerstein's points are less convincing than others: he attributes more significance, in terms of likely theatrical impact, to linguistic details than might be thought advisable; and he gives insufficient weight to the diversity of response to be expected from the Athenian audience. But, taken as a whole, his case seems to me impressive; not least because it engages with the detail of Aischylos' Greek. But does it actually support the conclusion that 'the audience . . . probably saw Apollo's argument as a clever and specious but fallacious piece of forensic pleading'? I do not see it like that. I believe that Sommerstein's marginalization of Apollo's theory as 'fallacious' fails to capture the *theatrical* centrality of Apollo's advocacy, at this point in this trilogy.

In the course of the *Oresteia* there are certain pivotal moments, moments of crisis, of indecision. One such moment is Agamemnon's at Aulis: Shall I be a deserter, thus abandoning a just expedition sanctioned by Zeus; or kill my daughter Iphigeneia? Somehow a decision is taken, thanks to a paradoxical act and a 'knocking sideways' of the wits. In the second play, another character, Orestes, has to face another impossible decision: kill my mother, or leave my father's honour unavenged? Somehow, a decision is taken: three lines from Pylades, recalling Apollo's injunction, tip Orestes' resolution in the direction of murder. And so to the third play. For the

[40] See in general G. E. R. Lloyd (1983) 86–111.

third time, matters are at a crisis, on a knife-edge. How to resolve the unresolvable dilemma about Orestes' crime? Somehow a decision is taken, thanks to an extraordinary, amazing, unpredictable intervention, a dramatic coup—neither something which (as the Zeitlin/Tyrrell/Brown approach might suggest) everybody really believed anyway, for that would drastically reduce the dramatic impact; nor something evidently fallacious—which would also reduce its impact. Rather, a triumph of *peithō* ('persuasion'), a theatrical sensation: not an answer to the unanswerable—for the unanswerable has no answer—but, in context, a brilliant piece of advocacy, just enough to tip the balance.

In this respect it resembles a famous scene from Shakespeare's *The Merchant of Venice* (Act IV, Scene 1):

> *Portia*: A pound of that same merchant's flesh is thine,
> The court awards it, and the law doth give it.
> *Shylock*: Most rightful judge!
> *Portia*: And you must cut this flesh from off his breast,
> The law allows it, and the court awards it.
> *Shylock*: Most learned judge! A sentence! Come, prepare!
> *Portia*: Tarry a little, there is something else.
> This bond doth give thee here no jot of blood;
> The words expressly are 'a pound of flesh'.
> Take then thy bond, take thou thy pound of flesh,
> But in the cutting it if thou dost shed
> One drop of Christian blood, thy lands and goods
> Are by the laws of Venice confiscate
> Unto the state of Venice.

Naturally, the Shakespearean scene too has been and should be read in relation to ideology (Christian versus Jew is the obvious polarity to explore first). But the shattering *theatrical* effect of the argument, coming, as it were, *ex machina*, is also very much part of the game. One editor, while noting that Portia's judgement combines strict observance of the law with respect for the principle of equity, suggests that 'what [Shakespeare] was pursuing was not legal theory but dramatic effect'.[41] Replace 'legal' with 'physiological', and the same may be said of Aischylos.

[41] Mahood (2003) 18.

5. CONCLUSIONS

First, one of Greek tragedy's defining characteristics is the peculiar blend of proximity and distance, in relation to time, space, and ideology, constituted by the myths re-enacted in the theatre. No myths are raw: all are cooked by the context. Proximity-and-distance is one of the key ingredients of tragic cookery.

Second, ideology in tragedy is not a unitary presence to be confirmed or subverted. It is fluid, subtle, informing the drama in numerous ways and at numerous levels, feeding back into society from the public festival of the Dionysia, and in turn nourished by particular streams (as with Anaxagoras' theory) which flow from society—streams which (to change the metaphor) are woven into the dramatic fabric, and situated in a theatrical as well as a social context.[42]

[42] I would like to thank the participants in a colloquium held at the Universidad Nacional de Educación a Distancia, Madrid, 2–5 March 1994, for their helpful comments; the remarks of Bernd Seidensticker were especially acute. Simon Goldhill and Vanda Zajko have also been kind enough to give me their reactions to the chapter, and I have done my best to take account of these. In addition, on a particular point I derived much benefit from a conversation with Thomas Johansen.

8

Bafflement in Greek Tragedy

The present chapter, like the previous two, discusses works by all three of the great Greek tragedians. But its scope is narrower than that of Chapters 6 and 7. Returning to an issue raised at the end of Chapter 6, I test the idea that tragic myth-telling may be characterized by a shared interest in the ultimate inexplicability of events.

A proper investigation into the possibility that Greek tragedies may in some respects be baffling—in the sense of not being fully interpretable—is an undertaking more appropriate for a long book than for a single chapter. To make the inquiry more manageable I shall concentrate on a more limited (though still broad) topic, by asking how far it is possible to give a satisfactory answer to the question: 'Why does what happens in a Greek tragedy happen?' I shall look at a range of contrasting plays, in the hope of putting together an analysis which, if not comprehensive, may at least be representative.

I begin with a work in which the account of why things happen seems to be, if not wholly consistent, then at least *reasonably* transparent: Aischylos' *Persians*.[1] In that play, a similar explanation for the defeat of the Persians by the Greeks is offered by several different characters. The Newsbringer ('Messenger'), the Queen Mother, the Chorus, and Xerxes all agree on the role of a *daimōn* ('divine power') or *theos/theoi* ('god', 'gods') in bringing about the Persian catastrophe.[2] A variant of the same view is expressed by the ghost of

[1] I have considerably modified the remarks which I made about *Persians* in the original version of this chapter, in order to do more justice, as I now think, to the play's complexity.

[2] Newsbringer: 345 (*daimōn*), 354 (*daimōn*), 373 (*theoi*), 454 (*theos*). Queen Mother: 294 (*theoi*), 472 (*daimōn*), 601 (*daimōn*), 845 (*daimōn*). Chorus: 515 (*daimōn*), 921 (*daimōn*). Xerxes: 911 (*daimōn*), 942 (*daimōn*).

Darius.[3] On hearing that Xerxes had tried to yoke the Hellespont, Darius concludes (725):

> Alas, there came a great divine power (*daimōn*) to rob him of his wits.

and a little later (742):

> When a man is himself eager, the god (*theos*) takes part too.

It must be conceded that the characteristics and source of the divine intervention in *Persians* are not entirely uniform, since there occurs what one might describe as a clarificatory shift (to put it no more strongly) from explanation in terms of a generalized *phthonos* ('envy'; e.g. 362) on the part of gods who deceive human beings and lead them on, to an affirmation of the specific function of Zeus as chastizer of the over-bold (especially 532–6, 827–8).[4] Human motivation too is recognized—not only the recklessness of Xerxes in overstepping divinely sanctioned limits, but also the courage of the Greeks.[5] But, allowing for these not inconsiderable nuances, the explanation which gradually takes hold is that Xerxes has transgressed and, as a result or as a concomitant, the gods have been instrumental in his destruction.

In certain other tragedies the explanation of why things happen is a good deal more intricate. I take as an example Sophokles' *Women of Trachis*. Who is responsible for the tragic events of this play?

(a) Is Deianeira responsible? It is evident that the sending of the poisoned robe is the direct prelude to Herakles' downfall. But this act is done in a spirit not of hostility but of desperate hopelessness, and ignorance, and love. Deianeira acts in the condition in which all mortals are forced to act: limited knowledge. Too late she recognizes what she has done.

(b) Is Herakles responsible? His pursuit of Iole, and his decision to introduce her into his own *oikos* ('household'), are the things which prompt Deianeira to take her own desperate remedy. Yet Herakles

[3] In the original version of this chapter I wrote of 'a view which is restated authoritatively by the ghost of Darius'. In the same vein R. Parker (2009, 128) argues that Darius speaks 'with absolute authority'. However I am now persuaded by the comments of Mark Griffith (discussion in Parker, ibid. 155–6) that even Darius' opinions need to be situated dramatically, *and thus qualified*.

[4] See Winnington-Ingram (1983, 1–2), who goes so far as to speak, not of a shift, but of a contradiction; cf. also Paduano (1978), esp. ch. 5, 'Zeus e la giustizia'.

[5] See the excellent remarks of Jouanna (1981, 4–7) about contrasting perspectives on the causation of the Persian defeat.

himself is not an entirely independent and free agent. As the News-bringer says, Lichas had announced that 'Eros alone of the gods bewitched Herakles' into sacking the city in which Iole lived (354–5); and in a choral ode the women of Trachis similarly sing about the great power of Aphrodite (497–502).

(c) Is Eros—or Aphrodite—then responsible for what happens? It is true that the chorus sings memorably about the power of Kypris (Aphrodite). But Sophokles does not portray Herakles and Deianeira as merely the puppets of love: what we see and hear about in *Women of Trachis* is a series of events in which, whatever involvement of divine powers there may be, we still see mortals deciding, and acting upon their decisions.

(d) How about the centaur Nessos, who had planted the piece of false information which led to Deianeira's fatal mistake? Is *he* responsible for what happens? In a sense it is that planted information which provides the catalyst for Herakles' downfall. But it would be grotesque to stress the role of the dead centaur to the exclusion of Herakles and Deianeira and the power of love. It is only because the relationship of Herakles and Deianeira is as it is that there is room for Nessos' scheme to operate.

(e) What of Iole? It is her introduction into the house which precipitates the disaster. But throughout she is presented, not as a causal agent, but as a passive victim—a victim of the power of love and the overwhelming violence of Herakles. Throughout the play she is silent—the still centre of the storm. It would again be absurd to regard this passive victim as 'responsible' for what happens.

(f) Lastly, Zeus. The concluding words of the play are:

k'ouden toutōn hoti mē Zeus

They are not easy to translate. 'Zeus is the cause of all this'? 'Zeus is at work in all this'? Literally: 'There is none of these things which is not Zeus.' But surely it would take a logician of a very literal-minded kind to infer from this that all the examples of human decision and choice witnessed in the course of the previous one and a half hours were really an illusion. It is true that in *Women of Trachis* the prophecies concerning the end of Herakles' troubles (155–72, 821–8, 1159–78) derive from Zeus, at his oracular shrine in Dodona. Nevertheless it is also true that at no point in the play have the will and purposes of

Zeus been in any way manifest; on the contrary, they have seemed inscrutably remote. Zeus cannot be simply 'blamed' for what has happened.

In fact, to go through the play apportioning blame in this way does not bear much relation to what is actually experienced in the theatre. There, the audience experiences the complex interplay of *all* the wills, human and divine, which I have been discussing: to isolate one of them is quite false to the complexity of the drama. What the audience senses is that these various wills and forces seem to be converging 'inevitably' (as we say) towards the tragically wasteful conclusion. This awful feeling of the inevitable convergence of the human and the divine is far more important than any mechanical apportionment of responsibility.

From the *relatively* uncomplicated case of *Persians* we have moved to the more complex situation in *Women of Trachis*. But even in *Women of Trachis*, it seems to me, we are dealing precisely with complexity rather than with a dramatic representation which resists explanation. However, we have by no means finished: for there are some tragedies which, in my view, do indeed resist explanation, either in whole or in part; that is, there are some moments in some plays—indeed some plays in their entirety—which are not just complex but actually baffling, either because there is insufficient evidence to decide upon an interpretation or (more interestingly) because there is too much evidence—contradictory evidence.

For a first example of a baffling moment we may turn to Euripides' *Bakchai*. The three central scenes in the play consist of confrontations between Dionysos and Pentheus. In the first of these scenes Pentheus believes himself to be in control, with Dionysos being led in as his prisoner. In the third of the scenes it is the god who is in control: Pentheus has been dressed in woman's clothing, and his behaviour is that of (in the words of E. R. Dodds) a 'giggling, leering creature' with whom Dionysos plays sadistically.[6] The transition between these two situations occurs in the middle scene—and it occurs instantaneously.[7] At line 809 Pentheus calls out to his attendants, 'Bring weapons out to me; and *you* [i.e. Dionysos] be quiet.' At line 811 Dionysos asks, 'Do

[6] Dodds (1960) 192.

[7] One critic who does not think it is a turning point is Oranje (1984) 82.

you want to see [the maenads] sitting together on the mountains?', to which Pentheus replies, 'Yes indeed! I would give a great weight of gold for it.' Between the two lines, Dionysos has uttered the monosyllable *ā*. What has happened?

Dodds (on lines 810–12) suggests that the exclamation here means 'Stop!'—which does not get us very far. Most critics agree that *ā* marks an important turning point (R. P. Winnington-Ingram: 'the exclamation marks a change in their relationship'; Jeanne Roux: 'Elle marque dans la pièce un tournant décisif'), but the nature of this change is far from clear. Winnington-Ingram suggests that the exclamation may 'perhaps' be accompanied by an 'intense stare and a grasping of Pentheus's hands, as [Dionysos] begins to exert some kind of psychic power over his victim'.[8] J. E. Sandys glosses the exclamation rather bathetically with: 'Suddenly a bright thought strikes the Stranger'; a more sophisticated interpretation would see in Pentheus a victim of hypnosis.[9] I have even heard it proposed that *ā* marks a moment when Dionysos metaphorically seduces Pentheus—a not wholly wrong-headed idea when one remembers Pentheus' awareness of the stranger's physical attractiveness (453) as well as the sexual dimension to Pentheus' imaginings about the maenads. However, such attempts to fill out the enigmatic text surely miss the point. We do not know what has happened to Pentheus in straightforward psychological terms, because what has happened to him cannot be accounted for in straightforward psychological terms: *ā* signifies the moment when the power of the god breaks out of its confines. It is an uncanny moment, a moment which is altogether too much to comprehend—and not only for the individual mortal who has to cope with it onstage: it is a moment ultimately baffling, which cannot be fully explained by the spectators in the theatre.[10]

An equally baffling and even more controversial moment occurs in the *parodos* of Aischylos' *Agamemnon*. The omen of the eagles' feast is one of the great Problems posed by the play. Why—countless hundreds of scholars have asked themselves—should (on Kalchas' interpretation) Artemis become angry with the leaders of the Greek expedition against Troy because of the fact that two eagles ominously

[8] Winnington-Ingram (1948) 102; Roux (1972) on line 810.

[9] See Sandys (1900) lv. Dodds (1960, 172) wisely advises against the hypnosis theory.

[10] The case for the indefinability of *ā* is well put by Goldhill (1986) 284–5.

devour a pregnant hare before the expedition departs (134–7)? Other versions of the myth give a clear reason for the hostility of Artemis—a reckless boast by Agamemnon about his hunting prowess, sometimes compounded by sacrilegious intrusion into Artemis' sacred grove (the *Kypria*; Sophokles' *Elektra*).[11] The *Oresteia* replaces the transgression with an omen which—so it has been usual to argue—contains the clues to the cause of Artemis' motive. However, the detective work has proved difficult. The anger has been related (to name only some of the more popular views) to her 'traditional' (and therefore to-be-read-into-the-text) partisanship for the Trojans;[12] to the imminent sacrifice of Iphigeneia;[13] to the future destruction of young and innocent life at Troy.[14] The debate continues, and shows no sign of resolution.[15] The difficulty is that at the heart of the search for a cause is a void: the link between the eagles and the Atreidai is one of analogy, so that it is enormously difficult to make a *causal* link between the Atreidai on the one hand and Artemis' loathing of the eagles' feast on the other.[16] My own view—and this, in the light of the argument so far, will come as no surprise—is that the causality must remain a mystery: we have here a case where the interrelations between humans and gods are ultimately baffling. One may well agree, therefore, with William Whallon when he states that the reason for Artemis' anger is 'a manifold problem, almost to be worked out by several kinds of analysis, but finally resistant to our efforts'.[17]

From two baffling moments let us turn to a baffling play. At the beginning of Euripides' *The Madness of Herakles*, the hero is away performing his twelfth, last, and most difficult Labour, the capturing of the multi-headed dog Kerberos from Hades. Meanwhile his father, his wife Megara, and their children have been kidnapped by the usurper Lykos, who is on the point of murdering them. Then, in the nick of time, Herakles arrives to save them. But, just as his prosperity

[11] See Peradotto (1969) 242.

[12] Lloyd-Jones (1962) 190.

[13] Whallon (1961) 81.

[14] Neitzel (1979) 16: 'In line 134 her motive is expressed clearly and explicitly: *oiktos*, "pity" [with the hare and her young; which means: with Troy and its inhabitants]' (my translation).

[15] For comments on the history of interpretations of the problem see Bollack and Judet de La Combe (1981) 175. Sommerstein (2010, 258–61) offers a recent, reasoned approach.

[16] Cf. Elata-Alster (1985) 28.

[17] Whallon (1980) 27.

and success seem to be at their height, the goddesses Iris and Lyssa appear above the house. Lyssa has been sent by Hera to make Herakles mad: and mad he is duly made. He kills his wife and children, and is only prevented from the ultimate crime of killing his own father by Athene, who hurls a rock at him and knocks him senseless. When he comes to, his shame is so great that he sees suicide as the only way out; but, in a deeply moving and humane end to the play, he is persuaded to go on living by his friend Theseus, who offers him hope, and a home, in Athens.

The problem is: what is the explanation for Herakles' madness? Iris announces that Hera wants to make Herakles guilty of shedding his children's blood; and that she, Iris, wants it too—a horribly capricious-sounding affirmation (831–2). But is there any more to the destruction of Herakles than the mere whim of the gods? Wilamowitz famously argued that Herakles' madness was an extension of his earlier violent and bloodthirsty career (cf. the reported remark of Amphitryon at 966–7: 'Surely blood-murder has not sent you mad?').[18] E. M. Blaiklock, in a book revealingly entitled *The Male Characters of Euripides: A Study in Realism*, accounted for Herakles' behaviour in terms of his suffering an epileptic fit; Blaiklock noted that epilepsy and 'greatness' are known on occasions to coincide, as with Julius Caesar, Mahomet, Peter the Great, Charles V, Napoleon, and Flaubert.[19] These interpretations are of a kind familiar to us from our discussion of the central confrontation scene in *Bakchai*—they are attempts to fill out the text with psychological explanations for which the evidence is either scarce (Wilamowitz) or absent (Blaiklock). Other scholars have tried to explain the madness with reference to Hera's resentment towards Herakles because he was the product of Zeus' extramarital affair with Alkmene.[20] It is worth pointing out, though, that this resentment is not actually very prominent in the play—though it certainly is mentioned, as one possible retrospective explanation for the catastrophe, after Herakles returns to sanity (e.g. 1308–12). One more possible means of explaining the madness is hinted at by Iris at 841–2:

[18] Wilamowitz-Moellendorff (1895) i. 128.

[19] Blaiklock (1952) 126–7. Mattes (1970, 83) found in the epileptic fit a model for the description of Herakles' madness.

[20] On Hera as a sender of madness, see Mattes (1970) 37–8.

> or the gods are nowhere,
> And mortal things will be great, if he does not pay the penalty.

But the penalty for what? To infer, as some scholars have done,[21] that the penalty is either for raising too high the condition of humanity, or else for Herakles' getting above himself in some vaguely hubristic sense, is not spelled out even in this line and a half, let alone anywhere else in the play.

In short: with *The Madness of Herakles*, as with certain aspects of *Bakchai* and *Agamemnon*, to admit to bafflement is, I would argue, not a fine-sounding cover-up for an inability to understand a dramatic problem, but rather the soundest and most faithful response to the complex evidence of the text.

Now in suggesting that bafflement should be seen as a justifiable reaction to certain tragedies I do not wish to be understood as advocating the 'infinite play of significances' view, a view which has become associated with the habit of thought known as 'deconstruction'. I start out from a premise which seems—to me at least—to be self-evident: that some things which happen in Greek tragedy are less difficult to understand than others. Take the joy of the abandoned Philoktetes as, in Sophokles' play, he hears the sound of Greek words being spoken (234). As a reader and spectator now, I feel—I think I can convince myself—enough continuity with that situation to comprehend and respond to the central emotions and ideas at work in it: the naïveté and gullibility and openness displayed by Philoktetes as a result of his isolation seem to me comprehensible, recognizable. I would qualify this in two ways. First there is a need, here as elsewhere in Greek tragedy, for anthropological spadework: for example, Philoktetes' isolation is expressed by his living in a cave, and this needs to be understood in terms of the specifically Greek symbolic landscape which includes (as well as caves) mountains, the sea, crossroads, the plain, the city, etc. Secondly, I am perfectly ready to admit that Philoktetes' reaction might well appear *hard* to understand in some other society than our own—a society of solo-habiting Polyphemoi, for instance. But, those qualifications apart, I would suggest that Philoktetes' joy is the very reverse of baffling.

[21] See refs. in Bond (1981) on 841f.

Nor, for that matter, is there much to be baffled by in the retort of the old but still spirited Oidipous at Kolonos: 'Suppose a man were trying to kill you, what would *you* do—ask him if he was your father?' (I paraphrase 992–4). I am not, then, saying that the whole of Greek tragedy is baffling. Nor am I saying that all scenes and plays which depict the interaction of the human and the divine are baffling (cf. the remarks above on *Persians* and *Women of Trachis*). What I am saying is that in some scenes, and indeed some plays—above all, scenes and plays which involve the juxtaposition of human and divine—it may be over-optimistic to seek, beyond the evidence of the text, to account fully for what is happening.

That it should be precisely in the area of the juxtaposition of human and divine that tragic bafflement may be located should cause no surprise. In Greek religion in general, encounters with the gods are always potentially dangerous, and the nature of the divine may be strange and inexplicable.[22] Ritual reflects the precariousness of the relationship by putting restrictions on the places and occasions when contact between humans and gods is possible, whether via the elaborate procedures associated with the consultation of oracles (typically located in remote, often mountainous areas) or through the carefully controlled and orchestrated act of communication with the gods known as sacrifice. In myths, comparably, encounters between gods and mortals are often thought of as occurring in areas outside the space normally occupied by the activities of household and village or city: Hesiod meets the Muses on Mount Helikon; Paris meets and judges the three goddesses on Mount Ida; Aphrodite has her brief encounter with Anchises on the same mountain; the affair between the Moon goddess and Endymion was conducted in a cave; and so on. Myths also regularly mark the dangers and unpredictability of encounters with the divine: witness the blinding of Teiresias, the thunderbolting of Semele, or Hippolytos' fatal meeting with the monstrous bull sent from the sea by Poseidon. What happens in tragedy is that these encounters across the boundary of mortality are scrutinized in the most striking way possible—by placing humans and gods side by side on the same stage (sometimes without the humans being aware of it, as in *Bakchai*). In this way the gods'

[22] Cf. the remarks of Gould (2001, 203–34) about the role of the gods as a means of imagining that which is alien and uncanny in experience.

unconfinability and unmanageability and unfathomability are seen at their most unnerving, and sometimes at their most baffling.

One final question imposes itself. If I am right about the prevalence of tragic bafflement, was this response also experienced by the original audiences of the tragedies?

Let us begin with the obvious point that not everyone in an audience, ancient or modern, reacts in the same way to what is on offer. In the case of the City Dionysia, one man has walked for hours to the centre of Athens from an outlying deme, not because he is much concerned with the finer points of theatrical performance—he is not—but because his son is in the chorus and he is tremendously proud of him. And here is a group from the island of Samos: they are in Athens on business, but today there is no one to do business *with*, as everyone is at the theatre—so they have come along too; and gladly so, because the famous Euripides is competing. And so it goes on: an audience is composed of persons with diverse degrees of enthusiasm, understanding, and commitment to the drama unfolding before them.

What concerns us then is not the hypothetical, collective response of the whole of an audience, but the varied reactions of some of its members. Within that more limited compass, can we assert with any plausibility that some members of ancient audiences may sometimes have experienced bafflement when faced with tragedy? There is surprisingly little direct evidence about fifth-century BC audience response to tragic drama, and what we do have is often hard to interpret. But there are certain things we can say with more or less probability. We can hardly doubt that ancient audiences listened to the *ideas* of the tragedians (cf. the frequent casting of poets in the role of teachers),[23] and were aware when those ideas differed from accepted tradition (as with the notice taken of Euripides—not least by Aristophanes—when he reflected new trends in religious belief). We can be sure too that discussions about the interrelations of human and divine causality will have been accessible to fifth-century audiences; one thinks, for example, of the arguments mounted by Gorgias in his *Encomium of Helen*, where what is at issue is precisely the question of what might have motivated Helen to abscond with Paris. But the suggestion that those audiences may specifically have

[23] The tradition which saw poets as teachers has (to me unconvincingly) been downplayed by Heath (1987), esp. 44–7.

experienced feelings of bafflement in the face of tragic drama is harder to prove.

There are, however, two points which may be relevant.

First: *within* many of the tragedies we find articulations of perplexity about how to understand what is happening, articulations which often come from the collective mouth of a chorus, whose role is commonly that of the confused bystander. A classic case is the song of the chorus of the eponymous hero's attendants in *Hippolytos*, unable to comprehend a situation in which their master has been cursed and banished by his father Theseus (1102–21):

> When I reflect that gods are concerned for human life,
> This thought brings relief in a time of trouble.
> Yet, though deep within me
> I cherish hope of a kind of understanding,
> I am baffled [*leipomai*, literally 'I fail, am left behind'] when I survey the mortal scene—
> On the one hand men's fortunes, on the other their deeds,
> Change follows change,
> Coming now from this side, now from that;
> Men's lives are uprooted, wandering is endless
> . . . .
> My mind is no longer clear;
> What I see is not what I expected.

One should not of course equate any single utterance within a tragedy with the play's 'message'; tragedies are too many-sided for that. In the case of *Hippolytos*, indeed, at various points the play attains—thanks above all to the initial and concluding interventions by Aphrodite and Artemis respectively—much greater clarity about causation than is implicit in the anxiety of the baffled chorus in the passage quoted above.[24] Nevertheless the chorus' words do at least present 'local' bafflement as the possible effect of the action upon a group of (within the dramatic context) 'ordinary' people.

Second: it seems to me that the producing of what I am calling bafflement could be regarded as particularly characteristic of Euripides. More even than Aischylos or Sophokles, Euripides loves to oblige his audience to look at an action first from one perspective,

[24] Which is *not*, of course, to suggest that the explanations given by either goddess are to be seen as 'the last word'.

and then from a different and contrasting one, so that their original assumptions about, for example, character, have to be reassessed. As Agamemnon is presented differently in *Agamemnon* and *Libation-Bearers*; as the broken Kreon of the end of *Antigone* differs from the tyrant portrayed earlier in the play; so in Euripides we find time and again the same phenomenon: Pentheus in *Bakchai*, Alkmene in *The Children of Herakles*, Jason, Hippolytos . . .[25] And even if it is maintained that such shifts are indicative of complexity rather than bafflement, it seems to me undeniable that there *are* Euripidean scenes, above all at the ends of his plays, which are desperately hard to come to terms with: that airborne escape by Medea,[26] or the extraordinary ending to *Orestes*, where Orestes is required to abandon on the instant his murderous intentions towards Hermione and to marry her instead. I would raise the possibilities (a) that bafflement is above all generated by Euripides; (b) that this might not only have been felt in antiquity, but might have been one reason for his being perceived by his contemporaries as a controversial and iconoclastic figure. But how could this be, given that, as I have argued, bafflement was a recurring feature of *all* tragedy? I agree with Donald Mastronarde when he writes: 'The concern with questioning, contingency, and double vision that is so prominent in Euripides is to be accepted as properly at home in the tragic tradition'.[27] But I would add that Euripides might have been felt to be pushing that which was 'at home' up to, and occasionally beyond, its limits. Whether the resulting sense of moral discomfort might have played a role in Euripides' (relative) lack of success in the dramatic competitions during his own lifetime[28] is a question which is easier to pose than to answer.[29]

[25] See Buxton (1982) 150–2. [26] See 110–16 above.

[27] Mastronarde (2010) 54.

[28] Though not afterwards, given the extent of revivals of his plays even as early as the fourth century BC: see Easterling (1993) 567, on the way in which Euripides soon came to prominence in 'the repertoire'.

[29] A version of this chapter was given as a lecture in the Hungarian Academy of Sciences in Budapest in 1987; in the same year a somewhat different version was presented at the universities of Newcastle upon Tyne and Reading. I am grateful to all three audiences for their valuable comments.

9

Blindness and Limits: Sophokles and the Logic of Myth

In each of Chapters 6–8, works by all three of the great Greek tragedians were discussed. In Chapters 9–11 the focus progressively narrows: from an analysis of a theme in the whole Sophoklean oeuvre (Chapter 9) we move to an account of one Euripidean play (Chapter 10), and then to an examination of just one theme in one play (Chapter 11). But this narrowing is only relative. In each of the final three chapters I seek to locate a particular dramatist's use of mythology within the wider cultural context.

To generalize about Aischylos is difficult; to generalize about Euripides is almost impossible; but to generalize about Sophokles is both possible and potentially rewarding. With Sophokles—or, rather, with the Sophokles of the seven fully extant tragedies—we can sense a mood, a use of language, and a style of play-making ('dramatic technique') which are largely shared by all seven works. Of these characteristics it is surely the mood which contains the quintessence of Sophoklean tragedy. My aim in the first section of this chapter will be to open the way to an appreciation of that mood by following up one of the most important themes in Sophokles: blindness. In the second section the scope of the inquiry will be widened: I shall show that, in using the blindness theme, Sophokles was drawing on a motif which was fundamental to a large number of mythical narratives told by Greeks from the time of Homer to that of Pausanias, and beyond. In the final section I shall return to Sophokles, placing him this time not against the background of the whole Greek mythical tradition but rather within the specific context of the fifth century BC, and attempting to overhear the individual dramatic 'voice' used by him as he explored the implications of blindness.

1. SOPHOKLES: BLINDNESS IN THE TRAGEDIES

As *Aias* begins, Odysseus is attempting to track down the play's eponymous hero, who is suspected of having done to death some beasts, together with their drovers, in the Greek camp near Troy. But the first words of the drama are spoken not by Odysseus but by Athene: 'Son of Laertes, I am always seeing you seeking to snatch some means of attacking your foes; and now again, at Aias' tent by the ships, . . . I see you tracking his footsteps' (1–7). Athene sees Odysseus. But Odysseus does not see Athene: 'Voice of Athene, dearest to me of the gods, how clearly I hear your utterance, even though you are invisible[1] to me' (14–16).[2] Exactly how this lack of visual reciprocity was enacted onstage is not relevant to us here;[3] what is relevant is that from the outset the goddess is presented as having the advantage over the mortal in respect of sight.

[1] The word *apoptos* can mean either 'seen afar off, only dimly visible' or else 'invisible'; see Jebb (1896) and Stanford (1963) ad loc. But here the context seems to require the meaning 'invisible', to provide a stronger contrast with the words of 'hearing' (*phthegma*, 'voice'; *phōnēma*, 'utterance'; *akouō*, 'I hear'). Kamerbeek (1953, ad loc.) opts unambiguously for 'hidden from view', and Garvie (1998, ad loc.) for 'invisible'; likewise Finglass (2011, 137).

[2] Taplin (1977, 116 n. 1) argues that lines 14–17 'say that Odysseus knows Athena so well that he can recognize her by her voice alone even when she is not visible—unlike the present occasion'. However, Jebb's comment (Appendix, on 15) on a similar suggestion by A. Müller remains valid: 'it is surely inconceivable that, if Odysseus *saw* Athena standing near him, he should say to her, "How clearly I hear thy voice, even when thou art unseen"'. The clause 'even when you are invisible' does indeed become weak if Sophokles intends the audience to regard Odysseus as being already able to see Athene.

[3] Discussions in Stanford (1963) on 15, and Calder (1965). The very existence of a fifth-century *theologeion*—the platform on which many scholars have put Athene during this scene—has been persuasively challenged by Taplin (1977), esp. 440–1. Perhaps the least implausible view of the staging is Stanford's: Odysseus is at first unable to see Athene, who is, however, on the scene just as he is. But gradually, presumably by moving uncertainly in her direction, he becomes able to see her, in time for the dialogue beginning at 36. There is no difficulty about the theatricality of this ('Characters in a play see what the playwright has them see, regardless of the realities of optics', Taplin (1977) 116 n. 1), nor about a mortal hearing but not seeing a divinity (cf. Eur. *Hipp.* 86). The problem is, rather, that the progress from invisibility to visibility is not charted in the text. This raises fundamental questions about the relation between text and staging, which we cannot go into here. (For an extreme but extraordinarily well-argued view, see Taplin (1977), 28–39.) What is certain is that the last word on the staging of the opening of *Aias* has not yet been said; for a sound and lucid review of the *status quaestionis*, see now Finglass (2011, 137–8).

Soon the blindness theme is developed further. In his anger at being deprived of the arms of Achilles, says Athene, Aias plotted murderous revenge on the Greek commanders, but (51–2):

> I kept him from his fatal gloating revenge, by
> Casting oppressive fancies upon his eyes

In fact, Athene interfered with Aias' sight so that he mistook animals for men, slaughtering and tormenting them instead of the Greek leaders. 'I will *show* you this madness of his,' she says; 'but do not be afraid' (69–70):

> I shall prevent the gleams of his eyes—which shall
> Be turned away—from seeing your face.

That is, she will disorient his vision. Later in the dialogue she repeats her promise in slightly different terms (85):

> I shall darken his eyes, (keen-)sighted though they are.

A god can do anything, comments Odysseus in reply. And Athene does indeed bring Aias onto the scene, a deluded victim, convinced that he has Odysseus in his power to do with as he likes—whereas in fact all he has in his tent is a captive animal. For in reality Odysseus is standing here before Aias, though invisible to him. As Athene is to Odysseus, so Odysseus is to Aias: superior, and sighted.

Having momentarily been able to view a mortal from a vantage point of godlike superiority, Odysseus is in a position to generalize about the whole human condition (125–6):

> I see that all we who are mortals are nothing but phantoms
> And insubstantial shadow.

It is the same insight as Kassandra's, just before she walks to her death in *Agamemnon* (1327–30): not only are mortals limited in comparison with gods; they are even, in a way, less real.

After the first scene in *Aias* blindness hardly recurs as a prominent theme, and it would be misleading to exaggerate its significance in this play. Nevertheless, its presence in that first scene serves to emphasize a crucial and recurring feature of the Sophoklean dramatic universe: namely, the feeling that human sight and insight are *limited* when compared with the sight and insight of the gods.

The play in which the metaphor of blindness is used to the most devastating effect in order to explore the limits of human insight is, of course, *Oidipous Tyrannos*. It will be sensible if we remind ourselves of two famous episodes: the confrontation between Teiresias and Oidipous, and the self-blinding of Oidipous.

At *OT* 284–5 the chorus introduces the possibility of consulting Teiresias with these words:

> I know that the vision of our lord Teiresias is
> Most like that of our lord Apollo

Although blind, Teiresias has insight greater than that of a man. He is thus at once less than, and greater than, a man. By contrast, Oidipous is no more than, and no less than, a man. As the priest said at 31–4, Oidipous was not regarded as the equal of the gods, but only as 'first of men'. Oidipous is sighted, as men are; yet he lacks insight into the truth about himself and the world, as all mortals are liable to lack such insight.[4] Oidipous is a paradigm of humanity (1193–6). Superficially, his fate is extraordinary; in reality, it is the distillation of common experience. The heroism and fragility of Oidipous' life are examples of what the heroism and fragility of *any* mortal life might be like.

Out of the contrast between Teiresias and Oidipous, Sophokles creates a complex web of ambiguity and paradox. The pattern of the web has been analysed by numerous critics, and we may content ourselves with a look at one or two relevant strands. First, an accusation which is as dire as it is (to Oidipous) opaque (366–7):

> *Teir*: I say that, unbeknown to yourself, you are in
> An obscene relationship with those closest to you, yet
> You do not *see* what wretchedness you are in.

A little later the mutual recriminations between the king and the seer draw heavily on the imagery of blindness (370–5):

> *Oid*: You do not have [that strength of truth], since
> You are blind in ears, in mind, in eyes.
> *Teir*: You are a poor wretch to be hurling that

[4] A word about the odd heresy which has Oidipous knowing the truth from the outset of the play (argued at book length by Vellacott (1971); see the detailed refutation by Vickers (1973), ch. 9, esp. 501–13, with 547–8 n. 9): (i) if Oidipous knows already, the imagery of blindness is wholly without point, and the self-blinding is as gratuitous an irrelevance as it is in Seneca's *Oedipus*; (ii) if Oidipous knows already, the play becomes a grubby and *unrepresentative* 'cover-up'.

> Reproach at me, since soon everyone will be
> Reproaching you in just the same terms.
> *Oid*: Endless night is your element—you could harm[5]
> Neither me nor anyone else who sees the light.

Soon Oidipous flies off at a tangent. It is, he imagines, *Kreon* who is behind Teiresias' allegations; Kreon wants the throne, and has suborned this magician (388–9):

> Who only has eyes for gain—he is blind in respect of prophecy.

Really stung now, Teiresias delivers one of the great speeches of ancient tragedy (408–28). Paradoxes and dark allusions come thick and fast (413):

> You are sighted, yet cannot see the calamity you are in

But in time things will be different (419):

> Now you see clearly; but afterwards you will see only darkness.

I turn now to a much later episode in the play: the self-blinding. How is it to be interpreted? 'We know today', observes Albert Esser, a medical doctor who has written about blindness in antiquity, 'that self-blinding in a state of emotional arousal is an act carried out only by the insane.'[6] The chorus would seem to confirm this at 1299–1300, when they ask, 'What madness came upon you?' Yet the overall picture drawn by Sophokles of Oidipous before and after the self-blinding is emphatically *not* that of a deranged man. The reasons given by Oidipous for putting out his own eyes have, indeed, an inexorable logic. At 1271–4 the messenger from the palace reports that, as Oidipous was doing the deed, he cried out that his eyes should no longer be able to look upon his crimes; before, his eyes had seen those they should not have seen, and failed to recognize those they ought to have recognized.[7] At 1371–83 Oidipous fills this out. Without eyes, he will not have to look upon his father and mother in

[5] The reading βλάψαι ('to harm') is to be preferred in 375, against the alternative βλέψαι ('to see'). So, rightly, e.g. Dawe (1984). In view of the dominant imagery of blindness and sight, it is easy to see how the error βλέψαι could creep in.

[6] Esser (1961) 67; my translation.

[7] As is very common in references to incest in *OT*, the language is difficult and contorted. In these cases scholars have too often sought to reduce the language to normality by altering the text.

Hades, nor to endure the intolerable sight of his children, nor to look at the places in Thebes from which he banished himself. In fact, the ideal for him would be to be deprived of *all* perception of the external world (1386–90), a world which can only remind him of the pain which his relationships with others have produced.

According to the case argued by Georges Devereux, Oidipous' own explanations of his self-blinding are unconvincing rationalizations: the deed is really to be interpreted as a symbolic castration.[8] Now psychoanalysis is at its weakest when it is made to explain everything, but at its strongest when it is used to explain only the unusual—and Oidipous' self-blinding is certainly unusual. Devereux cites an impressive number of stories from antiquity in which a person guilty of a sexual misdemeanour is punished with blinding.[9] In view of this evidence we cannot, I think, rule out the possibility that Oidipous' self-blinding might have been regarded as *appropriate* by reason of his having committed incest. However, the question to ask is not, 'Why did Oidipous blind himself?' but, 'Why did Sophokles represent Oidipous as blinding himself?' And a large part of the answer to that question is that it forms the culmination of the image-pattern of sight and blindness, with the implications of that pattern for the opposition insight/lack of insight.

Let us turn briefly to the other five plays. In *Antigone* Teiresias appears once more, but his importance is confined to the episode near the end of the play where he warns of the consequences entailed by Kreon's condemnation of Antigone. There is no all-pervasive use of the blindness motif comparable with that in *OT*, although in some of the verbal imagery there emerges a contrast between a matter-of-fact, practical ability to see, which Kreon possesses, and the power of insight, which he lacks.[10]

But it is in *Oidipous at Kolonos* that the relationship between blindness and insight is again examined in detail. At first, the audience is confronted with a helpless, blind old man. Soon it becomes plain that he has insight, greater than that of other mortals, into his own fate. And eventually, with a final, paradoxical turn of the screw, Sophokles has Oidipous behave as if he were physically sighted (1542–3):

> Follow me, children: for now I am revealed
> As your new guide, just as you guided your father.

[8] Devereux (1973). [9] Devereux (1973) 41. See also 192 below.
[10] See Goheen (1951) 84–6.

We must beware of turning what Sophokles is saying into an absurd philosophy of self-mutilation. He is not claiming that *only* the blind have insight—Antigone, Aias, Herakles, Philoktetes, and Neoptolemos all achieve knowledge of 'how the world is', and none of them is blind. (No more is Lear blind, unlike Gloucester.) Rather is it the case that, in some of Sophokles' works, blindness is a powerful verbal and visual *metaphor* for the limits of humanity, limits of which the dramatist wants his audience to be aware.

From *Women of Trachis*, *Philoktetes*, and *Elektra* the motif of blindness is as good as absent. But the opposition between insight and ignorance, and the related gap between reality and appearance, are powerfully present. A good example is *Women of Trachis*. Deianeira, Hyllos, and Herakles all advance from partial to fuller knowledge during the course of the action, yet in each case their greater insight comes too late to avert calamity. It is worth noticing the exclamation uttered by Herakles as the mention of Nessos tears away the veil obscuring the past: *iou iou* (1043). The same exclamation is uttered by Jocasta (*OT* 1071) and Oidipous (*OT* 1182) when they see 'how the pattern fits'. *Iou iou* marks a sudden release of energy, when the irony of partial knowledge is instantaneously discharged. With every Sophoklean character who learns more—or 'sees' more—after having achieved greater awareness, it is vital to be clear *what sort* of insight each gains. In the case of Oidipous in *Oidipous Tyrannos*, especially, we must be careful not to exaggerate or idealize what he learns into some kind of all-encompassing perception of the workings of the universe. He achieves no such perception. Yet it remains true that he does answer, with complete success, the much more limited question which he has set himself, namely that of his own identity. In *that* sense, his *iou iou* moment denotes a transition from blindness to insight.[11]

2. MYTH

Myth, language, and limits

Just as no utterance in Greek can be understood without reference to the grammar and syntax of Greek, so no Greek mythical narrative

[11] See further Buxton (1996) 48 n. 16.

makes proper sense unless it is seen as an element of an interrelated—i.e. not just random—whole. Accordingly, the next step in the argument will be to place Sophokles' treatment of blindness within the wider context of Greek myth. But before that I want briefly to develop the analogy made in the opening sentence of this paragraph.

Greek mythology is like a language—a set of conventions enabling meaning to be created and communicated. In order to comprehend how this language worked, we should like to be able to reconstruct its state at a whole series of different dates, and then describe in detail how one state changed into another over time. Unfortunately, the paucity of the evidence puts these objectives quite beyond our reach. So we are faced with a dilemma. If we try to recover the state of the language of myth as it was in (say) 400 BC, and if we refuse to include stories which are known to us only from sources dating from *after* 400 BC, then we shall have the satisfaction of being philologically impeccable, but we shall not get very far in compiling a vocabulary—let alone in writing a grammar—of Greek myth. On the other hand, if we welcome into one, undifferentiated, quasi-synchronic picture mythical items from early epic to Nonnos, then we run the risk (though, of course, some structuralists see it rather as an opportunity) of producing an account of a language which exists only in the mind of its grammarian.

I have stated this methodological division in a grossly 'ideal' way. In practice, the matter does not present itself as a cut-and-dried choice between chronology and structure; it is rather a question of *how much* to privilege chronological considerations at the expense of structural ones, or vice versa. In this chapter I follow the by no means original procedure of steering a middle course between the two extremes. The feasibility of this approach depends upon the fact that there are a lot of regularities in Greek mythical narratives, regularities which occur in authors of widely differing dates. (Whether we call these regularities 'patterns' or 'structures' does not, perhaps, make a lot of difference; but, while 'pattern' might tend to imply a superficial ordering, 'structure' conveys a sense of something more fundamental. For reasons shortly to be given, 'structure' will therefore be the more suitable term.) If we build up our grammar by gathering together the most prominent of these structures—without pretending that we shall be able to accommodate *every* version, since our knowledge will certainly be inadequate to cope with many local 'idioms'—then we may hope to make headway. In discovering the structures, we are revealing part of (in Saussurian terminology) *la langue*: in order to discover them, we have first to collect and scrutinize many specific mythical utterances, i.e. examples of (in the same terminology) *la parole*.

In the first section we looked at some 'utterances' about blindness. We turn now from *parole* to *langue*: that is, we attempt to reconstruct some of the mythical structures to which the utterances correspond, and in relation to which they have meaning.

In *Aias* gods and mortals are strongly distinguished in respect of their powers of sight. The distinction goes far beyond fifth-century Athens. Aristotle affirms that 'we allow to the gods the power to see all things' (*Poet.* 1454^{b}), and the point is made by numerous other writers.[12] While we should not interpret such statements as ascribing *infinite* powers of sight to the gods—infinity is not a concept relevant to the classical Greek pantheon, where 'each god found his limits in another god'[13]—the gap between god and man is, in this as in every sphere, a large one. The gods can lighten or darken human vision at will: Poseidon casts a mist over Achilles' eyes, and removes it when the danger to his favourite Aineias is over (*Il.* 20.321, 341). Usually mortals are limited in their vision, and may fail to perceive the difference between gods and men; but in exceptional circumstances they may be granted a temporary heightening of their powers of sight, as Athene enables Diomedes clearly to distinguish mortals from immortals on the battlefield (*Il.* 5.127–8). However, this is the exception which proves the rule: 'I gave them (*sc.* mortals) *blind* hopes', says Aischylos' Prometheus (*PV* 250).

Any attempt to infringe, or call into question, or render ambiguous the boundary between gods and men is potentially dangerous, as it puts in jeopardy one of the most fundamental category-distinctions in terms of which Greek culture is organized. A large number of Greek myths explore such dangerous situations, and a significant number of them involve blindness or blinding. It will be convenient to concentrate on two main types of myth: (a) those dealing with a character who, by virtue of his extraordinary power or insight, threatens to blur the distinction between god and man; (b) those narrating a specific infringement of the boundary between god and man, for example, stories of mortals who see immortals when they ought not to do so.

12 See Deonna (1965) 102–8.

13 Sabbatucci (1965) 207. Sabbatucci argues persuasively that it is only the *megaloi theoi* ('great gods') whose 'size' is infinite.

Poets, seers, and insight

Two sorts of person are repeatedly presented as blind in Greek myths: poets and prophets. Before considering possible explanations of this fact,[14] we shall review the main features of the evidence.

Firstly, poets. 'All these poets are blind', a character in Dio Chrysostom's thirty-sixth oration (10–11) is reported as saying, 'and they do not think it possible for anyone to become a poet otherwise.' 'That they have got from Homer', replies Dio, 'as though from ophthalmia.' The text is odd here,[15] but the sense is clear enough: the blind poet is a 'type' who goes back to Homer. In addition to Homer's own legendary blindness[16] there is of course that of the Phaiakian bard whom Homer describes, Demodokos. The pair of hexameters in which the origins of his blindness are alluded to convey a strong sense of the 'equivalence' of blindness and the power of song (*Od.* 8.63–4):

> whom the Muse loved exceedingly, yet gave
> him both good and evil: she deprived him of
> eyesight, but bestowed upon him the gift of sweet
> song.

According to this account, blindness and song are 'contemporaneous' attributes: neither precedes the other, both are basic to the singer's character. However, a late source (schol. Ov. *Ibis* 272) states that Demodokos was blinded after being defeated in a contest with the Muses. This is one of countless instances where we cannot be sure how old a particular version is: did Homer know of this story but prefer to ignore it, so as not to interfere with his idealized portrait; or is the scholiast's version a post-Homeric one, produced by either a 'correct' memory of a 'genuine' variant or an 'erroneous' confusion of Demodokos with other poets who had legendary musical contests with divinities? The question is insoluble. Fortunately, it is not very interesting either. What is much more interesting is that two variants of the Demodokos myth preserve a connection between poetry and blindness *although this connection is expressed in different ways at the*

[14] It *is* a fact, *pace* ch. 1 of Mahoney (1940).

[15] I follow von Arnim's reading, without conviction.

[16] *Hymn. Hom. Ap.* 172; Paus. 4.33.7 etc.; see Esser (1961) 10. A thoughtful and persuasive account of blindness as a central feature of Homer's poetic persona is available in Graziosi (2002) 125–63.

level of narrative. In one case the power of song precedes blindness, in the other there is no such priority. This is the first of several cases we shall meet in which motive, causality, and temporal priority appear to be variable in a way that more basic ('structural') associations are not.[17]

A few more myths linking blindness with poetry may be mentioned. The 'mythical' Thamyris and the 'historical' Stesichoros were both blinded because they overstepped particular limits (more on this below). By contrast, the early Lokrian poet Xenokritos was said to have been blind from birth.[18] (Once more, it is the fact of the association of blindness with poetry, rather than the narrative order in which this association is expressed, which we should be noticing.) Lastly, we ought not to pass over the fate of the tragedian Achaios who, it was said, lost his sight after being stung by bees.[19] This is a perfect example of the logic of myth. Bees are traditionally associated with the Muses (Ar. *Eccl.* 974), and are often linked with poets and others with power over words.[20] In being blinded by bees, a poet is being weakened by the very agency which represents his strength.

It goes without saying that not all Greek poets, real or imagined, were blind. Nevertheless, the frequency with which poetry and blindness are linked in traditional stories is too great to be attributable to chance. Exactly the same goes for prophecy and blindness. The most famous instance of the conjunction of the two is Teiresias.[21] The causal and chronological relationship between prophecy and blindness, and the reason for Teiresias' blinding, vary according to

[17] See Brisson (1976) 33, who mentions the 'mécanisme propre a tout recit, qui projette la simultanéité dans la succession, et qui transforme la relation en causalité'. Compare already Propp (1968) 75–8, who noted that functionally identical actions were coupled with extremely various motivations. The story of Daphnis exemplifies the same point. He was a fine singer, a follower of Artemis, and loved by a nymph (Diod. Sic. 4.84). As a punishment for being unfaithful to her, Daphnis was blinded and then turned to stone (Servius on Verg. *Ecl.* 8.68)—that is (by implication) he stopped singing immediately. Yet, according to another version, Daphnis went blind *and consoled his blindness with song*, although he did not live long afterwards (Philargyrius on Verg. *Ecl.* 5.20). Narrative details vary, more fundamental relationships remain stable.

[18] *FHG* ii. 221; cf. Plut. *De mus.* 9 (= *Mor.* 1134b).

[19] *TrGF* i. 20 Achaeus I, T 3a + b Snell.

[20] See *RE* iii, s.v. 'Biene', cols. 431–50 (Olck), esp. 447–8; also Waszink (1974).

[21] See Brisson (1976). The rigour with which the structuralist approach is applied by Brisson strikes me as positively algebraic in its formality, but there are many good things to be found in the book.

different versions current in antiquity. Kallimachos' fifth hymn told how Teiresias lost his eyesight because he saw Athene bathing, but then, at the intercession of his mother Chariklo, was granted the compensating gift of bird-prophecy. Another variant retained the same narrative order—first blindness, then the gift of prophecy—but altered the motive: Teiresias was blinded by Hera because he asserted that women gain more pleasure from the sexual act than men; but, as compensation, Zeus gave him the power to know the future (Ov. *Met.* 3.316–38; cf. Hyg. *Fab.* 75). A third version altered both narrative order and motive: Teiresias was blinded by the gods because he revealed (*sc.* as a prophet) divine secrets (Apollod. *Bibl.* 3.6.7). Yet, in spite of all the narrative variations, the association between blindness and prophecy remains constant.

We get the same sort of result if we look at the stories told about some lesser-known seers. Phormion, a fisherman from Erythrai, lost his eyesight but possessed the ability to dream prophetic dreams (Paus. 7.5.7). Ophioneus, a Messenian seer, was blind from birth (Paus. 4.10.6); then he regained his sight, but subsequently lost it again (Paus. 4.12.10; 13.3). Euenios lived at Apollonia on the Adriatic (Hdt. 9.93–4). While keeping watch over the sacred sheep of Helios, he fell asleep. Wolves killed many of the animals, and the angry citizens of Apollonia condemned the unfortunate watchman to be blinded. But then infertility came upon the land. On consulting oracles, the people learned that they had acted wrongly in blinding Euenios: the gods themselves had sent the wolves. The Apolloniats made their own (deceitfully meagre) reparations, while the gods compensated Euenios *by giving him the gift of prophecy.*[22] In the stories about Phormion, Ophioneus, and Euenios, the details of the narrative are individual in each case, but the structural relationship between prophecy and blindness is the same.

As a final instance of a blind seer we may take Phineus.[23] The various versions of the myth offer several different reasons for his blinding, and locate his receipt of the gift of prophecy at different points in the narrative. In Hesiod's *Megalai Eoiai* the story went that Phineus was blinded for showing Phrixos the way to Kolchis, while in

[22] On the story of Euenios, see the delightful article by Griffiths (1999); also Grottanelli (2003); Burkert (2007).

[23] See *RE* xx.1, s.v. 'Phineus', cols. 215–46 (Ziegler), esp. 225–30; Grégoire (1949) 78–95; Brisson (1976) 101–4.

the same poet's *Catalogue* Phineus himself chooses a long life in preference to a sighted one (Hes. frr. 157, 254 MW). Another variant, preserved by a scholiast on Apollonios Rhodios 2.178–82b (Wendel), attributes the blinding to Helios, on the ground that Phineus 'had preferred to be long-lived rather than sighted'. The Atthidographer Istros brought both Phrixos and Helios into the picture: Aietes, king of Kolchis, cursed Phineus for helping by his prophecies his foes the sons of Phrixos; and Helios, Aietes' father, fulfilled the curse by blinding Phineus (*FGrH* 334 F 67). In this variant, therefore, Phineus is explicitly stated already to possess the gift of prophecy *before* he is blinded. But the narrative order is not always like that. We know of one version according to which Phineus had the choice of either blindness with prophetic powers or a normally sighted but short life; in other words, neither blindness nor prophecy has priority.[24] However, with the most extensive surviving version of the Phineus myth, that recounted by Apollonios Rhodios at 2.178–497, we are back with a narrative in which prophetic powers precede blindness. Out of kindness (257) Apollo taught Phineus prophecy; but he abused the gift and, in a Prometheus-like gesture, disregarded Zeus by unerringly reporting the gods' 'sacred intention' to men (181–2). (The similarity with Apollodoros' version of the Teiresias myth is striking.) In return, Zeus blinded him and sent him a wearyingly long life.

All these variants—and there are several more which introduce still other motives for Phineus' blinding, for example that it was a punishment for having wrongly blinded his own children (Diod. Sic. 4.44.4)—show an unmistakable connection between blindness and prophecy. (No wonder that Oppian reports 'an incredible tale which has spread amongst men' to the effect that moles are descended from Phineus; and moles, as Aristotle wrote, 'cannot see' and have 'no eyes which can be detected externally'.)[25] Moreover, just as with poetry, the connection between prophecy and blindness exists at a deeper

[24] *Et. Gen.* s.v. ὀπίζεσθαι; see Wendel (1958), n. on Ap. Rhod. *Argon.* 178–82b, 13; *TrGF* iv on Soph. *ΦΙΝΕΥΣ* F 704–5 Radt. The continuation of the story in *Et. Gen.* is very odd—Pearson (1917) ii. 312 n. 3, calls it 'absurd'—for, when Phineus had opted for blindness with prophecy, 'for this reason Apollo was angry and blinded him'. For an attempt to explain this mythical *ill*ogic, see Ziegler's painstaking article (n. 23 above) 226.

[25] Opp. *Cyn.* 2.612–28, with n. ad loc. in Mair (1928); Arist. *Hist. an.* 491^b27–34. See Grégoire (1949) 78–95; Brisson (1976) 101–4.

level than the surface detail of narrative. Not *all* seers are sightless, of course, as may readily be gathered from Hopfner's list in his Pauly-Wissowa article on '*Mantike*'.[26] But, again as with poetry, the connection is too marked to be random. What is the explanation for it?

Let us consider first what we may call 'natural logic'. As the Greeks were well aware, a person bereft of external sight may naturally develop mental perceptiveness as a compensation. Thus Aristotle affirms that 'the blind remember better, being released from having their faculty of memory engaged with objects of sight' (*Eth. Eud.* 1248^{b}).[27] The attribution of insight, a 'sixth sense', to a blind person is therefore perfectly comprehensible.[28] But why the specific links with poetry and prophecy? Once more there are sound 'practical' reasons. The number of ways in which a blind man can earn his living in a society such as the ancient Greek one is extremely limited, but the profession of 'oral' bard is one which *is* available. (Many other cultures also know of the 'blind singer'.)[29] As for the blind seer, the closing of the eyes during trances may have played a part in the development of the type.[30]

But a more profound 'cultural logic' is also at work. Poets and seers have in common the power to see and know more than ordinary men. E. R. Dodds puts it well: 'Just as the truth about the future would be attained only if man were in touch with a knowledge wider than his own, so the truth about the past could be preserved only on a like condition. Its human repositories, the poets, had (like the seers) their technical resources, their professional training; but vision of the past, like insight into the future, remained a mysterious faculty, only partially under its owner's control, and dependent in the last resort on divine grace. By that grace poet and seer alike enjoyed a knowledge denied to other men.'[31] Indeed for Hesiod the link between poetry and prophecy was closer even than is implied in Dodds' words: the

[26] *RE* xiv.1, cols. 1258–88, at 1267–8.

[27] Trans. H. Rackham (1952). See also Plut. *De def. or.* 39 (= *Mor.* 432b).

[28] For parallels from other cultures, see Thompson (1955–8) D1820.1.1, F655.

[29] See Bowra (1952) 421–2; Grimm (1957) 426; Burke (1978) 99–100.

[30] Esser (1961) 101; Deonna (1965) 50–2. During initiation, the eyes of a Samoyed shaman were changed by a divine blacksmith: 'and that is why, when he shamanizes, he does not see with his bodily eyes but with these mystical eyes' (Eliade [1964] 42). NB also Mac Cana (1977) 94: 'even down to the seventeenth or eighteenth century Irish and Scottish poets continued to simulate the practice of the seer by composing their verse while lying on their beds in utter darkness'.

[31] Dodds (1951) 81.

Muses inspired him with a divine voice in order that he might celebrate not only the past but also 'that which is to be' (*Th.* 31–2). Poets and seers stand in an especially close relationship to the gods.[32] But, precisely for that reason, they blur the distinction between god and man. In order to preserve the distinction intact, special powers possessed by mortals are, in the logic of myth, balanced by special defects.[33]

This complementary coexistence of power and defect recurs often in Greek myth. To recall that Herakleitos was said to have had dropsy and to have lost his eyesight as a result, or to note that Demokritos was supposed by some to have blinded himself in order to retain the greatest possible capacity for reflection, ought to cause no surprise, since the philosopher too is a man with greater than normal insight.[34] But there is no need for us to restrict ourselves to insight, on the positive side of the equation, or to blindness, on the negative. Kassandra foresaw the future—but was not believed.[35] Tithonos' immortality set him above other men—but his extreme senility redressed the balance (cf. especially *Hymn. Hom. Aphr.* 218–38). Asklepios' raising of the dead threatened the fundamental distinction between gods and men—so Zeus' thunderbolt achieved the necessary restitution of order (e.g. Eur. *Alc.* 3–4, 122–9). Philoktetes' unfailing bow approximated him to the gods—but his wound made him little better than an animal.[36] Hephaistos, too, combined a physical defect with an exceptional power, being a superb smith, yet lame. His case is anomalous, for he, unlike the other defective figures just mentioned, is a full Olympian deity. But, bearing in mind that he has been described as 'a magician who paid for his knowledge with the soundness of his

[32] See J.-P. Vernant in Vernant et al. (1974) 12.

[33] Brisson (1976) 32. Brelich (1958, 244–8) has a fascinating discussion of mythical mutilations of the feet and eyes.

[34] Herakleitos: Diog. Laert. 9.4. Demokritos: Plut. *De curios.* 12 (= *Mor.* 521d). See also Cic. *Fin.* 5.87, *Tusc.* 5.114; Aul. Gell. *NA* 10.17.

[35] The *locus classicus* is Aesch. *Ag.* 1202–12. Here too the *motive* for the gift of prophecy to Kassandra, and the *moment* in the narrative at which the gift is given, vary according to different versions. In Apollodoros (*Bibl.* 3.12.5) the gift is a bribe offered by Apollo for her favours; but, in a version recorded in schol. *Il.* 7.44 (quoting Antikleides, *FGrH* 140 F 17), Kassandra and her twin brother Helenos both receive the gift *as children* when their 'organs of sense' are licked by serpents in a temple of Apollo. See Frazer (1921) on Apollod. *Bibl.* 3.12.5.

[36] Cf. E. Wilson (1952).

body',[37] and as a god with markedly *heroic* traits,[38] it is surely feasible to regard Hephaistos too as exemplifying the mythical structure in which we are interested.[39]

Boundaries and transgressions

In Greek myths certain sorts of action typically result in the blinding of the agent. Such actions involve the overstepping of limits. Consequently they are central to our theme.

(i) *Visual infringements against divinities.* 'The gods', says Hera, 'are hard to look upon in their full brightness' (*Il.* 20.131). Several myths take this further: not only is it 'hard' to look on gods, it is dangerous to do so. Epizelos, an Athenian, went blind after encountering an apparition (*phasma*) at the battle of Marathon (Hdt. 6.117). Philip of Macedon lost the eye with which he spied on his wife Olympias as she shared her bed with the god Ammon, who had taken the form of a serpent (Plut. *Alex.* 3). Erymanthos, a son of Apollo, saw Aphrodite bathing after her union with Adonis, and was blinded.[40] More famous is the case of Teiresias, who, as mentioned earlier, lost his eyesight as a consequence of seeing Athene bathing.[41] Sometimes it is not the seeing of a divinity but the seeing of a particularly numinous statuette which leads to the blinding of the transgressor. Thus Ilos seized the Palladion from Athene's shrine in Troy. The image 'might not be looked upon by a man', and Ilos was blinded. Exactly the same fate befell Antylus (or Metellus), who took the Palladion from the temple of Vesta at Rome.[42] Sometimes, again, it is not a question of seeing a divinity or a divine image but of

[37] Delcourt (1982) 11; my translation.

[38] Brelich (1958) 354–7.

[39] Ogden (1997, 35–7) argues that tales about Hephaistos exemplify another mythical structure, linking bastardy, lameness, and exposure. This is by no means incompatible with the structure I am identifying. In the view of Jan Bremmer (in Bremmer and Erskine (2010), 199–200) Hephaistos' lameness suggests social exclusion.

[40] Ptol. Heph. in Phot. *Bibl.* 190 pp. 146–7.

[41] The *locus classicus*, and indeed the reason for the fame of this myth, is Kallimachos' fifth hymn; see Bulloch (1985). For the variants, see Buslepp (1916–24b). There is a full discussion of the hymn in Kleinknecht (1939), reprinted in Skiadas (1975, 207–75).

[42] Both stories in Plut. *Parall. Graec. et Rom.* 17 (= *Mor.* 309f-310a).

entering a sanctuary which should not be entered. Soldiers of Alexander's army, bursting into the temple of Demeter at Miletos with the object of plundering it, were blinded there and then.[43] A certain Aipytos entered the temple of Poseidon Hippios at Mantineia. The sanctuary was one which no mortal had ever been allowed to penetrate. Aipytos was blinded, and died immediately, or soon afterwards (Paus. 8.5.4–5, 10.3).

One or two comments are in order about the myths adumbrated in the preceding paragraph. First, and importantly, it is not the case that blinding always follows an *intentional* infringement of the sphere of the divine. In Kallimachos' hymn, Teiresias 'saw *unwillingly* that which it is not permitted to see' (78); but, nevertheless, there was nothing that could be done to restore his sight: 'The laws of Kronos', says Athene, 'say this: whoever sees one of the immortals when the god himself does not choose—at a heavy cost shall he see what he sees' (100–2). The mere fact of transgressing a boundary which must not be transgressed is sufficient to entail punishment.

Secondly, it is plain that a number of the myths involve a gender boundary in addition to the boundary between gods and mortals. Stories about mortals seeing immortals bathing—and there are many such stories, some culminating in blinding, some in other forms of punishment (see below)—are normally of the form: male mortal sees female immortal. Furthermore, the goddesses about whom these narratives cluster are the virgin divinities Athene and Artemis.[44] Presumably the logic here is that, since these two goddesses have certain 'masculine' characteristics, represented by the trappings of war[45] on the one hand and the trappings of hunting on the other, then the penetration of this external masculinity through to the latent femininity beyond it amounts to a more radical infringement of divine identity than would be the case with the 'transparently'

[43] Val. Max., ed. C. Kempf (Teubner edn.) p. 13, 10.

[44] It is revealing that Eustathios' memory plays him false when he speaks of Kallimachos' story about Teiresias' having seen *Artemis* naked (*Comm. ad Hom. Od.* 10.492, 1665.47–8); see Brisson (1976) 52.

[45] Notice Prop. 4.9.57–8: Teiresias saw Pallas bathing 'when she had put aside the Gorgon'—that is, the shield bearing the image of the Gorgon, which would have rendered the punishment of blinding superfluous by *petrifying* the mortal gazing upon it.

feminine Aphrodite.[46] It is, then, appropriate that the distinctions between the respective provinces of Athene and Aphrodite are clearly marked in Kallimachos' hymn: no unguents or mirror for *Athene* (13–22).

Third, it should be noted that the overstepping of visual limits in myth is closely paralleled in certain ritual prohibitions. The danger associated with seeing gods and their images finds expression in prescriptions such as these reported by Pausanias: the image of Hera at Aigion in Achaia might be seen by no one but her priestess (Paus. 7.23.9); and similarly the image of Soteria in the same locality might be seen only by her priests (7.24.3). As for the infringement of gender boundaries, numerous Greek cults involved the exclusion of either males or females from all or part of the proceedings; and it may not be a coincidence that the majority of cults requiring the exclusion of men are for a female divinity (usually Demeter), while the majority of cults which exclude women are for male divinities.[47] That which is expressed in the language of myth by narratives of transgression and consequent mutilation is expressed in the language of ritual by prohibitions on behaviour. Both languages are rich, powerful, and vivid, so both can be made to say an enormous variety of things about the world. But both come back again and again to category distinctions vital to the cultural world as the classical Greeks assembled it: distinctions like those between god and man, male and female.

(ii) *Other infringements against divinities.*[48] We have already discussed the myth in which Teiresias was blinded for revealing the gods' secrets to men, and that in which Phineus suffered a comparable fate for divulging the gods' 'sacred intention'. A similar story was told about Anchises, who boasted of his union with Aphrodite: he was 'touched' by a thunderbolt, and so blinded.[49] Lykourgos, the mythical persecutor of

[46] Cf. Brisson (1976) 34. That Aphrodite, too, figures occasionally in these narratives (e.g. Erymanthos) is no cause for dismay. Dare one risk the heresy that Greek myths would be duller if *every* one of them could be fitted into a neatly organized scheme?

[47] See the catalogues in Wächter (1910) 125–34. Cf. Burkert (1985) 258–9 on the gender differentiation of roles in cult.

[48] See Gruppe (1906) 1002 n. 3.

[49] This version came in a poem of Theokritos, referred to by Servius on Verg. *Aen.* 2.35 and 687; cf. on 1.617. For the 'modes of action' of the thunderbolt, see Serv. on *Aen.* 2.649. Both *Hymn. Hom. Aphr.* 286–8 and Hyg. *Fab.* 94 refer to the thunderbolt

Dionysos, was blinded by Zeus as a punishment for his transgression (*Il.* 6.130–40).[50] To offend minor divinities was no safer. The Egyptian king Pheros lost his sight after he had hurled his spear into the Nile, which was flooding (Hdt. 2.111, cf. Diod. Sic. 1.59). Thamyris' challenge to the gods was of a different and more common type: he competed with them.[51] Specifically, he sought to defeat the Muses in a musical contest (e.g. *Il.* 2.594–600). Different accounts report different punishments for this recklessness;[52] but according to one common variant (e.g. Hes. fr. 65 MW) he was blinded.

Lastly, we must not omit the famous case of Stesichoros, who was said to have lost his sight because he slandered Helen, but to have regained it when he composed a palinode of recantation and apology.[53] What is the mythical logic here? Helen was worshipped as a goddess at a number of places in the Greek world; she was the daughter of Zeus; and she was the sister of the divine twins, Kastor and Polydeukes. Thus to offend her might be seen as equivalent to infringing the honour of other, more august deities in the pantheon. So Stesichoros, like Anchises, was guilty of broadcasting information detrimental to the reputation of a goddess; information, moreover, which in both instances involved a sexual indiscretion by the character concerned. This broadcasting may, in turn, be seen as a metaphorical extension of the literal voyeurism for which Teiresias and others were punished. There is more to the Stesichoros–Helen story than this, of course: for one thing, it represents an extremely interesting, 'reflexive' use of myth—myth itself being used to explore the ambiguous truth-status (from a certain point of view) of myth. But what matters for our present purposes is that, while retaining a marked

in connection with the punishment of Anchises; but neither mentions blindness explicitly. For Anchises' *lameness* (a variant 'paradigmatic' with blindness; see 192–7 below), cf. Austin (1964) on *Aen.* 2.649.

50 Even other divinities, of course, might incur the wrath of Zeus. Ploutos transgressed against Zeus' order in wanting to favour the just amongst mortals. For this quasi-Promethean attitude he was requited with blindness (Ar. *Plut.* 87–92).

51 See Weiler (1974) 66–72.

52 See *RE* v A. 1 s.v. 'Thamyris', cols. 1236–45 (Gebhard), at 1241–2; Woodbury (1967) 173 n. 33.

53 This is not the place to go into the hotly disputed questions of how many palinodes (one or two) there were, and, if two, what relation obtained between them. The relevant primary sources and testimonia are at *PMG* frr. 192–3. On blindness and Stesichoros, see Graziosi (2002) 147–50.

narrative individuality—indeed uniqueness—the essentials of the infringement-and-punishment sequence in the Stesichoros–Helen myth show strong similarities to the structures already familiar to us.

(iii) *Transgressions not directly involving divinities.* The myths reported in (i) and (ii) use blindness to stress the importance of the distinction between gods and men. While this is a major function of the blindness motif, it is not its only function. Several myths depict mortals *guilty of sexual transgressions against other mortals* being punished by blinding. A glance at Devereux's list reveals that the transgressions are extremely various: incest, adultery, rape, and seduction figure prominently.[54] In so far as the gods are guarantors of human morality, such crimes are, at one remove, infringements of the divine order; but it would be misleading for us to classify them with narratives of *direct* infringements of the honour and power of the gods. Perhaps a connection between 'sexual' and 'overstepping mortality' blindness (if I may use this shorthand) may be seen in the light of the consideration that, in ignoring the restrictions placed on human sexual conduct, the transgressor is occupying a territory of greater freedom of sexual relationships normally available only to the gods. However, I put this suggestion forward with diffidence; my principal concern remains those cases which seem to me to deal unambiguously with the limits of humanity, and the gap between men and gods.

Paradigms

One of the useful things about a grammar is that it gives rules about the 'substitutability' of words in a language. Given ἔλυσα (*elusa*, 'I released'), we can form ἔπαυσα (*epausa*, 'I caused to stop'); given a sentence in which *elusa* is grammatically correct, we can, by substitution, form a new sentence in which *epausa* is grammatically correct. Following the usage of structural linguistics, we may conveniently call this relationship of substitutability 'paradigmatic', whereas the relationship between the individual items in any one utterance is called, in the same terminology, 'syntagmatic'. Thus, in the well-formed

[54] Devereux (1973) 41. Devereux's analysis groups together indiscriminately—I use the word without pejorative overtones—transgressions against immortals and mortals alike. From *his* point of view, this classification makes sense.

sentence 'I called John', the relationship between 'I' and 'called' and 'John' is syntagmatic, whereas that between 'called' and (say) 'killed' is paradigmatic.

Myth, it was suggested earlier, may be thought of as a language; and the analogy can, without forcing, be extended to include paradigmatic and syntagmatic relationships.[55] A myth is a chain of narrative items, and each item exists in a relationship of potential substitutability with other items. To take an example:

(i) Man sees goddess naked {
(ii) a man is blinded
(ii) b man goes mad
(ii) c man becomes woman

The relationship between (i) and (ii) is syntagmatic, that between (ii) a and (ii) b and (ii) c paradigmatic.

The last stage in this inquiry into blindness in Greek myths will be to look at motifs which are structurally equivalent to—stand in a paradigmatic relationship with—blindness in certain types of narrative.

One such equivalent motif is madness. We found a clear case of this in *Aias*, where the hero's temporary departure from his senses manifests itself as an inability to see properly: his shameful deed is, in fact, the result of his mistaking one thing for another. Euripides gives us evidence for the same equivalence in *The Madness of Herakles* and *Bakchai*, since the awakenings of Herakles and Agaue from their respective bouts of madness are likened to a recovery of 'normal' vision (*HF* 1089) and to a 'clearer' seeing (*Ba.* 1267).[56] Then there are several myths about men who see a divinity (or the image of a divinity) which they ought not to see, and become not blind, but mad. Skamandros saw Rhea during the performance of her mysteries, and went mad (Ps.-Plut. *De fluv.* 13.1). Similarly, Haliakmon unwittingly observed the sacred union of Zeus with Rhea, and lost his senses forthwith (Ps.-Plut. *De fluv.* 18.1). When Astrabakos and Alopekos found the wooden image of Artemis Orthia at Sparta, they too went mad (Paus. 3.16.9). Equally unlucky was Eurypylos,

[55] For a syntagmatic/paradigmatic distinction applied to the analysis of myth, see e.g. Lévi-Strauss (1966), index s.v. 'syntagmatic'; Leach (1976) 15, 25–7.

[56] See Mattes (1970) 110.

who found an image of Dionysos in a chest at Troy. Pausanias—exemplifying the inexhaustible inventiveness of surface detail characteristic of Greek myth—tells us that Eurypylos became mad, and continued in that condition '*with a few lucid intervals*' (7.19.7). That such myths had a counterpart in ritual is as certain as these things can be: at Patrai there was a wooden statue of Dionysos which maddened anyone who saw it, and which might only be handled on one sacred night during the year.[57]

One last story should be mentioned as an illustration of the equivalence between madness and blindness. It concerns Dionysos' foe Lykourgos. According to Homer, as we saw above, Lykourgos' effrontery led to his being blinded. But another variant gave the punishment as madness.[58] After going out of his mind, Lykourgos mutilated his son by chopping off his limbs because he took him for a vine-stock—that is, he mistook one thing for another.

Other forms of diminution of the faculties function as paradigmatic equivalents of blindness. Dumbness is an example. Aelian (*NA* 11.17) illustrates the Homeric tag that 'the gods are hard to look upon in their full brightness' (*Il.* 20.131) with a story about a sacred snake which lived at Metelis in Egypt. An old and inquisitive servant conceived a desire to see the beast. He did so, suffering predictably dire consequences: he went mad, lost the power of speech, and dropped dead. This would seem to be a case of structural overkill.[59]

For a male, to be changed into a female represents a departure from normality which is the equivalent of being blinded, maddened, or struck dumb. The Cretan Siproites was changed into a woman after he had seen Artemis bathing (Ant. Lib. *Met.* 17),[60] while 'some say that [Teiresias], having seen Athene naked, became a woman' (Tzetzes *schol. in Lyk. Alex.* 683).

Some other equivalents of blindness are more drastic still. Iodama was priestess of Athene Itonia in Boiotia. She went into the sanctuary at night, and the goddess appeared before her: Iodama saw (met the eyes of) the Gorgon's head which was worked on to Athene's robe,

[57] Paus. 7.19–20; see Burkert (1985) 223, also 228–9 on the role of the *kistē*, a sacred basket which might not be opened, in the myth-and-ritual of the Arrephoria at Athens.

[58] E.g. Apollod. *Bibl.* 3.5.1; other references at Mattes (1970) 21.

[59] Cf. Daphnis (n. 17 above) who was blinded *and* turned to stone.

[60] The best edition and commentary on the *Metamorphoses* of Antoninus Liberalis is Papathomopoulos (1968).

and immediately turned to stone (Paus. 9.34.1).[61] Aktaion's end was just as abrupt, but more violent. He saw Artemis bathing in a spring, was changed by her into a stag, and was torn to pieces by his own hounds.[62] Semele saw Zeus in all his glory, but expired on the spot; as so often, narrative details vary: Apollodoros (3.4.3) says she died of fright; others (e.g. Eur. *Hipp.* 559–62; Hyg. *Fab.* 179) put her death down directly to the scorching of Zeus' lightning and thunderbolt.[63] Then there are several myths, parallel with that of Thamyris, about characters whose reckless challenges to divinities brought them either a total or a partial loss of their humanity. Marsyas dared to compete with Apollo in a musical contest: the god flayed him for his presumption.[64] The nine daughters of Pieros were changed into birds after they had challenged the Muses to a contest of song (e.g. Ant. Lib. *Met.* 9).[65] Equally unwise was the attempt of some Messapian shepherds to dance better than the Nymphs. Their clod-hopping performance (*amousos*, Ant. Lib. *Met.* 31) resulted, with no little irony, in their metamorphosis into trees.[66] Arachne overstepped the limits of humanity by seeking to out-weave Athene; for her pains she became that less-than-human weaver, the spider.[67] The 'grammatical' rule that an attempt to exceed human competence is followed by—or, in structural terms, is balanced by—a compensating and usually appropriate reduction in humanity is surely proved by an apparent exception: the Sirens. These half-birdlike, half-human creatures competed with the Muses at singing. As a consequence they lost their feathers (Paus. 9.34.3), so becoming less-than-normal birds.[68]

[61] The glance of *all* divinities, not just Gorgo, is fearsome and powerful; cf. Malten (1961) 12, on Homer. For petrifaction see *RE* vii, s.v. 'Gorgo', cols. 1630–55 (Ziegler), esp. 1638–9 ('Versteinerung'); Vernant (2006) 328; Forbes Irving (1990) 139–48; Buxton (2009), see index s.v. 'stone(s)'.

[62] The myth was very popular in antiquity; see Forbes Irving (1990) 197–201; Frontisi-Ducroux (2003) 95–143; Buxton (2009) 98–109.

[63] See Buxton (2009) 148–50, 158–9.

[64] See index to Weiler (1974) s.v. 'Marsyas'.

[65] Other references, with discussion, at Weiler (1974) 72–7.

[66] Weiler (1974) 90–1.

[67] Weiler (1974) 100–4.

[68] Sirens: Weiler (1974) 77–80; Aguirre Castro (1994); Jiménez San Cristóbal (2012) 139–42. Bettini and Spina (2007) present an engaging and idiosyncratic retelling/interpretation of the myth; cf. the review by Agapiou in *BMCR* 2007.11.20.

What conclusions are we to draw from these paradigmatic motifs? Three points may be made.

First, it is worth noticing that the same structural relationship which we observed in myths about people with special powers and special defects is also found in myths about people whose acts of transgression take them momentarily 'above' the limits of humanity and who are then reduced to a condition 'below' that of normal humanity. Both sorts of narrative mark the crucial significance of the boundary between god and man.

Secondly, we can use our findings to contribute towards an evaluation of a characteristically psychoanalytical approach to myth. In particular, what do we make of the equation, favoured by psychoanalytical critics, between blindness and castration? Writers who are unsympathetic to psychoanalysis tend to ignore this equation, while those who *are* so sympathetic usually assume the validity of the equation without argument. I think our analysis may help to clarify what is at stake in this polarization of methods. It is demonstrable that in some myths blinding is equivalent to metamorphosis from male to female. But a lot of other motifs are equivalent to blinding as well. In the logic of Greek myth as we have tried to uncover it, there is nothing *privileged* about the male/female metamorphosis vis-à-vis all the other equivalents. To regard blindness as merely 'standing for' castration is quite as arbitrary as to regard dumbness as 'standing for' madness. The *priority* of castration over blindness cannot be demonstrated from the Greek evidence.

Thirdly—and this is a conclusion which readers will certainly have formed already for themselves—it must be emphasized that we have very far from exhausted the richness of the corpus even of the blindness myths, let alone that of the paradigmatic equivalents. We have only intermittently raised the issue of why, in a given case, blindness is preferred to one of the other motifs. In order to answer this question properly we should need to devote to the equivalents as detailed a study as we gave to blindness. Again, we omitted to examine *where* blindings, maddenings, contests with gods, etc., take place.[69] That they usually happen in areas separate from the normal social space of the city, either in wild as opposed to civilized parts (mountain tops, glens, remote springs), or in special areas like

[69] I am indebted to my former pupil Rachel Morris for stressing to me the importance of this point.

sanctuaries, is an observation which needs to be set in the context of a wider study of the places in which mythical relations (e.g. sex) between gods and mortals occur. Such an undertaking, though it would definitely repay attention, is beyond our scope here.[70]

3. SOPHOKLES: FIFTH-CENTURY ATHENS AND THE LIMITS OF KNOWLEDGE

In using blindness as an image to represent the limits of humanity, Sophokles was making explicit something already implicit in the logic of Greek myth. But to say that tells us nothing about the 'tone of voice' used by the dramatist in developing this theme. In order to catch the particular quality of that voice, we must stop treating mythical variants as of equal worth irrespective of date and provenance, and focus once more on the time and place at which Sophokles was writing.

In fifth-century Athens the problem of human limits, like many other questions of profound intellectual significance, was subjected to a fresh and intelligent scrutiny. One sort of approach is exemplified by thinkers who observed and analysed the regularities in experience in order to be able to deal better with similar phenomena if ever they occurred again. The clearest instances of this are Thucydides, who consciously produced a 'possession for all time' (1.22.4); and the Hippokratic writers, whose meticulous classification of symptoms was designed to help subsequent doctors recognize comparable *tekmēria* ('signs') should they recur in the future. At bottom, the methods of Thucydides and the medical writers offered intellectual hope—hope that the boundaries of one man's or one generation's understanding might be exceeded thanks to the recording of accumulated experience for the use of posterity.

A contrasting attitude was adopted by certain philosophers. Gorgias affirmed that the foundations of human knowledge were shaky. Protagoras insisted on the *adēlotēs* ('lack of clarity') which affected men's knowledge of one major aspect of the world—divinity:

[70] Subsequently to the original publication of this article I have attempted to explore in some detail the significance of landscape in Greek myth: e.g. in Buxton (1994) 80–113, and in a number of chapters in the present volume.

'Concerning the gods, I have no way of knowing either that they exist, or that they do not exist, or what form they have: for there are many things which prevent knowledge, (namely) the unclarity (*sc.* of that which is to be known) and the fact that human life is short' (fr. 4 DK).[71] Man might be the measure of all things, but his insight was, at least in one respect, severely limited.

In so far as he, too, stressed the limitations of humanity, Sophokles might at first glance seem to exhibit an affinity with Protagoras; but nothing could be further from Protagorean scepticism about the gods than the world of Sophoklean drama. In fact, if we want a closer parallel to the Sophoklean attitude to limits, it can be found, not in the developments of speculative thought at Athens, but in the utterances of the oracle at Delphi. The characteristic Delphic response—a good instance is the reply given to Kroisos about crossing the river Halys (Hdt. 1.53; 91)—was ambiguous, turning the questioner back upon himself, beguiling his aspiration towards clear vision, denying him salvation.[72] The oracle *sēmainei* ('gives signs') (Herakleit. fr. 93 DK), but offers no guarantee that fallible humanity will interpret the signs correctly. (It is Zeus' will, says Phineus at Ap. Rhod. *Arg.* 2.314–16, that the clues offered to mankind by divination shall be *imperfect.*) Delphi starkly confronts man with his frailty. The plays of Sophokles and the pronouncements of Delphi alike convey a sense of the inscrutability of the gods, and of man's inability fully to grasp their will in time to avert disaster.[73]

In a way, then, Sophokles is merely filling out the implications of the mythical structures which we examined earlier, structures which express the importance of the gulf between men and gods. Yet that 'merely' already feels uneasy, and it certainly glosses over much that is essentially Sophoklean. For, at the same time as making his audience aware of human limits, Sophokles makes them aware also of what humans can achieve within and in spite of those limits. Just because the gods are remote, human character and human choices acquire greater significance.

[71] See C. W. Müller (1967). Only with Plato was the unclarity of everyday experience reconciled with the notion of an eternal and unchanging truth, a truth to be approached through the trained mind of the philosopher. In the simile of the cave in the *Republic*, the identity between ignorance and blindness and between knowledge and sight was used to affirm, not the weakness, but the transcendent power of man's vision. On philosophical aspects of visibility/invisibility see Schuhl (1953); Gernet (1981) 343–51.

[72] Sabbatucci (1965) 187–8.

[73] Cf. R. Parker (1999) 17.

This point is rather important, and it may be worth illustrating it briefly with reference to some of the plays. The first scene in *Aias* leaves us in no doubt of man's inferiority to the gods in respect of power—Athene spells this out with brutal clarity at 127–33; but the rest of the play shows us that, in spite of the limitations of our mortality, we do have the power to make fundamental moral choices. We can aspire to be fair and just, like Odysseus, or loyal, like Teukros; or we can be mean-spirited, like Menelaos and Agamemnon. And such choices *matter*. In *Elektra* we have, early on, a reference to the (much-debated) Delphic injunction upon Orestes to commit matricide; yet thereafter it is the *human* aspects of the action, such as the conflicts between Elektra and Chrysothemis and Elektra and Klytaimestra, and the impact upon Elektra of Orestes' 'death', which occupy the centre of the drama. *Philoktetes* is played out against the background of references to prophecies by the Trojan seer Helenos; yet the main significance of the play is created by the complex and shifting pattern of human choices, hesitations, and decisions enacted by Neoptolemos, Odysseus, and Philoktetes. *Oidipous at Kolonos* might at first glance seem to be an exception, in that Oidipous' passing apparently suggests that the limits of humanity are not as inflexible as all that. But we must beware of convincing ourselves that the play ends in a glorious apotheosis. After all, the voice which summons Oidipous is strange, allusive, and enigmatic, and gives no inkling of a majestic or godlike existence for him after his death.[74] In fact, as is usual with Sophokles, what is more to the point than the reaction of the gods is the reaction of the humans: and it is upon the behaviour of Oidipous towards his sons and daughters, their behaviour towards him, and the contrasting postures of Kreon and Theseus, that the dramatic weight falls.

Once we recognize that it is the *individual moral consequences* of the limitations of our common humanity which Sophokles invites his audience to ponder, we can see that he is not 'merely' reproducing a theme offered to him by the mythical tradition. Certainly, the basic nature of the relation between men and gods was built into the structures of Greek myth; but the delineation of character and the ascription of motive—in a word, the placing of the moral accent—all this lay with the dramatist.

[74] See Linforth (1951) 180–4.

And so we are back where we began this essay: with the mood of Sophoklean tragedy. It would be wrong to see him as an unrelievedly pessimistic writer. Suicides may be frequent in his plays, but the context in which they occur is neither godless nor meaningless. The gods' will may be hard for mortals to fathom, and it may not match human notions of what is just; but the gods are indisputably *there*, as ever-present, yet as distant, as the 'wheeling paths of the [Great] Bear' (*Trach.* 130–1).[75] However, it is not the gods who are the principal source of meaning in Sophokles: it is man. In the Sophoklean dramatic universe man does not passively accept his limitations: he demands, affirms, strives. With one or two exceptions (Deianeira, perhaps Philoktetes) his characters are not warm or lovable, but they do act with passionate and memorable intensity; and it is this intensity (which Bernard Knox has christened 'the heroic temper'),[76] together with a feeling that there *is* a divine will if only we could see it, that counterbalances the impression of man's limitations and produces the mood, poised somewhere between hope and despair, which we associate with Sophokles.[77]

Postscript 2012:

This chapter is by some distance the most elderly in the book, as its original version came out in 1980. However, it seems to have stood up gratifyingly well, and continues to be cited when the topic of blindness in antiquity is being discussed.[78] I was especially pleased to see that it found favour with Eleftheria Bernidaki-Aldous, whose book-length study (1990) was informed by direct personal experience, the author herself being blind. Moreover, though I did not know it at the time, I was to have my own indirect, existential brush with blindness, since my father was sightless for the last years of his life. Blindness may be a 'theme', but it is also much more than that.

[75] Cf. Lattimore (1958) 102. [76] Knox (1964).

[77] An early version of this chapter was read at a meeting of the Classical Society of King's College, Cambridge. I am most grateful to those who participated in the discussion, above all to Geoffrey Lloyd. Later drafts were put before research seminars in the Sociology and Classics departments at Bristol, and before the Oxford Philological Society. My thanks go to all who offered comments on these various occasions, in particular to John Gould and Christopher Rowe. Finally, I am indebted to Jan Bremmer and Fritz Graf, who were responsible for suggesting that I work up my ideas into a paper, and whose criticisms have been most valuable.

[78] See for example Létoublon (2010) and Tatti-Gartziou (2010).

10

Euripides' *Alkestis*: Five Aspects of an Interpretation

As should have become clear from Chapters 6, 8, and 9, the exploration of divine/human relationships in tragic myth-telling is profound and complex. I end this book with what I hope are two further demonstrations of this truth. The second of these, in Chapter 11, concerns a tragedy of unquestionable genius. The first, to which we turn now, focuses on a drama whose apparent simplicity belies an always challenging and sometimes brilliant reworking of mythology. Both plays illustrate the indispensability of situating Greek tragedy within its contemporary cultural context.

In this chapter I discuss five topics which seem to me to be of major importance for our interpretation of Euripides' *Alkestis*. Whereas many previous treatments have concentrated on matters of characterization, especially relating to Admetos, the emphasis of my own account will be different. Only the fourth of my sections will engage with the debate over character. For the rest, I shall be analysing the changing significance of the door in the visual stage action (Section 1), the boundary between life and death (Section 2), the role of Herakles (Section 3), and the tone of the work as a whole (Section 5). In keeping with the scope of this book, I shall from time to time explore certain 'themes', notably the house door, veiling, and silence.

1. THE DOOR OF THE HOUSE

The *skēnē* represents Admetos' palace at Pherai. In the centre is the door, the visual focus for most of the significant actions in the plot.

According to a stage direction recorded in the scholia, the play begins with the emergence of Apollo from the house. While it is impossible to demonstrate the correctness of such a direction, it is surely incontrovertible that such a beginning is symbolically appropriate. Apollo's identification with the fortunes of Admetos is now over: the presence of the god from above is to be replaced by that of the god from below. Thus at the end of the first scene, Apollo leaves by the side exit, but Thanatos enters the palace through the central doorway.[1]

When the chorus arrive they notice (98–103) that outside the door there is no sign either of hair cut in mourning or of a vessel of water—needed, after a death, so that those emerging can purify themselves before resuming contact with normality outside.[2] The reason for these absences is of course that Alkestis is still alive. When she has emerged, spoken, and died, she is carried back into the house; and the house door then takes on the significance which had been prefigured as Thanatos passed through it: it becomes the point of transition between the polluted interior and the non-polluted world outside.

With the arrival of Herakles on his way north, the significance of the door is intensified. In order to treat Herakles properly, i.e. as a *xenos* ('stranger', 'guest-friend') and *philos* ('friend', 'person who is near or dear') should treat his *xenos* and *philos*, Admetos must persuade him to enter the house—in spite of the evidence from Admetos' appearance that this is a place of mourning. (Incidentally, it is surely quite likely that a vessel of water *has* now been placed on stage outside the door.) The pivot of Admetos' persuasion of Herakles is linguistic: the woman who has died was *othneios* ('no blood relation') (532–3).[3] For the first of two occasions in the play, a man gets his *philos* to enter the house by deception, but for the best of motives.

After the carrying-out of Alkestis and the argument with Pheres, the next scene, between Herakles and the servant, goes back to the linguistic point which I have just mentioned, but with a different word in question. 'Why so gloomy?', asks Herakles; 'the *pēma* ('pain', 'grief') is *thuraion*' (778); 'the woman who died was *thuraios*' (805). 'She was only too *thuraios*', replies the servant (811). Herakles: 'These

[1] Apollo emerges from house: see Hourmouziades (1965) 162–3. Symbolism of Apollo leaving and Thanatos entering the house: Dingel (1967) 213, followed by Rivier (1972) 130. There is virtually nothing on *Alc.* in Haight (1950).

[2] Schol. *Alc.* 98, 99; Ar. *Eccl.* 1033; Poll. *Onom.* 8. 65–6; cf. Kurtz and Boardman (1971) 146, and R. Parker (1983) 35.

[3] See Steidle (1968) 146, with n. 76; L. P. E. Parker (2007) xii.

don't sound like *thuraia pēmata*' (814); and later, when he knows the true identity of the deceased: 'He persuaded me by saying it was a *thuraion kēdos* ('grief', 'funeral rites', 'dead person') that he was taking to the tomb' (828). *Thuraios* is, etymologically speaking, 'at, connected with, the door' (hence Hermes, that quintessential boundary-crosser, can be Hermes Thuraios).[4] But just as 'Go and see who's at the door' means 'Go and see who's *outside* the door', so *thuraios* can mean 'one connected with the outside', 'an outsider'.[5] And a wife is an 'outsider', brought across the threshold into the husband's house from outside.[6]

It is exactly this reference which becomes poignantly explicit in the next scene. Admetos, having just buried Alkestis, returns to confront the house door, now hateful to him because of yet another range of associations which the door has (861–2; 911):

> Alas, hateful approach, hateful sight of this house of bereavement!
>
> . . . .
>
> O form [perhaps: 'familiar form'; the Greek word is *schēma*] of my house! How can I enter?

He is reminded of that other time when he passed through the house door, when he and Alkestis, white-robed instead of black, surrounded not by lamentation but by marriage songs, together entered the house, with Admetos holding her hand—that is, her wrist—in his (917).[7]

As the door was a boundary-marker in the case of a death, so it was in the case of a wedding. A Greek wedding dramatized in ritual terms the transition of a woman from the *oikos* ('house') of her father to the *oikos*, or more specifically the bedroom, of her husband. The crossing of the threshold of the new *oikos* was one aspect of this transition. There was, so far as I know, nothing comparable to the Roman custom of carrying the bride over the threshold (thus marking the danger and significance of the passage);[8] and the door of the bridal chamber seems if anything to have been of more importance (it was outside *that* door that a *thurōros* ('door-keeper') was posted);[9]

[4] Hermes Thuraios: cf. Farnell (1896–1909) v. 66 n. 23, and Eitrem in *RE* viii. col. 777.

[5] Linguistic connections between words meaning 'door' and 'outside': see Benveniste (1973) 255–6.

[6] For the bride as 'stranger' in the house into which she marries, see Llewellyn-Jones (2003) 173.

[7] Groom holds bride *cheir' epi karpōi* ('hand upon wrist'): see Jenkins (1983); the significance of the gesture in *Alc.* is noted by Foley (1985) 87–8.

[8] Bride carried over threshold in Rome: references listed by Ogle (1911) 253.

[9] *Thurōros*: Sappho fr. 110 (a) and (b) *PLF*; Poll. *Onom.* 3.42; Hesych. s.v.; see also Theoc. *Id.* 15.77 with Gow (1952) ad loc. On *Thurōros* as the title of a play by

nevertheless, the crossing of the threshold of the house itself *was* marked in Greece, since it was there that the couple were welcomed by the groom's parents.[10]

Recalling his marriage, Admetos describes his present dilemma (941; 944):

> How shall I bear to go into this house?
>
> . . . .
>
> The desolation [or: loneliness] within will drive me out.

'But *outside*' (950) there will be weddings, social gatherings of women of Alkestis' age—and that too will be intolerable. Apollo's unique gift to Admetos has resulted in a unique dilemma.

But when all is said and done, *Alkestis* is not a tragedy, it is a non-satyric fourth play. And so we have the scene where Herakles returns with a veiled woman (see Section 2). He reproaches Admetos for entertaining him as if concerned only for a *thuraiou pēmatos* ('foreign grief') (1014)—a line unnecessarily deleted by Louis Méridier following Karl Lachmann—and he urges Admetos to take the woman into the house. When Admetos at last relents, Herakles goes further: Admetos must lead her in *with his own right hand*—enacting, of course, the entry of a bridal couple (1115). For the second time a *philos* is deceiving a *philos* in order to be kind—although in this case there is perhaps a fine balance between our sense of the pain of the deceived *philos* and our anticipation of his joy. But eventually Admetos looks at Alkestis' face; and what came perilously close to being a bitter parody of part of a wedding ceremony turns into a resolemnization of the union which only death has put asunder. From the beginning of the play the significance of the action of entering the house has varied as the house itself has successively become a place of death, hospitality, mourning, and marriage. At the end, the restored stability of the house is sealed by a definitive re-entry of Admetos and Alkestis over the threshold, as man and wife.

Menander, see Theodoridis (1977) 52–3. We may add that the literary lover/suitor only got as far as the *house* door, which was where he sang his *paraklausithuron*; cf. Copley (1956).

[10] Welcome by groom's parents: schol. Eur. *Phoen.* 344 (mother); loutrophoros, Berlin, Staatliche Museen F2372, illustration in Jenkins (1983) Fig. 1 = Daremberg/Saglio s.v. 'matrimonium', fig. 4866 = Oakley and Sinos (1993) Figs. 72–3 (mother and father); cup, Berlin, Staatliche Museen F2530, illustration in Oakley and Sinos (1993) Fig. 91 (mother); pyxis, Paris, Louvre L55, illustration in Oakley and Sinos (1993) Fig. 90 = *LIMC* 'Apollon' 849 (? mother and father). For a general account of doors (and windows) in Greek vase-painting, see Halm-Tisserant (1995).

2. LIFE AND DEATH

The relations between life and death in *Alkestis* are complex;[11] and perhaps the most interesting aspect of this complexity is the fact that, for virtually the whole of the play, Alkestis herself is presented as being between life and death. Before going inside the house, Thanatos says that the person whose hair his sword has consecrated (76) by cutting it is thenceforth dedicated to the gods below: so begins Alkestis' separation from life. In practically their first words the chorus express doubt about whether Alkestis is alive or dead (79–83). When a servant-girl comes out of the house, and the chorus ask her, 'Is she alive or dead?', they are told (141):

> It is possible to tell you that she is both alive and dead.

By her actions—washing herself as a preliminary to putting on the clothes in which she will die; praying to the hearth and adorning the altars of the other gods; bidding farewell to her bed, children, and servants—Alkestis shows that she is in the process of dying. It is not a physiological, 'Hippokratean' process ('seventh day: great chill; acute fever; much sweat; death'); rather it is a social process, involving severance from all the cultural ties which bind a person to life.[12] The counterpart to the social process of dying is the belief that death is not instantaneous, but a journey: so Alkestis sees a two-oared boat, and Charon calls, 'Why do you hesitate?' (252–5). The reference to Charon is significant: he, like Thanatos, is an *intermediate* agent of death.[13] Perhaps this makes the ultimate rescue more imaginatively credible: the dead woman has not yet been definitively incarcerated in Hades. Furthermore, although she dies at line 391, Alkestis in a way remains, even after that, between life and death. We have already been told (348–54) of Admetos' plan to give his wife a kind of continued existence by creating a lifelike statue of her; and when Herakles arrives and asks, 'How is your wife?', Admetos' reply ('She is alive, and no longer alive', 521) seems to perpetuate in a linguistic manner this ambiguity of Alkestis' status. Even at the very end of the play, when Death has been defeated, Alkestis is still not yet fully alive. As throughout the play, so at its end, she is poised on the

[11] Good remarks on this in Burnett (1965).
[12] On death as a process, see Garland (2001) 13.
[13] See Dale (1954) on 871.

boundary between life and death. To see how this can be so, it will be necessary to explore two themes: veiling and silence.

On the evidence of Admetos' words at 1050 ('She is young, *to judge from her clothing and appearance*') the scholiast inferred that Alkestis was veiled; and he was surely right. At 1121 Herakles instructs Admetos: 'Look at her'—and here Herakles will have unveiled her. (Compare Euripides' *The Madness of Herakles* 1227, where Theseus, unveiling the polluted Herakles, tells him: 'Look at me'.) The veil in *Alkestis* is powerful from the sheerly dramatic point of view, in that it makes possible the tense persuasion of Admetos by Herakles, which depends on Admetos' inability correctly to identify a woman—just as Admetos earlier persuaded Herakles when Herakles failed correctly to identify a woman.

But there is more to veiling than that. A veil often marks out an individual who is in a marginal or transitional state. Those in mourning veil themselves.[14] Those in the abnormal state of being polluted might cover their heads.[15] And of course veiling might mark a transition with quite different emotional resonances: as Kassandra says in *Agamemnon*, 'My oracle will no longer peep out from a veil like a newly married bride' (1178–9). That the bridal veil signals a transition is evident enough; but there is uncertainty over details. We know that the bride was veiled at the meal at her father's house,[16] but when did she *unveil?* In his 1982 account of the Anakalupteria, or Ceremony of Unveiling, John Oakley followed Ludwig Deubner in placing it at the house of the bride's father, i.e. *before* the procession to the new house.[17] However, not only is it more plausible on general grounds of ritual symbolism that the bride made the transition from house to house veiled,[18] but there are a considerable number of vases showing the bride in the bridal procession with her head still veiled, even if her face is visible.[19] Whenever the unveiling took place, it is clear

[14] Hom. *Il.* 24.93–4; *Od.* 8.92; *Hymn. Hom. Dem.* 40–2; Pl. *Phd.* 117c; etc.

[15] Eur. *HF* 1160–2, with Bond (1981) ad loc.

[16] Lucian *Symp.* 8: 'very carefully veiled'. An *onos* from Eretria (Beazley ARV^2 1250–1, 34; Arias and Hirmer [1962] pl. 203 = *LIMC* 'Alkestis' 3) shows Alkestis veiled in the company of women—possibly before the wedding.

[17] Deubner (1900); Oakley (1982). But in Oakley and Sinos (1993, 25) the stress is laid, rather, on the *inconsistency* about timing evidenced in the sources.

[18] So rightly Roussel (1950) 10.

[19] For vases depicting wedding processions see Haspels (1930); Boardman (1952) 34–5; Krauskopf (1977); Oakley and Sinos (1993) 26–34. Examples of 'veiled' bride – i.e. bride with head covered—in bridal procession: Berlin loutrophoros, Berlin cup,

that the moment when the groom saw the bride's face was an important one in the wedding ritual (one name for the gifts presented to the bride at the Anakalupteria was *optēria*, 'to do with seeing');[20] and realizing the importance of the moment of seeing the bride may sharpen our awareness of what is at stake in the unveiling in Euripides' play.[21]

What, then, of the veiled Alkestis? She is in a doubly transitional state. Firstly, she is still between death and life, between the other world and this.[22] Secondly, her new arrival at Admetos' *oikos* is like the prelude to a second marriage. There is no reason to believe that Alkestis' unveiling *before entering the house* represents a direct transcription of wedding ritual. Rather it would seem that the symbolism of unveiling is borrowed and adapted to fit the specific dramatic requirements of the play. Alkestis must unveil onstage (i.e. outside the house) because Admetos must recognize her onstage.

I have repeatedly spoken of Alkestis as a character poised between life and death. It remains to consider one last aspect of this point. 'You may speak to her,' Herakles tells Admetos, 'but it is not yet *themis* ('lawful') for you to hear her addressing you, until she has been deconsecrated from the gods below, when the third dawn comes' (1132; 1144–6). The connection between silence, covering the head,

and Louvre pyxis, as cited in n. 10 above; hydria from Orvieto (Florence, Mus. Arch. Naz. 3790 = *LIMC* 'Peleus' 208) showing Peleus and Thetis on marriage chariot, Beazley *ABV* 260, 30.

[20] Pollux *Onom.* 2.59, 3.36, cf. Deubner (1900) 148.

[21] Since I wrote the original version of this chapter, a major work on veiling in ancient Greece has appeared: Llewellyn-Jones (2003). He intriguingly (though perhaps not quite convincingly) suggests that we may need to allow for *several successive unveilings* in the course of the several days of wedding ceremonies. He argues further—and here I am quite sure he is right—that it is unwise to impose uniformity of procedure on what may have been a custom which had major local variations (227–48). I am encouraged that L.-J. accepts, as I did (and do), that 'the mask of the actor playing Alkestis must have been veiled at the crucial moment of her return from the dead in order for the scene to work and for Admetos to unveil her at line 1123' (107; cf. 234 with n. 114 on p. 254); see also Rehm (1994) 89 with 193–4 n. 23; Vérilhac and Vial (1998) 304–12. For a wholly unconvincing rejection of the idea of a veiled Alkestis, see Luschnig and Roisman (2003) 209–10. L. P. E. Parker (2007, on lines 1006–1158) rightly assumes that Alkestis is veiled, but makes the curious observation that '[t]here is no reason to ask why Alkestis is veiled'. On the contrary, there is every reason to ask that question, as Llewellyn-Jones (not cited by Parker) amply demonstrates, and as I myself (not cited either) have sought to argue.

[22] Eurydike too is veiled during her transition from death to life: see the fifth-century relief of Orpheus, Eurydike, and Hermes (known from Roman copies, cf. H. A. Thompson (1952), esp. 60–9, with pl. 17a, and E. B. Harrison (1964), with pl. 12d = *LIMC* 'Eurydike I' 5a).

and real or symbolic death is not unfamiliar to us. We think perhaps of Benedictine monks, who wear the hood over the head at all times when forbidden to speak; but when they take their final vows, they lie still and prostrate on a pall (not only physically resembling the dead but explicitly 'dying to the world') and have the hood pinned under the chin; they must then keep silence until the hood is unpinned—at Communion, on the third day afterwards.[23] From ancient Greece we have several examples of a congruence between veiling and silence.[24] Aischylos' Niobe sits veiled and silent until (on one reading of the text of the *Life of Aischylos*) the third day;[25] and his Achilles seems to have covered his head and been silent in both *Phrygians* and *Myrmidons*—his silence persisting in the latter case, apparently, till the third day.[26] Euripides' Phaidra is veiled and silent at one point in *Hippolytos* through shame at her polluting state; and it is her third day without food.[27] In *Alkestis* the congruence is only partial: the silence persists for three days *after* the unveiling. This is partly a matter of dramatic necessity: as we observed earlier, she *has* to unveil, but there is no compelling reason for her to speak. But her silence is appropriate in ritual terms too, since it marks her unusually anomalous condition. The words of a person in any state of pollution might be harmful to others: as Orestes says in *Eumenides*, 'the law is that the murderer be without speech until purified'.[28] But this applies a fortiori to Alkestis: she has died and been buried. Plutarch notes that anyone for whom carrying-out and burial had been performed, as though he were dead, was considered impure by the Greeks, and they would not let such a

[23] There are further links between the hood and 'death': the monk is surrounded, when prostrate, by 'catafalque' candles; and monks are buried with the hood *up*. (I am indebted for guidance here to the late Dr Ian Hammett.)

[24] See Montiglio (2000) 176–80; Llewellyn-Jones (2003) 269–74.

[25] *TrGF* iii. T1, 20–2, with p. 265 Radt; see Taplin (1972) 60–2. But the 'third day' detail is regarded as textually unsound by Radt (1981).

[26] The 'third day' detail is accepted for *Myrmidons* by Taplin (1972) 64 (cf. *TrGF* iii. *ΜΥΡΜΙΔΟΝΕΣ*, p. 239 Radt). In *Phrygians or The Ransom of Hektor* Achilles' motive for veiling seems to have been grief (*TrGF* iii. T1, 22–3 Radt); in *Myrmidons* it may have been because of his self-imposed marginality; see Taplin (1972) 76. Michelakis (2002, 36–7) convincingly interprets Achilles' crouching position and hiding of his face in *Myrmidons* as expressive of distress and anger, whereas his silence constitutes a deliberate weapon directed at those who seek to impose their will upon him.

[27] Eur. *Hipp.* 275.

[28] *Eum.* 448–50. For the converse see *Eum.* 276–7 and esp. 287: when Orestes' pollution has gone, he speaks 'from a pure mouth'. Note also Eur. *IT* 951 and 956, for the silence surrounding the polluted Orestes at Athens.

person associate with themselves or approach a temple; and Hesychios refers to a ceremony of re-enacted birth designed to admit the *deuteropotmos* ('one who, though supposed dead, reappears alive') back to life.[29] Did a symbolic silence figure in the ritual for managing such a rare and anomalous case, and was Euripides adapting that silence in *Alkestis*? There is, I think, no evidence; and the silence could just as easily have been Euripidean invention, appropriate because of Alkestis' still-dangerous link with the dead. Or could he, here too, have been borrowing from the wedding ritual? When the bride was veiled before the Anakalupteria, did she also have to keep silent, being restored to normal communication only after the unveiling? According to Pollux, an alternative name for the Anakalupteria gifts was *prosphthegtēria* ('gifts of salutation').[30] In any case, we would be dealing, not with a simple 'reflection' of ritual, but with its adaptation to the needs of a given dramatic context.

Even at the end, then, Alkestis is not yet fully alive. Through her fate, the relation between life and death is shown to be in certain respects ambiguous. Now closely related to this ambiguity is what seems to be an outright paradox. The plot is based on the assumption that Death will inevitably get what is due to him: if Admetos does not die, someone else must. Furthermore, there is in the course of the work a series of references to the *fixity* of the boundary between life and death: (a) the fate of Asklepios (3–4, 122–9; cf. 970) who raised the dead and was thunderbolted for it; (b) the emphatic words of Herakles at 528, 'Most people reckon there is a big difference between being alive and being dead'; (c) the attitude of the chorus: 'There is no way round Necessity' (962–72); 'You will not raise the dead' (985–6).[31] And yet *Alkestis* ends with the defeat of Thanatos and the restoration of Alkestis. Is the

[29] The revived dead: Plut. *Quaest. Rom.* 264f–265a; Hesych. s.v. '*deuteropotmos*'. See Betts (1965) and R. Parker (1983) 61.

[30] Pollux 3.36.

[31] A word needs to be added about Admetos' assertion (357–62) that, had he the voice of Orpheus, he would have gone down to charm the powers of the Underworld. One implication is, of course, that Admetos does *not* have the voice of Orpheus; hence the outlook in Admetos' own case would seem (as with the references to Asklepios) to be made even more pessimistic. On the other hand, it is not clear what version of the Orpheus/Eurydike story had the greater currency in Euripides' time—did he look back and lose her, or was his mission successful? If the latter alternative were being evoked, the reference to Orpheus might offer a small glimmer of hope that the boundary between life and death *can* be affected by human entreaty. On the ambiguities of the reference to Orpheus in *Alkestis*, see Graf (1987) 81.

boundary between life and death not, then, fixed, as we have been led to believe? On this paradox two things should be said.

First we must consider who it is that is apparently threatening the boundary between life and death. Of all the figures in Greek myth, Herakles is the one who seems to be licensed most regularly to push beyond boundaries. In particular, he breaks the confines of mortality in two ways: downwardly, by invading Hades and stealing Kerberos; and upwardly, by achieving acceptance into Olympos. In *Alkestis* the boundary between life and death is not abolished or redrawn: 'after' the action of the play, things will remain as they are. It is just that, in one exceptional case, the exceptional hero par excellence is able to intervene and postpone (but not, we imagine, cancel) the death of Alkestis.

This leads us to the second point. In the house of Admetos, normal life has at last, we must assume, been re-established. Normal life—and normal death: the recent suspension of normal relationships between life and death has, presumably, come to an end. From the beginning of the play, the relationship between life and death has been in an unusual state, with both the main characters poised in different ways between the two; finally, the usual distance between the extremes is restored.[32] Perhaps one respect in which *Alkestis* asserts itself as a 'fourth play' rather than a tragedy is that, at its conclusion, at least one ambiguity is resolved instead of being left open-ended.

3. HERAKLES

In order to appreciate Herakles' role in *Alkestis* it will be useful first to remind ourselves about his place within Greek mythology as a whole, and the literary tradition in particular.[33]

Herakles was the great 'helper' to whom one could appeal in time of trouble. Myths about him range widely: from the East to the far West, from (as we mentioned) the Underworld to Olympos. In other ways too he is associated with the limits of humanity: he is repeatedly connected

[32] Gregory (1979, 267) appropriately describes Herakles in this play as 'the restorer of differences'.

[33] One may consult Brelich (1958), Galinsky (1972), Silk (1985), and Stafford (2010) (with more bibliography cited in her n.1). The *LIMC* entries in vols. iv and v, and in *LIMC Supplementum 2009*, are monumental in all senses.

with animals, which he kills or controls; he has to deal with centaurs (incompletely human) and with Amazons (abnormally human). Sometimes, it is true, Herakles is situated in the social rather than the natural world, as when he sacks the cities of Troy and Oichalia. But here once more he is hardly a comfortably socialized being: he is a disrupter of civilization, a hero whose boundless violence can be a potential threat to order as well as (when he slays monsters) a supporter of it.

Literary representations of the hero are heterogeneous. It will be convenient to take three examples:

(a) *Praise-poetry.* In Pindar Herakles has an honoured place as a representative of athleticism, of *aretē* ('excellence'), and of a willingness to strive in order to deserve the reward of victory. In return for his exertions he attained peace and rest on Olympos, with Hebe by his side (*Nem.* 1.69–72). Such ambivalence as there is in the Pindaric Herakles[34] fades before the presentation of the hero as a shining example to emulate.

(b) *Tragedy.* Here Herakles is a much more paradoxical and ambiguous figure. In *Women of Trachis*, for instance, he is the monster-slayer who is himself a monster, the mighty hero who is brought so low as to be subservient to a woman (Omphale, Deianeira); in *The Madness of Herakles* he is the hero who is both son of a god and son of a man. In general, tragedy explores the darker and more problematic side of Herakles—he is a defender of civilization, yet he can kill his own wife and children, and is only just prevented from killing his father, Amphitryon.

(c) *Comedy.* Once more, of course, we have a different emphasis. In his *Learned Banqueters* Athenaios cites two comic authors who give complementary pictures of the gluttonous Herakles: 'Epicharmos, for example, says in his *Busiris*: "If you saw him eating, first of all, you'd die. His throat emits a roar, his jaw rattles, his molars resound, his canine teeth squeak, he snorts loudly, and he wiggles his ears."' And in Ion's satyr-play *Omphale* the audience heard that 'not content with the steaks, he ate the firewood and charcoal from the grill as well'.[35]

Where do we locate *Alkestis* in all this? The Herakles of this play combines the three types which we have reviewed. The mighty athlete

[34] Cf. Silk (1985) 7.
[35] *Deipn.* 411b–c; trans. slightly adapted from Olson (2008).

praised by Pindar is the heroic figure who strides boldly out to wrestle with Death. The fact that it is *with Death* that Herakles fights reminds us of the tragic Herakles, whose exploits so often have the profoundest implications for humanity and for the boundary between life and death. And the scene in which the bewildered servant reports the drunken misbehaviour of his unruly guest reminds us of the Herakles of comedy. But it is important that we do not misrepresent the balance between the three aspects of Herakles in *Alkestis*. In particular, we must realize that there is nothing tragic about Herakles' own position. He is on his way to Thrace to perform one of his Labours; that is, he is *in the middle* of his Labours. His situation is therefore unproblematic: only when his Labours are over, as in *The Madness of Herakles*, will his fate become precarious. In *Alkestis* he is merely in transit. The only tragic or near-tragic events with which he comes into contact are events in the life of the Thessalian household in which he is entertained.

One other question is worth asking before we leave Herakles: why is he not polluted either by entering the house of Admetos when the corpse is still inside, or by his wrestling match with Death? On the first point, no one in the play expresses any criticism of Admetos for exposing Herakles to possible pollution, so we can only conclude that no such pollution was felt to have been incurred—presumably because pollution most strongly affected the deceased's immediate kin, a group to which Herakles clearly did not belong.[36] As for the second point, I suggest that the reason why Apollo (like Artemis in *Hippolytos*) feels compelled to avoid a house where Death is present, while Herakles can go so far as to wrestle with Death, is that, in religious terms, the distance between Apollo and Death is greater than that between Herakles and Death: Apollo is a god of the above, Death a god of the below, and Herakles a figure whose activities span both spheres. With a splendidly structuralist logic, Herakles can operate where Apollo fears to tread.

4. ADMETOS AND HOSPITALITY

The issue of how we are to take the character of Admetos has come virtually to dominate criticism of the play. On the one hand, there are

[36] See Garland (2001, 41–2) on the varying relationship between pollution and degrees of kinship in Greece.

scholars who detect numerous hints that Admetos' willingness to accept his wife's sacrifice is represented by Euripides in a negative light.[37] On the other hand, there are those who prefer a 'naïve' reading, accepting the lines at face value rather than looking between and behind them. My own view coincides with the latter approach, and in particular with the excellent discussion by Anne Pippin Burnett.[38] I shall confine myself here to some specific comments in support of a 'non-ironical' reading of *Alkestis*.

A small but significant detail occurs in the scene where the servant tells the chorus about Alkestis' moving farewell to her children, marriage bed, and household slaves. Although the chorus are full of praise for Alkestis (150–1), they express sympathy for Admetos too (144):

> Poor wretch, what a man you are, what a woman you have lost!

It would have been perfectly possible for Euripides to have written a play in which Admetos appeared as unpleasantly insensitive as is Jason in *Medea*; but that is not what he has done. Again, nothing in the farewell scene between husband and wife can lead us to regard Admetos as a hypocrite, or to regard his grief as insincere. As a result of his generosity to a god, he has been given a gift; and the gifts of the gods, as Paris reminded Hektor (*Il.* 3.65), are not to be cast away. Apollo's gift to Admetos was life; and one of the play's paradoxes is that this life is no life at all without the person who made the life possible. But, for most of *Alkestis*, the result of the paradox is sympathy for Admetos, not censure of him. For most of *Alkestis* the question 'What do we make of a man who allows his wife to die so that he himself may live?' is simply not asked, because that is not what the play is mainly about.

[37] An example is W. D. Smith (1960), who sees the play's apparently positive verdict on Admetos undercut by 'a running commentary which hints at kinds of motivation and qualities of character beneath the surface' (134); on this reading Admetos emerges as 'self-centred, cowardly, and short-sighted' (129). For similarly unflattering views of Admetos, see von Fritz (1962) 256–321, esp. 310; Schwinge (1968) 109; Nielsen (1976).

[38] Burnett (1965), an article imperiously but quite unpersuasively dismissed by L. P. E. Parker (2007, xlviii–xlix). Another non-ironist is that fine Euripidean André Rivier (1972) and (1973). M. Lloyd (1985) and Thury (1988) also see ethical merits in Admetos. For Dyson (1988, 13), '[Admetos'] grief is genuine and his hospitality wholly admirable'.

The positive presentation of Admetos is maintained in the episode where he deceives Herakles into accepting hospitality. How are we to evaluate his decision to withhold the truth because he does not wish to fail in his obligations as a *xenos* ('guest-friend')?[39] Euripides does not present it as absurd or foolish. On the contrary, it is—as Herakles himself later recognizes (855–60)—the act of a noble man and a true friend. In a society such as that of ancient Greece, where travellers were bereft of all the social ties which made existence practicable when they were at home, the institution of *xenia* ('guest-friendship') was of enormous practical and emotional significance. Hence it was sanctioned by Zeus (Xenios) himself; and its obligations could be ignored only at great peril: in myth, those who break *xenia* invariably suffer for it, whether they are behaving as a wicked host in their own house (Tantalos) or as a wicked guest in the house of another (Paris). In presenting Admetos as a good *xenos* Euripides was reflecting a fundamental custom of Greek society; although the chorus is at first critical of Admetos, his explanation—he absolutely refuses to turn away a friend—convinces them, and they sing an ode in praise of his nobility.

Then, with a sharp contrast so typical of Euripides, we have the bitter scene between Admetos and Pheres. Now *for the first time* Euripides confronts us with the moral issue implicit in the starting point of the plot, namely: what do we make of a man who allows his wife to die so that he himself may live?[40] So far we have seen Admetos only as loving husband and noble host; now suddenly we are forced to look at the other side of the coin—to see him as a murderer (694–6):

> Shamelessly you strove to avoid death, and you are living past your appointed fate—having killed her.

Whether this scene can outweigh the positive evaluation of Admetos which the play has given us so far is perhaps something that each individual reader or spectator must answer for him-/herself; in my own view it certainly does not. The scene makes Admetos more complex, and therefore more interesting. We see his grief take a new direction, leading him to be fiercely aggressive to his own father. Hence his isolation becomes even more complete. The ground is thus

[39] On *xenia* in the play, see Stanton (1990) and, in relation to *charis*, Padilla (2000).

[40] On the radically new turn constituted by the Pheres scene, see Hose (2008) 47. Hose's discussion of the play (41–9) is thoroughly judicious.

prepared for the truly distressing scene beginning at line 861, when Admetos, returning after the funeral, comes face to face with the empty house. Here once more, as in the early part of the play, we must surely take Admetos' grief as sincere: there is more than a hint of real tragedy in his *arti manthanō* ('[Only] now do I realize it') (940).

How, finally, does the last scene of the play affect our view of Admetos? It is interesting that Herakles gently but firmly expresses criticism of Admetos for concealing the truth: 'I blame you, I blame you' (1017). The suggestion seems to be that true friendship in fact lies in something more than a mechanical returning of *charis* ('favour') for *charis*: it should involve a willingness to trust another person and to confide in them. But it is one of the numerous paradoxes of *Alkestis* that Herakles, in the very moment of blaming his *philos* for deceiving him, proceeds immediately to use deceit; and this brings us to the persuasion of Admetos by Herakles.

Could it be that Admetos' agreement to accept what he believes to be 'another woman' into his house is designed by Euripides to seem ironical in view of his earlier promise (328–31) not to remarry? It is of course hard to disprove such a suggestion conclusively; but certain considerations tell against it. Firstly, the resistance of Admetos is extremely lengthy. At line 1020 Herakles instructs him to look after the woman, but only at line 1108 does Admetos consent to her entry into the house; and not until 1118—almost exactly a hundred lines since the original instruction was given—does he reluctantly agree to take her in himself. Given the compression and stylization of stichomythia—one may contrast the mere fifteen lines which it takes Klytaimestra to persuade Agamemnon in *Agamemnon* (931–45)—Euripides can hardly be said to have portrayed Admetos acquiescing readily. Secondly, there is that much more pressure on Admetos to accept, because to refuse would be to refuse a *charis* to a friend—and throughout the play we have seen and heard of several such favours which have been presented in a positive light, most notably Alkestis' *charis* of life to Admetos and Admetos' *charis* of hospitality to Herakles. Thirdly, does it not make a difference that, because of what the audience knows but Admetos does not, the audience *wants* him to acquiesce? The desired outcome, the outcome which will restore the relationship torn by Alkestis' self-sacrifice and Admetos' grief, the outcome which will enable Herakles worthily to reciprocate Admetos' gift of hospitality—that outcome depends on Admetos' giving way. Often enough in his other works Euripides uses irony to expose the reality behind human pretension; but there is no reason why we should deny him the right to be unironical if that was what the drama required.

5. THE TONE OF *ALKESTIS*: TRAGEDY? COMEDY? 'FOURTH PLAY'?

Alkestis is unique amongst the surviving works of the Greek tragedians in that it is the only one of which we know both that it was put on fourth and that it was not a satyr-play. Scholars have tried to accommodate this uniqueness by inventing the term 'prosatyric'; but this does little more than remind us that there is an unusual phenomenon which needs explanation.[41] However, the impulse to coin such a term is not wholly misguided, since it reflects the importance of our being able to reconstruct the category—the mental 'heading'—to which the original audience would have ascribed the play. After all, some sense of what the Athenians would have expected from *Alkestis* is necessary before we can judge how far Euripides met, or perhaps challenged, those expectations. But how do we proceed if we have no other work which we can be certain is a non-satyric fourth play?

Faute de mieux we may consider satyr-plays themselves. To answer the question, 'What would the audience have expected from a fifth-century satyr-play?', we have to rely mainly on Sophokles' *Trackers* and Euripides' *Cyclops*, the only two examples to have survived in anything like complete form. The subject of *Trackers* is the theft of the cattle of Apollo by baby Hermes; helping in the quest for the lost beasts are Silenos and his sons the Satyrs. In other words the plot is, like the plots of tragedy, taken from the mythical past, but bursting into it is a disruptive and indeed farcical element. *Cyclops* too is set in the mythical past, and includes many of the features familiar from *Odyssey* 9: Polyphemos' cannibalism; Odysseus' trick with the name Outis ('Nobody'); the blinding; the escape. But into this traditional world of myth there bursts, as before, an element of disruptive farce; once again it is the lustful and cowardly Satyrs with their pot-bellied

[41] Sutton (1980, 184–90) suggests other possible candidates for the category 'pro-satyric'.

old father. Amongst many amusing moments perhaps the best is when Polyphemos, hopelessly drunk, ominously announces that he prefers boys to women, and carries off the alarmed Silenos into his cave to be his little Ganymede.

The rest of our evidence about satyr-plays,[42] meagre though it is, does not invalidate the assumption that the audience awaiting the start of such a work was expecting something set in the mythical past, but with a disruptively comical element breaking in to disturb the seriousness. But what about *non*-satyric fourth plays? While we really cannot be dogmatic about audience expectations in this case, it is at any rate interesting that in *Alkestis* too we find a combination of a mythical setting with an element of disruptive comedy, as Herakles totters on to the stage after enjoying himself in Admetos' wine store.

Alkestis is indeed a quite remarkably variegated work. It has many features in common with tragedy: an *oikos* is disrupted; a character is caught in dilemmas (be hospitable, or mourn; accept the gift of life and live emptily, or die and render the gift meaningless); events come to a crisis; a father and son are driven to a bitter scene of mutual recrimination; someone learns the truth too late. On the other hand, Herakles' riotous good spirits, and the loving reconciliation at the end, may make us think rather of comedy.[43] But it has to be said that the serious part of the play far exceeds the light-hearted. Could it be that Euripides was surprising his audience in 438 by providing something darker and more thought-provoking than they were expecting from a fourth play? We have no way of answering the question for certain.[44] It is better simply to rejoice in the particular—indeed unique—range of emotions and tones which make up this rich and complex masterpiece.[45]

[42] Collected and analysed in the introduction to Seaford (1984). See also Krumeich, Pechstein, and Seidensticker (1999); Voelke (2001).

[43] The *hypothesis* to the play observes that it has an ending which is *kōmikōteran* ('somewhat like comedy').

[44] Cf. the caution of Mastronarde (2010) 57: 'we unfortunately are uncertain how the "prosatyric" position of the play affected [contemporary] reception'.

[45] This is an expanded version of a paper given at the Hellenic Society Colloquium for Professor R. P. Winnington-Ingram; my thanks are due to the audience for their constructive comments, and in particular to Ian Jenkins for subsequent assistance. The same material also formed the basis of a lecture given in Greek in the Department of Classical Philology at Ioannina; the ensuing discussion was of great value to me, particularly the contributions by Mary Mantziou, Katerina Synodinou, Andreas Katsouris, and D. Sakalis.

11

Feminized Males in *Bakchai*: The Importance of Discrimination

Euripides' last and arguably greatest play resumes many of the themes explored in this book. The contrast between mountain and city provides the drama's topographical framework; the pervasive imagery drawn from the animal world—though this time the animals are lions, birds, fawns, bulls, and serpents, rather than wolves—shows once more how Greek myths 'think with' fauna; the name of the tragic hero, Pentheus (from penthos, *'grief') highlights the relationship between nomenclature and meaning; one of the central characters in the play is a blind prophet; and so on. But one issue which has not so far figured prominently in the book (though it was raised during the discussion of ideology in Chapter 7), an issue which has deservedly received a huge amount of scholarly attention in recent years, is also a crucial feature of* Bakchai*: gender. No book purporting to set myth and tragedy into context can afford to pass over such a matter.*

It is universally agreed that religion is the principal issue which Euripides' *Bakchai* is 'about'. The play, it is again universally agreed, confronts interpreters with two interrelated questions. The first is theological: what are the characteristics of the Euripidean Dionysos? The second concerns the god's worshippers: what is the nature of Dionysiac cult as it appears in this tragedy? As soon as scholars come to grips with these two questions in detail, however, the consensus evaporates.

On the theological point, the spectrum of starkly contrasting views is well enough known.[1] For R. P. Winnington-Ingram, 'Euripides

[1] For a helpful orientation up to the time when he was writing, see Oranje (1984) 7–19. Versnel (1990b, 96–205) is fundamental. Mills (2006, 80–102) is a more recent *mise au point.*

recognized, but hated Dionysos'.[2] No less forceful arguments have been mounted on the other side, often in conjunction with the idea that the (assumed) Euripidean 'scepticism' about the gods might have been reversed at the end of his career.[3] For E. R. Dodds, however, the Euripidean Dionysos was 'beyond good and evil', since the playwright intended 'to enlarge our sensibility' rather than to produce a pro- or anti-Dionysos tract.[4] Recent scholarship has tended to follow Dodds in concentrating less on the question of Euripides' attitude to Dionysos, and more on the complexity of the dramatic text.[5]

Regarding the god's worshippers, critical attention has focussed on the relationship between, on the one hand, Dionysiac cult as represented in the play, and, on the other hand, real-world Dionysiac cults, especially in relation to such high-octane issues as the presence or absence of *omophagia*, and conceivably cannibalism, in real-world rituals.[6] Against Dodds, who maintained, following Jane Harrison, that the tearing and ingestion of the god's surrogate by his worshippers constituted a central emotional element in the god's rite, Albert Henrichs and Dirk Obbink, among others, have argued for a more sceptical view.[7] Another issue which has been insistently pressed and contested has been the question of how far Dionysiac cult in the play reflects the language and action of Dionysiac mysteries. Richard Seaford, in particular, has repeatedly urged that we should note a significant similarity between the mythical dismemberment-and-reconstitution of Dionysos and the *sparagmos*-and-reassembly of Pentheus in *Bakchai*, a similarity which, according to Seaford, finds its analogue in the structure of the Dionysiac mysteries.[8]

Religion is not the only topic which modern critics have universally agreed to be fundamental to *Bakchai*: another is gender.[9] No one disputes the significant presence of certain themes in the play: the

[2] Winnington-Ingram (1948) 179; for the doxography of this view see Bierl (1991) 177 n. 2.

[3] See Roux (1972) 226–7; Bierl (1991) 177 n. 1.

[4] Dodds (1960) xlv–xlvii.

[5] On this scholarly trend, see Bierl (1991) 179–81.

[6] For a lively contribution to the debate, see Bremmer (1984).

[7] J. Harrison (1927) 118–19; Dodds (1951) 270–82, cf. Bremmer (1984) 267 with n. 2; Henrichs (1982) 143–7, with the long n. 53 on pp. 218–20; Obbink (1993); Seaford (1996) 37.

[8] See e.g. Seaford (1981) and (1996) 39–45.

[9] Cf. Mills (2006) 11–13.

disruptive role played by a community's women when they fall under the influence of Dionysos, an empowerment which enables them to reverse the 'natural' order and to rout men (emblematically, *Ba.* 763–4); the sensitivity of the ultra-masculine/militaristic leader Pentheus towards any hint of submission to women;[10] the strikingly and (to Pentheus) unnervingly feminine appearance of Dionysos in his role as 'the Stranger'; the feminizing of Pentheus by virtue of his wearing of the apparel which typifies the god's maenadic devotees. Yet here again, as soon as we move beyond the recognized generalities, scholarly voices are raised in dissonance. Interpretation of the bacchants' disruptiveness is inseparable from the controversy about how we are to explain the frequent occurrence of dominant, often threateningly aggressive behaviour by women as portrayed generally in myth and specifically in tragedy, and how such imagined behaviour relates to women's real-life 'secluded' role as evidenced by custom and law.[11] A second dispute concerns the absence or presence of women in the theatre of Dionysos, an issue which must inevitably affect how we reconstruct an ancient audience's reaction to the female and feminized characters in *Bakchai.*[12] Then again, Pentheus' cross-dressing finds itself at the centre of several interpretative debates, especially concerning theatricality, initiation, and psychology.[13] Gender is central to *Bakchai*, but *how* it is central is a far from settled question.

In the present chapter I discuss a circumscribed problem which impinges on both religion and gender: the feminization of male characters, both divine and human. Consideration of this limited issue will, however, enable us to examine a broader aspect of the interpretation of *Bakchai*, relating to differentiation. The several forms in which different dramatic characters imagine the god Dionysos as appearing, and the varied ways in which Euripides presents the categories of male and female as overlapping, have been widely taken to constitute yet

[10] See Bierl (1991) 205 n. 78.

[11] Bremmer (1984) sees maenadism as a temporary, legitimized escape from the normal confinement/seclusion of upper-class women's existence. For Zeitlin (1982), women who worship Dionysos are liberated, yet at the same time their perceived wildness confirms the threat they pose to men. On the generally problematic quality of the notion of 'seclusion', see above all Gould (2001) 112–57; though Gould's analysis, for all its originality, takes too little account of the difference between myth and *tragic* myth.

[12] Henderson (1991); contrast Goldhill in Easterling (1997) 54–68.

[13] See 233–7 below.

one more example of the play's general collapsing of distinctions (god/man/beast, mountain/city, old/young, hunter/prey, far/near, individual/group, native-born Greek/barbarian incomer, etc.) under the 'sign' of Dionysos.[14] For Simon Goldhill, 'Dionysos works to invert the oppositions by which the city defines itself, undermining differences'; for Jean-Pierre Vernant, through Dionysos' epiphany 'all the cut-and-dried categories and clear oppositions that impart coherence to our vision of the world lose their distinctiveness and merge, fuse, changing from one thing into another'; for Charles Segal, 'Dionysos operates as the principle that destroys differences'.[15] Such a view is the overwhelmingly dominant orthodoxy, and it has much to recommend it. Nevertheless I shall argue that, if we place exclusive emphasis on *Bakchai*'s dramatization of the collapsing of distinctions, we risk obscuring another fundamental aspect of the play's meaning, namely that which is concerned with the *upholding* of distinctions in spite of the enormous pressures pulling in the opposite direction. My argument will be that, in respect of feminization, we need to register both generic differences between gods and heroes, and specific differences between one god and another, one hero and another.

Concomitantly I shall insist that we must stress another differentiation: that between *this* retelling of a myth and all other actual and possible retellings. Tragedy is not the whole of mythology, nor is *Bakchai* the whole of tragedy. The fact that a mythological character is in some way associated with feminization elsewhere in Greek mythology *may* be relevant to this play, but is not necessarily so.

My overall case will therefore be that, in this of all plays—precisely because it is a work which often invites us to notice the eliding of distinctions—it is of cardinal importance to *discriminate*, in order to avoid what Nicole Loraux brilliantly called 'the vertigo of limitless association'.[16]

[14] Very widely, but not absolutely universally. I think here of a comment by Michelle Gellrich, that Dionysos 'does not so much destroy or confuse distinctions as configure the nondifferentiation out of which such distinctions eventually arise' (in Goff (1995) 53). I am grateful to Seaford (1996) 31 n. 25, for citing the comment, with due scepticism.

[15] Goldhill (1986) 266; Vernant in Vernant and Vidal-Naquet (1988) 398; Segal (1997) 234; cf. Henrichs in Carpenter and Faraone (1993) 24–6, citing a range of critics who take the 'subversion of opposites' approach.

[16] Loraux (1995) 120.

1. ZEUS

Whatever the explanation for Zeus' absence from the tragic stage as a directly participating character, his agency behind the scenes is felt in many tragedies, whether that agency is readily intelligible (as for example in *Prometheus Bound*) or whether he strikes the other characters—and the audience—as *somehow* active behind the scenes, but also inscrutable (as for example in *Women of Trachis*).[17] In *Bakchai*, the case differs from either of these models. With the exception of one passage, Zeus' agency comes across as insignificant for the development of the stage action, an insignificance which corresponds to the all-dominant, manipulative presence of his son Dionysos, beside whom everything else, even the power of the supreme god, seems unimportant. The solitary exception proves the rule. At line 1349 Dionysos, at last in epiphany, observes to Kadmos that 'Long ago my father Zeus nodded his assent to these things (*tade*)', where *tade* seems to embrace not only the play's action, in particular the self-vindication of Dionysos, but also the future events just predicted by Dionysos, and indeed the order of the cosmos within which such events can take place and, up to a point, have meaning.[18] What is significant for us here, however, is that, even as Dionysos alludes to Zeus' 'nodding' governorship of the cosmos, he also cites Zeus' role *as a parent*. *Bakchai* is a family drama: Semele is a mother, Pentheus a son and grandson, Kadmos a husband and grandfather, Agaue a daughter and mother, Dionysos a son—and Zeus is a parent. And in contrast to *Women of Trachis*, where the problematic involvement of Zeus in the unfolding of the play's total action is every bit as dramatically relevant as his father-son relationship with Herakles, in *Bakchai* Zeus' parenthood of Dionysos is his principal role. 'Parenthood'—not 'fatherhood'. Of course Zeus is Dionysos' father. But because he is an *immortal* father (cf. 1340–1), he is not limited by the constraints of merely human biology. And the most distinctive quality of Zeus' parenthood in *Bakchai* is that he is a mother.

[17] Dowden (2006, 112) speaks of tragic characters who 'struggle to find meaning in acute crises and grope for the mystery of Zeus'.

[18] *tade*: note the similarly charged demonstrative in the last line of *Women of Trachis*: '*k'ouden toutōn ho ti mē Zeus*', 'There is none of these things which is not Zeus.' (See 139 and 163–4 above.) 'Up to a point'; cf. the remark of Winnington-Ingram (1948, 146), quoted with evident approval by Dodds ad loc., that 'The appeal to Zeus is an appeal to ultimate mystery.'

In the first line of the play Dionysos describes himself as *Dios pais* ('son of Zeus'). For the chorus at 417 their beloved god is *ho daimōn ho Dios pais* ('the divinity, the son of Zeus'). At 581 Dionysos identifies himself as *ho Semelas, ho Dios pais* ('the son of Semele and of Zeus'). For the chorus at 603 Dionysos is *Dios gonos* ('offspring of Zeus'). In none of these cases, even 581, is it explicit that Zeus' role is here that of the father', though the balanced expression in 581 does strongly tend that way. At 1340–1 ('I, Dionysos, say this not as one sired by a mortal father, but by Zeus') and 1349 ('long ago my father Zeus nodded his assent to this'), sure enough, Zeus is unequivocally cited as Dionysos' father. But this is far from being the whole story. By recalling the myth of Zeus' sewing of the prematurely born Dionysos into his thigh, the chorus casts Zeus in the role of Dionysos' second mother. After the initial birth by Semele, 'whom once, when constrained in the pains of childbirth (*lochiais*), as the lightning-bolt of Zeus flew down, his mother cast forth from her womb and gave birth to him (*eteken*)' (88–92), a second parturition follows, with, this time, Zeus' body as the container of the baby: 'Zeus the son of Kronos instantly received him in the secret recesses of birth (*lochiais*), having concealed him in his thigh . . . He gave birth to him (*eteken*)' (94–9).[19] Within the play the authenticity of the event is contested, not only by Pentheus (242–7) but also by Teiresias (286–97), for whom the *mēros* ('thigh') detail can be explained away as a play on words. But such denials cut no ice with the chorus, who re-emphasize Zeus' maternal role when they go so far as to imagine the very words spoken by *Zeus ho tekōn* ('Zeus who gave birth'), as he summoned the newborn to enter his body: 'Come, Dithyrambos, enter this male womb of mine' (526–7). What kind of feminization is this? It is a matter, not of form or dress, but of function. Zeus does not *look* feminine; rather, at one key moment, he *acts* like a female in her physiologically most distinctive capacity.

Within the wider network of Greek mythology, Zeus' motherhood is not unique. The closest parallel is the birth of Athene: in that case, Zeus' swallowing of Metis leads to the parturition of Athene through the head.[20] The reason for Zeus' action lies, of course, in his wish to

[19] In 94, λοχίαις (*lochiais*) is preferred to the MSS reading λοχίοις (*lochiois*) by both Dodds and Diggle.

[20] Cf. the altar of Zeus Lecheates at Aliphera in Arkadia, the alleged location of the birth (Paus. 8.26.6).

avoid being supplanted by the child whom Metis is carrying in her womb. Nicole Loraux explains the logic: 'By incorporating the mother into himself, Zeus bypasses the [potentially threatening] son, who is replaced by a daughter totally devoted to the rights of the *anēr*.'[21] Loraux goes so far as to describe Zeus' 'maternities' as 'well-known'.[22] Perhaps, but not all scholars evaluate their importance in the same way. Ken Dowden's recent account of the supreme god understandably places enormous weight on Zeus' role as father of gods and men, but passes over the point about maternity.[23] At the other extreme, Marcel Detienne's brief entry on 'Zeus' in Bonnefoy's mythological dictionary devotes, with carefree idiosyncrasy, more space to this one trait than to all the others put together.[24] We need to strike a balance. In myth, Zeus' femininity, as incorporated in the act of child-bearing, is just one possible mode of action for the supreme god; it is not 'typical', since in terms of sheer quantity it is enormously outweighed by accounts of Zeus' serially adulterous fathering of offspring, presumably an expression of one sort of male fantasy about virility. Not typical: but it *is* a possibility, which extends his power rather than limiting it; it is, for example, perfectly compatible with his exercising of the supreme act of aggressive violence—the lightning strike—which he carries out in his role as the quintessentially virile lover of Semele.

Why is this possibility—the non-limiting maternalization of Zeus—highlighted in *Bakchai*? Surely because it suits the context of a play which explores in other ways too the overlap between the masculine and the feminine. Dionysos, the god who, as we shall see, also embodies elements of femininity but in his own quite different style, is born not from one womb but two.[25]

21 Loraux (1995) 13.

22 Loraux (1995) 12.

23 Dowden (2006) 29: 'The function that has above all preserved Zeus since Indo-European times is that of *father*' (italics in original).

24 Detienne (1981).

25 How unlike Athene, the ultra-masculine virgin who has no contact whatever with the female womb; cf. Burkert (1985) 143. NB about the possible connotations—initiatory?—of the wound in the thigh, I am not concerned here. On this see e.g. Burkert (1969) 23–5; Lambrinoudakis (1971); Bremmer (1978) 10–13; Obbink (1993) 78; see also my comments on Talos at 89 above.

2. TEIRESIAS AND KADMOS

'The two old men, Teiresias and Kadmos . . . dress as maenads and prepare to form a chorus'; they are, Simon Goldhill continues, 'old men dressed as women'.[26] These comments seem uncontroversial enough, and could be paralleled dozens of times in the scholarship on the play. For example, in his commentary Richard Seaford observes that Teiresias and Kadmos are 'dressed, like the maenads, with fawnskin, crown, and *thyrsos* (176–7)'.[27] As a description of what the two men are wearing this is entirely accurate: in lines 176–7 Teiresias indeed states that he and Kadmos have made a pact to bear the *thyrsos*, to wear the fawnskin, and to wreathe their heads with ivy. But what of the gloss 'like the maenads'? Clearly, Teiresias and Kadmos are marking themselves out *as adherents of Dionysos*, whose symbols—*thyrsos*, fawnskin, ivy—they sport. But these attributes are not exclusively the privilege of the god's *female* devotees: they may also be borne by the god's male celebrants: as described by Kyllene in Sophokles' *Trackers*, the satyrs worship Dionysos clad in fawnskins and holding *thyrsoi*.[28] Other characters in *Bakchai*—the chorus throughout, and Pentheus in one memorable scene—do indeed wear the full regalia of the maenad, which distinguishes them both as devotees of Dionysos and as female/feminized; but not Teiresias and Kadmos. György Karsai has it absolutely right when he speaks of the two old men 'déguisés en bacchants'—not 'en bacchantes'.[29] The point is easy to miss. Even that doyen of Dionysiac scholars Albert Henrichs was in two minds over the matter: whereas in one fine article he allowed himself inadvertently to say that 'Kadmos, Teiresias and Pentheus in Euripides's *Bakchai* dress as maenads',[30] in another he expressed the matter more accurately, referring to 'Kadmos and Teiresias, who carry thyrsi and wear fawnskins *without donning women's clothes*'.[31]

[26] Goldhill (1986) 273; cf. 262: 'the spectacle of the two old men, dressed as women'.

[27] Seaford (1996) on 170–369.

[28] *TrGF* iv. F 314, lines 225–6 Radt; see Easterling in Easterling (1997) 43.

[29] Karsai (1992) 201. So also, rightly, Hose (2008) 206: Teiresias is described as 'im Kostüm *eines* Bakchanten . . . und im gleichen Aufzug . . . der alte Kadmos' (my italics).

[30] Henrichs (1982) 224 n. 97.

[31] Henrichs (1984) 69; my italics.

Why does this matter? Because it highlights the importance of differentiation within this play. It is vital, in order to appreciate the way the play develops and the action builds to a climax, to note the difference between the appearance of Teiresias and Kadmos, on the one hand, and that of the chorus and Pentheus, on the other. Just as the Herdsman's description of the maenads will be trumped by the later narrative of the Newsbringer,[32] so the appearance of Teiresias and Kadmos—the willing, conscious pair of male devotees—will be thrown into relief by the later guise of Pentheus, comprehensively transvestite and out of his normal mind.

What impression do the appearance and demeanour of Teiresias and Kadmos make, if not one of transvestism? The text is unambiguous. The point which is repeatedly stressed is not their gender but their age. Teiresias refers to himself as a *presbus* ('old man'), and to Kadmos as *geraiterōi* ('older') (175); Kadmos' hair is grey (185); the theme of old age is a refrain: *gerōn geronti* ('an old man [leading] an old man') (186), *gerontes ontes* ('being old men') (189), *gerōn geronti* ('as an old man [I shall take along] an old man') (193), *gēras* ('old age') (204); the god does not distinguish between a man who is young and one who is *geraiteron* ('older') (206–7). When Pentheus arrives on the scene, not once does his mockery of the old men express itself as: 'Why are you dressed as women?' On the contrary, what rankles is their age: they are behaving indecorously, in a way unbefitting their years: *to gēras humōn . . . gēras polion* ('your old age . . . grey old age') (252, 258). Teiresias readily acknowledges his and Kadmos' age, but maintains that dancing for the god is an imperative (324). As the two leave the scene leaning on each other for support, their signature tune *geronte* ('two old men') echoes once more about them (365). *This* is why, from the point of view of ordinary civic behaviour, they can be seen as ridiculous. Seaford helpfully quotes a passage from Plato's *Laws* (665) in which Kleinias, reacting to the Athenian's suggestion that there should be a chorus of 'the third age' singing for Dionysos, exclaims: 'What? Please explain: a chorus of elderly men dedicated to Dionysos sounds a very odd idea, at any rate at first hearing.'[33] Bernhard Zimmermann accurately summarizes the point of the scene in *Bakchai*: 'Their Dionysiac costume and desire to dance are almost grotesquely incongruous with their frailness.'[34]

[32] See Buxton (1989); (1991) 41–6.

[33] Seaford (1996) on 170–369.

[34] Zimmermann (1991) 125.

Another issue needs to be addressed before we leave the alleged gender-crossing in the Euripidean presentation of Teiresias and Kadmos. If we move beyond this play to the wider network of Greek myth, we find, so far as I am aware, no connection whatever between Kadmos and feminization. But with Teiresias things are very different. In order to resolve their dispute about whether males or females enjoy sexual intercourse more, Zeus and Hera consult Teiresias who has, uniquely, experienced the act from both sides. In his no-holds-barred structuralist analysis of the Teiresias myth, Luc Brisson meticulously catalogued and examined different narratives of the episode in which Teiresias had changed sex from male to female as a result of (in the best-known version) striking two copulating snakes with his staff, and subsequently changed back from female to male when he did precisely the same thing on an identical occasion.[35] As always, there are variations: Teiresias either kills the snakes, or wounds them, or strikes them with his staff, or tramples them.[36] More intriguing are the variants according to which Teiresias directs his aggression first against the female (after which he himself becomes female), and then, in the mirror-episode, against the male (after which he becomes male again).[37] Equally revealing is the variant in which Teiresias becomes female *after seeing Athene naked*.[38] A mere *lapsus memoriae* on the part of a myth-teller? If so, it is a significant one, since the parallelism between the entwined snakes—masculine conjoined with feminine—and Athene—the masculine goddess par excellence—can hardly be missed.[39] Brisson cogently infers that Teiresias' role is as mediator both in the sphere of divination, between gods and humans, and in the sphere of gender, mediating between the sexes in his own person.[40]

This, then, is one aspect of Teiresias' mythical personality. But it is not the whole of that personality; nor should we regard it as necessarily relevant to every occurrence of this complex mythological

[35] Brisson (1976). [36] Brisson (1976) 24.

[37] Brisson (1976) 24–5, referring to his versions A07 (schol. Hom. *Od.* 10.492) and A08 (Eust. *Od.* 10.494): 'this first episode gains added coherence if Teiresias takes on the gender of the serpent which he has just attacked' (my translation).

[38] Brisson (1976) 52 with n. 25, on Tzetz. schol. *ad Lyc.* 683.

[39] See though the comments of Loraux (1995) 216–18, advising against a too ready assumption of Athene's bisexuality. The whole of Loraux's chapter on 'What Teiresias Saw' (211–26)—indeed the whole book from which it comes—repays careful study.

[40] Brisson (1976) 53.

figure in every narrative in which he occurs. In *Oidipous Tyrannos* what counts is Teiresias' capacity for divination, his simultaneous frailty and power, his proximity to and distance from the seat of political authority, and above all his blindness. In *Antigone* his role as a prophet and his relationship to the *polis* are again focal. And in neither case, I suggest, is his mythical history of gender-crossing of any dramatic relevance. It could be argued that the case is less clear-cut in *Bakchai*, because, elsewhere in the play, gender-crossing *is* obviously a dramatic issue. Nevertheless, nothing in the text of this scene entitles us to detect echoes of Teiresias' *own* gender-crossing. It would have been easy enough for Euripides to introduce it had he wished to do so—perhaps by making a link with those snakes which *are* of dramatic relevance (the snakes which play around the maenads; the snakes into which Kadmos and Harmonia will turn); but he did not do it. Not every myth about Teiresias should be made to tell the same story.[41]

3. DIONYSOS

Bakchai is dominated by changes of form, and many of these concern the god himself. At the start of the prologue he establishes that he has taken the *morphēn* ('form') of a mortal in exchange for that of a god (4), a point which he re-emphasizes at the end of the speech (since the audience needs to be in no doubt about it in order to grasp the logic of the plot): 'I have taken and keep the *eidos* ('look') of a mortal, and have altered my *morphēn* to the nature of a man' (53–4).[42] As the action unfolds, changes in the god's perceived form multiply. For Teiresias, Dionysos is a liquid, who/which can be poured out as a libation of wine (284). To the Servant he is a *thēr* ('wild beast') (436). The metaphor comes closer to reality when the god creates the semblance of a bull in order to delude his adversary (618); when Pentheus has fallen completely under the god's power, the final stage

[41] See 183–4 above for a discussion of Teiresias complementary to the present one, with particular attention to his blindness.

[42] This couplet alone should be enough to explode the fantasy interpretation (by Verrall and others) according to which the Stranger is a mere mortal adept of the god. If it is not enough, Dodds (1960, xlviii–l) completes the demolition.

of the imagined metamorphosis occurs: 'You seem to be leading me as a bull, with horns upon your head. Have you been a wild beast all along? At any rate, now you have become a bull (*tetaurōsai gar oun*)' (920–2). By implication, Pentheus has recognized the truth of Dionysos' words from an exchange during their first dialogue(477–8):

Penth: You say you saw the god clearly; how did he look?
Dion: However he wanted; I did not decide that.

Dionysos' form is mobile, fluid, and unbounded: as the chorus expresses it in the coda, *pollai morphai tōn daimoniōn* ('many are the forms of divinity') (1388).

One of these many possible *morphai* is that of femininity. Whereas the feminization of Zeus concerns function, that of Dionysos concerns form. The point of departure for *Bakchai*'s exploration of Dionysos' femininity is how his appearance is perceived—not his way of dressing, but something more intimate: the look of his face and body, especially his skin colour and hair. Even before the Stranger enters, Pentheus singles out aspects of the mysterious incomer's appearance which he has heard about (233) and which already fascinate him: long, fair, scented hair, and a vinous complexion, a look which lends him 'the graces of Aphrodite' (235–6). Pentheus categorizes the Stranger as *thēlumorphos* ('female in form') (353), a double-edged quality which makes him both resemble women and, allegedly, appeal to them sexually (353–4). This impression formed on the basis of hearsay is reinforced during the first dialogue between the king and his adversary. After a neutral's-eye-view confirmation by the Servant that the Stranger's appearance is *oinōpos* ('wine-coloured in complexion') (438) as well as an allusion to his smiling countenance, Pentheus gives his own face-to-face appraisal of the Stranger: attractive *hōs es gunaikas* ('[at least] in the eyes of women')—the double edge again—long hair 'full of desire', white skin: not the appearance of a (masculine) wrestler, but that of one in search of Aphrodite (453–9).

The perception of Dionysos as feminine is not, of course, confined to the Euripidean representation.[43] Evidence from many parts of the mythological tradition confirms that the god's gender might be seen as ambivalent, though the nature of this ambivalence, and the tone

[43] Some relevant scholarship: Delcourt (1961) 24–7; Otto (1965) 175–7; Bremmer (1999); M. Jameson in Carpenter and Faraone (1993) 44–64; Csapo (1997).

with which it is presented, varies greatly from context to context. In Aischylos' *Edonians* he is called by Lykourgos, evidently with contempt, *ho gunnis* ('the womanish man')—surely (though this is only a fragment) a close parallel to the situation in *Bakchai*.[44] The god's effeminacy gets the full comic treatment in Aristophanes' *Frogs*, in relation to his wearing of the *krokōtos* ('saffron-coloured robe').[45] In Philochoros he is called *thēlumorphos* ('female in form'); a line from an *Orphic Hymn* styles him *arsena kai thēlun, diphuē* ('male and female, two-natured').[46]

Walter Otto used a parallel from the world of heroes in order to illuminate Dionysos' femininity, noting that in the *Iliad* Paris is addressed by Hektor as *gunaimanes* ('woman-mad') (3.39)—the very epithet used of Dionysos in the first, fragmentary *Homeric Hymn* to the god (17).[47] However, the comparison needs to be handled with caution: a word can vary greatly in connotation, and even denotation, from context to context. In Hektor's mouth *gunaimanes* is an insult, being prefaced by the all-embracing rebuke *Duspari* ('ill-omened Paris'). In the *Hymn*, on the other hand, *gunaimanes* evidently expresses admiration for some aspect of the god's power. But this could well be a reference to Dionysos' tendency to drive women 'mad' in a sense quite other than the sexual sense—a reference to the general Dionysiac capacity to 'intoxicate'. In any case, far more important is the fact that Dionysos is a god and Paris a mortal man. To link a mortal man with 'woman-madness' is (at least in Hektor's eyes) to diminish his masculinity; but to link a god with the same quality may be a way of expressing awe for his power.

A feature of Dionysiac imagery which has sometimes been linked with his femininity is a shift in the iconographical tradition: although the god was at first represented as a bearded adult, around 425 BC this convention was decisively replaced by his depiction as a beardless youth.[48] This has been interpreted by some as a change from a 'more masculine' to a 'more feminine' Dionysos. Taking an assumed equivalence between femininity and youthful maleness as

[44] *TrGF* iii. F 61 Radt; cf. Ar. *Thesm.* 134–6.

[45] Ar. *Ran.* 46. On the complexity of the Herakles/Dionysos interplay here, see Loraux (1995) 129.

[46] Philochoros: *FGrH* 328 F 7; *Hymn. Orph.* 42.4.

[47] Otto (1965) 176.

[48] On all this, see the excellent paper by Tom Carpenter in Carpenter and Faraone (1993) 185–206.

his cue, Jan Bremmer identifies a pattern according to which certain mythological figures—he cites, among others, Theseus and Achilles—progress from a young and 'feminine' stage to a stage at which, as fully adult male warriors, they perform exploits in the world of action.[49] Bremmer detects the same pattern in the representation of Dionysos in general, and in *Bakchai* in particular. Now Theseus and Achilles are heroes, while Dionysos is a god. Can Bremmer's pattern span this fundamental divide? The stories that Dionysos was raised as a girl by Ino and Athamas (Apollod. *Bibl.* 3.4.3), and that he appeared to Minyas' daughters first in the form of a girl (Ant. Lib. *Met.* 10), certainly lend support to Bremmer's general case. But how relevant are these mythological episodes to *Bakchai*, in which they play no part? As always, we need to test an approach based on the mythical tradition against the evidence of each specific text.

Let us, then, turn back to *Bakchai*, and in particular to the dramatic context within which Dionysos' femininity is portrayed. For most of the characters the femininity of the god/Stranger goes unremarked, because it is not what strikes them as significant. It is principally Pentheus (although not exclusively he—cf. the Servant at 438) who focuses his perceptions on the physical look of the Stranger; and it is *exclusively* Pentheus to whom this look seems to evoke strong associations of the feminine. Even for Pentheus, however, that femininity is not a constant preoccupation: as the play progresses—and, in particular, after the earthquake and the manifestation of the bull—it will be the Stranger's wildness, and specifically his appearance as a bull (922), which force themselves onto the King's attention. The time when the Stranger's femininity does strike Pentheus is earlier in the tragedy, when the captive's compliance predominates over his aggression, and when Pentheus is in any case preoccupied by the issue of gender in quite another way—because the women's abandoning of the city constitutes a subversion of the established order. In other words, Dionysos' femininity, like that of the other characters in the play, is a theme moulded by and responsive to the needs of the drama.

[49] As Bremmer acknowledges (1999, 191–2), the case of Kaineus is more complex. The references to Theseus and Achilles are at Bremmer (1999) 199 n. 61.

4. PENTHEUS

From the point of view of stagecraft, and arguably from every other point of view as well, the feminization of Pentheus is the most powerful realization of the theme to be found anywhere in the play. In keeping with his desire to get close to the women topographically, Pentheus compliantly agrees to Dionysos' suggestion that he must also make himself resemble them physically. His dress will be the full, feminine, maenadic costume. Like Kadmos and Teiresias, Pentheus will carry the *thyrsos* and wear the fawnskin (835, 941–4). But, unlike them, he will also put on the full-length *peplos* (821, 833, 935–8), let his hair fall loosely (831, cf. 928–31; interpreted by Dodds as the wearing of a wig), and wear a belt (935) and, over his hair, a *mitra* ('headdress') (833, 929, 1115–16).[50] Again quite unlike the emphasis of the Teiresias and Kadmos scene, the verbal weight falls repeatedly upon the femininity of the deluded king. We find it in the preparatory dialogue scene before the dressing takes place: *es gunaikas ex andros telō?* ('am I to be counted as a woman instead of a man?') (822), *tina stolēn? ē thēlun?* ('What clothing? Female?') (828), *thēlun . . . stolēn* ('female clothing') (836 and 852), *gunaikomorphon* ('having the form of a woman') (855). We find it in the following dialogue, when Pentheus' costuming is completed: 'wearing the garb of a woman, a maenad, a bacchant' (915); 'How do I look? Do I not stand like Ino, or like Agaue . . . ?' (925–6). We find it in the chorus' triumphant cries as Pentheus is led off to the slaughter: *ton en gunaikomimōi stolai* ('the one in a costume which mimics women') (980).

Pentheus' transvestism has fascinated scholars.[51] The episode seems to act like a mirror, reflecting back to interpreters that which interests them most in Greek theatre and in Greek religion. Three examples of this mirroring correspond to influential interpretations which may be described respectively as 'theatrical', 'initiatory', and 'psychological'.

What interests Froma Zeitlin, in her book *Playing the Other*, is the theatrical, mimetic aspect of Athenian drama: above all, the implications of the twin facts that female characters, 'the radical

[50] Wig: Dodds (1960) on 831–3. *Mitra*: Brandenburg (1966) 62, 140; Bremmer (1999) 185; cf. Boardman and Kurtz (1986) 56.

[51] On transvestism as a general cultural phenomenon, see the splendid article by Miller (1999).

other', are astonishingly (in sociocultural terms) prominent in the plays, and that they are played by male actors.[52] What of the rather more elaborate kind of role reversal, that which involves a male actor impersonating a male character who dresses up as a woman? Writing of comedy (specifically *Women at the Thesmophoria*), Zeitlin observes that 'the exhibitionist donning of female costume focuses the problem of mimesis at its most ambiguous and most sensitive spot, where social and artistic rules are most in conflict with each other . . . [F]eminization attracts to itself all the scorn and abuse that the culture—and comedy—can muster.'[53] But not all representations of feminization should be seen as equivalent to each other. Zeitlin stresses the gulf in *Bakchai* between the feminizations of Dionysos and Pentheus: whereas the former manipulates his own femininity to gain mastery, the latter's powerlessness is enacted when he dresses up as a woman.[54] Zeitlin draws large conclusions from this and related evidence (evidence about, for example, 'masculine' women, and about the perceived association between women and 'artifice'): Dionysos, and his theatre, are profoundly linked with the feminine, which is 'a model of both weakness and strength'.[55] In Zeitlin's view we can use this paradox to help us address the vexed question of Greek drama's social function, by holding that 'theatre uses the feminine for the purposes of imagining a fuller model for the masculine self'.[56]

The keyword of the second approach is 'initiation'. Pentheus' robing as a woman has been seen as a failed rite of passage, reflecting actual Greek rituals involving cross-dressing. Charles Segal articulates this point of view: '[The robing scene] resembles a number of initiatory rites in classical Greece and elsewhere where the male initiand temporarily wears the clothing of the opposite sex, entering the liminal or in-between period in which he has no identity, or rather has both male and female identities at the same time, before the definitive passage to the male side.'[57] A variant of this position is adopted by Richard Seaford, who argues that 'in the *Bakchai* the adoption of maenadic dress by Pentheus, which is not required by the plot, is one of a whole series of his experiences that reflect mystic initiation'.[58]

[52] E.g. Zeitlin (1996) 346.
[53] Zeitlin (1996) 385–6.
[54] Zeitlin (1996) 342.
[55] Zeitlin (1996) 346, 345.
[56] Zeitlin (1996) 363.
[57] Segal (1997) 169.
[58] Seaford (1998) 129.

Thirdly, psychology. A variety of approaches might be included under this heading, embracing Pentheus' sexual motivation, his mental health, and the profiling of his authoritarian personality.[59] However, the most influential of these approaches is still that of Dodds, who read the representation of Pentheus in terms of repression and the unconscious. '[H]e is the dark puritan', Dodds wrote, 'whose passion is compounded of horror and unconscious desire.'[60] What enables Dionysos to bend Pentheus to his will is 'the Dionysiac longing' within the king, a longing which can be translated as 'a deeper, unacknowledged lust to pry into the women's doings'.[61] As for the dressing up of Pentheus in female garb, Dodds explains this in part as a reflection of cult: 'The specific ritual reason for the disguising of Pentheus is perhaps that the victim of the womanish god . . . must wear the god's livery', in part in terms of the horrific psychology of revenge and domination: 'the stage business with Pentheus' costume (925–44) is the counterpart of the stage business with the Stranger's costume at 493–7; for the outrage then done to his person the Stranger now takes a fantastic revenge on the pretext of playing the valet'.[62]

We can and should learn from each of these approaches; though I have some reservations.

Zeitlin's mimetic approach is, to me, more convincing when she moves from particular plays to large-scale generalizations, and less convincing when she redescends to the particular. Still, she valuably forces us to confront the cultural realities of a scene of male transvestism in *this* kind of theatre. The second approach, that via initiation, highlights a ritual pattern which is undeniably present in Greek culture, namely the use of gender reversal as a marker of change of status. However, we should note the criticisms of Peter Heslin, who rightly stresses the *variety* of contexts in antiquity for which we have evidence for male/female cross-dressing, a variety which does not lend itself to being reduced to the schema 'initiation to manhood', though it *is* more easily equated with a more general 'involvement in a rite of passage' (e.g. marriage or mourning).[63] As for the suggestion of

[59] Cf. the interpretations reviewed by Oranje (1984) 7–19.
[60] Dodds (1960) on 222–3.
[61] Dodds (1960) nn. on Scene 3 (c) (p. 172), and on 821–38.
[62] Dodds (1960) nn. on 854–5, and on Scene (4) 912–76 (p. 192).
[63] Heslin (2005) 211.

an initiation into the Dionysiac mysteries, the danger here is that one may overlook the glaring truth that an initiand's passage 'from anxiety to joy'[64] does not correspond to the emotional trajectory either of the *Bakchai* in particular or of tragedy in general: for in tragedy, death carries overwhelmingly more weight than salvation.[65]

Still compelling after half a century—and not incompatible with either of the other two approaches—is Dodds' psychologizing reading. It would certainly be possible to play the character of Pentheus this way in the theatre, and it would make a wonderful story for a director to tell; and in telling it she/he would not be going against the grain of the text. Indeed in the very words of the play we find that Pentheus displays an interest in sex and gender which at first seems to be belied by his public, authoritarian stance, but which later open the psychic gates to Dionysos' invasion. The wearing of female clothes offers a perfect corporeal analogue for what is happening to Pentheus' mind: his body will come to resemble what he has hitherto been fascinatedly rejecting. *Odit et amat.*

All I would myself add to these discussions of Pentheus' transvestism is the most obvious-sounding of points, which follows from my argument elsewhere in this chapter: that the king's cross-dressing must be seen in its dramatic context. Like the feminizations of Zeus and Dionysos, and like the (as I have argued) relative *non*-feminization of Kadmos and Teiresias, the feminization of Pentheus belongs at a certain phase of the plot, after which the play moves on. Already in that same ode where the chorus sings of *ton en gunaikomimōi stolai* ('the one in a costume which mimics women') (980), a shift is being prepared, as the bacchants imagine the words with which Agaue will react to being spied on: 'He is not born from the blood of women, but from a lioness, or he is descended from the Libyan Gorgons' (988–90). In the perception of the maenads of Kithairon, it is neither a woman nor a man who has come to disturb them, but a *thēr* ('wild beast') (1108). When he returns to normal consciousness Pentheus tries to dispel the illusion of his false identity—his identity as a woman—by

[64] Seaford (1994) 287.

[65] On Seaford's more general point, that Dionysiac ritual, above all Dionysiac mysteries, constitute the nucleus of the development of Athenian drama (Seaford (1994) 281), one may note this calmly shrewd comment: 'surviving Attic tragedy is not easily understood in relation to any master plot-pattern' (Easterling in Easterling (1997) 52). The identical comment might be made about some of the work of George Thomson, Seaford's direct intellectual ancestor.

removing the *mitra* (1115–16), in the hope of returning to his masculine state. But in vain: his head, ripped from his body, is 'like that of a mountain lion' (1141–2). One last time the chorus evokes Pentheus' wearing of *thēlugenē stolan* ('the clothing of womankind'), and wielding of the *thyrsos* (1156–8). But thereafter the king's feminization is forgotten. For the first part of the next scene he is to Agaue a wild beast, prey, something hunted, a lion (1202–15); to Kadmos he is a dead boy (1226). After Agaue's recognition of the truth, she too shrinks from the identification of the head with that of a lion (1284)—and certainly neither she nor anyone else refers to Pentheus' dressing up as a woman. While it is theoretically possible that some reference was made to Pentheus' transvestism in the lost part of the play, it is surely far more likely that the matter was ignored, the play's action and meaning having now passed beyond that point—beyond his feminization, beyond also his metaphorical transformation into a lion, and back to his starting point as a man: son, grandson, suffering human victim.

Zeus is not Dionysos. Zeus and Dionysos are not Teiresias, Kadmos, or Pentheus. Nor is any of the mortal characters like any other. In this highly discriminating play, the upholding of distinctions is every bit as crucial as the collapsing of boundaries.

5. FEMINIZATION AND THE TRAGIC TRADITION

The above account of *Bakchai* could be contextualized in many ways. One obvious context to choose is that of the remainder of the corpus of Greek tragedy. Gender, after all, is one of the great tragic themes: there is hardly a play which does not explore in some way or another the relationship between male and female.

A note frequently sounded in tragedy is that of the divide between the sexes. In *Seven against Thebes*, Eteokles maintains that it is for men to make sacrifice to the gods and to engage with the enemy; women should be quiet and stay in the house (*Sept.* 230–2).[66] In Aischylos' *Suppliants* the plot strongly contrasts the *thēlugenē stolon*

[66] Makaria in Euripides' *Children of Herakles* takes the identical view of a model woman's conduct (*Heracl.* 476–7), as does Aias in the play named after him (Soph. *Aj.* 293).

('company of females') of the Danaids with the *arsenoplēthē hesmon* ('crowding swarm of males') of the sons of Aigyptos (*Supp.* 28–30).[67] In Sophokles' *Elektra*, the eponymous heroine is told by her sister Chrysothemis that 'you are a woman, not a man, and weaker than your adversaries' (*El.* 997–8).

But tragedy would not be tragedy unless it also *explored* stereotypes, pushing them to or beyond their limits. In this spirit, tragedians often evoke various kinds of *overlap* between male and female. In *Agamemnon* the possibility that a woman can behave mannishly is raised from the outset in relation to Klytaimestra's *androboulon* . . . *kear* ('heart which deliberates like a man') (*Ag.* 11); the Chorus later praises her for talking like a prudent man: 'Lady, you speak wisely like a man of sense' (351); when in *Eumenides* Athene ultimately asserts the father's role against the mother's in parenthood, this is merely the culmination of a contrastive theme adumbrated repeatedly in the preceding action of the trilogy. *Medea* is rich in generalizations about women, but highlighted too is the possibility of reversals in gender expectations: 'It is the thoughts of *men* that are deceitful' (*Med.* 412). The issue of woman's cunning, on display throughout *Medea*, is present also in Euripides' *Suppliants*, where Aithra observes that such cunning may involve a subtle elision of the gender boundary: 'It is reasonable for women, if they are wise, to get everything done by men' (*Supp.* 41–2). In *Orestes*, when Elektra devises a plan to get the better of Menelaos by seizing his daughter Hermione, Orestes praises his sister in cross-gender terms: she possesses *phrenas* . . . *arsenas* ('the mind of a man'), yet her body shines out *en gunaixi thēleiais* ('among female women') (*Or.* 1204–5). What infuriates Oidipous in *Oidipous at Kolonos* is his sense that his sons are staying at home 'like maidens', whereas his daughters are out in the world helping their father through action (*OC* 337–45).

The preceding example from *Oidipous at Kolonos*, involving the image of the stay-at-home male, leads us to the particular kind of gender overlap which is my concern in this chapter: feminization. We can divide tragic feminization—apart from that in *Bakchai*—into two main types. The first is akin to the image of the (allegedly) cowardly stay-at-homes Eteokles and Polyneikes mocked by Oidipous. Its stereotypical embodiment is Aigisthos, styled by Kassandra as

[67] Cf. *Supp.* 392–3.

analkin ('cowardly') and *oikouron* ('a stay-at-home') (*Ag.* 1224–5) and, later in the trilogy, by Orestes as a woman with a mind that is *thēleia* ('female') (*Cho.* 304–5). The motif became Aigisthos' trademark. The Euripidean Elektra, gloating over his corpse, recalls that the Argives used to refer disparagingly to 'the woman's man', not 'the man's woman' (*El.* 931), and wishes that she herself may have a husband who is not *parthenōpos* ('of maidenly face'), and who possesses a masculine character (948–9).

The other type of tragic feminization relates to 'the heroic temper', Bernard Knox's term for the distinctive set of traits characteristic of the central figures in Sophoklean drama, rock-like when wheedled by the persuasions of lesser mortals or buffeted by the unforeseeable blows of misfortune.[68] In the case of heroic Sophoklean males, any weakening of their unshakeable resilience can seem to them to amount to a diminution of their masculinity. So it is for Aias, when he claims, or pretends, to be acquiescing in the wishes of Tekmessa: *ethēlunthēn stoma/pros tēsde tēs gunaikos* ('my mouth/speech has been feminized by this woman') (*Aj.* 651–2). On the whole, though, *Aias* is a man's play, and the gender divide remains strong throughout. The same cannot be said of *Women of Trachis.* Herakles, the archetype of male derring-do, twice undergoes subjection at the hands of a woman. The first instance is an episode reported rather than enacted, when we learn of his former year-long enslavement to the Lydian queen Omphale (*Trach.* 69–70, 252–7, 356–7). However, although other, predominantly later versions of the myth involve the fascinating extra detail of Herakles' exchanging of clothes with Omphale, Sophokles' version, perhaps more 'seriously', focuses not on cross-dressing but on slavery, a motif developed later in the play through the fate of captive Iole.[69] The second instance of feminization in the play grows out of the central action in which the pain-ridden Herakles is reduced to a husk of his former adventure-driven self. This reduction is described by Herakles through the explicit language of feminization. After asserting that 'a woman, female and with no masculine nature' has been alone responsible for his downfall, he likens his shouts and lamentations to those of a *parthenos* ('maiden'): in a word, he has become female: *nun d' ek toioutou thēlus hēurēmai talas* ('Now from such a thing [*sc.* from being a man who has endured

[68] Knox (1964).
[69] Motif of exchanging clothes: see Boardman (1994).

misfortune uncomplainingly] I am found to be a wretched womanish creature') (*Trach.* 1062–3; 1071–2; 1075).

Where do we place *Bakchai* against this background? Quite simply, there is nothing comparable to this play in the rest of the extant tragic tradition, in relation either to the multiplicity of types of feminization which it depicts, or to the dramatic prominence which the theme enjoys. Neither the Sophoklean depictions of the weakened, 'feminine' hero, nor the references to womanish-cowardly Aigisthos in various tragedies, can begin to rival the emotionally devastating power with which the feminization of a mortal is enacted through the transvestism of Pentheus—though *in comedy* there is no shortage of scene-stealing mortals who cross-dress. Again, the highlighting of the ambivalent appearance of Dionysos cannot be matched elsewhere in the extant tragedies—though *in comedy* we need look no further than *Frogs* for an equivalent. Could we say that Euripides was demonstrating his originality by pushing at the boundaries of the tragic genre (and, incidentally, stretching the boundaries of gender too) in ways which other tragedians did not? Even as we formulate such a suggestion, however, the fragment from Aischylos' *Edonians* mentioned above—in which Dionysos is slightingly called *ho gunnis* ('the womanish man')—should remind us, if reminder were needed, that what we have is merely a tiny sample of the total tragic corpus. Rather than hazarding a possibly illusory comparative point, then, I prefer to conclude with a comment on Euripides himself. To the very end of his career he retained an astonishing capacity to exploit and extend the possibilities of tragedy, in a continuing effort to draw out central human significance from the depiction of the paradoxical. The feminized male is a paradox; in *Bakchai* it is made to yield insights into the nature of existence, both human and divine.[70]

[70] Warm thanks go to Simon Goldhill and Edith Hall for originally commissioning this essay, and for commenting helpfully on successive drafts.

Envoi

I know how I would *like* this book to have been read. I would like my readers to feel that three objectives have been achieved. The first is that of highlighting certain structures—frameworks of thought and perception—within which Greeks told and listened to and read myths. The second is that of exploring unique examples of myth-telling, especially in tragedy but also in other genres too. The third is that of showing how those structures/frameworks and that uniqueness interrelate: the structures/frameworks constitute a language—to borrow a metaphor from my account in Chapter 9—which enables complex and powerful utterances to be made. In short, I would like this book to be read as a blend—and of course a successful blend—of, on the one hand, analyses of myth and, on the other hand, interpretations of literature and (less often) the visual arts.

There are two difficulties with this expression of authorial desire. To begin with, the patron saint of scholars is Narcissus. (Let us call him thus and not 'Narkissos', in recognition both of Ovid's definitive version, and of the form of the name under which the Complex has come to be known.) When we gaze at our own work, we tend to see its image reflected back to us in a benignly distorting mirror which removes blemishes and irons out wrinkles. (How else to account for the fact that in so many scholarly bibliographies—such as the present one—the author's own earlier writings figure so prominently?) Indeed the very act of selecting from one's own previous papers in order to produce a *Gesamtkunstwerk* could be seen as quintessentially narcissistic: the cream of the cream.

The second difficulty is that—fortunately—writers cannot control how they will be read. Therefore, rather than urging *per impossibile*, 'Read me like this', I end on a less dictatorial note, with the simple hope that my readers may derive from reading these chapters—however they read them—at least a little of the enjoyment which the author derived from writing them.

Details of Original Publication

1. 'Imaginary Greek Mountains', revised version of an article originally published in the *Journal of Hellenic Studies* 112 (1992), 1–15; reprinted with the kind permission of the Council of the Society for the Promotion of Hellenic Studies.
2. 'Wolves and Werewolves in Greek Thought', revised version of an article published in J. N. Bremmer (ed.), *Interpretations of Greek Mythology* (Croom Helm: Beckenham, 1987), 60–79; reprinted with the kind permission of Taylor and Francis Group.
3. 'Mythological Names: The Case of *melas*', revised and expanded version of an article originally published as 'The Significance (or Insignificance) of Blackness in Mythological Names', in J. Dijkstra, J. Kroesen, and Yme Kuiper (eds.), *Myths, Martyrs, and Modernity: Studies in the History of Religions in Honour of Jan N. Bremmer* (Brill: Leiden, 2010), 31–41, and, under the same title, in M. Christopoulos, E. D. Karakantza, and O. Levaniouk (eds.), *Light and Darkness in Ancient Greek Myth and Religion* (Lexington Books: Lanham, MA, 2010), 3–13; reprinted with the kind permission respectively of Brill and The Rowman and Littlefield Publishing Group.
4. 'The Myth of Talos: Vulnerability, *ichōr*, and Boundary-Crossing', revised version of 'The Myth of Talos', in C. Atherton (ed.), *Monsters and Monstrosity in Greek and Roman Culture* (Levante Editori: Bari, 2002), 83–112; reprinted with the kind permission of the publisher.
5. 'Movement and Stillness: Versions of Medea', revised version of an article originally published as 'How Medea Moves: Versions of a Myth in Apollonius and Elsewhere', in H. Bartel and A. Simon (eds.), *Unbinding Medea: Interdisciplinary Approaches to a Classical Myth from Antiquity to the 21st Century* (Legenda: London, 2010), 25–38; reprinted with the kind permission of the publisher.
6. 'Tragedy and Greek Myth', revised version of an article originally published in R. D. Woodard (ed.), *The Cambridge Companion to Greek Mythology* (Cambridge University Press: Cambridge, 2007), 166–89; reprinted with the kind permission of the publisher.
7. 'Time, Space, and Ideology: Tragic Myths and the Athenian *Polis*', revised version of an article originally published in J. A. López Férez (ed.), *Mitos en la literatura griega arcaica y clásica* (Ediciones Clásicas: Madrid, 2002), 175–89; reprinted with the kind permission of the publisher.

8. 'Bafflement in Greek Tragedy', revised version of an article originally published in *Mètis* 3 (1988), 41–51; reprinted with the kind permission of the editor of *Mètis*.
9. 'Blindness and Limits: Sophokles and the Logic of Myth', revised version of an article originally published in the *Journal of Hellenic Studies* 100 (1980), 22–37; reprinted with the kind permission of the Council of the Society for the Promotion of Hellenic Studies.
10. 'Euripides' *Alkestis*: Five Aspects of an Interpretation', revised version of an article originally published in *Dodoni: Philologia* 14 (1985), 75–89, and also in L. Rodley (ed.), *Papers given at a Colloquium on Greek Drama in honour of R. P. Winnington-Ingram* (Society for the Promotion of Hellenic Studies: London, 1987), 17–31; reprinted with the kind permission respectively of the editor of *Dodoni* and the Council of the Society for the Promotion of Hellenic Studies.
11. 'Feminized Males in *Bakchai*: The Importance of Discrimination', revised version of an article first published in S. D. Goldhill and E. Hall (eds.), *Sophocles and the Greek Tragic Tradition* (Cambridge University Press: Cambridge, 2009), 232–50; reprinted with the kind permission of the publisher.

Bibliography

Accorinti, D. (2010), 'La montagna e il sacro nel mondo greco', in A. Grossato (ed.), *La montagna cosmica*, Milan, 17–42.

Aguirre Castro, M. (1994), 'El tema de la mujer fatal en la *Odisea*', *CFC* n.s. 4: 301–17.

Albis, R. V. (1996), *Poet and Audience in the Argonautica of Apollonius*. Lanham, MD.

Alföldi, A. (1974), *Die Struktur des voretruskischen Römerstaates*. Heidelberg.

Arens, W. (1979), *The Man-Eating Myth: Anthropology and Anthropophagy*. New York.

Arias, P. E., and Hirmer, M. (1962), *A History of Greek Vase Painting*. London (translated and revised by B. B. Shefton).

Arnott, W. G. (1996), *Alexis: The Fragments*. Cambridge.

Astour, M. C. (1965), *Hellenosemitica: An Ethnic and Cultural Study in West Semitic Impact on Mycenaean Greece*. Leiden.

Austin, R. G. (1964), *P. Vergili Maronis Aeneidos Liber Secundus*. Oxford.

Avezzù, G. (2004), 'Mappe di Argo, nella tragedia', in P. A. Bernardini (ed.), *La città di Argo: mito, storia, tradizioni poetiche*. Atti del Convegno Internazionale (Urbino, 13–15 giugno 2002), Rome, 149–61.

Baladié, R. (1980), *Le Péloponnèse de Strabon*. Paris.

Baldry, H. C. (1965), *The Unity of Mankind in Greek Thought*. Cambridge.

Balensiefen, L. (1996), 'Achills verwundbare Ferse. Zum Wandel der Gestalt des Achill in nacharchaischer Zeit', *JDAI* 111: 75–103.

Bambeck, M. (1973), 'Das Werwolfmotiv im *Bisclavret*', *Zeitschrift für romanische Philologie* 89: 123–47.

Barney, R. (2001), *Names and Nature in Plato's Cratylus*. New York.

Battaglia, S. (1965), *La coscienza letteraria del Medioevo*. Naples.

Baxter, T. M. S. (1992), *The Cratylus: Plato's Critique of Naming*. Leiden.

Benveniste, E. (1973), *Indo-European Language and Society*. London (trans. of *Le Vocabulaire des institutions indo-européennes*, Paris, 1969).

Berger, J. (1972), *Ways of Seeing*. London.

Berman, D. W. (2002), '"Seven-Gated" Thebes and Narrative Topography in Aeschylus' *Seven against Thebes*', *QUCC* 71: 73–100.

——(2004), 'The Double Foundation of Boiotian Thebes', *TAPA* 134: 1–22.

——(2005), 'The Hierarchy of Herdsmen, Goatherding, and Genre in Theocritean Bucolic', *Phoenix* 59: 228–45.

——(2007), 'Dirce at Thebes', *G&R* 54: 18–39.

Bernal, M. (1991), *Black Athena: The Afroasiatic Roots of Classical Civilization*, ii. London.

Bernardini, P. A. (2000), 'La città di Tebe nell' *Eracle* di Euripide', in Bernardini (ed.), *Presenza e funzione della città di Tebe nella cultura greca*. Atti del Convegno Internazionale (Urbino 7–9 luglio 1997), Pisa and Rome, 219–32.

Bernbaum, E. (1997), *Sacred Mountains of the World*. Berkeley, CA (with a new Preface; originally San Francisco, CA, 1990).

Bernidaki-Aldous, E. A. (1990), *Blindness in a Culture of Light: Especially the Case of Oedipus at Colonus of Sophocles*. New York.

Berthold, O. (1911), *Die Unverwundbarkeit in Sage und Aberglauben der Griechen*. Giessen.

Bettini, M., and Spina, L. (2007), *Il mito delle Sirene. Immagini e racconti dalla Grecia a oggi*. Turin.

Betts, G. G. (1965), 'The Silence of Alcestis', *Mnemosyne* 18: 181–2.

Bierl, A. F. H. (1991), *Dionysos und die griechische Tragödie*. Tübingen.

Blaiklock, E. M. (1952), *The Male Characters of Euripides: A Study in Realism*. Wellington.

Boardman, J. (1952), 'Pottery from Eretria', *ABSA* 47: 1–48.

——(1994), 'Omphale', *LIMC* vii, 1: 45–53.

——, and Kurtz, D. C. (1986), 'Booners', *Greek Vases in the J. Paul Getty Museum. Occasional Papers on Antiquities* 2, Malibu, CA, 35–70.

Bodin, J. (1580), *De la démonomanie des sorciers*. Paris.

Bollack, J., and Judet de La Combe, P. (1981), *L'Agamemnon d' Eschyle. Le texte et ses interprétations, Agamemnon 1, première partie*. Cahiers de Philologie 6. Lille.

Bond, G. W. (1981), *Euripides: Heracles*. Oxford.

Borgeaud, P. (1988), *The Cult of Pan in Ancient Greece*. Chicago, IL (trans. of *Recherches sur le dieu Pan*, Geneva, 1979).

——(1999), 'Melampous and Epimenides: Two Greek Paradigms of the Treatment of Mistake', in J. Assmann and G. G. Stroumsa (eds.), *Transformations of the Inner Self in Ancient Religions*, Leiden, 287–300.

Boswell, J. (1988), *The Kindness of Strangers: The Abandonment of Children in Western Europe from Late Antiquity to the Renaissance*. Harmondsworth.

Bowie, A. M. (1993), *Aristophanes: Myth, Ritual and Comedy*. Cambridge.

Bowra, C. M. (1952), *Heroic Poetry*. London.

Boys-Stones, G. R. (2003), 'The Stoics' Two Types of Allegory', in Boys-Stones (ed.), *Metaphor, Allegory, and the Classical Tradition*, Oxford, 189–216.

Brandenburg, H. (1966), *Studien zur Mitra: Beiträge zur Waffen- und Trachtgeschichte der Antike*. Münster.

Brelich, A. (1955–7), 'Les Monosandales', *La Nouvelle Clio* 7–9: 469–84.

——(1958), *Gli eroi greci: un problema storico-religioso*. Rome.

——(1969), *Paides e parthenoi*. Rome.

Bremmer, J. N. (1978), 'Heroes, Rituals and the Trojan War', *Studi Storico-Religiosi* 2: 5–38.

——(1982), 'The Suodales of Poplios Valesios', *ZPE* 47: 133–47.

——(1983), 'The Importance of the Maternal Uncle and Grandfather in Archaic and Classical Greece and Early Byzantium', *ZPE* 50: 173–86.

——(1984), 'Greek Maenadism Reconsidered', *ZPE* 55: 267–86.

——(1987), *Interpretations of Greek Mythology*. Beckenham.

——(1991a), 'Walking, Standing, and Sitting in Ancient Greek Culture', in Bremmer and H. Roodenburg (eds.), *A Cultural History of Gesture*, Cambridge, 15–35.

——(1991b), 'Orpheus: From Guru to Gay', in P. Borgeaud (ed.), *Orphisme et Orphée*, Geneva, 13–30.

——(1997), 'Why Did Medea Kill her Brother Apsyrtus?', in Clauss and Johnston (1997) 83–100.

——(1999), 'Transvestite Dionysos', in M. W. Padilla (ed.), *Rites of Passage in Ancient Greece: Literature, Religion, Society* (= *Bucknell Review* 43, 1), Lewisburg, PA, 183–200.

——(2007), 'Myth and Ritual in Greek Human Sacrifice: Lykaon, Polyxena and the Case of the Rhodian Criminal', in Bremmer (ed.), *The Strange World of Human Sacrifice*, Leuven, 55–79.

——(2008), *Greek Religion and Culture, the Bible and the Ancient Near East*. Leiden.

——, and Horsfall, N. M. (1987), *Roman Myth and Mythography*, *BICS* Supplement 52.

——, and Erskine, A. (2010) (eds.), *The Gods of Ancient Greece: Identities and Transformations*. Edinburgh.

Brisson, L. (1976), *Le Mythe de Tirésias: essai d'analyse structurale*. Leiden.

Brunvand, J. H. (1981), *The Vanishing Hitchhiker*. New York.

Buck, C. D. (1949), *A Dictionary of Selected Synonyms in the Principal Indo-European Languages*. Chicago, IL.

Budelmann, F. (2006), 'The Mediated Ending of Sophocles' *Oedipus Tyrannus*', *MD* 57: 43–62.

Bulloch, A.W. (1985), *Callimachus: The Fifth Hymn*. Cambridge.

Burgess, J. (1995), 'Achilles' Heel: The Death of Achilles in Ancient Myth', *CA* 14: 217–44.

——(2009), *The Death and Afterlife of Achilles*. Baltimore, MD.

Burian, P. (1997), 'Myth into *Muthos*: The Shaping of Tragic Plot', in Easterling (1997) 178–208.

——(2009), 'Inconclusive Conclusion: The Ending(s) of *Oedipus Tyrannus*', in S. D. Goldhill and E. Hall (eds.), *Sophocles and the Greek Tragic Tradition*, Cambridge, 99–118.

Burke, P. (1978), *Popular Culture in Early Modern Europe*. London.

Burke, P. (2002), 'Context in Context', *Common Knowledge* 8.1: 152–77.

Burkert, W. (1969), 'Das Proömium des Parmenides und die Katabasis des Pythagoras', *Phronesis* 14: 1–30.

——(1970), 'La genèse des choses et des mots: le papyrus de Derveni entre Anaxagore et Cratyle', *Les Études Philosophiques* 25 (1970) 443–55.

——(1983), *Homo Necans: The Anthropology of Ancient Greek Sacrificial Ritual and Myth.* Berkeley, CA (trans. of *Homo Necans: Interpretationen altgriechischer Opferriten und Mythen*, Berlin, 1972; revised edn. 1997).

——(1985), *Greek Religion: Archaic and Classical.* Oxford (trans. of *Griechische Religion der archaischen und klassischen Epoche*, Stuttgart, 1977).

——(1996), *Creation of the Sacred: Tracks of Biology in Early Religions*, Cambridge, MA.

——(2007), 'Euenios der Seher von Apollonia und Apollon Lykeios: Mythos jenseits der Texte', in Burkert, *Kleine Schriften* vii: *Tragica et Historica* (ed. W. Rösler), Göttingen, 186–94 (orig. in *Kernos* (1997) 10: 73–81).

Burn, A. R. (1949), 'Helikon in History: A Study in Greek Mountain Topography', *ABSA* 44: 313–23.

——(1951), 'Thermopylae and Callidromos', in Mylonas, G. E. (ed.), *Studies Presented to David Moore Robinson on his Seventieth Birthday*, i, Saint Louis, MO, 480–9.

Burnett, A. P. (1965), 'The Virtues of Admetus', *CP* 60: 240–55 (reprinted in E. Segal, ed., *Euripides: A Collection of Critical Essays*, Englewood Cliffs, NJ, 1968, 51–69).

Burton, R. W. B. (1962), *Pindar's Pythian Odes: Essays in Interpretation.* Oxford.

Buslepp, K. (1916–24a), 'Talos', in Roscher v: cols. 22–37.

——(1916–24b), 'Teiresias', in Roscher v: cols. 178–207.

Buxton, R. G. A. (1981), review of V. Citti, *Tragedia e lotta di classe in Grecia*, *JHS* 101: 172.

——(1982), *Persuasion in Greek Tragedy: A Study of Peitho*. Cambridge.

——(1989), 'The Messenger and the Maenads: A Speech from Euripides' *Bacchae* (1043–1152)', *Acta Antiqua* 32: 223–34.

——(1991), 'News from Cithaeron: Narrators and Narratives in the *Bacchae*', *Pallas* 37: 39–48.

——(1992a), 'Le Centaure anglais: l'espace "initiatique" dans *Henri IV* de Shakespeare', in A. Moreau (ed.), *L'Initiation*, Montpellier, ii, 153–61.

——(1992b), 'Iphigénie au bord de la mer', *Pallas* 38: 209–15.

——(1994), *Imaginary Greece: The Contexts of Mythology.* Cambridge.

——(1996), 'What Can You Rely on in *Oedipus Rex*?', in Silk (1996) 38–48.

——(2000a), 'Les Yeux de Médée: le regard et la magie dans les *Argonautiques* d'Apollonios de Rhodes', in A. Moreau and J.-C. Turpin (eds.), *La Magie*. Actes du Colloque International de Montpellier, 25–27 mars 1999, ii, 265–75.

——(2000b) (ed.), *Oxford Readings in Greek Religion*. Oxford.

——(2006), 'Weapons and Day's White Horses: The Language of *Ajax*', in I. J. F. de Jong and A. Rijksbaron (eds.), *Sophocles and the Greek Language: Aspects of Diction, Syntax and Pragmatics*, Leiden, 13–23.

——(2009), *Forms of Astonishment: Greek Myths of Metamorphosis*. Oxford.

Bynum, C. W. (2001), *Metamorphosis and Identity*. New York.

Cadell, H., and Rémondon, R. (1967), 'Sens et emplois de *τὸ ὄρος* dans les documents papyrologiques', *REG* 80: 343–9.

Calame, C. (1986), 'Le Nom d'Oedipe', in B. Gentili and R. Pretagostini (eds.), *Edipo: Il teatro greco e la cultura europea*, Rome, 395–407.

——(1995), *The Craft of Poetic Speech in Ancient Greece*. Ithaca, NY (trans. of *Le Récit en Grèce ancienne*, Paris, 1986; revised edn. Paris, 2000).

——(2000), 'Iô, les Danaïdes, l'extérieur et l'inflexion tragique', in Calame, *Poétique des mythes dans la Grèce antique*, Paris, 117–44.

Calder, W. M. (1965), 'The Entrance of Athena in *Ajax*', *CP* 60: 114–16.

Campbell, D. A. (1992) (ed.), *Greek Lyric* iv: *Bacchylides, Corinna, and Others*. Cambridge, MA.

Campbell, M. (1983), *Studies in the Third Book of Apollonius Rhodius' Argonautica*. Hildesheim.

Carpenter, T. H., and Faraone, C. A. (1993) (eds.), *Masks of Dionysus*. Ithaca, NY.

Carrière, J.-C., and Massonie, B. (1991), *La Bibliothèque d'Apollodore*. Paris.

Carter, D. M. (2011) (ed.), *Why Athens? A Reappraisal of Tragic Politics*. Oxford.

Cartledge, P. (1993), *The Greeks: A Portrait of Self and Others*. Oxford.

Caskey, J. L., and Amandry, P. (1952), 'Investigations at the Heraion of Argos, 1949', *Hesperia* 21: 165–221.

Chantraine, P. (1968–80), *Dictionnaire étymologique de la langue grecque: histoire des mots*. 4 vols. Paris.

Charles, J. A. (1980), 'The Coming of Copper and Copper-Base Alloys and Iron: A Metallurgical Sequence', in Th. A. Wertime and J. D. Muhly (eds.), *The Coming of the Age of Iron*, New Haven, CT, and London, 151–81.

Christopoulos, M., Karakantza, E. D., and Levaniouk, O. (2010) (eds.), *Light and Darkness in Ancient Greek Myth and Religion*. Lanham, MD.

Citti, V. (1978), *Tragedia e lotta di classe in Grecia*. Naples.

Clauss, J. J., and Johnston, S. I. (1997) (eds.), *Medea: Essays on Medea in Myth, Literature, Philosophy, and Art*. Princeton, NJ.

Colgrave, B. (1956), *Felix's Life of Saint Guthlac*. Cambridge.

Conte, G. B. (1994), *Genres and Readers*. Baltimore, MD.

Cook, A. B. (1894), 'Descriptive Animal Names in Greece', *CR* 8: 381–5.

——(1914–40), *Zeus: A Study in Ancient Religion*. 3 vols. Cambridge.

Cook, R. M. (1972), *Greek Art: Its Development, Character and Influence*. London.

Copley, F. O. (1956), *Exclusus Amator: A Study in Latin Love Poetry*. American Philological Association Monographs 17. Madison, WI.
Cox, G. W. (1883), *An Introduction to the Science of Comparative Mythology and Folklore*. 2nd edn. London.
Croally, N. (1994), *Euripidean Polemic*. Cambridge.
Crotty, K. (1982), *Song and Action: The Victory Odes of Pindar*. Baltimore, MD.
Csapo, E. (1997), 'Riding the Phallus for Dionysus', *Phoenix* 51: 253–95.
——, and Slater, W. J. (1994), *The Context of Ancient Drama*. Ann Arbor, MI.
Dale, A. M. (1954), *Euripides: Alcestis*. Oxford.
Dasen, V. (2004) (ed.), *Naissance et petite enfance dans l'Antiquité*. Actes du colloque de Fribourg, 28 novembre—1er décembre 2001. Fribourg and Göttingen.
Davies, J. G. (1962), *The Architectural Setting of Baptism*. London.
Dawe, R. D. (1984), *Sophoclis tragoediae*, i. 2nd edn. Leipzig.
Delcourt, M. (1982), *Héphaistos, ou la légende du magicien*. 2nd edn. Paris.
——(1961), *Hermaphrodite. Myths and Rites of the Bisexual Figure in Classical Antiquity*. London (trans. of *Hermaphrodite. Mythes et rites de la bisexualité dans l'Antiquité classique*, Paris, 1958).
Denniston, J. D., and Page, D. L. (1957), *Aeschylus: Agamemnon*. Oxford.
Dent, A. (1974), *Lost Beasts of Britain*. London.
Deonna, W. (1965), *Le Symbolisme de l'œil*. Paris.
Detienne, M. (1981), 'Zeus. L'Autre. Un problème de maïeutique', in Y. Bonnefoy (ed.), *Dictionnaire des mythologies et des religions des sociétés traditionnelles et du monde antique*, Paris, ii, 554.
——, and Svenbro, J. (1979), 'Les Loups au festin ou la cité impossible', in Detienne and J.-P. Vernant (eds.), *La Cuisine du sacrifice en pays grec*, Paris, 215–37.
Der Kleine Pauly: Lexikon der Antike (1964–75). 5 vols. Stuttgart.
Deubner, L. (1900), '*ΕΠΑΥΛΙΑ*', *JDAI* 15: 144–54.
Devereux, G. (1973), 'The Self-Blinding of Oidipous in Sophokles: *Oidipous Tyrannos*', *JHS* 93: 36–49.
Dickie, M. (1990), 'Talos Bewitched: Magic, Atomic Theory and Paradoxography in Apollonius *Argonautica* 4.1638–88', in F. Cairns and M. Heath (eds.), *Papers of the Leeds International Latin Seminar*, 6, Leeds, 267–96.
——(2010), 'Lucian's Gods: Lucian's Understanding of the Divine', in Bremmer and Erskine (2010) 348–61.
Dierse, U. (1982), 'Ideologie', in O. Brunner, W. Conze, and R. Koselleck (eds.), *Geschichtliche Grundbegriffe*, Stuttgart, iii, 131–69.
Dillon, J. E. M. (1989), *The Greek Hero Perseus: Myths of Maturation*. Unpubl. Oxford D.Phil. Thesis.
Dingel, J. (1967), *Das Requisit in der griechischen Tragödie*. Diss. Tübingen.

Dodd, D. B., and Faraone, C. A. (2003) (eds.), *Initiation in Ancient Greek Rituals and Narratives.* London.
Dodds, E. R. (1951), *The Greeks and the Irrational.* Berkeley, CA.
——(1960), *Euripides: Bacchae.* 2nd edn. Oxford.
Douglas, A. (1993), *The Beast Within: Man, Myths and Werewolves.* London.
Douglas, M. (1954), 'The Lele of the Kasai', in D. Forde (ed.), *African Worlds,* Oxford, 1–26.
Dover, K. J. (1980), *Plato: Symposium.* Cambridge.
Dowden, K. (2006), *Zeus.* London.
Dozeman, T. B. (1989), *God on the Mountain. A Study of Redaction, Theology and Canon in Exodus 19–24.* Atlanta, GA.
Ducrey, P. (1985), *Guerre et guerriers dans la Grèce antique.* Paris.
Duminil, M.-P. (1977), 'Le Sens de *ichōr* dans les textes hippocratiques', in R. Joly (ed.) *Corpus Hippocraticum. Actes du colloque hippocratique de Mons (22–26 septembre 1975),* Mons, 65–76.
——(1983), *Le Sang, les vaisseaux, le coeur dans la Collection hippocratique. Anatomie et physiologie.* Paris.
Dunbar, N. (1995), *Aristophanes: Birds.* Oxford.
Dyson, M. (1988), 'Alcestis' Children and the Character of Admetus', *JHS* 108: 13–23.
Easterling, P. E. (1985), 'Anachronism in Greek Tragedy', *JHS* 105: 1–10.
——(1993), 'The End of an Era? Tragedy in the Early Fourth Century', in Sommerstein et al. (1993) 559–69.
——(1997) (ed.), *The Cambridge Companion to Greek Tragedy.* Cambridge.
——(2005a), '"The Speaking Page": Reading Sophocles with Jebb', in C. A. Stray (ed.), *The Owl of Minerva: The Cambridge Praelections of 1906, PCPhS* Suppl. vol. 28, 25–46.
——(2005b), 'The Image of the *Polis* in Greek Tragedy', in M. H. Hansen (ed.), *The Imaginary Polis,* Copenhagen, 49–72.
Elata-Alster, G. (1985), 'The King's Double Bind', *Arethusa* 18: 23–46.
Eliade, M. (1954), *The Myth of the Eternal Return.* New York.
——(1964), *Shamanism: Archaic Techniques of Ecstasy.* London (trans. of *Le Chamanisme et les techniques archaïques de l'extase,* Paris, 1951).
Elliger, W. (1975), *Die Darstellung der Landschaft in der griechischen Dichtung.* Berlin.
Engels, D. (1980), 'The Problem of Female Infanticide in the Greco-Roman World', *CP* 75: 112–20.
Esser, A. (1961), *Das Antlitz der Blindheit in der Antike.* 2nd edn. Leiden.
Fagles, R. (1966), *Aeschylus: The Oresteia.* Harmondsworth.
Fantuzzi, M. (2004), 'Performance and Genre', in Fantuzzi and R. L. Hunter (eds.), *Tradition and Innovation in Hellenistic Poetry,* Cambridge, 1–41.
Faraone, C. A. (1987), 'Hephaestus the Magician and Near Eastern Parallels for Alcinous' Watchdogs', *GRBS* 28: 257–80.

Farnell, L. R. (1896–1909), *The Cults of the Greek States*. 5 vols. Oxford.

Federico, E. (1989), 'Talos: funzione e rifunzionalizzazioni di un mito eteocretese', *Annali dell' Istituto Universitario Orientale (Sezione di Storia Antica e Archeologia)* 11: 95–120.

Feeney, D. C. (1991), *The Gods in Epic: Poets and Critics of the Classical Tradition*. Oxford.

Fehling, D. (1974), *Ethologische Überlegungen auf dem Gebiet der Altertumskunde*. Munich.

Finglass, P. J. (2009), 'The Ending of Sophocles' *Oedipus Rex*', *Philologus* 153: 42–62.

——(2011), *Sophocles: Ajax*. Cambridge.

Fitzgibbon, C. (1971), *Red Hand: The Ulster Colony*. London.

Flint, V., Gordon, R., Luck, G., and Ogden, D. (1999), *Witchcraft and Magic in Europe*, ii: *Ancient Greece and Rome*. London.

Foley, H. P. (1985), *Ritual Irony: Poetry and Sacrifice in Euripides*. Ithaca, NY.

Fontaine, J. (1981), 'Aux Sources de la lexicographie médiévale: Isidore de Séville, médiateur de l'étymologie antique', in Y. Lefèvre (ed.), *La Lexicographie du latin médiéval et ses rapports avec les recherches actuelles sur la civilisation du Moyen Âge*, Paris, 97–103.

Forbes Irving, P. M. C. (1990), *Metamorphosis in Greek Myths*. Oxford.

Fowler, R. L. (1995), 'Greek Magic, Greek Religion', *ICS* 20: 1–22 (reprinted in Buxton (2000b) 317–43).

——(2010), 'Gods in Early Greek Historiography', in Bremmer and Erskine (2010) 318–34.

Fraenkel, E. (1957), *Horace*. Oxford.

Franco, C. (2003), *Senza ritegno: Il cane e la donna nell' immaginario della Grecia antica*. Bologna.

Frazer, J. G. (1898), *Pausanias's Description of Greece*. 6 vols. London.

——(1921), *Apollodorus: The Library*. 2 vols. Cambridge, MA.

Freeden, M. (2003), *Ideology: A Very Short Introduction*. Oxford.

Frisk, H. (1960–72), *Griechisches etymologisches Wörterbuch*. 3 vols. Heidelberg.

Fritz, K. von (1962), *Antike und moderne Tragödie*. Berlin.

Frontisi-Ducroux, F. (1975), *Dédale. Mythologie de l'artisan en Grèce ancienne*. Paris.

——(2003), *L'Homme-cerf et la femme-araignée*. Paris.

Galinsky, G. K. (1972), *The Herakles Theme*. Oxford.

Gantz, J. (1976), *The Mabinogion*. Translation. Harmondsworth.

Gantz, T. (1993), *Early Greek Myth: A Guide to Literary and Artistic Sources*. Baltimore, MD.

Garland, R. (2001), *The Greek Way of Death*. 2nd edn. Ithaca, NY.

Garlipp, P., Gödecke-Koch, T., Dietrich, D. E., and Haltenhof, H. (2004), 'Lycanthropy—Psychopathological and Psychodynamical Aspects', *Acta Psychiatrica Scandinavica* 109, 1: 19–22.

Garvie, A. F. (1998), *Sophocles: Ajax*. Warminster.

Gejvall, N.-G. (1969), *Lerna*, i: *The Fauna*. Princeton, NJ.

Genette, G., et al. (1986), *Théorie des genres*. Paris.

Gennep, A. van (1909), *Les Rites de passage*. Paris.

Gentili, B., et al. (1995), *Pindaro: Le Pitiche*. Milan.

Georgoudi, S. (1974), 'Quelques problèmes de la transhumance dans la Grèce ancienne', *REG* 87: 155–85.

Gerhardt, T. (1977), 'Der Werwolf im Groschenroman', *Kieler Blätter zur Volkskunde* 9: 41–54.

Gernet, L. (1981), *The Anthropology of Ancient Greece*. Baltimore, MD (trans. of *Anthropologie de la Grèce antique*, Paris, 1968).

Ginouvès, R. (1962), *Balaneutikè. Recherches sur le bain dans l'Antiquité grecque*. Paris.

Ginzburg, C. (1983), *The Night Battles: Witchcraft and Agrarian Cults in the Sixteenth and Seventeenth Centuries*. London (trans. of *I benandanti: stregoneria e culti agrari tra Cinquecento e Seicento*, Turin, 1966).

Goff, B. (1995) (ed.), *History, Tragedy, Theory: Dialogues on Athenian Drama*. Austin, TX.

Goheen, R. F. (1951), *The Imagery of Sophocles' Antigone*. Princeton, NJ.

Golden, M. (1981), 'Demography and the Exposure of Girls at Athens', *Phoenix* 35: 316–31.

Goldhill, S. D. (1986), *Reading Greek Tragedy*. Cambridge.

——(1987), 'The Great Dionysia and Civic Ideology', *JHS* 107: 58–76 (reprinted in Winkler and Zeitlin (1990) 97–129).

Gomme, A. W. (1945), *A Historical Commentary on Thucydides*, i. Oxford.

Gould, J. (2001), *Myth, Ritual, Memory, and Exchange: Essays in Greek Literature and Culture*. Oxford.

Gow, A. S. F. (1934), '*Ἴυγξ, ῥόμβος, rhombus, turbo*', in *JHS* 54: 1–13.

——(1952), *Theocritus*. 2nd edn. 2 vols. Cambridge.

Graf, F. (1985), *Nordionische Kulte*. Schweizerisches Institut in Rom.

——(1987), 'Orpheus: A Poet among Men', in Bremmer (1987) 80–106.

Graves, R. (1960), *The Greek Myths*, i. Revised edn. Harmondsworth.

Graziosi, B. (2002), *Inventing Homer: The Early Reception of Epic*. Cambridge.

Grégoire, H. (with R. Goossens and M. Mathieu) (1949), *Asklèpios, Apollon Smintheus et Rudra: Études sur le dieu à la taupe et le dieu au rat dans la Grèce et dans l'Inde*. Académie Royale de Belgique, Classe des Lettres et des Sciences morales et politiques. Mémoires xlv.1.

Gregory, J. (1979), 'Euripides' *Alcestis*', *Hermes* 107: 259–70.

Grene, D., and Lattimore, R. (1958) (eds.), *The Complete Greek Tragedies: Euripides*, iii. Chicago, IL.

Griffin, J. (1980), *Homer on Life and Death*. Oxford.

Griffiths, A. (1999), 'Euenius the Negligent Nightwatchman (Herodotus 9.92–6)', in R. G. A. Buxton (ed.), *From Myth to Reason? Studies in the Development of Greek Thought*, Oxford, 169–82.

Grimm, W. (1957), *Die deutsche Heldensage*, 4th edn. Darmstadt.

Grottanelli, C. (2003), 'Evenius Becomes a Seer (Herodotus 9.93–5). A Paradoxical Initiation?', in Dodd and Faraone (2003) 203–18.

Gruppe, O. (1906), *Griechische Mythologie und Religionsgeschichte*. Munich.

Guillén, C. (1971), *Literature as System: Essays toward the Theory of Literary History*. Princeton, NJ.

Haight, E. H. (1950), *The Symbolism of the House Door in Classical Poetry*. New York.

Hall, E. (1996), 'Is there a *Polis* in Aristotle's *Poetics*?', in Silk (1996) 295–309.

——(2010), 'Medea and the Mind of the Murderer', in H. Bartel and A. Simon (eds.), *Unbinding Medea: Interdisciplinary Approaches to a Classical Myth from Antiquity to the 21st Century*, London, 16–24.

Halliwell, S. (1998), *Aristotle's Poetics*. 2nd edn. Chicago, IL.

——(2002), 'Mimesis and the Best Life: Plato's Repudiation of the Tragic,' in Halliwell, *The Aesthetics of Mimesis: Ancient Texts and Modern Problems*, Princeton, NJ, 98–117.

Halm-Tisserant, M. (1995), '*Exo—Entos*—De l'ambiguïté des portes et des fenêtres dans la peinture de vases grecque', *REA* 97: 473–503.

Halstead, P. (1987), 'Traditional and Ancient Rural Economy in Mediterranean Europe: *plus ça change*?', *JHS* 107: 77–87.

Hansen, P. A. (1983), *Carmina epigraphica graeca*, i. Berlin.

Hansen, W. F. (2010), 'Unverwundbarkeit', in *Enzyklopädie des Märchens*, Berlin, xiii: 1239–48.

Harf-Lancner, L. (1985), 'La Métamorphose illusoire: des théories chrétiennes de la métamorphose aux images médiévales du loup-garou', *Annales E.S.C.*, 40: 208–26.

Harrison, E. B. (1964), 'Hesperides and Heroes: A Note on the Three-Figure Reliefs', *Hesperia* 33: 76–82.

Harrison, J. (1927), *Themis: A Study of the Social Origins of Greek Religion*. 2nd edn. Cambridge.

Hartog, F. (2001a), *Le Miroir d'Hérodote: Essai sur la représentation de l'autre*. 2nd edn. Paris.

——(2001b), *Memories of Odysseus: Frontier Tales from Ancient Greece*. Edinburgh (trans. of *Mémoire d'Ulisse: Récits sur la frontière en Grèce ancienne*, Paris, 1996).

Haspels, C. H. E. (1930), 'Deux fragments d'une coupe d'Euphronios', *BCH* 54: 422–51.

Haupt, M. (1869), 'Excerpta ex Timothei Gazaei libris de animalibus', *Hermes* 3: 1–30.

Heath, M. (1987), *The Poetics of Greek Tragedy*. London.

Henderson, J. (1987), *Aristophanes: Lysistrata.* Oxford.
——(1991), 'Women and the Athenian Dramatic Festivals', *TAPA* 121: 133–47.
Henrichs, A. (1978), 'Greek Maenadism from Olympias to Messalina', *HSCP* 82: 121–60.
——(1982), 'Changing Dionysiac Identities', in B. F. Meyer and E. P. Sanders (eds.), *Jewish and Christian Self-Definition*, London, iii, 137–60.
——(1984), 'Male Intruders among the Maenads: The So-Called Male Celebrant', in H. D. Evjen (ed.), *MNHMAI: Classical Studies in Memory of Karl K. Hulley*, Chico, CA, 69–91.
Hermann, G. (1819), *Über das Wesen und die Behandlung der Mythologie. Ein Brief an Herrn Hofrath Creuzer.* Leipzig.
Heslin, P. J. (2005), *The Transvestite Achilles: Gender and Genre in Statius' Achilleid.* Cambridge.
Hickey, K. (2011), *Wolves in Ireland: A Natural and Cultural History.* Dublin.
Himmelmann, N. (1980), *Über Hirten-Genre in der antiken Kunst.* Opladen.
Hodkinson, S. (1988), 'Animal Husbandry in the Greek Polis', in Whittaker (1988) 35–74.
Höfer, O. (1902–9), 'Perdix', in Roscher iii, 2: cols. 1946–55.
——(1916–24), 'Tallaios', in Roscher v: cols. 21–2.
Hopkinson, N. (1988), *A Hellenistic Anthology.* Cambridge.
Hose, M. (2008), *Euripides: Der Dichter der Leidenschaften.* Munich.
Hourmouziades, N. C. (1965), *Production and Imagination in Euripides.* Athens.
Hughes, D. D. (1991), *Human Sacrifice in Ancient Greece.* London.
Hunter, R. L. (1993a), *Apollonius of Rhodes: Jason and the Golden Fleece.* Oxford.
——(1993b), *The Argonautica of Apollonius: Literary Studies.* Cambridge.
Hurst, A., and Schachter, A. (1996) (eds.), *La Montagne des Muses.* Geneva.
Hutchinson, G. O. (1988), *Hellenistic Poetry.* Oxford.
Huxley, G. L. (1978), '*ΟΡΟΣ ΘΕΟΣ* (Maximus Tyrius 2.8)', *Liverpool Classical Monthly* 3: 71–2.
Irwin, E. (1974), *Colour Terms in Greek Poetry.* Toronto.
Jaccottet, A.-F. (2003), *Choisir Dionysos. Les associations dionysiaques ou la face cachée du dionysisme.* 2 vols. Kilchberg.
Jaeger, W. (1947), *The Theology of the Early Greek Philosophers.* Oxford.
Janko, R. (1992), *The Iliad: A Commentary. Vol. IV: Books 13–16.* Cambridge.
Jeanmaire, H. (1939), *Couroi et Courètes.* Lille.
Jebb, R. C. (1896), *Sophocles: The Plays and Fragments. Part VII. The Ajax.* Cambridge.
Jenkins, I. D. (1983), 'Is there Life after Marriage? A Study of the Abduction Motif in Vase Paintings of the Athenian Wedding Ceremony', *BICS* 30: 137–45.

Jiménez San Cristóbal, A. I. (2012), 'Las Sirenas', in A. Bernabé and J. Pérez de Tudela (eds.), *Seres híbridos en la mitología griega*, Madrid, 113–51.
Johnston, S. I. (1995), 'The Song of the *Iynx*: Magic and Rhetoric in *Pythian* 4', *TAPA* 125: 177–206.
——(1999), *Restless Dead: Encounters between the Living and the Dead in Ancient Greece*. Berkeley, CA.
Jordan, D. R. (1988), 'New Archaeological Evidence for the Practice of Magic in Classical Athens', in *Praktika tou XII Diethnous Synedriou Klasikes Archaiologias*, Athens, iv, 273–7.
Jost, M. (1985), *Sanctuaires et cultes d'Arcadie*. École française d'Athènes, Études Péloponnésiennes 9. Paris.
——(1992), 'La Légende de Mélampous en Argolide et dans le Péloponnèse', in M. Piérart (ed.), *Polydipsion Argos. Argos de la fin des palais mycéniens à la constitution de l'État classique*. École française d'Athènes, Paris, 173–84.
Jouanna, J. (1981), 'Les Causes de la défaite des Barbares chez Eschyle, Hérodote et Hippocrate', *Ktèma* 6: 3–15.
Kamerbeek, J. C. (1953), *The Plays of Sophocles. Part 1, The Ajax*. Leiden.
Kamptz, H. von (1982), *Homerische Personennamen: Sprachwissenschaftliche und historische Klassifikation*. Göttingen.
Kanavou, N. (2011), *Aristophanes' Comedy of Names: A Study of Speaking Names in Aristophanes*. Berlin.
Karsai, G. (1992), 'Tirésias dans les *Bacchantes*', in A. Moreau (ed.), *L'Initiation*, Montpellier, i, 199–208.
Katz, J. T. (2010), 'Etymology', in A. Grafton, G. W. Most, and S. Settis (eds.), *The Classical Tradition*, Cambridge, MA, 342–5.
Kearns, E. (2004), 'The Gods in the Homeric Epics', in R. Fowler (ed.), *The Cambridge Companion to Homer*, Cambridge, 59–73.
Khatchatrian, A. (1962), *Les Baptistères paléochrétiens*. Paris.
Kingsley, P. (1995), *Ancient Philosophy, Mystery, and Magic: Empedocles and Pythagorean Tradition*. Oxford.
Kleinknecht, H. (1939), '*ΛΟΥΤΡΑ ΤΗΣ ΠΑΛΛΑΔΟΣ*', *Hermes* 74: 301–50.
Klinck, R. (1970), *Die lateinische Etymologie des Mittelalters*. Munich.
Knox, B. M. W. (1964), *The Heroic Temper: Studies in Sophoclean Tragedy*. Berkeley, CA.
——(1979), *Word and Action: Essays on the Ancient Theater*. Baltimore, MD.
Konstan, D. (2001), *Pity Transformed*. London.
Kossatz-Deissmann, A. (2009), 'Thanatos', *LIMC Supplementum 2009*, 1: 473.
Kourouniotis, K. (1904), '*Ανασκαφαὶ Λυκαίου*', in *ArchEph* 153–214.
——(1905), '*Κατάλογοι Λυκαιονικῶν*', *ArchEph* 161–78.
——(1909), '*Ανασκαφὴ Λυκαίου*', *Praktika* 185–200.
Kovacs, D. (2009), 'Do We Have the End of Sophocles' *Oedipus Tyrannus*?', *JHS* 129: 53–70.

Kraus, W. (1984), 'Götter und Menschen bei Homer', in Kraus, *Aus Allem Eines. Studien zur antiken Geistesgeschichte*, 15–27. Heidelberg (reprinted from *Wiener Humanistische Blätter* 18 (1976) 20–32).

Krauskopf, I. (1977), 'Eine attisch schwarzfigurige Hydria in Heidelberg', *AA*, 13–37.

Krumeich, R., Pechstein, N., and Seidensticker, B. (1999) (eds.), *Das griechische Satyrspiel*. Darmstadt.

Kullmann, W. (1992), 'Gods and Men in the *Iliad* and *Odyssey*', in Kullmann, *Homerische Motive: Beiträge zur Entstehung, Eigenart und Wirkung von Ilias und Odyssee*, 243–63. Stuttgart (reprinted from *HSCP* 89 (1985) 1–23).

Kuper, A., and Kuper, J., (1985) (eds.), *The Social Science Encyclopaedia*. London.

Kurtz, D. C., and Boardman, J. (1971), *Greek Burial Customs*. London.

Lacey, W. K. (1968), *The Family in Classical Greece*. London.

Lambrinoudakis, V. (1971), *ΜΗΡΟΤΡΑΦΗΣ*. Athens.

Lane Fox, R. (1986), *Pagans and Christians*. London.

Langdon, M. K. (1976), 'A Sanctuary of Zeus on Mount Hymettos', *Hesperia* Suppl. 16.

——(2000), 'Mountains in Greek Religion', *CW* 93: 461–70.

Lanza, D. (1977), *Il tiranno e il suo pubblico*. Turin.

Lattimore, R. (1958), *The Poetry of Greek Tragedy*. Baltimore, MD.

Lauter, H. (1985), *Der Kultplatz auf dem Turkovuni, MDAI(A) Beiheft* 12. Berlin.

Leach, E. R. (1976), *Culture and Communication: The Logic by which Symbols are Connected*. Cambridge.

Lehmann, W. P. (1986), 'Latin *aeger* "sick" and its Proto-Indo-European Context', in A. Etter (ed.) *o-o-pe-ro-si: Festschrift für Ernst Risch zum 75. Geburtstag*, Berlin, 85–9.

Lesky, A. (1973), 'Eine neue Talos-Vase', *AA* 88: 115–19.

Létoublon, F. (2010), 'To See or Not to See: Blind People and Blindness in Ancient Greek Myths', in Christopoulos, Karakantza, and Levaniouk (2010) 167–80.

Leventi, I. (1994), 'Talos II', *LIMC* vii, 1: 837.

Levi, P. (1971), *Pausanias: Guide to Greece*. 2 vols. Harmondsworth.

Lévi-Strauss, C. (1966), *The Savage Mind*. London (trans. of *La Pensée sauvage*, Paris, 1962).

Lienhardt, G. (1961), *Divinity and Experience: The Religion of the Dinka*. Oxford.

Linforth, I. M. (1951), 'Religion and Drama in *Oedipus at Colonus*'. Univ. Calif. Publ. in Cl. Phil. 14, 4: 75–191.

Lissarrague, F. (1980), 'Iconographie de Dolon le loup', *RA*, 3–30.

Livrea, E. (1973), *Apollonii Rhodii Argonauticon Liber Quartus*. Florence.

Llewellyn-Jones, L. (2003), *Aphrodite's Tortoise: The Veiled Woman of Ancient Greece*. Swansea.

Lloyd, G. E. R. (1968), *Aristotle: The Growth and Structure of his Thought*. Cambridge.

——(1983), *Science, Folklore and Ideology: Studies in the Life Sciences in Ancient Greece*. Cambridge.

Lloyd, M. (1985), 'Euripides' *Alcestis*', *G&R* 32: 119–31.

Lloyd-Jones, H. (1962), 'The Guilt of Agamemnon', *CQ* 12: 187–99.

Loraux, N. (1993), *The Children of Athena*. Princeton, NJ (trans. of *Les Enfants d'Athéna*, Paris, 1981).

——(1995), *The Experiences of Tiresias*. Princeton, NJ (trans. of *Les Expériences de Tirésias*, Paris, 1989).

Lucas, D. W. (1972), *Aristotle: Poetics*. Corrected edn. Oxford.

Lurje, M. (2004), *Die Suche nach der Schuld: Sophokles' Oedipus Rex, Aristoteles' Poetik und das Tragödienverständnis der Neuzeit*. Munich and Leipzig.

Luschnig, C. A. E., and Roisman, H. M. (2003), *Euripides' Alcestis*. Norman, OK.

Mac Cana, P. (1977), *The Mabinogi*. Cardiff.

McLeod, M. D. (1981), *The Asante*. London.

Mahoney, H. M. (1940), *The Blind Man in Greek Legend and Literature*. Diss. Fordham, NY.

Mahood, M. M. (2003), *Shakespeare: The Merchant of Venice*. Updated edn. Cambridge.

Mainoldi, C. (1984), *L'Image du loup et du chien dans la Grèce ancienne d'Homère à Platon*. Paris.

Mair, A. W. (1928), *Oppian, Colluthus, Tryphiodorus*. London.

Malten, L. (1961), *Die Sprache des menschlichen Antlitzes im frühen Griechentum*. Berlin.

Manuwald, B. (1989), *Studien zum Unbewegten Beweger in der Naturphilosophie des Aristoteles*, Abhandlungen der Geistes- und Sozialwissenschaftlichen Klasse, Nr. 9. Mainz.

Martin, R. (1974), *L'Urbanisme dans la Grèce antique*. 2nd edn. Paris.

Mastronarde, D. J. (2010), *The Art of Euripides: Dramatic Technique and Social Context*. Cambridge.

Mattes, J. (1970), *Der Wahnsinn im griechischen Mythos und in der Dichtung bis zum Drama des fünften Jahrhunderts*. Heidelberg.

Mech, L. D. (1970), *The Wolf: The Ecology and Behavior of an Endangered Species*. New York.

——(1991), *The Way of the Wolf*. Stillwater, MN.

——, and Boitani, L. (2003) (eds.), *Wolves: Behavior, Ecology and Conservation*. Chicago, IL.

Meier, C. (1993), *The Political Art of Greek Tragedy*. Oxford (trans. of *Die politische Kunst der griechischen Tragödie*, Munich, 1988).

Merlen, R. H. A. (1971), *De Canibus: Dog and Hound in Antiquity*. London.

Meuli, K. (1975), *Gesammelte Schriften*, i. Basel.

Meyer, C. (1884), *Der Aberglaube des Mittelalters und der nächstfolgenden Jahrhunderte*. Basel.

Michelakis, P. (2002), *Achilles in Greek Tragedy*. Cambridge.

Miller, M. C. (1999), 'Reexamining Transvestism in Archaic and Classical Athens: the Zewadski stamnos', *AJA* 103: 223–53.

Mills, S. (2006), *Euripides: Bacchae*. London.

Mirto, M. S. (2010), 'Il dio nato due volte: l'etimologia nelle *Baccanti* tra fede religiosa e critica del mito,' *Philologus* 154: 3–24.

Molinier, A. and Molinier-Meyer, N. (1981), 'Environnement et histoire: les loups et l'homme en France', *Revue d' histoire moderne et contemporaine* 28: 225–45.

Montiglio, S. (2000), *Silence in the Land of Logos*. Princeton, NJ.

——(2005), *Wandering in Ancient Greek Culture*. Chicago, IL.

Moreau, A. (1994), *Le Mythe de Jason et Médée: le va-nu-pied et la sorcière*. Paris.

Moret, J.-M. (1984), *Oedipe, la Sphinx et les thébains*. Geneva.

Müller, C. W. (1967), 'Protagoras über die Götter', *Hermes* 95: 140–59.

Müller, F. M. (1895), *Chips from a German Workshop*. New edn., iv. London.

Müller, K. O. (1825), *Prolegomena zu einer wissenschaftlichen Mythologie*. Göttingen.

Nehamas, A. (1992), 'Pity and Fear in the *Rhetoric* and the *Poetics*', in A. O. Rorty (ed.), *Essays on Aristotle's Poetics*, Princeton, NJ, 291–314.

Neitzel, H. (1979), 'Artemis und Agamemnon in der Parodos des aischyleischen *Agamemnon*', *Hermes* 107: 10–32.

Newlands, C. E. (1997), 'The Metamorphosis of Ovid's Medea', in Clauss and Johnston (1997) 178–208.

Nielsen, R. M. (1976), 'Alcestis: A Paradox in Dying', *Ramus* 5: 92–102.

Ninck, M. (1921), *Die Bedeutung des Wassers im Kult und Leben der Alten*, *Philologus*, Supplbd. 14.2. Leipzig.

Nisetich, F. J. (1980), *Pindar's Victory Songs*. Translation. MD.

Oakley, J. H. (1982), 'The Anakalupteria', *AA*: 113–18.

——, and Sinos, R. H. (1993), *The Wedding in Ancient Athens*. Madison, WI.

Obbink, D. (1993), 'Dionysus Poured Out: Ancient and Modern Theories of Sacrifice and Cultural Formation', in Carpenter and Faraone (1993) 65–86.

Ogden, D. (1997), *The Crooked Kings of Ancient Greece*. London.

Ogle, M. B. (1911), 'The House-Door in Greek and Roman Religion and Folk-Lore', *AJP* 32: 251–71.

O'Hara, J. J. (1996), *True Names: Vergil and the Alexandrian Tradition of Etymological Wordplay*. Ann Arbor, MI.

O'Higgins, D.M. (1997), 'Medea as Muse: Pindar's *Pythian* 4', in Clauss and Johnston (1997) 103–26.

Olson, S. D. (2008), *Athenaeus: The Learned Banqueters*, iv. Cambridge, MA.

Onians, R. B. (1954), *The Origins of European Thought about the Body, the Mind, the Soul, the World, Time and Fate*. 2nd edn. Cambridge.

Opelt, I. (1966), 'Etymologie', *Reallexikon für Antike und Christentum* vi: cols. 797–844.

Oranje, H. (1984), *Euripides' Bacchae: The Play and its Audience*. Leiden.

Ortalli, G., (1973), 'Natura, storia e mitografia del lupo nel Medioevo', *La Cultura* 11: 257–311.

Osborne, R. (1987), *Classical Landscape with Figures*. London.

——(1993), 'Competitive Festivals and the Polis: A Context for Dramatic Festivals at Athens', in Sommerstein et al. (1993) 21–38.

Otten, C. F. (1986) (ed.), *A Lycanthropy Reader: Werewolves in Western Culture*. Syracuse, NY.

——(2002) (ed.), *The Literary Werewolf: An Anthology*. Syracuse, NY.

Otto, W. F. (1965), *Dionysus: Myth and Cult*. Bloomington, IN (trans. of *Dionysos: Mythos und Kultus*, Frankfurt am Main, 1933).

Oudemans, Th. C. W., and Lardinois, A. P. M. H. (1987), *Tragic Ambiguity*. Leiden.

Padel, R. (1990), 'Making Space Speak', in Winkler and Zeitlin (1990) 336–65.

Padilla, M. (2000), 'Gifts of Humiliation: *Charis* and Tragic Experience in *Alcestis*', *AJP* 121: 179–211.

Paduano, G. (1970), 'L'episodio di Talos: osservazioni sull'esperienza magica nelle *Argonautiche* di Apollonio Rodio', *Studi classici e orientali* 19/20: 46–67.

——(1978), *Sui Persiani di Eschilo: problemi di focalizzazione drammatica*. Rome.

Page, D. L. (1953), *Corinna*. London.

——(1955), *Sappho and Alcaeus*. Oxford.

Papadopoulos, J. K. (1994), 'Talos I', *LIMC* vii, 1: 834–7.

Papathomopoulos, M. (1968), *Antoninus Liberalis: Les Métamorphoses*. Paris.

Parke, H. W. (1967), *The Oracles of Zeus*. Oxford.

Parker, L. P. E. (2007), *Euripides: Alcestis*. Oxford.

Parker, R. (1983), *Miasma: Pollution and Purification in Early Greek Religion*. Oxford.

——(1996), *Athenian Religion: A History*. Oxford.

——(1999), 'Through a Glass Darkly: Sophokles and the Divine', in J. Griffin (ed.), *Sophokles Revisited: Essays Presented to Sir Hugh Lloyd-Jones*, Oxford, 11–30.

——(2005), *Polytheism and Society at Athens*. Oxford.

——(2009), 'Aeschylus' Gods: Drama, Cult, Theology', in *Eschyle à l'aube du théâtre occidental.* Entretiens sur l'Antiquité classique lv, Vandoeuvres-Geneva, 127–64.

——(2011), *On Greek Religion*. Oxford.

Pastoureau, M. (2001), *Blue: The History of a Color*. Princeton, NJ (translation of *Bleu: Histoire d'une couleur*, Paris, 2000).

——(2009a), *Black: The History of a Color*. Princeton, NJ (translation of *Noir: Histoire d'une couleur*, Paris, 2008).

——(2009b), *Le Cochon—Histoire d'un cousin mal aimé*. Paris.

Patterson, C. (1985), '"Not Worth the Rearing": The Causes of Infant Exposure in Ancient Greece', *TAPA* 115: 103–23.

Pearson, A. C. (1917), *The Fragments of Sophocles*. 3 vols. Cambridge.

Pease, A. S. (1961), 'Notes on Mountain Climbing in Antiquity', *Appalachia* 132: 289–98.

Peradotto, J. J. (1969), 'The Omen of the Eagles and the *ΗΘΟΣ* of Agamemnon', *Phoenix* 23: 237–63.

Pfeiffer, R. (1968), *History of Classical Scholarship from the Beginnings to the End of the Hellenistic Age*. Oxford.

Pfister, F. (1951), 'Die Reisebilder des Herakleides', *Sitzungsberichte der Österreichische Akademie der Wissenschaften* 227, 2.

Pfuhl, E. (1923), *Malerei und Zeichnung der Griechen*. 3 vols. Munich.

Philippson, A. (1950–9), *Die griechischen Landschaften*. Frankfurt am Main.

Piccaluga, G. (1968), *Lykaon: un tema mitico*. Rome.

Pickard-Cambridge, A. (1988), *The Dramatic Festivals of Athens*, 2nd edn., revised by J. Gould and D. M. Lewis. Oxford.

Pimlott, D. H. (1975) (ed.), *Wolves*. Morges.

Pirenne-Delforge, V. (1993), 'L'Iynge dans le discours mythique et les procédures magiques', *Kernos* 6: 277–89.

Platnauer, M. (1938), *Euripides: Iphigenia in Tauris*. Oxford.

Pluskowski, A. (2006), *Wolves and the Wilderness in the Middle Ages*. Woodbridge.

Pollard, J. (1977), *Birds in Greek Life and Myth*. London.

Pritchett, W. K. (1965), *Studies in Ancient Greek Topography*, i. Berkeley, CA.

——(1971–91), *The Greek State at War*. 5 Parts (Part I first published as *Ancient Greek Military Practices*). Berkeley, CA.

——(1982), *Studies in Ancient Greek Topography*, Part IV (*Passes*). Berkeley, CA.

Propp, V. (1968), *Morphology of the Folktale*. Austin, TX (revised trans. of *Морфология сказкн*, Leningrad, 1928).

Rackham, H. (1952), *Aristotle: The Athenian Constitution. The Eudemian Ethics. On Virtues and Vices*. London.

Rackham, O. (1990), 'Ancient Landscapes', in O. Murray and S. Price (eds.), *The Greek City from Homer to Alexander*, Oxford, 85–111.

Radke, G. (1936), *Die Bedeutung der weissen und der schwarzen Farbe in Kult und Brauch der Griechen und Römer*. Berlin Diss. Jena.

Radt, S. L. (1981), '*Vita Aeschyli* § 6: ἕως τρίτου μέρους/ἕως τρίτης ἡμέρας', *ZPE* 42: 1–7.

Rank, L. P. (1951), *Etymologiseering en verwante verschijnselen bij Homerus*. Assen.

Redfield, J. M. (1975), *Nature and Culture in the Iliad: The Tragedy of Hector*. Chicago, IL.

Rehm, R. (1994), *Marriage to Death: The Conflation of Wedding and Funeral Rituals in Greek Tragedy*. Princeton, NJ.

——(2002), *The Play of Space: Spatial Transformation in Greek Tragedy*. Princeton, NJ.

——(2003), *Radical Theatre: Greek Tragedy and the Modern World*. London.

Rhodes, P. J. (1981), *A Commentary on the Aristotelian Athenaion Politeia*. Oxford.

Richardson, N. J. (1974), *The Homeric Hymn to Demeter*. Oxford.

——(1993), *The Iliad: A Commentary. VI: Books 21–24*. Cambridge.

Rivier, A. (1972), 'En marge d'*Alceste* et de quelques interprétations récentes', *MH* 29: 124–40.

——(1973), 'En marge d'*Alceste* et de quelques interprétations récentes' (Fin), *MH* 30: 130–43.

Robert, L. (1949), 'Épitaphe d'un berger à Thasos', *Hellenica* 7: 152–60.

——(1955), 'Dédicace d'un berger', *Hellenica* 10: 28–33.

——(1966), 'Inscriptions d'Aphrodisias: première partie', *AC* 35: 397–432.

Robertson, C. M. (1977), 'The Death of Talos', *JHS* 97: 158–60.

Rodighiero, A. (2011), 'The Sense of Place: *Oedipus at Colonus*, "Political" Geography, and the Defence of a Way of Life', in A. Markantonatos and B. Zimmermann (eds.), *Crisis on Stage: Tragedy and Comedy in Late Fifth-Century Athens*, Berlin, 55–80.

Romilly, J. de (1968), *Time in Greek Tragedy*. Ithaca, NY.

Ronay, G. (1972), *The Dracula Myth*. London.

Roscher, W. H. (1896), *Das von der "Kynanthropie" handelnde Fragment des Marcellus von Side. Abh. der Königl. Sächs. Ges. Wiss., phil.-hist. Cl.*, 17. Leipzig.

Rosenstock, H. A., and Vincent, K. R. (1977), 'A Case of Lycanthropy', *American Journal of Psychiatry* 134, 10 (October): 1147–9 (reprinted in Otten (1986) 31–3).

Rosner, E. (1955), 'Die Lahmheit des Hephaistos', *Forschungen und Fortschritte* 29: 362–3.

Roussel, P. (1950), 'La Famille athénienne', *Lettres d'humanité* 9: 5–59.

Roux, J. (1972), *Euripide: Les Bacchantes*, ii. Paris.

Rutherford, R. B. (1992), *Homer: Odyssey Books XIX and XX*. Cambridge.

Rydberg, V. (1889), *Undersökningar i germanisk mythologi*, ii. Stockholm.

Sabbatucci, D. (1965), *Saggio sul misticismo greco*. Rome.

Saïd, S. (1993), 'Tragic Argos', in Sommerstein et al. (1993) 167–89.

Sandys, J. E. (1900), *The Bacchae of Euripides*. 4th edn. Cambridge.

Sartre, M. (1979), 'Aspects économiques et aspects religieux de la frontière dans les cités grecques', *Ktèma* 4: 213–24.

Sassi, M. M. (2001), *The Science of Man in Greece*. Chicago, IL (trans. of *La scienza dell'uomo nella Grecia antica*, Turin, 1988).

Schama, S. (1995), *Landscape and Memory*. London.

Schibli, H. S. (1990), *Pherekydes of Syros*. Oxford.

Schmitt, J.-C. (1983), *The Holy Greyhound: Guinefort, Healer of Children since the Thirteenth Century*. Cambridge (trans. of *Le Saint lévrier: Guinefort, guérisseur d'enfants depuis le XIIIe siècle*, Paris, 1979).

Schnapp, A. (1973), 'Représentation du territoire de guerre et du territoire de chasse dans l'oeuvre de Xénophon', in M. I. Finley (ed.), *Problèmes de la terre en Grèce ancienne*, Paris, 307–21.

Scholz, H. H. (1937), *Der Hund in der griechisch-römischen Magie und Religion*. Berlin.

Schoo, J. (1936–7), 'Vulcanische und seismische Aktivität des ägäischen Meeresbeckens im Spiegel der griechischen Mythologie', *Mnemosyne*, 3rd series, no. 4: 257–94.

Schuhl, P. M. (1953), '*Adèla*', *Annales publiées par la Faculté des Lettres de Toulouse (Homo: Études philosophiques)* 1: 85–93.

Schwinge, E.-R. (1968), *Die Verwendung der Stichomythie in den Dramen des Euripides*. Heidelberg.

Sconduto, L. A. (2008), *Metamorphoses of the Werewolf: A Literary Study from Antiquity through the Renaissance*. Jefferson, NC.

Scott, K. (1929), 'Plutarch and the Ruler Cult', *TAPA* 60: 117–35.

Seaford, R. (1981), 'Dionysiac Drama and the Dionysiac Mysteries', *CQ* 31: 252–75.

——(1984), *Euripides: Cyclops*. Oxford.

——(1994), *Reciprocity and Ritual: Homer and Tragedy in the Developing City-State*. Oxford.

——(1996), *Euripides' Bacchae*. Warminster.

——(1998), 'In the Mirror of Dionysos,' in S. Blundell and M. Williamson (eds.), *The Sacred and the Feminine in Ancient Greece*, London, 128–46.

——(2006), *Dionysos*. London.

Sedley, D. (1998), 'The Etymologies in Plato's *Cratylus*', *JHS* 118: 140–54.

——(2003), *Plato's Cratylus*. Cambridge.

Segal, C. (1982), 'Etymologies and Double Meanings in Euripides' *Bacchae*', *Glotta* 60: 81–93.

——(1986), *Pindar's Mythmaking: The Fourth Pythian Ode*. Princeton, NJ.

——(1997), *Dionysiac Poetics and Euripides' Bacchae*. Expanded edn. Princeton, NJ.

Senn, H. A. (1982), *Were-Wolf and Vampire in Romania*. New York.

Sergent, B. (1986), *Homosexuality in Greek Myth*. Boston (trans. of *L'Homosexualité dans la mythologie grecque*, Paris, 1984).

Siegel, R. E. (1972), 'Galen's Concept of Bloodletting in Relation to his Ideas on Pulmonary and Peripheral Blood Flow and Blood Formation', in A. G. Debus (ed.), *Science, Medicine and Society in the Renaissance: Essays to Honor Walter Pagel*, London, i, 243–75.

Silk, M. S. (1985), 'Heracles and Greek Tragedy', *G&R* 32: 1–22.

——(1996) (ed.), *Tragedy and the Tragic: Greek Theatre and Beyond*. Oxford.

Simon, E. (1992), 'Melampous', *LIMC* vi, 2: 405–10.

Sinn, U. (2000), 'Greek Sanctuaries as Places of Refuge', in Buxton (2000b) 155–79 (orig. publ. in N. Marinatos and R. Hägg, eds., *Greek Sanctuaries: New Approaches*, London, 1993, 88–109).

Skiadas, A. D. (1975), *Wege der Forschung: Kallimachos*. Darmstadt.

Skydsgaard, J. E. (1988), 'Transhumance in Ancient Greece', in Whittaker (1988) 75–86.

Smith, J. Z. (1982), *Imagining Religion: From Babylon to Jonestown*. Chicago, IL.

Smith, W. D. (1960), 'The Ironic Structure in *Alcestis*', *Phoenix* 14: 127–45.

Sommerstein, A. H. (1989), *Aeschylus: Eumenides*. Cambridge.

——(1990), *The Comedies of Aristophanes*, vii: *Lysistrata*. Warminster.

——, Halliwell, S., Henderson, J., and Zimmermann, B. (1993) (eds.), *Tragedy, Comedy and the Polis*. Bari.

——(2010) (ed.), *Aeschylean Tragedy*. 2nd edn. London.

Sourvinou-Inwood, C. (1979), *Theseus as Son and Stepson*. London.

Sparkes, B. A. (1996), *The Red and the Black: Studies in Greek Pottery*. London.

Spencer, D. (2010), *Roman Landscape: Culture and Identity*. Greece and Rome New Surveys in the Classics, 39. Cambridge.

Stafford, E. (2010), 'Herakles between Gods and Heroes', in Bremmer and Erskine (2010) 228–44.

Stanford, W. B. (1963), *Sophocles: Ajax*. London.

——(1983), *Greek Tragedy and the Emotions: An Introductory Study*. London.

Stanton, G. R. (1990), '*Φιλία* and *ξενία* in Euripides' *Alkestis*', *Hermes* 118: 42–54.

Steidle, W. (1968), *Studien zum antiken Drama*. Munich.

Sternbach, L. (1886), 'Beiträge zu den Fragmenten des Aristophanes', *WS* 8: 231–61.

Stinton, T. C. W. (1965), *Euripides and the Judgement of Paris*. London.

Stoll, H. W. (1890–4), 'Kres', in Roscher ii, 1: col. 1419.

Storey, I. C. (2011), review of N. Kanavou, *Aristophanes' Comedy of Names: A Study of Speaking Names in Aristophanes*, in *BMCR* 2011.10.39.

Suard, F. (1980), '*Bisclauret* et les contes du loup-garou: essai d'interprétation', in *Mélanges de langue et littérature françaises du Moyen Age et de la Renaissance: offerts à M. Charles Foulon*, Liège, ii, 267–76.

Summers, M. (1933), *The Werewolf*. London.

Sutton, D. F. (1980), *The Greek Satyr Play*. Meisenheim am Glan.

Taplin, O. (1972), 'Aeschylean Silences and Silences in Aeschylus', *HSCP* 76: 57–97.

——(1977), *The Stagecraft of Aeschylus*. Oxford.

——(1978), *Greek Tragedy in Action*. London.

——(2010), 'Echoes from Mount Cithaeron', in P. Mitsis and C. Tsagalis (eds.), *Allusion, Authority, and Truth: Critical Perspectives on Greek Poetic and Rhetorical Praxis*, Berlin, 235–48.

Tatti-Gartziou, A. (2010), 'Blindness as Punishment', in Christopoulos, Karakantza, and Levaniouk (2010) 181–90.

Theodoridis, C. (1977), 'Bemerkungen zu den griechischen Komikern', *ZPE* 26: 49–54.

Thompson, H. A. (1952), 'The Altar of Pity in the Athenian Agora', *Hesperia* 21: 47–82.

Thompson, S. (1955–8), *Motif-Index of Folk-Literature*. Revised edn. 6 vols. Copenhagen.

Thordarson, F. (1972), 'Die Ferse des Achilleus—ein skythisches Motiv?', *Symbolae Osloenses* 47: 109–24.

Thury, E. M. (1988), 'Euripides' *Alcestis* and the Athenian Generation Gap', *Arethusa* 21: 197–214.

Todorov, T. (1982), *La Conquête de l'Amérique: La question de l'autre*. Paris.

Turner, V. (1967), *The Forest of Symbols: Aspects of Ndembu Ritual*. Ithaca, NY.

Tyrrell, W. B., and Brown, F. S. (1991), *Athenian Myths and Institutions: Words in Action*. New York.

Ullmann, M. (1976), 'Der Werwolf. Ein griechisches Sagenmotiv in arabischer Verkleidung', *Wiener Zeitschrift für die Kunde des Morgenlandes* 68: 171–84.

Uría Varela, J. (1997), *Tabú e eufemismo en latín*. Amsterdam.

Usener, H. (1896), *Götternamen. Versuch einer Lehre von der Religiösen Begriffsbildung*. Bonn.

Veenstra, J. R. (2002), 'The Ever-Changing Nature of the Beast: Cultural Change, Lycanthropy and the Question of Substantial Transformation (from Petronius to Del Rio)', in J. N. Bremmer and J. R. Veenstra (eds.), *The Metamorphosis of Magic from Late Antiquity to the Early Modern Period*, Leuven, 133–66.

Vellacott, P. (1971), *Sophocles and Oedipus*. London.

Verbruggen, H. (1981), *Le Zeus crétois*. Paris.

Vérilhac, A.-M., and Vial, C. (1998), *Le Mariage grec du VIe siècle av. J.-C. à l'époque d'Auguste*. Athens and Paris.

Vernant, J.-P. (2006), *Myth and Thought among the Greeks*. New edn. New York (trans. of *Mythe et pensée chez les Grecs*, Paris, 1965).

——, et al. (1974), *Divination et rationalité*. Paris.

——, and Vidal-Naquet, P. (1988), *Myth and Tragedy in Ancient Greece*. New York, trans. of (i) *Mythe et tragédie en Grèce ancienne*, Paris, 1972, and (ii) *Mythe et tragédie en Grèce ancienne, Deux*, Paris, 1986.

Versnel, H. S. (1990a), 'What's Sauce for the Goose is Sauce for the Gander: Myth and Ritual, Old and New', in L. Edmunds (ed.), *Approaches to Greek Myth*, Baltimore, MD, 25–90.

——(1990b), *Inconsistencies in Greek and Roman Religion*, i. *Ter Unus*. Leiden.

Vian, F. (1952), *La Guerre des Géants*. Paris.

——(1990) (ed.), *Nonnos de Panopolis: Les Dionysiaques*, XXV–XXIX. Paris.

Vickers, B. (1973), *Towards Greek Tragedy*. London.

Vidal-Naquet, P. (1986a), *The Black Hunter: Forms of Thought and Forms of Society in the Greek World*. Baltimore, MD (trans. of *Le Chasseur noir: formes de pensée et formes de société dans le monde grec*, Paris, 1981).

——(1986b), 'The Black Hunter Revisited', *PCPhS* 32: 126–44.

Voelke, P. (2001), *Un Théâtre de la marge. Aspects figuratifs et configurationnels du drame satyrique dans l'Athènes classique*. Bari.

Vollgraff, W. (1914), 'Novae inscriptiones Argivae', *Mnemosyne* 42: 330–54.

Vries, J. de (1961), *Forschungsgeschichte der Mythologie*. Freiburg.

Wächter, Th. (1910), *Reinheitsvorschriften im griechischen Kult*. Giessen.

Walsh, P. G. (1997), *Cicero: The Nature of the Gods*. Oxford.

Waszink, J. H. (1974), *Biene und Honig als Symbol des Dichters und der Dichtung in der griechisch-römischen Antike*. Opladen.

Weiler, I. (1974), *Der Agon im Mythos: Zur Einstellung der Griechen zum Wettkampf*. Darmstadt.

Wendel, C. (1958), *Scholia in Apollonium Rhodium vetera*. 2nd edn. Berlin.

West, M. L. (1966), *Hesiod: Theogony*. Oxford.

——(1983), 'Tragica VI', *BICS* 30: 63–71.

——(2007), *Indo-European Poetry and Myth*. Oxford.

Whallon, W. (1961), 'Why is Artemis Angry?', *AJP* 82: 78–88.

——(1980), *Problem and Spectacle: Studies in the Oresteia*. Heidelberg.

Whitehead, D. (1986), *The Demes of Attica 508/7—ca. 250 B.C.: A Political and Social Study*. Princeton, NJ.

Whittaker, C. R. (1988) (ed.), *Pastoral Economies in Classical Antiquity*. Cambridge.

Wiedemann, T. E. J. (1986), 'Between Men and Beasts: Barbarians in Ammianus Marcellinus', in I. S. Moxon, J. D. Smart, and A. J. Woodman (eds.), *Past Perspectives: Studies in Greek and Roman Historical Writing*, Cambridge, 189–201.

Wilamowitz-Moellendorff, U. von (1895), *Euripides: Herakles*. 2nd edn. 2 vols. Berlin.
——(1931–2), *Der Glaube der Hellenen*. 2 vols. Berlin.
Willetts, R. F. (1962), *Cretan Cults and Festivals*. London.
Wilson, E. (1952), 'Philoctetes: The Wound and the Bow', in Wilson, *The Wound and the Bow: Seven Studies in Literature*, London, 244–64.
Wilson, P. (2000), *The Athenian Institution of the Khoregia: The Chorus, the City and the Stage*. Cambridge.
——(2011), 'The Glue of Democracy? Tragedy, Structure, and Finance', in Carter (2011) 19–43.
Winkler, J. J. (1980), 'Lollianos and the Desperadoes', *JHS* 100: 155–81.
——, and Zeitlin, F. I. (1990) (eds.), *Nothing to Do with Dionysos?* Princeton, NJ.
Winnington-Ingram, R. P. (1948), *Euripides and Dionysus*. Cambridge.
——(1983), 'Zeus in *Persae*', in Winnington-Ingram, *Studies in Aeschylus*, Cambridge, 1–15.
Wörner, E. (1897–1902), 'Oinopion', in Roscher iii, 1: cols. 791–8.
Woodbury, L. (1967), 'Helen and the Palinode', *Phoenix* 21: 157–76.
Woodward, I. (1979), *The Werewolf Delusion*. New York.
Zacharia, K. (2003), *Converging Truths: Euripides' Ion and the Athenian Quest for Self-Definition*. Leiden.
Zaganiaris, N. J. (1980), 'Le Chien dans la mythologie et la littérature gréco-latines', *Platon* 32: 52–87.
Zeitlin, F. I. (1978), 'The Dynamics of Misogyny: Myth and Mythmaking in the *Oresteia*', *Arethusa* 11: 149–84 (reprinted in Zeitlin (1996) 87–119).
——(1982), 'Cultic Models of the Female: Rites of Dionysus and Demeter', *Arethusa* 15: 129–57.
——(1990), 'Thebes: Theater of Self and Society in Athenian Drama', in Winkler and Zeitlin (1990) 130–67.
——(1996), *Playing the Other: Gender and Society in Classical Greek Literature*. Chicago, IL.
Zimen, E. (1981), *The Wolf: His Place in the Natural World*. London (trans. of *Der Wolf: Mythos und Verhalten*, Vienna, 1978).
Zimmermann, B. (1991), *Greek Tragedy: An Introduction*. Baltimore, MD (trans. of *Die griechische Tragödie: Eine Einführung*, Munich, 1986).
Ziolkowski, T. (1983), *Varieties of Literary Thematics*. Princeton, NJ.

Index

Page numbers in *italics* refer to illustrations; 'fn' indicates a footnote

abnormal generation 90, 91
Achaios 183
Acharnians (Aristophanes) 12
Achilles 21, 70, 89, 92, 93, 95, 118, 123, 175, 181, 208, 232
acropolis 10, 13, 15
Admetos 201, 202, 203, 204, 205, 206, 207, 209, 210, 212–16, 217
Adonis 89, 188
Aegeus 61
Aelian 35, 38
Aesop 36
Agamemnon 122, 123, 130, 131, 141, 143, 158, 166, 172, 199, 215
Agamemnon (Aischylos) 17, 94, 122, 130, 132, 141, 143, 151, 153, 165, 168, 172, 175, 206, 215, 238
Agatharchides 88
Agaue 27, 132, 133, 223, 233, 236, 237
agriculture 48
Aias 88, 92, 139, 140, 142, 144, 147, 151, 175, 179, 239
Aias (Sophokles) 54, 128, 139, 141, 142, 151, 174, 181, 193, 199, 239
Aietes 185
Aigeus 107, 109, *110*, 128
Aigina 11
Aigisthos 153, 238, 239, 240
Aigyptos, sons of 129, 238
Aiolos 58
Aipytos 189
Aischylos *Agamemnon* 17, 94, 122, 130, 132, 141, 143, 151, 153, 165, 168, 172, 175, 206, 215, 238; *Edonians* 231, 240; *Eumenides* 142, 148, 150, 154, 156, 157, 208, 238; *Libation-Bearers* 54; *Myrmidons* 208; *Niobe* 208; *Oresteia* 135, 136, 143, 149, 151, 156, 158, 166; *Persians* 61, 150, 161–2, 164, 169; *Phrygians* 208; *Prometheus Bound* 132, 135, 136, 223; *Seven against Thebes* 237; *Suppliants* 129, 149, 237
Aison, son of 75
Aithra 238
Akeso 57
Aktaion 17, 19, 21, 27, 48, 195
Alexander ('the Great') 95, 96
  ankle wound 95
Alkaios 37
Alkestis (Euripides) 2, 201–17
Alkibiades 147
Alkinoos 104, 125, 129–30fn
Alkmene 167, 172
Alkyoneus 59
Alopekos 193
Ammon 188
Amphion 19
Amphitrite *80*
Amphitryon 122, 132, 167, 211
Anakalupteria 206, 207, 209
Anaxagoras 15, 157, 160
Anchises 16, 21, 169, 190, 191
Anchisia, Mount 13
Andokides 12
Andromache 130
Andromache (Euripides) 142
Androphagi 42
animal skins 23, 24
ankle 5, 75, 76, 78, 81, *84*, 87, 89, 92–4, 95, 97, 105
Antigone 139, 148, 178, 179, 229
Antigone (Sophokles) 139, 148, 150, 172, 229
Antinoos 66
Antipater 39, 41
Antoninus Liberalis 17
Antylus 188
Apatouria 68fn
Aphrodite 21, 55, 61, 62, 63, 68, 94, 122, 124, 136, 137, 140, 163, 169, 171, 188, 190, 230
Apollo 15, 16, 18, 28, 55, 57, 59, 61, 130, 132, 133, 135, 136, 138, 140, 142, 156, 157, 158, 176, 185, 188, 195, 202, 204, 212, 213, 216

Apollodoros (author of *Library of Mythology*) 49, 55, 68, 69, 78, 92, 185, 195
Apollodoros (author of *On the Gods*) 55
Apollonios of Rhodes *Argonautika* 74–6, 77, 78, 83, 84, 86, 87, 91, 92, 94, 95, 96, 97, 99–105, 106, 109, 110, 113, 114, 116, 124, 125, 185
Apsyrtos 104, 116, 125
Arachne 48, 195
Aratos *Phainomena* 17
Archidamian war 12
Areopagos 151
Arete 104
Argo 17, 74, 103, 104, 105, 124, 125, 126
Argonautika (Apollonios of Rhodes) 74–6, 77, 78, 83, 84, 86, 87, 91, 92, 94, 95, 96, 97, 99–105, 106, 109, 110, 113, 114, 116, 124, 125, 185
Argonauts 74, 75, 100, 124
Argos 15, 17, 37, 70, 130, 131, 143, 148, 149, 152
Ariadne 77, 104, 125
Aristaios 21
Aristophanes 12, 134; *Acharnians* 12; *Banqueters* 62; *Clouds* 158; *Frogs* 231, 240; *Lysistrata* 67, 68, 69; *Wasps* 69; *Women at the Thesmophoria* 234
Aristotle 38, 40, 41, 117, 149, 157, 181, 185, 186; *Poetics* 65, 145, 146; *Rhetoric* 146
Arkadia 15, 18, 22, 39, 41–50, 55, 62
Arkas 24, 46, 48
Arkesilaos of Cyrene 123, 124
Arrian 10
arsenic poisoning 91fn
Artemidoros 62
Artemis 15, 18, 55, 136, 137, 141, 142, 143, 147, 165, 166, 171, 189, 193, 194, 195, 212
Asante 18
Asklepios 19, 21, 187, 209
Astour, Michael 59
Astrabakos 193
astu 10, 12, 27, 78
Astyanax 130, 147
Atalante 22, 68, 69
Ate 61
Athamas 37, 232
Athenaios *Learned Banqueters* 147, 211
Athene 15, 17, 64, 100, 122, 130, 135, 136, 138, 139, 140, 141, 142, 147, 150, 167, 174, 175, 181, 184, 188, 189, 190, 194, 195, 199, 224, 228, 238
Athens 12, 67, 82, 114, 117, 121, 126, 129, 130, 148, 149, 150, 151, 152, 153, 155, 167, 170, 181, 197–200
Atlas 16
Atreidai 166
Atreus 65
Attica 12, 19, *83*, *84*, 109, *112*, 123, 149
Augustine 44, 46
Aulis 126, 143, 149, 158
Autolykos 17, 38, 53, 66
Avezzù, Guido 149

Bad-tempered Man (Menander) 19
bafflement 5, 161–72
Bakchai (Euripides) 1, 2, 18, 26, 29, 131, 132, 133, 142, 148, 164, 167, 168, 169, 172, 193, 219–40
Balensiefen, Lilian 92
Banqueters (Aristophanes) 62
bathing 45, 184, 188, 189, 194
Baxter, Timothy 56
Bdelykleon 69
beacons 14, 17
bees 183
Berger, John *Ways of Seeing* 154
Berman, Daniel 149
Bernal, Martin *Black Athena II* 59
Bernardini, Paola Angeli 149
Bernidaki-Aldous, Eleftheria 200
Berthold, O. 87, 88
Bion *Lament for Adonis* 17
birds 70, 71, 81, 94, 138, 195, 219
  see also crow, eagle, partridge
Bisclavret (Marie de France) 44
black/blackness 4, 53–71
  see also melas
blacksmith 91, 91fn, 187
'Black Hunter' (according to P. Vidal-Naquet) 66, 67, 68, 69
Blaiklock, E. M. *The Male Characters of Euripides* 167
blindness/blinding 2, 4, 91fn, 169, 173–200
Bloch, Marc 3
blood 64, 95, 116, 126, 141

blood-letting 93, 96
Bodin, Jean 44
Boiotia 37, 67, 194
Borgeaud, Philippe 49
Boswell, John 19
boukol(ik)oi 25
boundary-crossing 2, 45, 51, 88, 90, 95, 96, 129, 130, 153, 169, 188–92, 203, 238
bread-making 48
Brelich, Angelo 88, 89, 92
Bremmer, Jan 4, 60, 89, 92, 232
Bromios 26
bronze statues 86, 87
Brown, Frieda S. 156, 157, 159
bulls 99, 101, 103, 109, *111*, 125, 219
Burgess, Jonathan 92
Burke, Peter 3
Burkert, Walter 59–60
Burn, A. R. 13
Burnett, Anne Pippin 213

Calame, Claude 60, 90 *The Craft of Poetic Speech* 60
cannibalism 43, 51, 216, 220
castration 91fn, 178, 196
Catalogue (Hesiod) 185
Caucasus 135, 149
cave 11, 23, 24, 137, 168, 169, 198fn, 217
centaurs 19, 88, 211
Chalkiope 100
charcoal-burners 12, 22
Charon 205
Charybdis 97
Cheiron 21, 23, 24
chorus 28, 54, 67, 69, 128, 129, 130, 140, 141, 143, 148, 150, 161, 163, 170, 171, 176, 177, 202, 205, 209, 213, 214, 224, 226, 227, 230, 233, 236, 237, 238
Chrysostom, Dio 13
Chrysothemis 199, 238
Cicero *On the Nature of the Gods* 56
Circe 104, 116, 125
Citti, V. *Tragedia e lotta di classe in Grecia* 154
city 10, 13, 15, 21, 23, 24, 25, 26, 27, 28, 29, 30, 48, 129, 130, 131, 148, 151, 153, 168, 196, 219, 222
Clouds (Aristophanes) 158
comedy 64, 69, 134, 211, 217, 234, 240
compass 82, 83
context 2, 3
Cook, A. B. 15, 86
Corinth 27, 114, 117, 126, 127, 128, 149, 152
Corinthian messenger 28
Cotta 56
cowardice 64, 238, 239, 240
Cox, G. W. 58
Crete 74, 75, 77, 78, *79*, 79, *80*, 82, 86, 89, 105
Crimea 149
Croally, Neil 149
cross-dressing 221, 234, 235, 236, 239
  see also transvestism
crossing the threshold 203, 204
crow, 61, 62fn
cults 15, 23, 24, 25, 39, 43, 45, 62, 63, 64, 190, 219, 220, 235
cunning 38, 39, 238
Cyclops 16, 66, 78, 149
Cyclops (Euripides) 16, 149, 216

Daidalos 82, 83, 85
Daidalos (Sophokles) 78
Danaids 129, 238
Danaos 37
dancing 24, 25, 26, 195, 227
Dardanos 20
Darius, ghost of 162
dark *see melas*
death 19, 30, 45, 46, 61, 62, 75, 81, 92, 93, 95, 126, 129, 130, 136, 139, 147, 153, 175, 195, 199, 202, 203, 204, 212, 214, 236
  in *Alkestis* 205–10
deconstruction 5
deer 12, 13
Deianeira 29, 104, 116, 117, 162, 163, 179, 200, 211
Delos 41
Delphi 13, 27, 123, 149, 152, 198
deme 12, 146, 170
Demeter 15, 26, 62, 63, 189, 190
Demetrios of Phaleron 35
Demodokos 182
Demosthenes 12
desert 11
Detienne, Marcel 225
Deukalion 17, 20, 55
Devereux, Georges 178, 192
Diana 56
Dickie, Matthew 76

Dieuchidas of Megara 70
Dika/Dike 17, 54
Dikaiopolis 12
Dikte 20, 74
Dinka 18
Diodoros 82, 83
Diogenes Laertios 61
Diomedes 94, 181
Dionysos 15, 18, 24, 25, 26, 27, 28, 67, 70, 77, 104, 121, 131, 132, 133, 140, 142, 151, 153, 155, 164, 165, 191, 194, 219–37
  see also femininity
Dioskouroi 61
Ditanu 60
Dodds, E. R. 164, 165, 186, 220, 235, 236
Dodona 29, 70, 71, 138, 163
Dog Star 23
dogs 19, 36, 51, 75, 105
  see also Kerberos
Dolios 65
Dolon 38, 54
dolos see trickery
Doripe 70
dumbness 194, 196
Duminil, Marie-Paule 94

eagle 135, 143, 165, 166
Easterling, Pat 148
Edonians (Aischylos) 231
effeminacy 63, 231
Egypt 11, 37, 59, 70, 149, 191, 194
  origin of Greek names 59
Eira 13
Elektra (Euripides) 142, 239
Elektra (Sophokles) 166, 179, 199, 238
Elias, Mount 11
Elysian Fields 125
Encomium of Helen (Gorgias) 170
Endymion 17, 21, 169
Enodia 61
Eos 58
ephebe/*ephebeia* 46, 66, 67, 153
Epicharmos 211
Epidemics (Hippokratic) 95
epilepsy 167
Epizelos 188
Erichtho 117
Eros 99, 100, 163
Erymanthos 18
Esser, Albert 177
Eteokles 54, 237, 238
Etna, Mount 14, 16
etymology 55, 56, 57, 58, 59
Eudoxos 15
Euenios 184
Eumaios 24
Eumenides (Aischylos) 142, 148, 150, 154, 156, 157, 208, 238
Eupeithes 66
Euripides 22, 134, 142, 143, 240; *Alkestis* 2, 201–17; *Andromache* 142; *Bakchai* 1, 2, 18, 26, 29, 131, 132, 133, 142, 148, 164, 165, 166, 167, 168, 169, 172, 193, 219–240; *Cyclops* 16, 149, 216; *Elektra* 142, 239; *Helen* 26; *Hippolytos* 122, 136, 142, 146, 147, 150, 153, 171, 208, 212; *Ion* 54, 137, 142; *Iphigeneia in Tauris* 142; *The Madness of Herakles* 122, 132, 150, 166–8, 193, 206, 211, 212; *Medea* 126, 127, 128; *Orestes* 142, 238; *Phoenician Women* 19, 54; *Rhesos* 38, 54; *Suppliants* 151, 238; *Trojan Women* 18, 130, 142, 147, 149, 151
Europa 75
Eurymachos 65
Eurypylos 193, 194
Eurysakes 147
Eurytos 57
Eusebios 17
Evans-Pritchard, Edward 3
evil eye 76, 84

fauna 3, 34, 219
fawnskin 226, 233
Federico, Eduardo 89, 90, 92
femininity 221, 225, 228, 230, 231, 232, 233, 234, 240
feminization 4, 221, 222, 224, 228, 230, 233, 234, 236, 237–40
fire-signalling 14, 17
fleeces 23, 24, 106
forest 18
Frogs (Aristophanes) 231, 240
Frontisi-Ducroux, Françoise 83
Furies 135, 136, 142

Gelanor 37
gender 189, 190, 219, 220, 221, 228, 229, 230, 232, 235, 236, 237, 238, 239, 240
genitals 93, 94

genre 3fn
Gerania 17
Gernet, Louis 5
giant(s) 16, 59, 73, 105
Golden Ass, The (Apuleius) 44
Golden Fleece 74, 99, 103, 106, *111*, 123
Goldhill, Simon 150, 153, 155, 222, 226
Gorgias 170, 197
Gorgon 194
Graves, Robert *The Greek Myths* 59

Hades 62, 75, 105, 150, 166, 178, 205, 210
Haimon 148
Haimos 14
Haliakmon 193
Halys 198
hare 67, 143, 166
Harmonia 229
Harrison, Jane 220
Hebe 211
Hekabe 130
Hekate 62, 100, 101, 103, 116
Hektor 54, 123, 130, 147, 213, 231
Helen 122, 170, 191, 192
Helikon, Mount 10, 13, 16, 17, 18, 23, 25
Helios 15, 61, 105, 113, 184, 185
Henrichs, Albert 220, 226
Hephaistos 77, 89, 91, 187, 188
Hera 21, 23, 37, 41, 61, 70, 100, 101, 104, 122, 125, 132, 140, 167, 184, 188, 190, 228
Herakleides 23
Herakleitos 187
Herakles 17, 29, 30, 88, 104, 117, 122, 132, 133, 138, 139, 140, 141, 149, 162, 163, 166, 167, 168, 179, 193, 201, 202, 204, 206, 207, 209, 210–12, 214, 215, 217, 223, 239
  in comedy 211
  in Pindar 211
  in tragedy 211
  Labours of 122, 166, 212
  madness 167, 168
  murder of wife and children 122, 167
herdsmen 11, 16, 17, 20, 21, 24, 25, 227
  see also shepherds
Hermann, Gottfried 57
Hermes 15, 16, 20, 22, 28, 38, 135, 136, 142, 203, 216
Herodotos 42, 70, 133
heroism 123, 125, 127, 176
Hesiod 21, 48, 55, 71, 77, 169, 184, 185, 186; *Catalogue* 185; *Megalai Eoiai* 184; *Theogony* 133, 135; *Works and Days* 133
Heslin, Peter 235
Hesychios 86, 209
Hippokratic treatises 5, 93, 95, 97, 197
Hippolytos 22, 48, 59, 122, 142, 147, 153, 169, 171, 172, 208, 212
Hippolytos (Euripides) 122, 136, 142, 146, 147, 150, 153, 171, 208, 212
Homer 63, 64, 182; *Iliad* 13, 19, 21, 38, 62, 64, 94, 123, 135, 147, 231; *Odyssey* 18, 38, 53, 54, 61, 64, 65, 66, 71, 99, 123, 135, 216
Homeric Hymn to Dionysos 231
Homeric Hymn to Hermes 135
homosexuality 79, 89, 90, 91
hoplite 14
horses 59
  white 61
  wild 19
hospitality 201
  abuse of 48
  Admetos and 212–16
Hourmouziades, N. C. 149
hunting 12, 13, 17, 21, 22, 27, 67, 68, 75, 89, 136, 166, 189, 222, 237
Hygieia 57
Hyginus 49, 92
Hyllos 30, 139, 179
Hymettos, Mount 15
Hyperboreans 41
Hypsipyle 104

Iaso 57
ichor 94–6
Ida, Mount (in Crete) 10, 20
Ida, Mount (near Troy) 16, 17, 19, 20, 21
ideology in tragedy 152–60
Ikarios 25
Iliad (Homer) 13, 19, 21, 38, 62, 64, 94, 123, 135, 147, 231
Ilos 188
incest 178, 192
infants, abandonment of 19, 20
initiation 45–7, 89–90, 234, 235, 236
  see also ephebe/*ephebeia*
Ino 232
insight vs lack of sight 175, 176, 177, 178, 179

invulnerability 81, 87, 88, 92, 102, 103, 125
see also vulnerability
Io 132
Iodama 194
Iole 162, 163, 239
Iolkos 21, 114, 117, 125, 126
Ion 77, 138, 211
Ion (Euripides) 54, 137, 142
Iphigeneia 141, 158, 166
Iphigeneia in Tauris (Euripides) 142
Iris 142, 167
Istros 185
Ithaca 53, 61
Ithome, Mount 13, 20
ivy 26, 226

Jason 21, 64, 81, *84*, *85*, 89, 99, 100, 101, 102, 103, 104, 107, 109, *111*, *112*, 115, 116, 117, 123, 124, 125, 126, 127, 128, 130, 172, 213
and bulls 99, 103, 109, *111*, 125
and Sown Men 99, 103
in Apollonios 124–6
in Pindar 124–6
Jocasta 123, 179
Jupiter 56

Kadmos 26, 27, 132, 223, 226–9
daughters of 26
Kaineus 88, 92
Kalchas 143, 165
Kallimachos *Fifth Hymn* 184, 189, 190
Kallisto 22
Kamikoi (Sophokles) 85
Karsai, György 226
Kassandra 130, 132, 144, 153, 175, 187, 206, 238
Kastor *80*, 81, *83*, *84*, 142, 191
Kenaion 138
Kephalos 58
Kerberos 122, 166, 210
Keres 75
Kinaithon 77
Kinesias 69
Kithairon, Mount 10, 13, 16, 17, 18, 19, 21, 22, 23, 26, 27, 28, 29, 131, 140, 236
Kleitor 15
Klytaimestra 94, 122, 127, 131, 153, 199, 215, 238
Knox, Bernard 147, 200, 239
Kolchians 104, 105, 125, 130fn
Kolophon 61
Koronis 62
krater *80*, 81, *83*, *84*, 93, 109, *110*, *111*, *113*, 113, *115*
Kratylos (Plato) 19, 55, 56, 65
Kreon (Corinthian) 126
Kreon (Theban) 28, 129, 139, 148, 151, 172, 177, 178, 199
Kreousa 137, 138
Kres 77, 81
Kronos 10, 54, 75, 189
Kteatos 57
Kybele 26
Kyknos 92
Kyllene, Mount 20, 21
Kynthos, Mount 10
Kypris 163
Kyrene 22

Laios 79, 90, 91, 123, 151
Lakonians 13
lameness 83, 90, 91, 91fn, 187
Lament for Adonis (Bion) 17
landscape 2, 3, 9–31, 131, 168
Langdon, Merle K. 15
language system of Greek myth 2
Latmos, Mount 17
Laws, The (Plato) 20, 227
Leach, Edmund 63
Learned Banqueters (Athenaios) 211
Lele 18
Lemnos 128, 149, 151
leprosy 63, 71
Leto 41
Leuke 62
leukos 60–71
Leukothea 54
Lévi-Strauss, Claude 2
Libation-Bearers (Aischylos) 54
Library of Mythology (Apollodoros) 55
Lienhardt, Godfrey 18
Life of Apollonios of Tyana (Philostratos) 15
lions 27, 40, 88, 69, 76, 88, 236, 237
Llewellyn-Jones, Lloyd 4
Loraux, Nicole 148, 222, 225
Lucan 117
Lucian 13, 22, 134
Lucius (character in *The Golden Ass*) 44
Luna 56
lycanthropy 41, 42

Lykaion, Mount 10, 14, 20, 21, 23, 47, 48, 50
Lykaon 21, 43, 48, 49, 50
  sons of 49
Lykos 17, 166
Lykourgos 19, 190, 194, 231
Lysistrata (Aristophanes) 67, 68, 69
Lyssa 132, 142, 167

madness 22, 24, 37, 128, 132, 134, 142, 167, 175, 177, 193, 194, 196, 231
Madness of Herakles, The (Euripides) 122, 132, 150, 166–8, 193, 206, 211, 212
maenads 22, 25, 26, 140, 165, 226, 227, 229, 236
magic 76, *80*, 100, 102, 106, 110, 113, 114, 117, 118, 177, 187
Mainoldi, C. 37
Malinowski, Bruno 3
Mantinea 62, 189
Marathon, battle of 188
marginality 67, 128
Marie de France *Bisclavret* 44
Markellos of Side 42
marriage 21, 45, 46, 127, 129, 203, 204, 207, 235
  see also wedding
Marsyas 48, 195
masculinity 189, 221, 225, 228, 230, 231, 234, 237, 239
Mastronarde, Donald 172
Medea 74, 75, 76, 78, *80*, 81, *83*, 83, 99, *109*, *114*, 121, 123, 124, 125, 126, 127, 128, 130, 150, 172, 213, 238
  and Jason 99, 100, 101, 102, 103, 104, *111*, *112*
  as sorceress 107, 116
  dreams 101
  drugs 101, 102, 103, 104, 107
  eyes 101, 102, 103
  failed poisoning of Theseus *110*, 116
  infanticide 126, 127
  in Apollonios 99–107, 109, 116, 124–5
  in Euripides 107, 114, 115, 126, 127, 128
  in flight 110, *114*, 114, *115*, 116, 172
  in movement 99–118
  in Ovid 107, 114
  in Pindar 107
  in Seneca 107, 114, 115
  infanticide *108*
  murder of Apsyrtos 116
  murder of Pelias 124
  spell on Talos 105
  uncanny powers 99, 101, 102, 110
Medea (Euripides) 126, 127, 128
Megalai Eoiai (Hesiod) 184
Megaros 17
Mekone 48
Melainai 68
Melampous 70, 71
Melanaigis (epithet of Dionysos) 68
Melanion 67, 68, 69
  in Apollodoros 68, 69
  in Aristophanes 68, 69
Melanthios 65, 66, 71
Melantho 65, 66, 71
Melanthos 66, 67, 68, 69
melas 53–71
  names involving 65–71
Menander (*Bad-tempered Man*) 19
Menelaos 199, 238
Merchant of Venice, The (Shakespeare) 159
Messenians 13, 62
metal, mountains as source of 11
metamorphosis 21, 24, 42, 44, 46, 49, 50, 69, 81, 83, 114, 132, 195, 196, 230
Metamorphoses (Ovid) 48, 83, 107, 114
Metis 224, 225
Miletos 17, 189
Mimas 59
mimetic approach to drama 233, 235
Minos 77, 78
Minotaur 122
misogyny 67, 68, 69
mitra 233, 237
Moliones 57
monsters 30, 73, 122, 211
Montesarchio krater *81*, 93
Montiglio, Silvia 4
moon 43, 106, 169
moonlight 17, 42
'Mother' goddess 15
mountains 4, 10–31, 131, 219
  botanical research 14
  cults 15–16, 22–5
  dance for Dionysos 24, 25
  humans meet gods on 169
  in myth 16–22
  in tragedy 25–30
  observing the heavens 15

mountains (*cont.*)
  place of refuge 13, 17
  reversals 21–2
  sanctuaries for the gods 15–16, 18
  'smiters' 12
  tourism 14
  warfare 13, 14
mourning 26, 61, 62, 63, 118, 127, 202, 204, 206, 235
movement 4, 99–118
Müller, Karl Otfried *Prolegomena zu einer wissenschaflichen Mythologie* 58
Müller, Max 58
'Muse of Flame' 12
Muses, the 18, 20, 21, 23, 169, 182, 183, 187, 191, 195
muthos 67, 145
Myrmidons 35
mythological names and meaning 53–71
myths as refractions 18

names/naming 4, 19
  and meaning 53–71, 219
Nausikaa 66
Nausithoos 66
Neoptolemos 130, 142, 144, 153, 179, 199
Nessos 29, 116, 163, 179
Nestor 19
Neuri 42
Newlands, Carole 107
Newsbringer, The (Messenger) 126, 139, 161, 163, 227
Nikandros 17
Niobe 118
Niobe (Aischylos) 208
Noemon 66
nomenclature *see* names/naming
Nonnos 25, 133, 180
Nymphs 17, 18, 195
Nysa 18

Obbink, Dirk 220
Odysseus 24, 53, 54, 61, 64, 65, 66, 89, 97, 123, 130, 135, 141, 174, 175, 199, 216
Odyssey (Homer) 18, 38, 53, 54, 61, 64, 65, 66, 71, 99, 123, 135, 216
Oidipous 19, 28, 54, 89, 90, 122, 128, 129, 131, 140, 143, 144, 176, 177, 178, 179, 199, 238
  self-blinding 176, 177, 178
Oidipous at Kolonos (Sophokles) 129, 169, 178, 199, 238
Oidipous Tyrannos (Sophokles) 16, 27, 28, 29, 122, 128, 131, 140, 143, 153, 176, 179, 229
Oinopion 77
Oita, Mount 21, 29
old age 227
Olympia 10
Olympians (divinities) 18, 59, 61, 136, 156, 187
Olympias 188
Olympos, Mount 10, 18, 20
omophagia 220
Omphale 211, 239
On Animals (Timotheos of Gaza) 36
On the Gods (Apollodoros) 55
On the Nature of Man (Hippokratic) 93
On the Nature of the Gods (Cicero) 56
Onchestos 19
Onians, R. B. 4
Ophioneus 184
oracle 45
  see also Delphi, Dodona
Oreads 17
Oresteia (Aischylos) 135, 136, 143, 149, 151, 156, 158, 166
Orestes 19, 35, 39, 127, 136, 151, 158, 159, 172, 199, 208, 238, 239
Orestes (Euripides) 142, 238
oros 10–31
  see also mountains
Orpheus 22, 209fn
Othrys, Mount 17, 18
Otto, Walter 231
outsiders 12, 19, 24, 37, 39, 46, 128, 203
  wolves as outsiders 36
Ovid *Metamorphoses* 48, 83, 107, 111

Padel, Ruth 149
Pagasai 125, 126
Palaiphatos 78, 92
Palladion 188
Pamphile 44
Pan 15, 17, 18, 19, 21, 28
Panakeia 57
Pandora 60, 133
Pangaion, Mount 11, 19, 22
Paris (Trojan prince) 16, 19, 21, 22, 93, 122, 169, 213, 214, 231
Parke, H. W. 70
Parnassos, Mount 10, 13, 17, 18, 20

Parnes, Mount 19
Parthenion, Mount 19, 21
partridge 81, 83, 93
Pastoureau, Michel 4
pasturage 11, 26, 35
Patroklos 17, 62
Pausanias 10, 13, 14, 19, 24, 25, 37, 43, 44, 46, 48, 61, 62, 173, 189, 190, 194
Pelasgos 24, 48, 129, 151
Peleus 17, 21
Pelias 64, 104, 110, 114, 124
daughters of 114, 116
Pelion, Mount 10, 17, 21, 23, 24, 25
Penelope 65, 66
Pentelikon, Mount 11, 15
Pentheus 19, 22, 27, 29, 48, 132, 140, 164, 165, 172, 219, 220, 221, 223, 224, 226, 227, 229, 230, 232, 233–7
Persians 13, 161
Persians (Aischylos) 61, 150, 161–2, 164, 169
Phaiakia(ns) 66, 104, 125, 182
Phaidra 22, 122, 140, 208
Phainomena (Aratos) 17
Phaistos *79*
Pherai 149, 201
Pherekydes of Syros 54
Pheres 202, 214
Pheros 191
Phigalia 62
Philip II of Macedon 188
Philip V of Macedon 14
Philippides 21
Philo 14
Philochoros 231
Philokleon 69
Philoktetes 81, 89, 128, 144, 149, 168, 179, 187, 199, 200
Philoktetes (Sophokles) 128, 149, 150, 153, 179, 199
Philostratos *Life of Apollonios of Tyana* 15
Phineus 106, 184, 185, 190, 198
Phoenician Women (Euripides) 19, 54
Phokians 13
Phormion 184
Phrixos 184, 185
Phronios 66
Phthia 149
Physkos 25
Pieria 16, 20
Pieros, nine daughters of 195
Pindar 21, 22, 38, 54, 55, 64, 107, 123
Jason and the Golden Fleece 123–6
pity-and-fear 145, 146
plains 10
Plato 38, 43, 44, 55, 65, 123fn, 198fn
Kratylos 19, 55; *The Laws* 20, 227; *Sophist* 38
Pliny the Elder 14, 43, 44, 45, 46
plurality 73
Plutarch 35, 39, 95, 208
Poetics (Aristotle) 65, 145, 146
poetry and blindness 181, 182, 183
poets in Greek myth 182–8
poison 91fn, 104, 109, *110*, 116, 126, 127, 162
polis 2, 10, 21, 26, 27, 28, 29, 130, 131, 145, 146, 148, 149, 150, 152, 156, 229
see also city
pollution 28, 62, 140, 150, 202, 206, 208, 212
Pollux 209
Polydeukes *80*, 81, *83*, *84*, 191
Polyneikes 54, 129, 139, 238
Polyphemos 217
Polyxena 93
Pontinos, Mount 15
Pontonoos 66
Poseidon 54, 57, 61, 62, 63, *80*, 130, 133, 135, 142, 147, 169, 181, 189
potter's wheel 82, 83
Priam 123, 131
Proitos, daughters of 22, 70, 71
Prokris 22, 58
Prometheus 48
Prometheus Bound (Aischylos) 132, 135, 136, 223
prophecy 45, 177, 183, 184, 185, 186
Protagoras 197
psychological approach to drama 235, 236
punishment 48, 122, 132, 135, 185, 189, 191, 192, 194
Pylades 158
Pylos 70
Pyrrha 20, 55
Pythagoras 15, 54, 61
Pythian Odes see Pindar

Radke, Gerhard 60, 63
ram 23, 61, 109, *112*
rape 59, 122, 137, 192
reception theory 2

Rehm, Rush 3
religion 25, 59, 60, 86, 100, 137, 143, 169, 219, 220, 221, 233
reversals 21, 24, 238
Rhadamanthys 59, 77, 78, 79, 89
Rhea 193
Rhesos 17, 54
Rhetoric (Aristotle) 146
rituals 22–5, 44, 45, 47, 48, 50, 61, 63, 64, 131, 138, 142, 169, 194, 207, 208, 209, 220, 234, 235
  Arkadian 45, 46
  initiation 45
  Lykaion 46, 47, 49, 50
  of transition 45
  Pelion 23, 24, 25
  reinterpretation 46
  separation 46
role reversal 234
Roux, Jeanne 165
Ruvo di Puglia *80*, 110
Rydberg, Viktor 58

sacrifice 23, 30, 43, 45, 48, 61, 62, 63, 86, 141, 143, 150, 166, 169, 213, 237
Saïd, Suzanne 149, 152
Salamis 61
Samothrace 20
Sandys, J. E. 165
Santorini 86
Saturn 56
Schoo, J. 86
Scythia 42
sea deities 57, 62, 63, 168
  see also Poseidon
Seaford, Richard 149, 150, 220, 226, 234
Segal, Charles 222, 234
Selene 17, 21
Selloi 29, 70
Semele 49, 169, 195, 223, 224, 225
Sergent, Bernard 90
serpent 103, 104, 106, 109, *111*, 112, 188, 219
  see also snake(s)
Seven against Thebes (Aischylos) 237
sex/sexuality 90, 91, 93, 94, 136, 137
Shakespeare, William 159
sheepskins 24, 48
shepherds 12, 13, 17, 22, 24
  see also herdsmen
ships 64, 66, 99, 105, 128, 130, 174
  see also Argo
sight 2, 174, 175, 176, 177, 178, 181
silence 4, 206, 207, 208, 209
Silenos/Silenoi 78, 216, 217
Simaitha 116
Simonides 78
Siproites 194
Sirens 195
sitting 4, 118
skin colour 63, 64
Skinner, Quentin 3
Skylla 97
Sladek, John 73
slaves 103, 150, 153, 213
snake(s) 21, 103, 128, 193, 194, 228, 229
  see also serpent
Sokrates 19, 55, 65
Solon 35
Sommerstein, Alan 157, 158
song 16, 103, 147, 171, 182, 195
Sophist (Plato) 38
Sophokles 134, 143, 173–200
  Aias 54, 128, 139, 141, 142, 151, 174, 181, 193, 199, 239; *Antigone* 139, 148, 150, 172, 229; *Daidalos* 78; *Elektra* 166, 179, 199, 238; *Kamikoi* 85; *Oidipous at Kolonos* 129, 169, 178, 199, 238; *Oidipous Tyrannos* 16, 27, 28, 29, 122, 128, 131, 140, 143, 153, 176, 179, 229; *Philoktetes* 128, 149, 150, 153, 179, 199; *Trackers* 226; *Women of Trachis* 29, 30, 104, 116, 138, 162, 163, 164, 169, 179, 211, 223, 239
Soteria 190
Sown Men 99, 103, 132
space in tragedy 148–52
Sparta 193
spell(s) 75, 105, 106
Sphinx 19, 122
spider 195
sovereignty 124, 135
standing 4
stereotypes, explored in tragedy 238
Stesichoros 183, 191, 192
stillness 4, 103, 106, 107, 117, 118
Skamandros 193
stone, mountains as source of 11
Strabo 10, 89
structure/structuralism 1, 2, 4, 173–200
Styx 92

suicide 61, 122, 129, 139, 141, 153, 167, 200
Suppliants (Aischylos) 129, 149, 237
Suppliants (Euripides) 151, 238

Talos 2, 5, 73–97, *79, 80, 82, 84,* 105
 Athenian 81, 82, 83, 85
 Cretan 76, 77, 78, 79, 83, 85
 death 81
 homosexuality 79, 89, 90
 made of bronze 74, 75, 76, 77, 78, 81, 85, 90
 origins of myth 86–7
 Perdix 81
 wings *79,* 79
Tantalos 48, 214
Taplin, Oliver 149
Taygetos, Mount 18
Teiresias 17, 21, 26, 28, 48, 61, 139, 176, 177, 178, 183, 184, 185, 188, 189, 191, 224, 226–9, 233, 236, 237
Tekmessa 239
Telemachos 66
Telephos 19
Teukros 199
Thamyris 183, 191, 195
Thanatos 81, *85,* 202, 205, 209
Thebes 17, 21, 26, 27, 28, 29, 122, 129, 131, 143, 149, 150, 151, 152, 178
theme(s) 4
Theogony (Hesiod) 133, 135
Theokritos 24, 116
Theophrastos 12, 14
Theseus 61, 77, *109,* 109, *110,* 116, 122, 125, 130, 136, 144, 148, 150, 151, 167, 171, 199, 206, 232
Thessaly 70
Thetis 21
thigh 89, 93, 224
Thornax, Mount 21
Thracian(s) 14
Thucydides 197
thunderbolt 29, 49, 169, 187, 190, 195, 209
thyrsos 226, 233, 237
timber 11, 12, 17
time in tragedy 146–8
Timon 69
Timotheos of Gaza *On Animals* 36
Titans 15, 18, 60, 135
Tithonos 187
Titthion 19
Tmolos, Mount 18, 26
town *see astu*
Trachis 21, 29, 149, 152
Trackers (Sophokles) 226
tragedy 2, 3, 5, 20, 21, 28, 29, 54, 107, 121–240 *passim*
 and boundaries 2, 201–17, 219–40
 and Greek myth 121–44, 145–60
 audience response 170
 bafflement 161–72
 conflict among gods 135–7
 criticism of gods 137–9
 feminization and 237–40
 Greek vs Barbarian in 130, 222
 human choice in 140–1
 ideology in 152–60
 location of 128–33
 portrayal of gods in 133–44
 responsibility for actions in 161, 162, 163
 selection of myth in 122, 128
 space 148–52
 time 146–8
transgression against the gods 48
transhumance 11, 16
transvestism 227, 233, 235, 236, 237, 240
 see also cross-dressing
travel 13, 17
trickery 37, 38, 67, 150
Trojan horse 17
Trojan Women (Euripides) 18, 130, 142, 147, 149, 151
Troy 17, 21, 122, 130, 143, 149, 151, 152, 165, 166, 174, 188, 194, 211
Trozen 147, 149, 150
Tyrrell, W. Blake 156, 157, 159

(un)certainty principle 5
Underworld 61, 62
Usener, Hermann 57

Vari, cave 11
veiling 4, 204, 206, 207, 208, 209
Vernant, Jean-Pierre 90, 147, 155, 222
Vidal-Naquet, Pierre 66, 67, 68, 69, 149, 155, 222
vulnerability 4, 87, 88, 93, 96, 128
 in ankle 92–4
 in lower limbs 89–92
 see also invulnerability

walking 4
Walsh, Peter 56

wandering 4
warfare, mountains in 13, 14
Wasps (Aristophanes) 69
water 64; in ritual 44, 45, 202
weaving 24, 48
wedding 203, 204, 207, 209
  see also marriage
werewolves 14, 23, 41–51
  see also wolves
Whallon, William 166
white/whiteness 4, 60–71
  see also leukos
Wilamowitz-Moellendorff, U. von 16, 94, 167
Willetts, R. F. 86
Winnington-Ingram, R. P. 165, 219
wolves 4, 14, 21, 23, 33–51, 57, 184, 219
  see also werewolves
women 22, 24, 25, 26, 27, 67, 68, 69, 70, 104, 116, 130, 131, 133, 148, 152, 163, 184, 190, 204, 217, 221, 226, 227, 230, 231, 232, 233, 234, 235, 236, 237, 238
Women at the Thesmophoria (Aristophanes) 234
Women of Trachis (Sophokles) 29, 30, 104, 116, 138, 162, 163, 164, 169, 179, 211, 223, 239
wood, mountains as source of 11, 12, 17
woodcutters 12, 17, 75
Works and Days (Hesiod) 133

Xanthos 67
Xenokritos 183
Xenophanes 117
Xenophon 12, 22, 35
Xerxes 161, 162
Xouthos 54

Zeitlin, Froma 149, 151, 152, 156, 159, 234; *Playing the Other* 233
Zethos 19
Zeus 15, 16, 20, 23, 25, 29, 30, 39, 48, 49, 61, 70, 75, 77, 86, 133, 135, 136, 138, 139, 156, 158, 162, 163, 164, 167, 184, 185, 187, 191, 193, 195, 198, 214, 223–5, 228, 230, 236, 237
  altar on acropolis, Athens 15
  god of rain and lightning 15, 17
  Ram god 23
  temple at Argos 15
  temple at Akragas 15
  turned into cuckoo 21
Zimmermann, Bernhard 227
Ziolkowski, Theodore 4

Printed and bound by CPI Group (UK) Ltd, Croydon, CR0 4YY